German Soldiers and the Occupation of France, 1940–1944

From 1940 to 1944, German soldiers not only fought in and ruled over France, but also lived their lives there. While the combat experiences of German soldiers are relatively well documented, as are the everyday lives of the occupied French population, we know much less about occupiers' daily activities beyond combat, especially when it comes to men who were not top-level administrators. Using letters, photographs, and tour guides, alongside official sources, Julia S. Torrie reveals how ground-level occupiers understood their role, and how their needs and desires shaped policy and practices. At the same time as soldiers were told to dominate and control France, they were also encouraged to sightsee, to photograph and to "consume" the country, leading to a familiarity that often limited violence rather than inciting it. The lives of these ordinary soldiers offer new insights into the occupation of France, the history of Nazism and World War II.

Julia S. Torrie is a professor of history at St Thomas University. Her publications include *"For Their Own Good": Civilian Evacuations in Germany and France, 1939–1945* (2010).

Studies in the Social and Cultural History of Modern Warfare

General Editor

Jay Winter, *Yale University*

Advisory Editors

David Blight, *Yale University*

Richard Bosworth, *University of Western Australia*

Peter Fritzsche, *University of Illinois, Urbana-Champaign*

Carol Gluck, *Columbia University*

Benedict Kiernan, *Yale University*

Antoine Prost, *Université de Paris-Sorbonne*

Robert Wohl, *University of California, Los Angeles*

In recent years the field of modern history has been enriched by the exploration of two parallel histories. These are the social and cultural history of armed conflict, and the impact of military events on social and cultural history.

Studies in the Social and Cultural History of Modern Warfare presents the fruits of this growing area of research, reflecting both the colonization of military history by cultural historians and the reciprocal interest of military historians in social and cultural history, to the benefit of both. The series offers the latest scholarship in European and non-European events from the 1850s to the present day.

A full list of titles in the series can be found at:
www.cambridge.org/modernwarfare

German Soldiers and the Occupation of France, 1940–1944

Julia S. Torrie

St Thomas University, New Brunswick

CAMBRIDGE
UNIVERSITY PRESS

CAMBRIDGE
UNIVERSITY PRESS

University Printing House, Cambridge CB2 8BS, United Kingdom

One Liberty Plaza, 20th Floor, New York, NY 10006, USA

477 Williamstown Road, Port Melbourne, VIC 3207, Australia

314-321, 3rd Floor, Plot 3, Splendor Forum, Jasola District Centre, New Delhi - 110025, India

79 Anson Road, #06-04/06, Singapore 079906

Cambridge University Press is part of the University of Cambridge.

It furthers the University's mission by disseminating knowledge in the pursuit of
education, learning and research at the highest international levels of excellence.

www.cambridge.org
Information on this title: www.cambridge.org/9781108457590
DOI: 10.1017/9781108658935

© Julia S. Torrie 2018

First published 2018
First paperback edition 2020

A catalogue record for this publication is available from the British Library

Library of Congress Cataloging in Publication data
Names: Torrie, Julia S. (Julia Suzanne), 1973- author.
Title: German soldiers and the occupation of France, 1940-1944 /
  Julia S. Torrie, St Thomas University, New Brunswick.
Description: First edition. | Cambridge ; New York, NY : Cambridge University
  Press, [2018] | Series: Studies in the social and cultural history of modern
  warfare | Includes bibliographical references and index.
Identifiers: LCCN 2018021294| ISBN 9781108471282 (hardback : alk. paper) |
  ISBN 9781108457590 (pbk. : alk. paper)
Subjects: LCSH: France–History–German occupation, 1940-1945. | Germany.
  Heer–Military life–History–20th century. | Soldiers–Germany–History–20th
  century. | Germans–France–History–20th century. | France–History–
  German occupation, 1940-1945–Social aspects.
Classification: LCC DC397 .T67 2018 | DDC 940.53/44–dc23
  LC record available at https://lccn.loc.gov/2018021294

ISBN 978-1-108-47128-2 Hardback
ISBN 978-1-108-45759-0 Paperback

Contents

List of Figures *page* vi
Acknowledgements vii
List of Abbreviations x
List of Recurring Personalities xi
Map xiii

Introduction 1

1 Occupations, Past and Present 27

2 Consuming the Tastes and Pleasures of France 61

3 Touring and Writing about Occupied Land 92

4 Capturing Experiences: Photography and Photo Books 128

5 Rising Tensions 165

6 *Westweich?* Perceptions of "Softness" among Soldiers
in France 192

7 Twilight of the Gods 221

Bibliography 252
Index 272

Figures

1.1 School map showing German borders and "cultural"
    area in 1500   *page* 39
1.2 Soldiers at the Tomb of the Unknown Soldier   53
2.1 Soldier bearing parcels   70
2.2 Soldiers in a perfume shop   89
3.1 Guide to Paris for Germans, 1940   117
3.2 *Der deutsche Wegleiter*   119
4.1 Domestic scene   129
4.2 "Peacefully rests the lake"   139
4.3 "Booty"   140
4.4 Soldiers on the Eiffel Tower   142
4.5 Clearing the "Vieux Port" neighbourhood, Marseilles   145
4.6 "France's fighters"   147
4.7 "Soldiers"   148
4.8 "Frenchmen on 'cable watch'"   149
4.9 Fishing for shrimp   151
4.10 With Hitler in the West   153
4.11 Soldiers in front of the Eiffel Tower   154
4.12 Landscape on the Orne River   156
4.13 France: a book of images   158
4.14 "Paris 1940, Montmartre"   159
4.15 Soldiers with women in front of the Moulin Rouge   160
4.16 Lothar-Günther Buchheim's Paris   162
6.1 Soldier's guide to Warsaw   200

Acknowledgements

It is a great pleasure to recognize the assistance I have received in completing this book. From the beginning, generous support from the Alexander von Humboldt-Foundation and St Thomas University made it possible to spend extended periods of time researching in European archives, and writing. During sabbatical leaves, the Albrecht-Ludwigs Universität, Freiburg and the Eberhard Karls Universität, Tübingen welcomed me as a visiting researcher in 2008–9 and 2015–16 respectively. I am grateful to Ulrich Herbert in Freiburg, whose advice helped give this project early form. In Tübingen, Anselm Doering-Manteuffel, Johannes Grossmann, and their colleagues made me feel at home as I finished the draft manuscript.

Staff at many libraries and archives gave helpful advice and pointed the way to important sources. Alongside the Bundesarchiv (Berlin-Lichterfelde, Freiburg and Koblenz), the Staatsbibliothek (Berlin), Akademie der Künste (Berlin), Archives Nationales (Paris), Bibliothèque Nationale (Paris), Mémorial (Caen), and University of New Brunswick Archives and Special Collections (Fredericton), I particularly want to thank Margot Blank at the Deutsch-Russisches Museum Karlshorst (Berlin), Jutta Jäger-Schenk and Gerhard Seitz at the Deutsches Tagebucharchiv (Emmendingen), Irina Renz at the Württembergische Landesbibliothek, Bibliothek für Zeitschichte (Stuttgart), and Hasso Spode of the Historisches Archiv zum Tourismus (Berlin). Armin Musterle offered crucial assistance with archival research in Freiburg.

At Cambridge University Press, I am grateful to Michael Watson, as well as to Ruth Boyes and Shaheer Husanne for production and Tasha Goddard for her copy-editing expertise. Material that appears in revised form in Chapter 4 was originally published as "Visible Trophies of War: German occupiers' photographic perceptions of France, 1940–44," in *The Ethics of Seeing: 20th Century German Documentary Photography Reconsidered.* Edited by Jennifer Evans et al., 108–37. New York: Berghahn Books, 2018. Chapter 3 is derived, in part, from an article published in the *Journal of Tourism History* 3:3 (Nov. 2011), available online at http://dx.doi.org/ 10.1080/1755182X.2011.628057 Heino Wetjen kindly allowed me to reproduce an image from his father's photo album and Christian Wolter permitted me to quote from family letters held at the Deutsche Tagebucharchiv, Emmendingen. I have endeavoured to contact all copyright holders for permission to use materials in this book, and I encourage any I may have missed to contact me at jtorrie@stu.ca.

Segments of this research were tested out and refined through presentations at venues too numerous to name. My understanding of soldiers' photography grew enormously through conversations at the 2013 conference "The Ethics of Seeing: 20th Century German Documentary Photography Reconsidered" (German Historical Institute, London). I especially want to thank the conference organisers and participants, including Paul Betts, Jennifer Evans, Elizabeth Harvey, Stefan-Ludwig Hoffmann, and Julia Adeney Thomas. In Germany, Petra Bopp generously shared her unparalleled knowledge of soldiers' amateur photographs, invited me to present my research at the Stadtmuseum Oldenburg, and read much of the material that became Chapter 4.

I am grateful for the ongoing encouragement of David Blackbourn, Robert Gellately, Charles Maier, and Susan Pedersen, all of whom have supported my work for many years. I also want to extend warm thanks to friends and colleagues who furthered this project in manifold ways, including Shelley Baranowski, Amy Bell, Chad Denton, Nicole Dombrowski-Risser, Sarah Fishman, Olivier Fourcade, Rainer Hudemann, Talbot Imlay, Fabian Lemmes, Kenneth Mouré, Eric Kurlander, Sandra Ott, Andrew Port, Raffael Scheck, Valentin Schneider, Nathan Stolzfus, Fabien Théofilakis, Lisa Todd, Fabrice Virgili, Maude Williams, and Nicholas Williams. All shared their thoughts and suggestions unstintingly.

This book could not have come to fruition without the daily kindness and encouragement of cherished colleagues at St Thomas University: in the History Department, Research Office, and beyond. I would also like to thank the historians of the University of New Brunswick, where I am an honorary research associate, and the document delivery staff at the Harriet Irving Library.

For many years, the Brinkmann family have offered friendship, kindness and a home away from home in Germany. More recently, Johannes and Sonja Grossmann and their sons Moritz and Noah gave me and my family a wonderful introduction to Tübingen. In France, Anne-Marie and Patrick Hébert, and Thérèse Eustache and Claude Quinette have given their whole-hearted support, both practical and moral, as the book took shape. Closer to home, Catherine and Matthew Ellis have shared good humour, wide-ranging conversation and cocktails. My parents, Amelia and James Torrie, continue to encourage me in everything that I do. I am profoundly grateful to them, and to Eloïse and Adélaïde, a good part of whose childhood has coincided with the gestation of this book. Without them, and especially without Frédéric, who combines historical acuity, archival stamina, and so much more, this book would have been inconceivable.

Abbreviations

AA	Politisches Archiv des Auswärtigen Amtes, Berlin
ADP	Archives Départementales, Paris
AN	Archives Nationales, Paris
BArch	Bundesarchiv, Berlin, Freiburg, Koblenz
BfZ SS	Württembergische Landesbibliothek, Bibliothek für Zeitgeschichte, Sammlung Sterz, Stuttgart
BfZ SSch	Württembergische Landesbibliothek, Bibliothek für Zeitgeschichte, Sammlung Schüling, Stuttgart
DAF	Deutsche Arbeitsfront (German Workers' Front)
DTA	Deutsches Tagebucharchiv, Emmendingen
MBH	Militärbefehlshaber Frankreich
NSFO	Nationalsozialistische Führungsoffizier (National Socialist Leadership Officer)
NSV	Nationalsozialistische Volkswohlfahrt (National Socialist People's Welfare Organization)
PK	Propagandakompagnie
SS	Schutzstaffel
TNA	The National Archives, Kew
UNBASC	University of New Brunswick Archives and Special Collections, Fredericton

Recurring Personalities

Full names have been used wherever possible.

Walter Bargatzky (1910–98), a member of the German administrative staff in Paris, worked in the department responsible for legal matters ("Justiz"). He was linked to the 20 July 1944 plot against Hitler, though was not one of its leaders, and wrote a memoir about his experiences in occupied France that was published in 1987.

Heinrich Böll (1917–85) was stationed in France in 1940, and again in 1942–3, before being sent to the Eastern Front. After the war, he became a well-known West German novelist.

Lothar-Günther Buchheim (1918–2007) was a propaganda company member, author and photographer, who served notably in Brittany and collected material that inspired the post-war feature film, *Das Boot*.

Hans-Peter Eckener (1910–44), who was from an artistic family in Stuttgart, served in Brittany and visited Paris as part of a soldiers' tour group in October 1941. Later transferred to the Eastern Front, he died there in February 1944.

Kurt F. (1909–44) fought in France in 1940, and then took part in the invasion of the Soviet Union in 1941. Wounded in the Ukraine, he convalesced in Germany and then was again sent to France. In 1944, he was stationed in Hungary, then transferred back to the West. He died in Normandy two days after the Allied invasion.

Johannes Gutschmidt (1876–1961) was a veteran of World War I who arrived in France in the summer of 1940 to command a prisoner of war camp near Le Mans. He later commanded several other camps in Poland and the Soviet Union.

Alfred Haas (?–1942) was a lieutenant in the Luftwaffe. He was stationed at Arcachon in 1940 and later deployed to Poland, where he visited the Warsaw ghetto. He died on the Eastern Front in February 1942.

Ernst Jünger (1895–1998), a well-known author who served in the military administration in Paris, was sent briefly to the Eastern Front, and later published his recollections of the period.

Hans Klumpp (1917–2008) had been in the army since 1938. Musically inclined, he was a life-long bachelor from Karlsruhe who became a teacher after the war. In December 1941, he requested leave to pursue medical studies. The leave was not granted, though he later worked in a field hospital.

Bernhard Schulz (1913–2003) was born in the village of Lindlar (Bergisches Land) and served as an occupier in the Cherbourg area, as well as on Alderney (British Channel Islands). He wrote letters home to Gerda, his future wife, in Osnabrück. After publishing short stories and several books during the war, he pursued a postwar career as a journalist and author.

Friedrich Siebert (1888–1950), from Wurzburg, was commander of the Forty-Fourth Infantry Division, stationed notably at La Rochelle in 1940–41. He then served on the Eastern Front and ended his career at the rank of General.

Klaus Peter Suhrkamp (1920–2004) was wounded in northern France in 1940. After his recovery, he served in France for several months before being sent to Poland. Son of the publisher Peter Suhrkamp, he kept a war diary from 1940 to 1942.

Fritz Swoboda (1922–2007) was an SS-Oberscharführer from Austria who was stationed in Prague, and later involved in anti-partisan operations in France, where he was taken prisoner in 1944 at the age of 22.

Wilhelm Unverzagt (1900–71) was a lawyer who was head of personnel management for the Reichsbahn (German national railway) until he lost his position on political grounds in 1938. During the war, he worked for the Reichsbahn in Russia and in France.

Map

Map of occupied France showing its division into various zones.
Julian Jackson, France: The Dark Years, 1940–44 (Oxford: Oxford University Press, 2001).

Introduction

In the verdant woods outside Cherbourg in Normandy, walkers sometimes stumble on a mysterious site. Almost overgrown by weeds,
brambles, and moss, a large concrete rectangle lies hidden among the
trees. It is about twenty metres long and ten wide, full of water and
trailing vines. Along each end of the structure are four evenly-spaced
blocks with angled tops. They look like short podiums that have been
turned around so that their top surface slants towards the water. These
blocks give the first clue to the structure's purpose, for they look as
though they were designed as diving platforms for racing swimmers to
take flight. A closer look reveals that they are in fact starting blocks, for
the structure is an open-air swimming pool, nestled deep in a valley and
fed by a local stream. According to a chiselled marking nearby, the pool
was built by the German army and inaugurated in 1942, midway through
the occupation of France. Not far away, a small house-like building, a
pillbox with loopholes in the sides, stands guard over the site that was
located near a German encampment.[1]

The swimming pool is a curiosity, one of thousands of concrete
structures dating from World War II that still mark the landscape of
France. Many such structures are bunkers, gun emplacements and
observation posts that line especially the English Channel and Atlantic
coasts. Some are in farmers' fields, others in towns and villages, and still
more on beaches, where they are slowly sinking into the sea. Remnants of
the German defences are everywhere, though they are left out of most
visitors' beach photographs, and rarely appear in any but the most
specialised tourist guides.

The swimming pool is in many ways a stranger sight, and one that
raises more troubling questions. Rather than conjuring up expected

---

[1] The site is near Sideville, Manche. Difficult to find, it is described here: Thierry Dubillot,
"La piscine aux Allemands veut se faire oublier," *Ouest France*, 26 September 2013,
www.ouest-france.fr/la-piscine-aux-allemands-veut-se-faire-oublier-92375.

images of armed watchfulness or the heated exchanges of battle, it suggests leisure, relaxation, and even fun. A first visit to the site is jarring because it draws attention away from the obviously warlike and exploitative aspects of military occupation and invites one to think of occupiers in a different light. As they exercised or rested by that pool, enjoying its cool water on a summer's day in pastoral Normandy, what were these soldiers thinking? How did they conceive of defeated France, and what did they imagine they were doing there as World War II went on?

The pool is a reminder that for four years, German soldiers not only stood guard over and fought in France, but also lived their lives there. They were trained and equipped first to invade Britain and, when that proved impossible, they fortified France and prepared to respond to the Allies' inevitable attempt to reconquer the European continent. Some men acted directly to claim local resources, to crush opposition, to oppress, persecute and deport France's Jewish population, and to track down and murder members of the resistance. Others condoned these actions. Some took on administrative tasks, managing the army itself and France's occupation by overseeing government and industry to ensure the maximal exploitation of economic and labour reserves. Some men were posted to France for weeks; others stayed for months and even years, interspersed with tours of duty to other Fronts.

As part of the larger history of National Socialist (Nazi) expansionism and oppression in World War II, the combat experiences of German soldiers are relatively well documented. The same is true of Germany's role in persecuting France's Jewish population, and of Adolf Hitler's efforts to exploit the land and its labour force. However, we know much less about German occupiers' everyday activities beyond combat, especially when it comes to men who were not top-level administrators. What were the attitudes of ground-level occupiers, and how did these shape the way the occupation unfolded? How did soldiers approach occupying a place that, to many men, seemed deeply attractive, and offered unprecedented opportunities for consumption, leisure and sightseeing? Although some occupiers harboured scorn for France that was nourished by National Socialist propaganda, most also recognised that they were fortunate to be stationed in a country that seemed remarkably calm and "peaceful." Better still, France offered a panoply of pleasures that victorious incoming soldiers found easy to access. Soon after the 1940 invasion ended, for instance, an exhilarated occupier, Kurt F., wrote home to his parents about the fabulous food and drink he was enjoying, and commented that "when it comes to provisions, we live here like the Lord

God in France."[2] Although the exact origins of the German phrase F. used, *"leben wie Gott in Frankreich "* ("living like God in France") are unclear, in everyday parlance, it describes taking advantage of the good life. The term is a cliché, but it was frequently used by soldiers during the occupation, sometimes to the frustration of the military authorities. Freighted with aspirational, idealising qualities, it encapsulated many men's approach to France – a place where it seemed possible, if only for a few hours, to relish simple joys and get away from the war.[3]

From the summer of 1940 onwards, occupiers visited and enjoyed France's varied landscapes, consumed French goods, and profited from the country's many opportunities for leisure and pleasure. They also took vast numbers of photographs, developing through these and their letters, diaries, and even publications, a narrative about the occupation that depicted Germans not as barbaric oppressors, but as welcome guests. In this narrative, the occupiers were open-minded, culturally sophisticated visitors, whose wartime victories had confirmed the superiority of their National Socialist worldview, and whose leadership would help the French, weakened, degenerate and abandoned by their leaders, become junior members of a Nazi-dominated Europe.

With the loss of the war, this narrative was rightfully consigned to the proverbial dustbin of history, but some of its elements proved remarkably long-lasting. Even today, in casual conversation in France, the occupiers' behaviour is often described as having been "correct."[4] Among both the French and the Germans, the occupation is remembered as relatively "gentle," despite its well-documented and omnipresent exploitation. The violence and brutality of its final phase are viewed as the exception rather than the rule.

In light of these notions, we might ignore the "softer" aspects of the occupation, dismissing them as frivolous or shying away from them as misguided efforts to hold a genteel fig leaf over the "real," brutal face of Hitler's war. Yet doing so would be a mistake, for wars consist not only of combat, but also of administration and occupation, of brief moments of leisure and pleasure, of the men behind the lines as well as those

---

[2] Kurt F., 1 July 1940, (DTA: 270/1). F. was born in Bremen in 1909, studied pharmacy and worked in a chemical factory in Berlin before being called up. He fought in the West in 1940, remained in France as an occupier until June 1941, fought in the Soviet Union for two years, was wounded, and, after a period of convalescence in 1943, was posted back to France in 1944. He died at Sourdeval, Manche on 8 June 1944.

[3] Robert Gildea, *Marianne in Chains: In Search of the German Occupation 1940–45* (London: MacMillan, 2002), 71; Ludger Tewes, *Frankreich in der Besatzungszeit 1940–1943* (Bonn: Bouvier, 1998), 388.

[4] Tewes, *Frankreich*, 388.

at the front. As Craig Gibson has emphasised in his book on British soldiers in France in World War I, "the soldier's experience of soldiering needs to be defined rather more broadly than his experience of combat."[5] Examining the lives of men behind the lines, their leisure and pleasures, the experiences and worldviews of occupiers, reveals a different and more complex face of conflict.

Furthermore, what happens away from the front-lines and in occupied areas can, and does, influence the course of major events. Managing occupations, and above all, managing occupiers, are challenging and important tasks. A more nuanced and three-dimensional picture of German policy towards occupied France emerges when one takes into account the complexities of managing an occupying army of between 35,000 and nearly 100,000 men, depending on the time period.[6] This book offers a corrective to high-policy-focused standard accounts by rendering ground-level occupiers visible and bringing their role in shaping the occupation of France to light.

Occupiers from the highest officers down to the lowest-ranking privates found France remarkably appealing and sought to make the most of its opportunities for leisure, consumption, and even tourism while they could. They lived, in a very real sense, between the pillbox and the swimming pool, between violence and leisure, between their duties as combatants, and the pull of the good life. The tension that this occasioned played itself out in thousands of individual choices between indifference and possessive entitlement, proximity and distance, restraint and brutality, that coloured the occupation's every facet.

To investigate soldiers' roles as occupiers, and how their approaches and behaviour shaped the occupation, the book asks three levels of question. The first level has to do with occupation experiences. Although it is generally recognised that officers, particularly the top brass in Paris, lived well, to what extent was this true of lower-ranking troops beyond the capital? How did ground-level soldiers approach occupation, and what was it like to be in France as an occupier? To answer these first questions, the book analyses occupiers' experiences, demonstrating notably that leisure, consumption and tourism were integral to the project of occupation. Sources such as letters and diaries, as well as amateur

---

[5] Craig Gibson, *Behind the Front: British Soldiers and French Civilians, 1914–1918* (Cambridge: Cambridge University Press, 2014), 21.

[6] These numbers refer to men under the command of the Militärbefehlshaber Frankreich. The low figure dates from summer 1942, while the high figure corresponds to the period just before the Allied landing in Normandy. See discussion of numbers in Peter Lieb and Robert O. Paxton, "Maintenir l'ordre en France occupée: Combien de divisions?," *Vingtième Siècle* no. 112 (2011): 124–5.

photographs, offer new perspectives on how occupiers saw themselves and understood their role.

Delving deeper, the book explores, secondly, how Hitler's regime instrumentalised soldiers' activities. It lays out a circular dynamic of appropriation and reappropriation in which official propaganda picked up and exploited impulses from soldiers, who then drew on propaganda themes in their own visual and written productions, which in turn became sources for new propaganda initiatives. Soldiers' initial leisure, consumption, and tourism-based approach to occupation was allowed to persist because these activities offered numerous advantages to the regime. Suggesting that Germans were doing nothing more than enjoying France, admiring its monuments and appreciating its food and consumer goods raised a smokescreen of civility that helped to hide the occupation's exploitative core.[7] Occupiers' enjoyment of France, which was shared through letters, images and shipments of goods to their families at home, lubricated overall consent for Hitler's rule. Above all, allowing France to persist as a comparatively "peaceful" place enabled its ongoing use for rest and relaxation, regrouping and retraining tattered units from the Eastern Front. A period of time spent recuperating in France became arguably one of the most common wartime experiences for soldiers, and the respite offered by leisure, consumption, and tourism in France thus undergirded violence and brutality elsewhere.

If allowing for leisure and pleasure offered advantages, these activities also threatened to become liabilities over the longer-term. Maintaining a balance between benefit and risk, a growing challenge, is explored through three separate problems in the third level of analysis. The first problem had to do with differences between relatively comfortable France and the unprecedented horror of the Eastern Front; the second was linked to growing resistance activity, and the third stemmed from differences in culture between long-term occupiers and incoming troops in 1944. All three problems threatened to destabilise the occupation and forced a reevaluation of the desirable balance between leisure and violence in occupied France.

While occupiers in the West were relaxing and taking in the pleasures of France, from June 1941 onward, soldiers in the East were facing some of the most difficult and brutal fighting Germans had ever seen. Looking

---

[7] "Smokescreen" is employed in the sense used by Birthe Kundrus, who cites the importance of the Nazi regime's "smokescreen of solicitude" in ensuring popular consent for Hitler's rule. "Greasing the Palm of the Volksgemeinschaft? Consumption under National Socialism" in *Visions of Community in Nazi Germany: Social Engineering and Private Lives*, ed. Martina Steber and Bernhard Gotto, 2014, 166–9.

westwards, men on the Eastern Front were justifiably envious, and they came to believe that their own difficulties were being aggravated by lazy, relaxed attitudes in rear areas, especially in France. Many soldiers had already spent time in France, and some like Kurt F. made direct comparisons between their experiences there and the terrible conditions they faced in the East. Such comparisons were never advantageous to the French occupiers, and a widespread belief arose that troops in the West were becoming soft; feminised by living too well for too long a time. In their letters, men in the East complained about the *Etappengeist* (spirit of the rear) as opposed to *Kampfgeist* (fighting spirit) of men in France, and described them as "*westweich*," soft (*weich*) from being too long in the West.

The notion that soldiers in the West were going soft led to repeated attempts to reduce administration staff and to limit the amount of time individuals spent in France. Younger, fitter administrators were rotated out for compulsory spells in the East, and a special commission on rationalising manpower was sent to France to comb through the administration, root out inefficiencies and redeploy as many fit men as possible to the front-lines. Taking soldiers' mobility into account and viewing the French occupation not in isolation, but as part of a much larger European conflict, new themes like these emerge.

A second problem that made it difficult for administrators to decide how to "pitch" the occupation was that from mid-1941, resistance groups stepped up their attacks on German forces. Facing demands from Berlin to respond harshly, the Militärbefehlshaber, Otto von Stülpnagel, prevaricated. Cracking down on resistance activities would upset a delicate equilibrium in France. Not only would it make the French less willing to collaborate with Germany, but it would also get in the way of the country's continued exploitation both through "hard" forms of despoilment and through the "soft" methods of leisure, consumption, and tourism. In his self-justifying resignation letter to General Wilhelm Keitel in February 1942, Stülpnagel underlined that he had always striven to maintain "calm and order" in France in order to exploit the country "in the most useful and extensive way" for the German war effort.[8] "Calm and order" were necessary for extensive exploitation and, despite Stülpnagel's efforts, the challenge of finding a balance between stability and repression troubled the occupation to its bitter end. It affected not only the fraught relationship between Paris and Berlin, but also interactions between different levels of the occupation

---

[8] MBH to Keitel Nr. 11/42, 15 February 1942 (BArch: RW 35/1).

apparatus and incoming troops when the German presence in France was contested on the battlefield in 1944.

Occupiers' main tasks had always been to exploit French resources while defending French territory against opponents of the occupation and Allied attack. Most of the time, this meant exercising, watching and waiting, but in June 1944, American, British and Canadian forces landed on the beaches of Normandy. Recognising that war in western Europe came nowhere near the levels of violence that were commonplace in the eastern Europe, historians debate the degree to which the battle in France in 1944 was fought conventionally, or was ideologically driven. For the most part, units proceeded conventionally, but there were moments of excessive violence and atrocities against civilians. In the most detailed analysis of anti-partisan fighting and combat in France to date, historian Peter Lieb shows that the worst atrocities in France were committed by SS units, and that beyond these groups, regular army forces that had experienced difficult rear-guard action and anti-partisan warfare on the Eastern Front tended to behave most brutally.[9] Beyond these explanations, which suggest that levels of brutality were determined by the combat experiences of the troops and their ideological conviction, how did the experience of having been an occupier shape soldiers' tendency (or not) towards extreme violence? In some cases, Bertram Gordon has suggested, the closer, deeper knowledge of France that longer-term occupiers enjoyed seems to have served as a brake on violence.[10] There was a noticeable difference in culture between occupation administrators, many of whom were older men who had been brought in from civilian posts, and younger incoming troops.[11] While the former had spent months, if not years, in one place, and generally sought stable relations with local people to facilitate smooth exploitation, the principal task of the latter was making war. Active troops, notably those recently arrived in the West, were often scornful of longer-term occupiers. In 1944, the widespread perception that occupiers in the West were going soft, developed into a World War II equivalent of the "stab-in-the-back" myth that was retailed in the interwar period to explain Germany's 1918 loss. Now, the notion that occupiers were *westweich*

---

[9] Peter Lieb, *Konventioneller Krieg oder NS-Weltanschauungskrieg?: Kriegführung und Partisanenbekämpfung in Frankreich 1943/44* (Munich: R. Oldenbourg, 2007). See historiographical discussion later in this introduction.

[10] Bertram Gordon, "Warfare and Tourism: Paris in World War II," *Annals of Tourism Research* 25, no. 3 (1998): 628–31, 633.

[11] Thomas J. Laub, *After the Fall: German Policy in Occupied France, 1940–1944* (New York: Oxford University Press, 2010), 44–5.

shaped interpretations of new setbacks in France and elsewhere. This perception may also have spurred on greater violence among some men arriving in France in the desperate 1944 efforts to shore up German defences and retain Hitler's western prize. Viewing troops in the West as soft made it easier for incoming men, particularly members of Waffen-SS and elite units, to turn to extreme methods to show that, unlike the occupiers, they were "hard" and knew how a "real" war should be fought.[12] In examining responses to three sets of problems, therefore, the third level of analysis takes up questions about the interaction of leisure and violence, suggesting that, while a closer relationship with France fostered through leisure and pleasure sometimes held back violence, at other times the idea that some men were enjoying themselves excessively drove others to violent acts.

As it explores three levels of questions about occupiers' approaches and experiences, the management of these experiences, and the effects of "soft" interactions with France on the course of the war, the book addresses three broad historical fields: the history of the German occupation of France; the history of tourism, consumption, and leisure; and the history of Nazism and World War II. In terms of the first, it brings ground-level occupiers into an account that has hitherto been dominated by the policy-making activities of elite administrators in Paris. The need to ensure that occupying soldiers felt satisfied and France remained available as an essential rest area for front-line troops shaped the occupation throughout. Uncovering the everyday experiences of occupying a country that was viewed, before the war, as a virtual equal and an attractive destination complicates the standard picture of the occupation years. A focus on ground-level soldiers also brings out their mobility, and the permeability of France as part of a much larger European and global war.

Second, by considering occupying soldiers as tourists, and as consumers of goods and leisure opportunities, the book adds depth to the history of tourism, consumption, and leisure in wartime. It argues that pastimes such as sightseeing and photography served as crucial tools for coming to terms with France and one's role as an occupier. Such activities were also instrumentalised by the regime to increase support for

---

[12] See Ch. 7, Lieb, *Konventionneller*, 383, 506. On "hardness," see Thomas Kühne, *Kameradschaft. Die Soldaten des nationalsozialistischen Krieges und das 20. Jahrhundert* (Göttingen: Vandenhoeck & Ruprecht, 2006), 142, 148–53; Sönke Neitzel and Harald Welzer, *Soldaten: Protokolle vom Kämpfen, Töten und Sterben* (Frankfurt, M: Fischer Taschenbuch, 2012), 387–8.

Hitler's dictatorship. Historians of Nazism often raise questions about consent, and in that context, this research demonstrates how leisure and consumption, especially in western-occupied areas, contributed to maintaining soldiers' morale and became part of the larger reward system of the Third Reich.

Finally, one of the most significant debates about Nazism and World War II concerns the nature of the war Germans fought – whether, and to what extent, it was conventional or ideologically driven. Looking at France, specifically, and focusing on ground-level soldiers' attitudes, this book interrogates the character of the war in the West, and identifies factors that may have served either as precipitants or as brakes on violence. It explores not only the overt, but also the underlying types of violence present during a military occupation, turning attention to these more subtle forms alongside the open hostility that characterised German actions in France, especially after 1943.

The scholarship of the German occupation of France is marked by a divide between research about Germany's role in France, on the one hand, which tends to focus on high policy and, on the other hand, works about France and French life during the occupation which, though they may use a social and cultural-historical approach, attend primarily to the French, leaving German soldiers, as historian Philippe Burrin has put it, "a faint shadow in the background."[13] This book cuts across this framework, offering the first social and cultural history of the occupation of France that gives depth and colour to ground-level occupiers.

Historians who have studied the occupation from a German point of view have done so primarily by elucidating the workings of the Militärbefehlshaber in Paris (MBH): his staff, their relationships with other instances in Paris, and their conflicts with Berlin. Hans Umbreit's work marked out this path in the 1960s, and two valuable recent contributions,

---

[13] Burrin linked this tendency to the new focus on France brought about by the publication of Robert O. Paxton's landmark work *Vichy France: Old Guard and New Order, 1940–1944*. "Writing the History of Military Occupations" in *France at War: Vichy and the Historians* (Oxford: Berg, 2000), 77–8; Robert O. Paxton, *Vichy France: Old Guard and New Order, 1940–1944* (New York: Knopf, 1972). Examples include David Drake, *Paris at War: 1939–1944* (Harvard University Press, 2015); Julian Jackson, *France: The Dark Years, 1940–1944* (Oxford: Oxford University Press, 2001); Ronald C. Rosbottom, *When Paris Went Dark: The City of Light under German Occupation, 1940–1944* (New York, NY: Little, Brown and Company, 2014). Cf. Talbot Imlay, "The German Side of Things: Recent Scholarship on the German Occupation of France," *French Historical Studies* 39, no. 1 (February 2016): 185; Julia S. Torrie, *"For Their Own Good": Civilian Evacuations in Germany and France, 1939–1945* (New York: Berghahn Books, 2010), 9.

by Allan Mitchell and Thomas Laub, do not fundamentally challenge this paradigm.[14]

Laub's study of German policy-making offers an insightful and thorough top-down analysis of decisions made in Paris. With the exception of high-level administrators, however, the military appears as a monolith, and lower-ranking soldiers are largely absent. The focus on high policy means that this book tends to overlook the extent to which the need to "manage" ground-level troops in France, and Europe-wide, influenced policy making. Arguing that "left to its own devices, the military administration established a standard of conduct that was undoubtedly severe but largely unadulterated by Nazi ideology," Laub views the Militärbefehlshaber as defending a traditional style of warfare between nation states against the racially-charged understanding of war favoured by Hitler and his closest allies.[15] Understandably, since ground-level occupiers are not his focus, Laub tells us little about how occupying soldiers experienced the occupation, how and to what degree their attitudes and needs coloured it, and what role this occupation played in the larger pursuit of the war.

Mitchell, for his part, focuses on Paris and offers a compelling analysis especially of economic issues and the organisation of German policy against French Jews. Unlike most accounts, Mitchell's includes brief consideration of soldiers' everyday activities such as tourism, visits to restaurants, and German cultural productions, all of which he interprets as attempts to retain a sense of normalcy and show that Germans were "comfortably in charge" in France.[16] On the whole, Mitchell's work, which also highlights the daily interactions of French and German administrators, offers a well-rounded picture of occupation, but his focus on Paris is limiting, and occupiers' leisure activities deserve more attention, for they went well beyond simply retaining a sense of normalcy to have a major impact on the running of the occupation itself.

German high-policy decisions and events in Paris mattered, of course, but they took place within a broader context. That context included the relationship among German offices in Paris, between Paris and Berlin, and also between Paris and ground-level occupiers spread across France. Troops on the ground were the foundation of a kind of pyramid that

---

[14] Laub, *After the Fall*; Allan Mitchell, *Nazi Paris: The History of an Occupation, 1940–1944* (New York: Berghahn, 2008); Hans Umbreit, *Der Militärbefehlshaber in Frankreich 1940–1944* (Boppard am Rhein: H. Boldt, 1968).
[15] Laub, *After the Fall*, 17.   [16] Mitchell, *Nazi Paris*, 123.

involved low- and higher-level administrators, the Militärbefehlshaber and other German instances in Paris (notably the police and SS, and the German embassy) at the next level, and Berlin at the top.

To get a sense of the bottom level of this pyramid, Ludger Tewes consulted soldiers' letters and, in the late 1980s, interviewed former occupiers about their experiences.[17] His rather impressionistic account is based on rich sources, but it is problematic first because it mixes primary sources from the war era rather indiscriminately with postwar oral accounts, and secondly because it covers only the period from 1940 to 1943. Omitting the last and harshest months of the occupation gives a false sense of its trajectory and cuts off any opportunity to examine connections between the pleasures of the first years and the changed climate of the final period.

Although Tewes's work remains the only large-scale, systematic attempt to get at occupiers' everyday lives and attitudes, other accounts give helpful insights. In particular, Robert Gildea's masterful regional study of relations between the French and Germans in the Loire area was the first to delve into the everyday interactions of these two groups in a way that gave depth to German characters as well as French.[18] Gildea's move away from Paris and the high-policy approach shed new light on Franco-German interactions, and a great deal more could be written about the interactions that Gildea brought to light. Before that project can be realised, however, we need to know more about the German side of the unequal German–French equation.

Putting German soldiers in the foreground thus offers new perspectives, and paints a more nuanced portrait of how occupation policies and practices developed. Another contribution this book makes to the history of the French occupation stems from its approach to occupied France not as a closed system, but as one element in the much larger zone of Nazi-occupied Europe. Contemporaries did not compartmentalise the war into national boxes as subsequent historiography has typically done – for them, it was a German war Europe-wide. Spending time as an occupier in France was, after a stint on the Eastern Front, perhaps the most common experience for a German soldier. Soldiers lived in France before, after, or between tours of duty in the East and elsewhere, and there was significant transfer between these areas. This mobility is recognised in broader accounts of Germans' war experiences, such as Nicholas Stargardt's remarkable tapestry of war and Home-Front lives, and books

---

[17] Tewes, *Frankreich*.   [18] Gildea, *Marianne*.

about soldiers' fighting experiences, such as Ben H. Shepherd's work.[19] However, with the exception of Lieb's research, it has yet to make its way into the more specific historiography of the German occupation of France.

In the context of an emerging historiography about the National Socialist empire Europe-wide, this book focuses on France while under-lining the permeability of this zone to outside pressures, whether these stemmed from German manpower requirements for the Eastern Front, morale at home in the Reich, or the need to maintain France as a rest area for convalescent and war-weary troops.[20] Policy in France was not determined simply through bilateral exchanges between Paris and Berlin. Rather, complex negotiations attempted to balance the well-being and discipline of men on the ground, the needs of local German adminis-trators, the search for relative autonomy on the part of the Militärbefehlshaber in Paris, directions handed down from Berlin, and forces deriving from the war effort as a whole.

While they were in France, Germans played out their hegemony in manifold ways, including through diverse modes of consumption, tour-ism, and leisure. Being able to live "like God in France" and to send parcels of luxury goods home to one's family constituted important rewards for soldiers. Examining the nature and value of these rewards adds shading to the somewhat polarised historiography of German con-sumption in wartime. Occupiers' consumption took many forms that were all, to varying degrees, exploitative. These went from conventional shopping with a highly advantageous exchange rate, through tourism as a displaced form of consumption, to the consumption of sexual "services" through prostitution in military bordellos.[21] Less conventional types of consumption, such as pillaging, were officially frowned upon, but often

---

[19] Ben H. Shepherd, *Hitler's Soldiers: The German Army in the Third Reich* (New Haven, CT: Yale University Press, 2016); Nicholas Stargardt, *The German War: A Nation under Arms, 1939–45* (London: Bodley Head, 2015).

[20] On German-occupied Europe, see notably Shelley Baranowski, *Nazi Empire: German Colonialism and Imperialism from Bismarck to Hitler* (Cambridge: Cambridge University Press, 2010); Peter Fritzsche, *An Iron Wind: Europe under Hitler* (New York: Basic Books, 2016); Mark Mazower, *Hitler's Empire: How the Nazis Ruled Europe* (New York: Penguin Books, 2009).

[21] Consumption, including the consumption of sexual "services" is examined Chapter 2. As Imlay points out, because of the power imbalance in play, "a transactional frame" may be more appropriate than a romantic one for viewing intimate relations between the Germans and the French. Imlay, "German Side," 208. On tourism as a form of consumption, see Shelley Baranowski, *Strength through Joy: Consumerism and Mass Tourism in the Third Reich* (Cambridge: Cambridge University Press, 2004), especially Ch. 6.

tolerated because, like others, they helped to keep soldiers satisfied and fostered consent for the regime.

As they consumed experiences, soldiers often took photographs. With each snapshot, they laid claim to France, exercising both the privilege of looking at conquered land, and a freedom to photograph out of doors that had been denied the French population since mid-September 1940. Photographs helped establish a narrative of dominance that was reinforced through tourism and the production of "France books," discussed in Chapter 3, that retold the story of the invasion and occupation from a German perspective.

Historian Götz Aly has argued that offering Germans consumer goods as compensation for their sacrifices was one of the key methods Hitler used to ensure overall consent for his regime.[22] For Aly, the fact that Hitler facilitated consumption not only in France, but also in other occupied areas, enabled Germans to avoid privations and live relatively well during the war. Critics of Aly's interpretation, such as Adam Tooze, have maintained that Aly underestimated the level of wartime sacrifice made by "ordinary" Germans, not just oppressed minorities such as Jews and foreign workers, to support war and genocide. These critics have highlighted inequalities of distribution that caused tension among citizens, and argued that Germans were not nearly as well off during the war as Aly claims.[23]

Even Tooze, however, admits that Aly's elucidation of the microeconomics of plunder is valuable.[24] Aly shows that providing ready access to material goods fostered a positive relationship between the German people and the Nazi regime. Leaving calculations of the exact economic value of pillage and shopping, and their contribution to the German war effort to specialists in these issues, and without seeking to argue that consumption formed the sole basis of popular support for the regime, it is clear that opportunities for consumption in occupied areas served as

---

[22] Götz Aly, *Hitlers Volksstaat: Raub, Rassenkrieg und nationaler Sozialismus* (Frankfurt am Main: S. Fisher, 2006); Götz Aly, *Hitler's Beneficiaries: Plunder, Racial War, and the Nazi Welfare State*, trans. Chase Jefferson (New York: Picador, 2008).

[23] See notably Christoph Buchheim, "Der Mythos vom „Wohlleben." Der Lebensstandard der deutschen Zivilbevölkerung im Zweiten Weltkrieg," *Vierteljahrshefte für Zeitgeschichte* 58, no. 3 (July 2010): 299–328; J. Adam Tooze, *The Wages of Destruction: The Making and Breaking of the Nazi Economy* (New York: Penguin USA, 2008). Aly's reponse to critics can be found in *Volksstaat*, 365–97. Kundrus summarises the debate in Kundrus, "Greasing the Palm," 159–60.

[24] J. Adam Tooze, "A New Look at Nazi Plunder," *The Telegraph*, 9 August 2007. See also J. Adam Tooze, "What Held Nazi Germany Together? The Aly-Tooze Debate Revisited," *Adam Tooze* (blog), 25 January 2017, www.adamtooze.com/2017/01/25/what-held-nazi-germany-together-the-aly-tooze-debate-revisited/.

lubricants for consent. The actual cost of the perfume, gloves and lingerie that soldiers brought home from France was not the main point – what mattered was that they carried or mailed these goods home in such large quantities that the occupation administration was compelled to establish department stores in Paris and other cities specifically to fill soldiers' needs. Although soldiers' "wild" purchasing, their black marketeering and outright pillage threatened to disrupt the orderly economic exploitation of France, their easy access to French goods was allowed to continue, for it gave their families unprecedented access to these goods as well. Whether they were luxuries or basic items like butter, which occupiers shipped home from France right through the summer of 1944, consumer goods constituted an important "perk" that bolstered popular morale and support for Hitler's war. Such items may have had little real economic impact, but they had a great deal of emotional and psychological impact, and this insight is the key to reconciling this book's focus on the micro-level and Tooze's macro-argument that pillage and shopping had no effect on the economics of war. The importance of both pillage and shopping lay in their value as tangible rewards for continuing to fight the war. It could be argued, moreover, that the greater the sacrifices Germans made at home, the more important compensations such as the ability to consume in the occupied territories became.

Moving beyond the strongly opposed positions of Aly and Tooze, Birthe Kundrus has highlighted the role of German citizens as consumers, and called for more research into their reactions to Nazi policies. Drawing on the work of historians such as Shelley Baranowski and S. Jonathan Wiesen, she encourages scholars to attend to the features of "a specific Nazi model of a modern consumer culture" and to the behavior and agency of Germans as consumers.[25] Looking at consumption in occupied France helps move this agenda forwards by reading this consumption as consumption and not only as plunder or exploitation, and by interrogating its gendered aspects. Many accounts view soldiers' consumption in France straightforwardly as plunder, reading it only in the context of war and spoliation.[26] Characterising it this way removes it from the broader history of consumption and leisure, and the roles of these pastimes in supporting consent for the regime. Occupiers'

---

[25] Kundrus, "Greasing the Palm," 161.

[26] Gilles Perrault and Pierre Azema, for example, reprinted images of Germans shopping in France and noted, as Aly and also Klaus Latzel have, that because of the exchange rate and price controls, this shopping was tantamount to plunder. Klaus Latzel, *Deutsche Soldaten – nationalsozialistischer Krieg? Kriegserlebnis – Kriegserfahrung, 1939–1945* (Paderborn: Schöningh, 1998), 136–8; Gilles Perrault and Pierre Azema, *Paris under the Occupation* (New York: Vendome Press, 1989), 74–5.

extensive shopping, eating and other types of consumption are a reminder that these activities persisted on a large scale despite wartime. They also shed light on male consumption, specifically, a relatively understudied phenomenon.[27] A broader reading of wartime shopping as a form of consumption, rather than simply pillage, and with attention notably to gender, offers new perspectives.

Alongside consumption, this book also speaks to historical scholarship on tourism, specifically. Baranowski has underlined that consumption must be understood in its broadest sense, with attention to the consumption of experiences, and in particular to tourism, as modes of consuming that satisfied many of the same impulses as shopping but did not rely on the purchase of material goods.[28] One of the reasons that tourism persisted until the very end of the occupation, long after material goods became scarce, was precisely because it had become such a useful form of displaced consumption.

Although war and tourism are usually considered separate, if not completely opposed, they are linked in many ways. No place illustrates the affinities and points of contact between tourism and war, tourism and military occupation better than France. Germans on all fronts engaged in sightseeing, but this activity was nourished in France by the country's previous reputation as a cultural destination. The fact that the occupation was long and comparatively peaceful in its early years also made tourism an attractive pastime. The appeal of tourism among occupiers is confirmed by evidence from soldiers' letters, diaries and photographs, not to mention the publication under German auspices of more than thirty guides to, and books about, Paris and various French cities and regions between 1940 and 1944.[29]

Bertram Gordon was the first historian to draw attention to the extent of German tourism in occupied France. Using it as a window into German attitudes, he suggested links between Germans' appreciation of France as tourists and their unwillingness to destroy it in 1940 and during the 1944 retreat.[30] Rudy Koshar discussed soldier tourism in *German Travel Cultures*, while Alon Confino analysed it in the context

---

[27] The historiography of gender and consumption began with women, and is only now beginning to take a wider approach. Tina Dingel, "Consumption in Nineteenth- and Twentieth-Century Germany: A Historiographical Essay," *Cultural & Social History* 2, no. 2 (May 2005): 248.

[28] Baranowski, *Strength*.

[29] These guides were part of the group of "France books" discussed in Chapter 3.

[30] Bertram Gordon, "Ist Gott Französisch? Germans, Tourism and Occupied France 1940–1944," *Modern and Contemporary France* NS 4, no. 3 (1996): 287–98; Gordon, "Warfare and Tourism."

of *Vergangenheitsbewältigung* (coming to terms with the past) in West Germany.[31] Tourism plays a role in most histories of Paris during the occupation, but such accounts rarely give it the attention it deserves, and their focus on the capital leaves the impression this activity was restricted to the City of Light alone.[32]

This book takes research on tourism and occupation in new directions by reading documents originating with soldiers alongside published sources that reflect the regime's attempts to instrumentalise tourism. Touristic attitudes were evident from the occupation's outset, and soldier-generated sources reveal how they emerged from below even as they were being promoted from above, creating a mutally-reinforcing circle of appropriation and reappropriation that disseminated particular "stories" about what Germans were doing in France. Tourism occurred throughout the occupied zone, and to a lesser extent in the unoccupied zone as well. The diaries and memoirs of the Paris elite only hint at the vast extent of this activity. Though senior military administrators and others with longer-term postings had more opportunities to enjoy this form of leisure than others, tourism was a fundamental part of occupiers' experience wherever they were stationed, regardless of rank. A wide range of soldiers' letters and diaries, as well as the photographs addressed in Chapter 4, reveal a touristic engagement with France so extensive that it is a fundamental key to understanding occupiers' attitudes towards the country, and to how they both construed and constructed the occupation of a place so attractive in so many ways.

Within the broader historiography of National Socialism and World War II, the study of occupier tourism has been hampered not only by the overall lack of scholarship on the "German side" of the occupation, but also by a persistent misapprehension that studying tourism is frivolous or unimportant in the context of National Socialist crimes.[33] Even the apparently trivial, however, has historical relevance. As the historian of tourism, Hasso Spode, pointed out in a review of Baranowski's important work on mass tourism and leisure in the Third Reich, concentrating only on genocide makes the broad-based approval National Socialism enjoyed in Germany after 1933 difficult to explain, and the

---

[31] Alon Confino, "Traveling as a Culture of Remembrance: Traces of National Socialism in West Germany, 1945–1960," *History & Memory* 12, no. 2 (2001): 92–121; Rudy Koshar, *German Travel Cultures* (Oxford: Berg, 2000).

[32] See, e.g. Mitchell, *Nazi Paris*; Drake, *Paris at War*.

[33] Kristin Semmens, *Seeing Hitler's Germany: Tourism in the Third Reich* (New York: Palgrave MacMillan, 2005), ix.

regime as a whole easy to view as exceptional.[34] In addition to serving very practical purposes during the occupation, detailed below, soldiers' tourism, like their consumption, was part of the larger rewards system of the Third Reich.[35] For some soldiers, the opportunity to see new land-scapes and peoples in France, and to a lesser extent elsewhere, provided a kind of compensation, albeit incomplete, for the sacrifices of war.

Understanding more about how consumption and leisure interacted with violence speaks to scholarly debates about National Socialism and the war in the West more generally. Recent scholarship has led to a recognition that the occupation of France was more violent than previously imagined, though it did not reach the levels of violence that were commonplace in the East until the summer of 1944, if then.[36] Looking at soldiers on the ground advances these discussions in two principle ways. First, it allows us to learn more about the attitudes that underlay occupiers' acts of overt violence; and second, it paints a more nuanced portrait of the various types of subtle, underlying violence that military occupation involved.

Since the 1970s and 1980s, both scholarly and public discourses have revised the traditional image of a Wehrmacht disassociated from National Socialist crimes. Though initial research focused on the Eastern Front, a reevaluation of the war in the West is underway. Raffael Scheck, for example, has documented German soldiers' murder of some 1,500 to 3,000 French African soldiers in 1940, suggesting that the West represented a 'missing link' on the road towards full brutalisation of troops moving into the Soviet Union in 1941.[37] Ahlrich Meyer and Regina Delacor have argued that the war in the West was more ideologically-driven than hitherto believed, while Gaël Eismann's analysis of German security policy underlines the common ground between police and military instances.[38] Eismann depicts the conflict in the West neither as

---

[34] Hasso Spode, review of Strength through Joy: Consumerism and Mass Tourism in the Third Reich, by Shelley Baranowski, *Journal of Social History* 41, no. 4 (2008): 1074–6.

[35] Baranowski, *Strength*.

[36] Gaël Eismann, *Hôtel Majestic: Ordre et sécurité en France occupée (1940–1944)* (Paris: Tallandier, 2010), 363.

[37] Raffael Scheck, *Hitler's African Victims: The German Army Massacres of Black French Soldiers in 1940* (Cambridge: Cambridge University Press, 2006). See also Raffael Scheck, *French Colonial Soldiers in German Captivity during World War II* (Cambridge: Cambridge University Press, 2014).

[38] Regina Delacor, "Weltanschauungskrieg im Westen: zur Rolle der Wehrmacht bei Geiselexekutionen im besetzten Frankreich 1941/42," *Militärgeschichtliche Zeitschrift* 62, no. 1 (2003): 71–99; Eismann, *Hôtel Majestic*; Ahlrich Meyer, *Die deutsche Besatzung in Frankreich, 1940–1944: Widerstandsbekämpfung und Judenverfolgung* (Darmstadt: Wissenschaftliche Buchgesellschaft, 2000).

completely conventional, nor as so violently genocidal as that of the East. Peter Lieb, for his part, has examined the fight against the French resistance in 1943 and 1944 and shown that as many as 16,000 partisans were murdered.[39] Without absolving the Wehrmacht of co-responsibility for brutality, Lieb ultimately concludes that it fought a harsh but conventional war in France. Though Lieb differentiates Wehrmacht activities from those of the ideologically-charged Waffen-SS responsible for the worst excesses, his research nonetheless contributes to the re-evaluation of both Wehrmacht and Waffen-SS in the West.

What has been missing from these debates, however, is more detailed examination of soldiers' overall attitudes. Instead of studying soldiers' actions to derive a sense of the worldview that underlay them, as Lieb does using a military-historical approach, this book strives to understand soldiers' attitudes directly to learn more about why they exercised greater violence in some circumstances than in others. Looking at attitudes in the East, Klaus Latzel has demonstrated that soldiers' preconceived ideas influenced how they saw and treated local populations.[40] Latzel's comparison of soldiers' letters from World War I and II reveals that a combination of interwar racialist thinking and six years of National Socialist government had radicalised soldiers' views, justifying German domination in the East and making extreme brutality conceivable. In the West where, despite debates about the degree to which the war was ideologically driven, there is no question that brutality did not reach levels common elsewhere until very late, the standard explanation is that Germans continued to harbour a basic respect for France and its people. As Ulrich Herbert has written, occupiers' own "estimation" of particular countries' "political-cultural value" determined their policies.[41] Beyond the reasonable assumption that Germans did not see most French as fundamentally inferior, however, historians have not investigated the bulk of occupiers' attitudes further.

It is, of course, difficult to get inside the heads of occupying soldiers. My attempt to do so has benefited from insights offered by Sönke Neitzel and Harald Welzer, as well as Felix Römer, who have used a mixture of historical and social psychological methods, in the former case, and more conventionally historical ones in the latter, to learn more about soldiers' worldview and attitudes by analysing transcripts from covert Allied

---

[39] Lieb, *Konventionneller.*   [40] Latzel, *Deutsche Soldaten.*
[41] Ulrich Herbert, "Die deutsche Militärverwaltung in Paris und die Deportation der französischen Juden" in *Von der Aufgabe der Freiheit: Politische Verantwortung und bürgerliche Gesellschaft im 19. und 20. Jahrhundert*, ed. Christian Jansen, Lutz Niethammer, and Bernd Weisbrod (Berlin: Akademie, 1995), 437.

recordings of German prisoner of war conversations.[42] Whereas their books deal primarily with attitudes towards combat, fighting and dying, the focus here is on occupation, and on differences in approach between combat troops and longer-term occupiers.

Based on analysis of all four years of occupying France, this book argues that Germans' often long and relatively "peaceful" period of acquaintance with France, their conception of themselves as model occupiers, and the knowledge of specific localities they obtained through everyday interactions with the land and its people factored into their reluctance to use high levels of violence as the occupation came to a close. Vacillations in policy and practice, not to mention local variations in levels of brutality in 1943 and 1944 can at least partly be explained by the ongoing tension between the desire to enjoy France and to maintain it as a quiet rear area for rest and relaxation, and a blunter, more direct approach to controlling the territory and its population through violence. Those occupiers who had been in France longer tended to favour the former approach, while incoming troops who had faced setbacks in the East preferred the latter. Looking at the French occupation from the point of view of occupying soldiers elucidates forms of German hegemony and factors in violence, adding depth and detail to debates about the nature of the war in the West. Bringing ground-level occupiers into the account, drawing attention to the roles notably of consumption and leisure in fostering support for the regime, and investigating factors that may have precipitated violence in the last weeks of the war in France, this book contributes to the intertwined historiographies of the German occupation of France; consumption, leisure, and tourism; and Nazism and World War II.

It should be clear from the above that this is not a military history in the traditional sense, with a focus on combat operations, nor does it offer a play-by-play account of the German occupation of France.[43] The book focuses on the experiences and attitudes primarily of regular army troops, offering a history of the occupation from below. There are occasional sources from the navy and air force, but most material pertains to the ground forces of various ranks and formations. Members of the Waffen-SS appear notably in Chapter 7, which deals with the reconquest of France by the Allies. The book pays little attention to other Germans

---

[42] Neitzel and Welzer, *Soldaten*; Felix Römer, *Kameraden: Die Wehrmacht von Innen* (München: Piper, 2012).

[43] Readers seeing more conventional military histories should consult e.g. Lieb, *Konventioneller*; Peter Lieb, *Unternehmen Overlord: Die Invasion in der Normandie und die Befreiung Westeuropas* (München: C.H.Beck, 2015); Shepherd, *Hitler's Soldiers*. For German policy in France, see Laub, *After the Fall*; Mitchell, *Nazi Paris*.

who were not under the direct oversight of the military, such as the police under Reinhard Heydrich's direction, or the representatives of the Organisation Todt, which built many of the defensive structures of the Atlantic Wall. Female clerical and communications auxiliaries, and civilian staff, such as that of the embassy or the Rohstoff-Handelsgesellschaft (ROGES), a raw materials purchasing agency, appear occasionally, but they are not the main subjects of this work.

Military administrators' voices are heard relatively frequently, since they tended to be the men who spent the most time in France. Administrators, who were often drawn directly from civilian posts, were somewhat older, and better educated than run-of-the-mill troops.[44] This background colours the sources. At the same time, since this work puts ground-level occupiers in the foreground, I have deliberately sought out letters, diaries and photographs from a range of low-ranking soldiers and staff across France.[45] To answer questions about attitudes and worldview, consumption activities, violence, and leisure, much of the available evidence is anonymous, or nearly so. Where a soldiers' rank or location could be determined, it is included, but most letters do not contain this information, which was censored. Full names are used when the terms of archival access allowed; in other cases, authors of primary sources are identified by first name and initial.

Censorship and the accompanying self-censorship are among the well-recognised problems of soldiers' letters.[46] Even if they were able to, soldiers often did not choose to share with their families the most brutal and violent aspects of their lives, and they wrote what they thought their audiences wanted to hear. Occupiers sometimes put pen to paper to get particular worries off their chests, but they were also representing themselves to their families, telling a story about events that was shaped by expectations about what constituted an interesting narrative worthy of

---

[44] Laub, *After the Fall*, 45.

[45] Rather than characterising the men of a particular unit or formation, or analysing a specific collection of sources exhaustively, the sources were sampled and selected according to their relevance for answering the book's overall questions, as outlined above.

[46] On the potential and problems of soldiers' letters, see Veit Didczuneit, Jens Ebert, and Thomas Jander, *Schreiben im Krieg – Schreiben vom Krieg: Feldpost im Zeitalter der Weltkriege* (Essen: Klartext, 2011); Hewitson M, "'I Witnesses': Soldiers, Selfhood and Testimony in Modern Wars," *German History* 28, no. 3 (2010): 310–25; Latzel, *Deutsche Soldaten*. A collection of such letters from France was recently published as: Aurélie Luneau, Jeanne Guérout, and Stefan Martens, eds., *Comme un allemand en France: lettres inédites sous l'occupation 1940–1944* (Paris: L'Iconoclaste, 2016).

being written down.[47] Diaries, in theory more reliable because they were not intended to be shared, also involved the distillation of experience and the representation of what took place. Like other types of sources, these so-called "ego-documents" must be read with sensitivity to their limitations, and they are more useful for the broad analysis of attitudes and perceptions, than for establishing the specifics of particular incidents. As Nicholas Stargardt has written, such sources are valuable "to explore the subjective dimensions of social history," for they enable historians to establish "how people judged and understood events while they were unfolding around them and before they knew the eventual outcome."[48]

Amateur photographs, an equally important and virtually unexploited source for the history of the occupation, pose many of the same problems as other so-called "ego-documents," as well as other difficulties of their own. Although images are often included in scholarly publications to illustrate and provide evidence, they are only beginning to be read with the same critical eye as textual sources, as constructions rather than reflections of reality. Which way the camera pointed, the approach and lighting that were used matter, and what was left out of the frame can reveal as much as what was included. To understand photographs requires interrogating the authorial "voice," asking not only what occupiers photographed, but also why they photographed it, and what was unique or specific about the ways in which occupiers photographed France. This process is complicated by the fact that photographs are often completely anonymous. Many soldiers did not own cameras, and sharing and copying images in order to build personal albums was a widespread practice. Thus, even if there is a name on a snapshot, we cannot be certain that all the photographs in a particular album were taken by the album's "author." Photographs nonetheless offer a new source base that is especially valuable for identifying broad themes in soldiers' perceptions of the occupation and their own roles as occupiers.[49]

To complement the written "ego-documents" and visual sources upon which this book is based, Chapter 7 draws on information from

---

[47] Thomas Kühne, "Kameradschaft: 'das Beste im Leben des Mannes:' Die deutschen Soldaten des Zweiten Weltkriegs in erfahrungs- und geschlechtergeschichtlicher Perspektive," *Geschichte und Gesellschaft* 22, no. 4 (1996): 522, note 77. Cf. Birgit Beck, *Wehrmacht und sexuelle Gewalt: Sexualverbrechen vor deutschen Militärgerichten 1939–1945* (Paderborn: Schöningh, 2004), 76–7.
[48] Stargardt, *German War*, 1.
[49] The historiography of soldiers' amateur photography and the advantages and challenges of using these sources are addressed in greater detail in Chapter 4.

conversations recorded among German prisoners of war (POWs) and analysed by scholars Neitzel and Welzer.[50] Most of these POWs were held at the Trent Park and Latimer camps in the United Kingdom and at Fort Hunt, VA, facilities for prisoners deemed to be of particular interest to the Allies. The men's conversations were recorded covertly for intelligence purposes, and the 16,960 British transcripts and 3,298 American files available to historians represent a broad cross-section of soldiers.[51] The recorded exchanges took place among prisoners, and some involved individuals who the POWs believed to be fellow prisoners, but who were informers working with the Allies. The fact that the transcripts document spontaneous conversations, social psychologist Welzer argues in an invaluable analysis of these reports prepared with historian Neitzel, gives them an unmediated, uncensored quality not present in soldiers' letters.[52] Still, the presence of fellow soldiers in the room shaped the conversations in other ways – for example by exaggerating elements of posturing, and displays of military masculinity. The British and American transcripts offer a new and different "insider" perspective on the lives of soldiers of all ranks that is helpful notably for interrogating men's attitudes towards other soldiers, and the factors that may lead to extreme violence.[53] The objective in using these and other sources that originated with the soldiers themselves is to listen to and analyse as many voices as possible. Sometimes, the same individual appears several times in the course of the book; more often, the voices are singular interjections that nonetheless represent broad themes in the data.

Beyond documents and images from ground-level occupiers, which form the core of the evidence, this book also draws on German, French and some British record sources to frame events and to explore how policy-makers responded to and tried to shape Germans' overall approach to France. Other material that illustrates the regime's instrumentalisation of leisure, consumption and tourism comes from newspapers, notably those for soldiers, like *Der Durchbruch: Soldatenzeitung an den Westfront*. Chapter 3 examines over thirty publications that, following

---

[50] The transcripts are excerpted and analysed in Neitzel and Welzer, *Soldaten*; Römer, *Kameraden*.

[51] The sample reflects the fact that some types of soldier (e.g. front soldiers, U-boat men, airmen) were more likely to be taken prisoner than others, and it includes no individuals who fought only on the Eastern Front. The British intelligence-gatherers tended to focus on officers, while American practitioners included more lower-ranking soldiers. On the representative quality of the data as well as the advantages and disadvantages of these sources, see Neitzel and Welzer, *Soldaten*, 423–30.

[52] Neitzel and Welzer, *Soldaten*, 7.

[53] Johannes Hürter, "Foreword" in Römer, *Kameraden*, 7.

Britta Schilling's "Africa books," I have called "France books."[54] These were tour guides and commemorative books that, like the literature on Germany's lost colonies in Africa that Schilling studies, sought to position the German conquest of France within a larger "world-historical" framework and offered soldiers and their families a kind of blueprint, or set of frames, through which to interpret French experiences. "France books" encouraged occupiers to celebrate how the French defeat had upended the Treaty of Versailles and returned Germany to its powerful position in Europe. These books also taught soldiers to see themselves as noble and fair warriors whose presence on French soil was justified, and intended to be long-lasting.

The book's overall approach is thematic, and it unfolds in a loosely chronological order. Chapter 1 examines German views of France as the occupation began. In particular, it underlines the role that memories of World War I and the Nazi-tainted scholarly discourse of *Westforschung* (research on the West) played in shaping Germans' perceptions of themselves and France as a new occupation got underway. Celebrating their victory as a vindication after the defeat of 1918, occupiers at the same time sought to counter the stereotype, reinforced by World War I, that they were barbarians. To this end, they emphasised their interest in cultural and historical monuments in France, especially those that, like Gothic cathedrals, could be viewed as part of a Germanic heritage in western Europe. As it establishes German perceptions of the neighbour across the Rhine, the chapter draws attention to a Ministry of the Interior memorandum uncovered in the early 2000s, which confirms that, based on supposed "historical" claims, the Germans contemplated annexing large portions of eastern France in 1940.[55] This goal informed their interactions with the land and the civilian populations in these areas. More generally, Chapter 1 shows how past interactions with France, whether "positive" from a German perspective, or negative, formed an important basis for policy-making and practices.

Chapter 2 is the first of three chapters dealing with how Germans approached the occupation. This segment focuses on consumption and leisure, including activities like shopping, eating, and fraternisation.

---

[54] Britta Schilling, *Postcolonial Germany: Memories of Empire in a Decolonized Nation* (New York, NY: Oxford University Press, 2014).

[55] *Wilhelm Stuckart draft plan for Germany/France frontier*, University of New Brunswick, Fredericton, Archives and Special Collections (UNBASC): BC MS/186,1. Peter Schöttler, "Eine Art 'Generalplan West': die Stuckart-Denkschrift vom 14 Juni 1940 und die Planungen für eine neue deutsch-französische Grenze im zweiten Weltkrieg," *Sozial.Geschichte* 18, no. 3 (2003): 83–131.

Historian Götz Aly has argued that Germans' widespread purchasing and pillage in occupied territories helped underpin popular support for the National Socialist regime. Chapter 2 explores this notion, interpreting occupiers' acquisitiveness not only as plunder but also as shopping. Although shopping is a leisure activity typically associated with women rather than men, and with peacetime rather than war, soldiers' letters are replete with references to the food, clothing, and other goods they purchased and sent home to the Reich. As mentioned earlier in this introduction, occupiers' consumption was so extensive that the German authorities established soldiers' department stores to allow occupiers to purchase commodities like perfume and lingerie without interfering with the regime's attempts to control the economy. A similar rationale underpinned official tolerance of French cabaret entertainments and the establishment of Wehrmacht bordellos, designed to reduce fraternisation and make it easier to monitor and channel occupiers' desire to consume French sexual "wares" as well. As it examines how consumption and leisure were deployed strategically to shape soldiers' interactions with France, this chapter draws attention not only to ruptures, but also to continuities between war and peacetime habits.

Like consumption and leisure, the tourism discussed in Chapter 3 was both encouraged and closely monitored by occupation authorities. Tourism helped men feel at home on foreign soil, and smoothed the transition from fighting to relatively static occupying modes. Germans had visited France and admired its monuments before the war; now, these activities continued under particularly favourable conditions. Similar to the "Africa books" that commemorated Germany's colonial exploits, special publications for occupying soldiers used a travel-guide format to direct soldiers' gaze at particular sights, and to transmit ways of seeing, understanding, and remembering France that aligned with a National Socialist worldview. Tourism, like consumption, was a benefit of conquest that occupiers were encouraged to enjoy and to share with their families in the form of letters and photographs. Carefully managed by the authorities, it became a valuable tool to mould occupiers' perceptions.

Chapter 4 turns to photography, which many occupiers used to record their experiences. In France, there was clear dissonance between what soldiers were actually doing – occupying a neighbouring country militarily and oppressing its population – and the way they constructed their role in both amateur photography and official publications. This chapter asks how photography aligned with conquest and what it reveals about occupiers' own perceptions of their role. Why was photography so appealing to occupying soldiers, and why did they favour motifs that made it look as though France was at peace, not war? What did it mean, moreover, to photograph Frenchmen who appeared to be relaxing while eating oysters, but had actually been requisitioned against their will to guard German communications cables? Once taken, how did these, and other seemingly benign images work with other materials to shape ideas about, and memories of, the German experience in France?

Chapter 5 turns to the violence that grew in France from late 1941 onwards. An initial segment surveys discussions about German responses to French resisters' first assassinations of occupying soldiers. Scholars debate whether, and if so how, these assassinations and the Militärbefehlshaber's attempts to navigate between local needs and demands from Berlin served as a trigger for the deportation of France's Jews.[56] In this context, this chapter explores how the need to maintain France as a stable area for rest and relaxation influenced the Militärbefehlshaber's decision-making process. Later, the chapter addresses the overall response to rising insecurity in France, asking what impact growing resistance had on the typical German soldier, and how the occupation authorities shifted their policies in response to resistance attacks.

Chapter 6 sets the French occupation in the context of the wider war, and soldiers' experiences on the Eastern Front, in particular. Many men moved back and forth between France and other fronts several times in the course of the conflict, a mobility that has been largely overlooked in the historical literature about the French occupation. This chapter looks at soldiers' responses to their unprecedented mobility, and the use of France as a "safe" area for rest, relaxation, and regrouping combat units. In the context of Eastern-Front experiences, it examines the highly influential notion that occupiers were going "soft" from being too long in the West. Why did both rank and file and upper echelons of the military leadership seem to think that soldiers in France were becoming feminised and losing their military strength? Here, the question of whether the occupiers in France actually were going soft is less important than the issue of why contemporaries thought they were, and how this perception shaped the occupation through, notably, attempts to manage manpower as Germany experienced increasing losses.

As it traces the end of the war in France, Chapter 7 takes up the question of how leisure activities like tourism and consumption

---

[56] Delacor, "Weltanschauungskrieg"; Herbert, "Militärverwaltung"; Ahlrich Meyer, *Die Besatzung*; Christopher Neumaier, "The Escalation of German Reprisal Policy in Occupied France, 1941–42," *Journal of Contemporary History* 41, no. 1 (2006): 113–31.

interacted with violence. This chapter builds on recent research into the German army's brutality to contend that while longer-serving occupiers may have been less likely to lash out violently against the French, the perception that precisely these occupiers had gone "soft" served as a catalyst to violence among "newer" reinforcements moving in from the Eastern Front. Using recorded conversations among prisoners of war alongside official reports compiled by members of the military administration after they had withdrawn from France, this chapter investigates an apparent "culture clash" between long-serving occupiers and newly arrived men. It returns to the notion of "softness" that often emerged in occupiers' explanations of what they thought had gone wrong. Bringing the book to a close, a brief conclusion summarises and restates the main arguments. Attention to ground-level occupiers' perceptions and experiences, and to the interaction of consumption, leisure and tourism with violence deepens our understanding of occupation policy and practices. Using a bottom-up approach, this study offers new perspectives on the German occupation of France, the history of Nazism and on World War II.

1 Occupations, Past and Present

Hans Klumpp, a radio operator with Infantry Regiment 75, entered France on 16 May 1940. He and his comrades crossed the Meuse River by rubber dinghy near the town of Revin in the central segment of the German Front, then paused to let their vehicles join them over a temporary bridge. While they were waiting, Klumpp confided to his diary, the soldiers helped themselves to motorbikes for their unit, as well as fresh underwear from local shops. They saw their first prisoners of war, including French African soldiers and, later that day, they observed Belgian civilian refugees returning home. Revin was "pretty heavily touched. No windowpanes left whole," and the next town, Maubert-Fontaine, offered "a sad picture." They passed fallen French soldiers, and arrived at midnight in the village of Girondelle having travelled "40–45 km." The roadsides were lined with "a few pieces of artillery and many vehicles, emptied, [with] linens, French helmets, ammunition . . . cows, rabbits, hens, pigs, all running around confusedly. An incredible muddle!"[1] The unit continued to advance for the next few days, then stopped to await further orders. Bored by sudden inactivity, Klumpp wrote that "we sit around lamely, [and] try to sleep. After all, you can't just eat all day." Having stuffed himself with French food and felt sick for twenty-four hours, he resolved to be more reasonable. The following days were marked by additional plundering and the decision to grow a small moustache. Continuing to mix the mundane and the extraordinary, Klumpp commented on the incongruously fine weather that served as a backdrop to the battle.[2]

Soon, Klumpp and his fellow soldiers were moving forwards again. Reims fell and, on their way to the Marne River, the troops stopped at a place called Romery.[3] Klumpp recounted that, "[t]he companies went

---

[1] Hans Klumpp, diary 1938–48, 16 May 1940 (Deutsches Tagebucharchiv [DTA]: 1942).
[2] Klumpp, diary, 8 June 1940 (DTA: 1942).
[3] Romery, near Damery on the Marne, is misidentified in the diary as Donnery. Klumpp, diary, 11 June 1940 (DTA: 1942).

in, and everything was calm. Suddenly shots rang out from every cellar. Many [were] wounded. It was terrible. We pulled back out of the village, which was burning in some places, to higher ground, where we spent the night." Shaken by the engagement, the soldiers' mood darkened when they had withdrawn, and "[a]n incredible fury against the French manifested itself among us. Some prisoners of war were with us. It wouldn't have taken much, and we would have shot them. The civilian prisoners were put up against a wall. After such meanness, there's no 'pardon' anymore."[4] Barely able to restrain themselves from killing uniformed prisoners protected by the laws of war, the furious combatants showed no mercy towards civilians.[5] Klumpp and his unit clearly believed they had been attacked by partisans, the much-feared "franc-tireurs" who were rumoured to lurk in French villages.[6] The following day, as if making a deliberate contrast with the previous night's brutality, Klumpp noted abruptly that he had had a "very good" conversation with three French prisoners of war who had even praised his accent.[7]

Within a couple of weeks, the battle for France was over. The soldiers found more permanent quarters and established everyday routines. Like many men, Klumpp was billeted in a local household where he had further opportunities to practise his French. Sometimes there were amusing instances of miscommunication, such as when he and his comrades tried to explain to a returning civilian that they had fed the man's dog in his absence. The Frenchman, clearly fearing the worst, understood to the contrary that the soldiers had devoured the dog themselves.[8] By early July, Klumpp reported with satisfaction that "[m]y French is getting better each day, yes, now I can measure the value of being able to make myself understood by the population."[9] The men had stopped outright plundering for the time being, but given the inflated exchange rate of 20 francs to one Reichsmark, even normal shopping was highly

---

[4] "Pardon" is rendered in French in the original. Klumpp, diary, 11 June 1940 (DTA: 1942).

[5] During the 1940 campaign, incidents in which German soldiers or SS men killed civilians occurred, though they were rare. Lieb, *Konventionneller*, 15–20.

[6] Fears of franc-tireurs went back to the Franco-Prussian war, 1870–71, when French citizens and irregular units had attacked German forces. According to the 1902 German guidelines for the conduct of war, still used in 1940, officers could court-martial and shoot franc-tireurs. Scheck, *Hitler's African Victims: The German Army Massacres of Black French Soldiers in 1940*, 74, 85, 87.

[7] Klumpp, diary, 12 June 1940 (DTA: 1942).

[8] Klumpp, diary, 22 June 1940 (DTA: 1942). Occupiers' weak language skills were a frequent source of humour at the beginning of the occupation, their linguistic fumbling serving as a metaphor for their early attempts to muddle through in a new environment. See, e.g. articles in *Der Vormarsch*, 21 June and 30 June 1940 (BArch: RHD 69/50).

[9] Klumpp, diary, 3 July 1940 (DTA: 1942).

profitable for the Germans. Klumpp noted that, "[w]e live very cheaply here in France ... so for example socks cost thirty-five pfennigs, a shirt forty pfennigs ... a cup of coffee seven pfennings, the best bottle of wine two Reichsmarks, etc., like God in France!"[10]

The alternation of excitement and boredom; remorseless plunder and eager consumption; the fine weather, friendly conversations and sudden, vengeful brutality reported in Klumpp's diary are typical of German soldiers' accounts of entering France in 1940.[11] These early experiences open up themes that can be traced in many further sources, offering evidence of attitudes, perceptions and behaviours that coloured the German occupation of France through the next four years. Still, while the peaks and dales of battle had become familiar to men like Klumpp by the end of the French campaign, occupation itself presented less-accustomed terrain. What underlying ideas about France did occupying soldiers and officers carry with them as they built a new occupation from the ground up? How did they perceive the country, and its relationship to its perennial rival and neighbour, Germany?

To see France as the soldiers saw it and to understand how their perceptions and experiences influenced occupation projects, we begin by examining the attitudes that Germans brought with them as they moved west. This chapter first summarises ideas about France that were current in the interwar period before turning to a Ministry of the Interior document, known as the Stuckart memorandum, that shows how geo-topographical and long-term "historical" claims were deployed to justify occupation and even the potential annexation of large portions of eastern France in 1940.[12] Although the annexation was never carried out, this memorandum represents one extreme of National Socialist plans for the country. The arguments that underlay it reflect an influential current of opinion that informed German interactions with France and its population.

The Stuckart memorandum drew on long-term historical precedents to make present-day claims on France, but shorter-term historical precedents and memories were also important in shaping the German approach to occupation. World War I was especially significant, for the

---

[10] Klumpp, diary, 5 July 1940 (DTA: 1942).
[11] Klumpp, who was 22 in 1940, had been in the army since 1938. He was a life-long bachelor from Karlsruhe who became a teacher after the war. In December 1941, he requested leave to pursue medical studies. The leave was not granted, though he later worked in a field hospital (DTA: 1942).
[12] *Wilhelm Stuckart draft plan for Germany/France frontier* [henceforth Stuckart memorandum], University of New Brunswick Archives and Special Collections (UNBASC): BC MS/186,1. See Schöttler, "Generalplan West."

memory of this conflict, little more than two decades past, loomed large in 1940. Its echoes were everywhere as sons followed in their veteran fathers' footsteps and some men even returned in person to occupy lands they had fought for in their youth. Victory over France carried particular symbolic weight, vindicating Germans for their loss in 1918 and the "shameful" Treaty of Versailles.

Even as they basked in their triumph, however, Germans also strove to counter the long-standing stereotype, reinforced during World War I, that they were barbarians.[13] Purporting to have established a new, National Socialist–style occupation that broke with vindictive habits of the past, they called for "correct" behaviour from individual occupiers. At the same time, they emphasised German cultural sophistication through staged public admiration of selected historical monuments which, like the Gothic cathedrals, could be stretched to become part of a shared Franco-German heritage. Hoping to establish positive relations with local people at the ground level, moreover, some men took the notion of a shared past further, suggesting that there might be a kind of camaraderie between themselves and French veterans of World War I. The German authorities, for their part, took a dim view of such camaraderie, for it implied too much common ground between occupiers and the defeated population.

Over the next four years, steering a path between cordiality and openness, on the one hand, and dominance and ruthless exploitation, on the other, became the occupation's chief internal challenge. Managing the French, about which we know a great deal, was just part of the story – managing the German occupiers themselves presented an equally great, though less widely recognised, test. Focusing on the Stuckart memorandum and the varied resonances of World War I, this chapter shows how long- and short-term memories and historical precedents coloured how Germans began to navigate the tension between admiring and enjoying French pleasures, and controlling French territory while profiting from its many resources. In a brief concluding segment, this

---

[13] John Horne and Alan Kramer have examined stories about German brutality in Belgium and France in World War I "German 'Atrocities' and Franco-German Opinion, 1914: The Evidence of German Soldiers' Diaries," *Journal of Modern History* 66, March (1994): 1–33; *German Atrocities 1914: A History of Denial* (New Haven, CT: Yale University Press, 2001). Brutality associated with the German occupation of East European territory during the same period perhaps also contributed to these popular memories, though this is difficult to judge because, as Jay Winter has pointed out, the experiences of soldiers and civilians on the Eastern Front have been almost completely buried since the conflict. Jay Winter, *Remembering War: The Great War between Memory and History in the Twentieth Century* (New Haven, CT: Yale University Press, 2006), 80–81.

chapter also introduces the occupation apparatus, the soldiers, and some of the ideas that German administrators developed to underpin their hegemony.

Compared to the invasion of Poland, the outcome of the battle in the West had been less certain. Hitler and his military staff were prepared to occupy the Netherlands and Belgium, but they had not foreseen a large-scale military occupation of France. Indeed, the Germans were probably as surprised by their victory in 1940 as the French, and there were no unified plans for occupied areas.[14]

To address this situation, some local *Wehrmacht* authorities reached for older plans that had been prepared for the 1914–18 conflict, when Germany had occupied Belgium and a section of Northern France.[15] Many others improvised, drawing on longer-term models where possible, and relying on French civil servants and police to do most of the day-to-day running of French affairs. As they improvised, occupiers' presence in France rested on the conviction that they belonged there, on land legitimately claimed by the Reich in the latest phase of a long-running rivalry with France for control over west-central Europe. Men like Hans Klumpp may have understood things in simpler terms – they had won the battle and now enjoyed the spoils of war – but they were part of a much larger project to legitimise German hegemony and build a model occupation in the West.[16]

In the interwar period, German attitudes towards France had generally been positive, if somewhat contradictory. Adolf Hitler himself had little good to say about France and decried the fawning franco-philia of the German-language press, but his views represented just one extreme of a fuller range of opinion about Germany's neighbour.[17] Generally speaking, Germans admired French culture,

---

[14] Richard Cobb, *French and Germans, Germans and French: A Personal Interpretation of France under Two Occupations 1914–1918/1940–1944* (Hanover, NH: University Press of New England, 1983), 57; Ahlrich Meyer, "Grossraumpolitik und Kollaboration im Westen: Werner Best, die Zeitschrift 'Reich – Volksordnung – Lebensraum' und die deutsche Militärverwaltung in Frankreich 1940–42" in *Modelle für ein deutsches Europa: Ökonomie und Herrschaft im Grosswirtschaftsraum*, ed. Horst Kahrs et al., Beiträge zur nationalsozialistischen Gesundheits- und Sozialpolitik 10 (Berlin: Rotbuch, 1992), 44; Schöttler, "Generalplan West," 83.

[15] Cobb, *French and Germans*, 41.

[16] The notion that Germany would be a superior, more chivalrous occupying power had considerable traction, as outlined in this chapter. "Model occupation" is also the title of a book on the Channel Islands under German control, where similar forces were at work on a smaller scale in a British context. The Germans administered the Channel Islands as part of the French department of Manche. Madeline Bunting, *The Model Occupation: The Channel Islands under German Rule, 1940–1945* (London: Pimlico, 2004).

[17] Adolf Hitler, *Mein Kampf*, 11th edn. (Munich: Franz Eher Nachf., 1942), 58, 696 ff.

yet vilified French decadence. They lauded the timelessness of "eternal" France, while complaining about its purportedly unchanging backwardness. Perhaps the preeminent "expert" on France was Friedrich Sieburg, whose work remained influential throughout the occupation.[18] Prior to the war, Sieburg's attitude was fond, even gently mocking. He wrote of France's faults as endearing foibles and seemed to affirm the attraction of a Gallic lifestyle model that was not based on modern efficiency alone. In France, as Sieburg put it, "the statistics are wrong, but all the measures are right."[19]

Through Sieburg's well-known work, Germans arriving in France in 1940 were primed to perceive the country as a backward but often delightful counter-model to the hustle and bustle of German modernity. Theoretically, at any rate, defeat had confirmed German superiority, but French charms remained. Midway through the occupation, Lieutenant Winfried A. summed up common perceptions when he wrote that "[a] Frenchman says: I am alive and that's lovely, and in order to make it lovely, he knows how to turn pleasure into the more important part [of life]. Not much bothers him from the inside. He looks outside and likes what he sees. He loves wine, a sense of equilibrium, and he loves love. We're also alive, but we ask why, we look for truth, meaning..."[20] For all their charm, the French were seen as superficial, and although Germans may have secretly admired the Gallic ability to shrug expansively and enjoy life, they also believed that their own soul was deeper and they had greater things to accomplish.

Such comments echoed Sieburg's ideas, and they point to fundamental ambiguities in the overall attitudes of the Third Reich towards France. Victory over the French in 1940 carried special value, for it vindicated Germans for the loss of World War I and the humiliations of the Treaty of Versailles. It was France's turn to be the underdog, but at the same time, long-standing respect and admiration for French culture got in the way of pure vengeance. In contrast to attitudes towards Poland, for

---

[18] Wolfgang Geiger, *L'image de la France dans l'Allemagne nazie 1933–1945* (Rennes: Presses Universitaires de Rennes, 1999), 17–40; Gordon, "Ist Gott Französisch? Germans, Tourism and Occupied France 1940–1944."

[19] Friedrich Sieburg, *Gott in Frankreich: Ein Versuch* (Frankfurt am Main: Societäts-Verlag, 1931). Although he had always suggested that France would have to change in order to keep up with modern, dynamic Germany, during the occupation Sieburg's attitudes hardened. In 1941, he declared before the "Groupe Collaboration" in Paris that "My experiences with France have made me into a fighter and a National Socialist." Sieburg, 199.

[20] Winfried A., war letters 1942–4, 22 April 1943 (DTA: 1908).

example, which were marked by a clear and ruthless sense of superiority, in the West, Germans were less sure of where they stood. They blended scorn for France's current government with admiration for "eternal France" and its cultural achievements.[21]

These ambiguities that were an underlying current throughout the occupation found early expression in plans about what to do with French territory. Did it make more sense to segment the country and weaken it so that it would never again challenge German dominance, or to retain it as a semi-independent and collaborating ally? Since Hitler himself apparently vacillated about how to treat Germany's defeated neighbour, the beginning of the occupation was marked by a lack of clarity about which approach to take.[22]

In the first uncertain weeks, German officials produced several texts that considered what to do with France.[23] Perhaps the most intriguing of these was a memorandum signed by Hitler's Minister of the Interior, Wilhelm Stuckart, that was long thought to have disappeared.[24] The precise authorship of the document remains unclear, but it is strongly linked to Hans Globke, a young Ministry of the Interior staff member who, though dogged by controversy about his career during the Third Reich, later served as Secretary of State and "right-hand man" to West German Chancellor Konrad Adenauer in the 1950s and early 1960s.[25] The document is significant not because it established a policy that was followed to the letter, but rather because it serves as a gloss on German views of France at the dawn of the occupation and illustrates the role that geo-topographical and long-term historical arguments played in lending

---

[21] On German views of France over the longer term, see Geiger, *L'image*, especially ch. 6.; Michael E. Nolan, *The Inverted Mirror: Mythologizing the Enemy in France and Germany 1898–1914* (New York: Berghahn Books, 2004).

[22] Meyer, "Grossraumpolitik," 44; Schöttler, "Generalplan West," 83.

[23] BArch: R 43 II/676; Schöttler, "Generalplan West," 103–4.

[24] Schöttler, 83–131. Cf. Umbreit, *Militärbefehlshaber*, 54–5. A copy of the document thought to have been Hitler's own can be found in the Beaverbrook Collection at Harriet Irving Library, University of New Brunswick, Fredericton, Canada (UNBSC: BC MS/186). Details of the document's provenance are given in the German version of British reporter Sefton Delmer's autobiography, where the document is reprinted in full, as it is in Schöttler's article cited above. Sefton Delmer, *Die Deutschen und ich* (Hamburg: Nannen, 1962), 667, 767–97.

[25] In 1962, as Adenauer and Charles de Gaulle were preparing to sign the Elysée Treaty, Globke denied authorship of the document. He claimed it had been produced before he had been made responsible for issues stemming from the armistice with France beginning in June 1940. In fact, Globke was responsible for "Western questions" in the Ministry of the Interior before 1 July 1940, making his assertion questionable. Schöttler, "Generalplan West," 92–3. Cf. Delmer, *Die Deutschen und ich*, 767. For a fuller discussion of the document's authorship, see Schöttler, "Generalplan West," 90, 102 ff.

an air of inevitability and a sense of entitlement to Germans' presence west of the Rhine.[26]

The tone of the Stuckart memorandum, dated 14 June 1940, was scholarly rather than overtly propagandistic or vindictive. Its message was nonetheless clear – Germany had long-standing and legitimate claims in western Europe: France's position henceforth must be subordinate to Germany's in every respect, and its resources exploited for the benefit of the Reich alone. The memorandum argued that the western powers' goal in World War I had been to return Germany to its fragmented state after the Thirty Years' War (1618–48) and to make the Rhine River into the Franco-German border along its full length. As a result, Germany had the right to go back centuries when drawing its own German-French border, back to a time when "the border with France lay where, according to natural circumstances, it must lie."[27] Modern political borders made no sense, serving only to rein in German ambitions.

With the restoration of putative "natural" borders in mind, the memorandum laid out four principles. First, a new border must align with regional geographic features. Second, German people should not be left "outside" the Reich. Third, Hitler's Germany must acquire the whole of the economic zones seen as belonging to "central Europe." Finally, a new border should secure for the Reich "natural and strategically necessary" defence lines in the West.[28] Developing each of these principles in greater detail, the text used geo–topographical arguments to contend that the true border between "Mitteleuropa" and "Westeuropa" (central Europe and western Europe), and thus between Germany and France, was not the Rhine River itself, but rather the Rhine River basin writ large, including the drainage basins of the Meuse and Scheldt rivers. Since the Ardennes formed part of the same formation of slate hills as Germany's Eifel and Luxemburg's Ösling region, they too should be considered part of "Mitteleuropa." Further south, the Vosges, and even the Jura ranges, similarly corresponded to the relief of the Black Forest on the Rhine's opposite side. Topographical arguments suggested that expanding the Reich's borders westwards would bring them into better alignment with the earth's natural features. Nature itself demanded that the artificial state borders of the past be redrawn.[29]

Alongside geography and topography, history was marshaled to support redrawing Germany's frontiers. Following the 843 division of Charlemagne's empire into three parts, the easternmost segment of the empire

---

[26] On German plans for France more generally, see Laub, *After the Fall*, ch. 2.
[27] UNBASC: BC MS/186, 1.   [28] UNBASC: BC MS/186, 1.
[29] UNBASC: BC MS/186, 2–9.

had quickly swallowed up the middle part, resulting (so the document maintained) in a German-French border that "prevailed without fundamental alteration until the occupation of the bishoprics of Metz, Toul and Verdun (1552), and even until the Peace of Westfalia [1648]."[30] Individual German rulers continued to control areas west of the Rhine for many years thereafter; quite apart from the much-contested Alsace and Lorraine, the county of Montbéliard (German Mömpelgard), for example, had belonged to the house of Württemberg, and was only turned over to France in 1801. Through the centuries, French leaders had continually tried to claim that the Rhine was the eastern edge of France, despite the fact that France's "natural" borders lay further west. Buffer states established in the lands that ran westwards from the Rhine to encompass the Ardennes and Vosges had never survived. "The Rhine has always been the German river of fate," this section of the document concluded portentously, for "if both of its banks and the lands that belong to its drainage basin lie uncontestedly in German hands, then a time of German greatness is upon us; if they are in French hands, then we are living through times of Germany's most profound debasement."[31] Speaking more generally, the historian Shelley Baranowski has pointed out that Germany was marked in the longer term by a "tension of empire," which combined "the aspiration to imperialist expansion and the simultaneous fear of dissolution at the hands of its imperialist rivals."[32] Exhibiting this tension, the Stuckart memorandum used a language of extremes to reinforce the notion that either Germany must expand westwards, or it would be doomed, its rightful territorial possessions swallowed up by France and its Allies.

Developing this polarised position, the Stuckart memorandum brought linguistic, racial, and even architectural arguments to bear. Not only would a new, more westerly border correspond better to the natural features of the area, but it would also resolve long-standing linguistic, cultural, and even "racial" tensions. Buildings and artwork clearly evinced the original Germanic character of these regions, for "we must recall the Gothic, that is to say German, town halls of many Belgian and French cities, and the Gothic cathedrals of Paris, Reims, Amiens, etc."[33] Alongside the French, many Germans, Flemish people, and Alsacians lived in the areas to be taken over by the Reich.[34]

---

[30] UNBASC: BC MS/186, 10.
[31] This section is annotated with a double red line in the margin of the original. UNBASC: BC MS/186, 12.
[32] Baranowski, *Nazi Empire*, 4.   [33] UNBASC: BC MS/186, 14.
[34] While the memorandum maintained that the need to include the Flemish population "in the Greater German space requires no additional justification," the Walloons were a somewhat

The memorandum argued, further, that racial mixing had critically weakened the French heartland. Given its low birthrate and low population density, "France has a suction effect on the neighbouring states like a vacuum."[35] Without large numbers of immigrants, the French economy would be unable to function, and the presence of some 7–8 million non-French individuals was evidence that the country "is no longer either willing or able to fill and exploit its own space with its own people."[36] Had the political history of the area been different, the labour of the many German and Flemish people who kept the French economy running would have served Germany instead. "Drawing the new border must create permanent change here," the memorandum maintained, "by making space, that ultimately can not be populated, cultivated and exploited by the French, available to the German people to be settled and won back as German land [Volksboden.]"[37] French people presented no obstacle to these plans, for "[t]he French population that is settled in these areas today can mostly be resettled and find sufficient space to establish and feed itself in the depopulated French interior."[38] As in eastern Europe, local citizens would be pushed out of the way, crowded together in areas that Germans regarded as under-populated, in order to make space for German expansion.

The memorandum concluded by noting that controlling the western heights of the Ardennes, the centuries-old transit route through the "Burgundian gates" at Belfort, and other key areas would place important strategic defense points in German hands.[39] The new border

more problematic element; in the end, it argued that Walloons were neither French nor German, but a separate and older racial group that had only recently come under French influence. The border should be redrawn without special regard for these individuals. UNBASC: BC MS/186, 19–20; Peter Schöttler, "Die historische 'Westforschung' zwischen 'Abwehrkampf' und territorialer Offensive" in *Geschichtsschreibung als Legitimationswissenschaft 1918–1945*, ed. Peter Schöttler (Frankfurt am Main: Suhrkamp, 1997), 217, 219.

[35] UNBASC: BC MS/186, 24.

[36] UNBASC: BC MS/186, 25. Reiterating a long-expressed mixture of disdain and resentment about France's use of colonial troops, the document also noted that "[a]bove all, France is no longer able to defend its territory through its own strength. Rather, it must draw on masses of coloured people, perhaps the most obvious sign of its decline." UNBASC: BC MS/186, 24–5.

[37] UNBASC: BC MS/186, 25.   [38] UNBASC: BC MS/186, 25.

[39] After detailing exactly where a new Franco-German border should be drawn, the document enumerated the extensive resources present in the zones to be transferred to Germany: the population, urban areas, roads, navigable waterways, railways, roads, mines, industrial facilities, and forests. Lest the memorandum leave any doubt in readers' minds about the utility of annexing these territories, the text noted bluntly that, "the areas that are to be separated are economically the most valuable parts of France." UNBASC: BC MS/186, 36.

it proposed would resolve centuries-old conflict over the borderlands and create a lasting frontier to "allow for peaceful development in the West."[40]

As this overview suggests, the memorandum's arguments were geo-topographical, racial and economic rather than diplomatic or military. Indeed, the Stuckart memorandum was closely linked to the long-standing field of German borderland research known as *Westforschung* (loosely: "Western Studies").[41] *Westforschung* became especially popular in German universities in the interwar period, where it was deployed to undermine the legitimacy of the French occupation of the Rhineland. Over time, *Westforschung* expanded to legitimise German claims to France itself. Its counterpart was the rather better-known *Ostforschung* ("Eastern Studies") devoted to substantiating German ambitions in eastern Europe.[42] In both cases, researchers employed "scientific" methods in fields like history, geography, archaeology, and linguistics, to support the political and racial agendas of the day. The Stuckart memorandum names key *Westforscher* as authorities to add weight to its arguments about where a "natural" German-French border should lie.[43]

---

[40] UNBASC: BC MS/186, 38.

[41] On Westforschung, see Burkhard Dietz, Helmut Gabel, and Ulrich Tiedau, *Griff nach dem Westen* (Waxmann Verlag, 2003); Schöttler, "historische 'Westforschung'"; Michael Fahlbusch and Ingo Haar, ed., *German Scholars and Ethnic Cleansing 1919–1945* (New York: Berghahn Books, 2005); Michael J. Wintle, *Imagining Europe: Europe and European Civilisation as Seen from Its Margins and by the Rest of the World, in the Nineteenth and Twentieth Centuries* (Bern: Peter Lang, 2008), 84 ff.; Matthias Middell, "Konjunktur der Wissenschaftsgeschichte: Beobachtungen und Problematisierungen anhand neuer Veröffentlichungen zur völkischnationalistischen Historiographie in Deutschland" in *"Westforschung" – Eine Diskussion zur völkisch-nationalistischen Historiographie in Deutschland – H-Soz-u-Kult Review Symposium*, ed. Vera Ziegeldorf and Matthias Middell, vol. 2, Veröffentlichungen von Clio-Online, 2003, 3–14, http://hsozkult.geschichte.hu-berlin.de/rezensionen/type=revsymp&id=320; Peter Schöttler, *Geschichtsschreibung als Legitimationswissenschaft 1918–1945* (Frankfurt am Main: Suhrkamp, 1997); Schöttler, "Generalplan West."

[42] Michael Burleigh, *Germany Turns Eastwards: A Study of Ostforschung in the Third Reich* (Cambridge: Cambridge University Press, 1988). Since the later 1990s, there have been ongoing and sometimes heated debates about the role played by academic researchers in supporting the political and racial agendas of the Third Reich. These have centred on Ostforschung, exploring Westforschung to a lesser extent. For an overview, see Middell, "Konjunktur der Wissenschaftsgeschichte: Beobachtungen und Problematisierungen anhand neuer Veröffentlichungen zur völkischnationalistischen Historiographie in Deutschland."

[43] UNSBASC: BC MS/186, 2. The document cites Otto Schlüter (1872–1959), a geographer who focused on "settlement geography" (Siedlungsgeographie), and a professor at Halle University from 1911; Friedrich Metz (1890–1969), a geographer who specialised in "settlement geography" and Westforschung, Professor at Freiburg university from 1935: as well as Franz Steinbach (1895–1964), an historian and specialist in the history of the Rhine region as well as Westforschung, Professor at Bonn University from 1928; and Karl Linnebach (1879–1961), an historian and specialist in the history of

Although the memorandum might be interpreted as an attempt by the proponents of Westforschung to push forwards their ideas in a friendly political climate, historian Peter Schöttler contends that the process actually worked the other way around, as the researchers provided "scholarly" justifications for pre-existing notions.[44] The idea that Germany's western border with France needed readjustment had broad currency. On 20 May, for example, well before the armistice with France was signed, General Jodl noted in his service diary that Hitler had imagined moving the Franco–German border significantly to the west.[45] Hitler's new border was based on the idea that France should "return" to Germany the lands it had held for the last 400 years.[46] This was a nationalist position with roots dating back to the Napoleonic wars that enjoyed considerable support in Germany.[47] It aligned comfortably with the ideas of Westforschung proponents, whose thinking was well-known to the German public by the mid-1930s. A 1937 historical atlas meant for school use included several maps that showed Germanic languages and "German cultural land" (Kulturboden) significantly further to the west, not to mention the east, than the political borders of the day.[48] One of these maps reminded readers of where the German empire's political border lay in 1500, inviting them to note its "better" alignment with the full extent of "German cultural land" (Figure 1.1).[49] Although Britain had been considered Germany's "true" enemy before 1939 – a circumstance that had helped reign in the most overt anti-French, anti-Belgian expansionist polemics – by the late 1930s, it was commonly accepted in Germany that "Germanic" settlements had existed well to the west of Germany's current borders, and arguably as far south as the Loire river.

Once Germany began to move into France, the overtly annexationist implications of these notions could be given free expression. Taking control of the country, Germany established a series demarcation lines to organise and monitor various regions. In addition to the well-known

the Rhine region as well as military history, archivist at the Reich Archives in Potsdam. Schöttler, "Generalplan West," 111.

[44] Schöttler, "Generalplan West," 97–8. Schöttler, 97–8.

[45] Diensttagebuch Jodl, entry for 20 May 1940, cited in *International Military Tribunal Nuremberg*, vol. 28 (Nuremberg, 1948), 431.

[46] Schöttler, "Generalplan West," 97.

[47] Wolfgang Hans Stein, "Archive als Objekt von Kulturimperialismen: Französische Archive in Deutschland – deutsche Archive in Frankreich" in *Archiv und Gedächtnis: Studien zur interkulturellen Überlieferung*, ed. Michael Espagne, Katharina Middell, and Matthias Middell (Leipzig: Leipziger Universitätsverlag, 2000), 102.

[48] Max Pehle et al., ed., *Historischer Schul-Atlas*, 54th edn. (Leipzig: Velhagen und Klasing, 1937), 1, 123, 140.

[49] Pehle et al., 140.

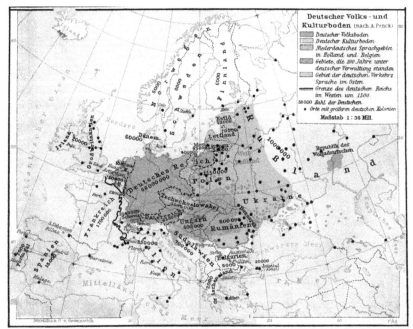

Figure 1.1 Map from a school atlas showing the political border of the German empire in 1500 and inviting readers to note its "better" alignment with "German cultural land."
Max Pehle et al., ed., *Historischer Schul-Atlas*, 54th edn. (Leipzig: Velhagen und Klasing, 1937), 140.

demarcation line that separated the nothern and western parts of France, occupied directly by the Germans, from the southeastern areas ruled by the satellite government of Maréchal Pétain, a Führer decree at the time of the armistice established a "Northeastern Line" (Nordostlinie) that corresponded almost exactly to the new border laid out in the Stuckart memorandum.[50] (See "Reserved" or "Forbidden" zone on map at the beginning of this book.) Despite vociferous French objections, the line was retained until the night of 17–18 December, 1941, when it was eliminated

---

[50] An occupation administrator noted in his final report in 1944 that, "[t]he political reasons that led to [the line's] creation were never made known." Final report by military administrator von Teuchert, 30, 5 January 1945 (BArch: RW/246); Schöttler, "Generalplan West," 97.

without explanation. Rumours that Germany planned to annex the area flourished, reinforced by the fact that French civilians who had fled it during the 1940 "Exodus" were forbidden to return there until February 1943.[51] In the interim, the shadowy Ostland company became active in the area. It emanated from the Reich Ministry of Food (Reichsernährungs-ministerium) and by January 1941, controlled some 70,000 hectares of French agricultural land, mainly in the departments of Ardennes and Meuse.[52] The Stuckart memorandum thus helped to underpin concrete plans for the exploitation and annexation of northeastern France.[53]

---

[51] In reality, exceptions to this rule were made almost immediately, since it was in Germany's interest to allow miners, doctors, policemen, French administrators, and their families to return. See final report by military administrator von Teuchert, 30, 5 January 1945 (BArch: RW/246). Still, Germany continued to use demarcation lines to sift through the French population. See Nicole Dombrowski Risser, *France under Fire: German Invasion, Civilian Flight and Family Survival during World War II* (Cambridge University Press, 2012), ch. 7.

[52] There is little historical research on the Ostland GmbH, which was distinct from the segment of German-occupied Soviet areas later called the Reichskommissariat Ostland. The Ostland company had been formed to manage land in occupied Poland. Jacques Mièvre, *L'"Ostland" en France durant la seconde guerre mondiale: une tentative de colonisation agraire allemande en zone interdite* (Nancy: Université de Nancy II, 1973), 24. It claimed to be managing "abandoned" French land according to the terms of the armistice, but was understood by the French to be a private business exploiting for Germany the lands in the restricted northeastern zone. Elmar Michel, "Allgemeiner Rückblick," undated final report [1944], 20 (BArch: RW 35/244). By January 1941, the Ostland controlled some 70,000 hectares of French agricultural land, mainly in the departments of Ardennes and Meuse. Mièvre, 34. Although the German seizure of lands slowed down after June 1941, the Ostland continued to make claims on individual properties into the spring of 1944, such that it is estimated to have taken over some 170,000 hectares all-told. Mièvre, 56, 58. The owners of these lands who were not already absent were typically expelled. As part of the occupation's growing repression, moreover, Gäel Eismann has shown that in August 1941, the MBH contemplated sending 5,000 arrested Jews to work on farms managed by the Ostland company. "Représailles et logique idéologico-répressive. Le tournant de l'été 1941 dans la politique répressive du Commandant militaire allemand en France," *Revue historique*, no. 669 (January 2014): 113. All of this activity lent credence to French fears that the area was about to be annexed. Mièvre, *Ostland*, 146. To respond to French concerns and further occlude the nature of Ostland's activities, it was renamed Landbewirtschaftungs-GmbH in 1941, and later also known as the Reichsland. MBH, Verwaltungsstab Abt. Wi III, Tgb. Nr. 2264/4, Re: "Landwirtschaftung in der Sperrzone," 21 June 1941 (Archives Nationales, Paris [AN]: 40 AJ/450). See also Margot Lyautey, "L'Ostland en France pendant la Seconde Guerre Mondiale" (M.A. thesis, Ecole des Hautes Etudes en Sciences Sociales, 2017).

[53] It seems, moreover, that when a first version of the memorandum did not go far enough, notably in annexing territory along the English Channel coast, Hitler requested the document be redrafted to include these areas. While all but one of the maps associated with the original memorandum have been lost, the one that does survive, in the files of the German–French armistice commission, gives a clear indication of where the new border was to lie. The map is reprinted in Schöttler, "Generalplan West," 108. See also introductory note to UNBASC: BC MS/186 by Sefton Delmer and interrogation of

Equally significantly for the further course of the occupation, the memorandum synthesised geo-topographical and historical arguments that were common currency in Germany in the late 1930s and that formed part of the "knowledge" about France that Germans brought with them when they entered the country. Helping to legitimise and justify occupation, these ideas offered a framework through which to perceive France and its inhabitants. When German soldiers visited the great Gothic cathedrals as part of the widespread tourism detailed in Chapter 3, for example, they saw them not as a product of French ingenuity, but as part of a German inheritance. Suggesting that German involvement in western Europe went back many centuries, that Germans had a long-standing claim on French soil, and that the French were in any case wasting key European resources, the memorandum made this most recent invasion seem legitimate, even necessary, and contributed to making soldiers feel "at home" in foreign territory.

The Stuckart memorandum drew on a long timespan to argue for Germany's continuous presence on west-central European soil, conveniently shorn of its ties to France, but shorter-term historical arguments, notably linked to World War I, also shaped occupiers' attitudes. When the German advance into France ended with armistice in 1940, World War I was less than a generation past. Both specific, personal experiences and broader public memories of the conflict were omnipresent as the Wehrmacht began a new and much more extensive occupation of French territory. On a private level, memories of World War I helped individual soldiers overcome dislocations accompanying their transition from the German homeland to French landscapes, from battle to occupation. Publicly, the occupation authorities invoked World War I to give "added value" to the 1940 victory. From a German perspective, the successes of 1940 redressed the balance of Franco–German rivalry, and the Third Reich milked to the fullest this opportunity to "revise" the Treaty of Versailles.

For the French, memories of World War I, and especially the German occupation of parts of northeastern France during that conflict, were far from positive. French recollections of past German atrocities, although sometimes exaggerated, influenced reactions to a renewed invasion, and the German approach on the ground in 1940 was designed to counter

---

Hans Globke by Commander Graff, 25 September and 13 October 1945, *International Military Tribunal Nuremberg*, vol. 37 (Nuremberg, 1949), 218, 222.

these negative popular memories.[54] Boasting that a National Socialist occupation represented a break with vindictive models of the past, the Wehrmacht sought to counter the commonly-held notion that Germans were barbaric. Organised tourism and other forms of cultural appreciation were deployed to convince the French, and the Germans themselves, that they were behaving differently this time around.

At least as problematic as Germans' reputation for being barbarians was the fact that, for veterans on both sides, remembered experiences from World War I might actually represent common ground. Shared recognition of the conflict's unprecedented brutality had served as a bridge-builder in the 1920s, embodied in the reconciliatory "Spirit of Locarno." Now, since shared memories of war might encourage fellow-feeling with the French and fraternisation, the occupation authorities sought ways to control these memories. Managing the memories of World War I, whether divergent or shared, became important to the long-term success of a renewed occupation.[55] The following section traces how memories of World War I played out among occupying soldiers, and examines how Hitler's regime tried to instrumentalise those memories to solidify its hold over the country.

Upon entering France in 1940, the occupiers' potentially tricky transition from war to relative peace and their assumption of new duties were eased by the fact that many had been to the country before. The connections between the Germans and the French ran deeply, making this encounter seem, for many, a renewal of acquaintances, rather than a fresh introduction. When he first met the German Field Commander

---

[54] Annette Becker, "From War to War: A Few Myths, 1914–1942" in *France at War in the Twentieth Century: Propaganda, Myth and Metaphor*, ed. Valerie Holman and Debra Kelly (New York: Berghahn, 2000), 25; Cobb, *French and Germans*, 53.

[55] Although much of the historiography of memory and myth in modern Europe revolves around World War I, the impact of World War I's memories on World War II's occupations, in both eastern and western Europe, has yet to be fully explored. Richard Cobb's comparison of the two twentieth-century French occupations suggests the extent of overlap between 1914 and 1940. Cobb weaves echoes of 1914–18 into the backdrop of the second occupation, but does not give a detailed account of the instrumentalisation of 1914–18 memories by the second occupation regime. *French and Germans*. Annette Becker, for her part, has looked at how the French understood memories of World War I, but made only brief references to the German side. Becker, "From War to War: A Few Myths, 1914–1942." On memory and World War I, see especially Paul Fussell, *The Great War and Modern Memory* (Oxford: Oxford University Press, 2013); George L. Mosse, *Fallen Soldiers: Reshaping the Memory of the World Wars* (Oxford: Oxford University Press, 1990); Pierre Nora, *Les Lieux de mémoire*, 7 vols. (Paris: Gallimard, 1984); Jay Winter, *Sites of Memory, Sites of Mourning: The Great War in European Cultural History* (Cambridge University Press, 1998). On memory and the East European war experience, 1914–18, see Jay Winter, *Remembering War: The Great War between Memory and History in the Twentieth Century*.

Karl Hotz of Nantes, for example, Frenchman Edmund Duméril noted that Hotz had visited France for the first time during the Paris exhibition in 1900 and "that Paris had amazed him."[56] Hotz had learned French in Switzerland and as a soldier stationed in then-German Metz before fighting in World War I. After 1918, Hotz had studied law at Tübingen under some of the same instructors Duméril had gotten to know while he was a scholar of German at Tübingen a few years later. The paths of the two men neared one another at several points, though they had not actually crossed before 1940. Although this example involves a mature officer who had been sent to France specifically because of his prior knowledge of the country and a Frenchman chosen as a mediator because he spoke German, it highlights the mutual familiarity that favoured cordial relations between occupiers and occupied populations at the local level.[57]

Both younger and older soldiers had occasionally travelled or studied in France prior to the war, but knowledge of the country was most common among World War I veterans like Hotz. The diaries and memoirs of older men typically begin with a nostalgic reference to World War I, or often close with a train journey through landscape familiar from the trenches. Major General Friedrich Siebert, for instance, could not help but think of World War I as he passed through the forest of Blincourt on his way into France.[58] POW camp Commander Johannes Gutschmidt noted in his war diary in March 1941 that he had passed through Villers Cotterets, where he had been shot in the head in 1918.[59] A veteran named Folkers, who came to France to provide war relief to civilians as part of the National Socialist People's Welfare Organisation (Nationalsozialistische Volkswohlfahrt, or NSV), emphasised that he had always wanted to revisit the places where he had fought in World War I.[60] He was delighted to "have been granted the good fortune to work at least another four weeks in the area where I was privileged to fight for Germany in the World War of 1914–18."[61] For men like Folkers, occupation meant an eagerly-awaited chance to revisit the stomping grounds

---

[56] Edmond Duméril, diary entry for 24 and 25 June, 1940, *Journal d'un honnête homme pendant l'Occupation: juin 1940–août 1944*, ed. Jean Bourgeon (Thonon-les-Bains: Albaron, 1990), 31.

[57] Hotz later became the first high-ranking officer killed by French resisters outside Paris. See Chapter 5. Longer-term connections between Germans and the French are explored notably in Cobb, *French and Germans*.

[58] Friedrich Siebert, *Westfeldzug 1940*, entry for 11 June 1940 (BArch: N 586/3).

[59] POW camp Commander Johannes Gutschmidt, *Kriegstagebuch*, March 1941 (BArch: Msg. 1/257).

[60] The NSV's deployment in France is discussed later in this chapter.

[61] Folkers, report on his experiences, 27 November 1940 (BArch: NS 37/2065).

of their youth. Having conquered and occupied part of France before made it easier to imagine holding the whole country, and Folkers was among those Germans who saw their previous knowledge of France as a kind of credential that added to their authority.[62] New experiences of France were framed by the past, and became part of a longer continuum of hostile and friendly relations across the Rhine.

If private memories of World War I lent France a familiarity that eased individual transitions from soldier to occupier, publicly such familiarity was overlaid by distancing and the concept of vindication, which was used to justify occupation. It was only right, Hitler's propagandists argued, that France should be occupied by Germany. Not only were the loss of the war and the subsequent Versailles Treaty widely seen as unjust, but in the years that followed 1918, Germans in the Rhineland had been directly occupied by their "hereditary enemy" (Erbfeind), the French. A new occupation of France, this time more complete, seemed essential to right past wrongs.

This framing of the victory and subsequent occupation as vindication was nowhere more apparent than in propaganda surrounding Hitler's visit to France in late June 1940. Official photographer Heinrich Hoffmann published a popular collection of glossy images, *Mit Hitler im Westen (With Hitler in the West)*, to commemorate the Western campaign and Hitler's whirlwind tour (Figure 4.10).[63] The collection drew direct links to World War I, for instance by juxtaposing an image of Hitler with his infantry comrades at Fromelles in 1916 with an image of him standing in the same spot in 1940.[64] Hitler toured the battlefields, and a few pages later he was shown inside the Strasbourg cathedral in "reclaimed" Alsace. The volume then moved on to Paris with pictures of Hitler in front of the Eiffel tower, visiting Napoleon's tomb at the Invalides, and seeing the Opera Garnier. Images of the capital's treasures were followed by pictures of more practical spoils of war: piles of guns and tanks of oil.[65] The book included a segment on Compiègne and the signing of the 1940 armistice, which documented not only the ceremony proper, but also the German delegation's formal departure from the site with the caption "The dishonour of Compiègne 1918 [has been] erased."[66] Linking past losses and present victories, the volume traced Hitler's own rise from humble World War I infantryman to national leader, connecting his personal successes with the German nation's path

---

[62] Folkers, report on his experiences, 27 November 1940 (BArch: NS 37/2065).
[63] Heinrich Hoffmann, *Mit Hitler im Westen* (Munich: Zeitgeschichte Verlag, 1940).
[64] Hoffmann, *Mit Hitler*, 103.   [65] Hoffmann, *Mit Hitler*, 110–15.
[66] Hoffmann, *Mit Hitler*, 122.

from brutal warfare through the humiliation and suffering of defeat, to rebirth and conquest.[67]

In fact, for the losers as well as the winners, World War I's battlefields had already become popular tourist sites in the interwar period. After 1940, many occupiers followed in Hitler's footsteps by touring the battlefields – not only veterans, but also men too young to have lived through the previous conflict themselves.[68] Compiègne which, in contrast to the battlefields, had not been a major site of German interwar tourism, now became a desirable destination.[69]

Even as occupiers drew, through tourism, abstract connections between German experiences in France in 1914–18 and those of the present day, there were very real continuities between this new occupation and those of previous eras. The Kommandant of the northeastern French city Roubaix, for example, was the nephew of the man who had been appointed to administer that city in 1914. According to historian Richard Cobb, the 1940 Kommandant arrived well-armed with his uncle's file listing subversive individuals, and promptly arrested many of the same men.[70] Such continuities were not limited to the northeastern French zone either, for General Field Marshal Fedor von Bock noted on 18 June 1940 that his army group's high command was housed at the Hotel Trianon in Versailles, the exact place where the German delegation had been accommodated during treaty negotiations in 1919. Harkening back to an even earlier conflict, von Bock remarked that his men had found office space at the local prefecture, which had been the German headquarters in 1870/71.[71] Memories, sightseeing, and the physical occupation of spaces with historical meaning combined to give a sense of continuity, even inevitability, to this renewed occupation.

---

[67] On Hitler, memory and the myths of World War I, see Bernd Hüppauf, "Langemarck, Verdun and the Myth of a New Man in Germany after the First World War," *War & Society* 6, no. 2 (1988): 70–97.

[68] Becker, "From War to War: A Few Myths, 1914–1942," 24; Matti Münch, *Verdun: Mythos und Alltag einer Schlacht* (Munich: Martin Meidenbauer, 2006), 462, 479.

[69] The 1931 Baedeker guide to the Paris region refers to the signing of the armistice in small print only (406), though it describes the city of Compiègne itself thoroughly. In contrast, the battlefields near Verdun (452–7) and Reims (440–45) each receive a five-page treatment, new in that edition (v). Karl Baedeker, *Paris und Umgebung: Chartres, Fontainebleau, Senlis, Reims, Verdun*, 20th edn. (Leipzig: Karl Baedeker, 1931). In 1941, in addition to being given tours of Paris and Versailles, officer trainees in Paris were taken to Compiègne. Kommandant von Gross-Paris, Kommandostab, Zeiteinteilung für den Ic-Lehrgang vom 16 February–25 February 1941 (AN: 40 AJ/873).

[70] Roubaix was in the northeastern French area that the Germans attached to Belgium for the purposes of occupation. Cobb, *French and Germans*, 41.

[71] Generalfeldmarschall Fedor von Bock, *Tagebuchnotizen aus der Zeit als Oberbefehlshaber der Heeresgruppe Nord im Westen, 1939–45*, 18 June 1940 (BArch: N 22/5).

Rather than a temporary aberration, these echoes of the past, like the geo-topographical and historical arguments of the Stuckart memorandum, encouraged Germans to see their presence in France as normal. In the same way, there was more than simple vindication behind Hitler's decision to hold the 1940 armistice-signing ceremony in the forest of Compiègne in the same railway car where the armistice ending World War I had been signed. Layering the present over the past in the same physical spaces obscured the past and reinforced the notion that a German presence in France was the new status quo. Hindsight makes us aware that the occupation of France lasted only four years, but in 1940, neither occupiers, nor occupied people, possessed this knowledge.

If establishing the 1940 occupation was made easier by the fact that Germans had been in France before, and a renewed occupation restored German honour after the indignities of Versailles, other echoes of World War I were less easy to domesticate. As mentioned earlier in this chapter, one of the enduring stories about the "Great War" was that the occupation of Belgium and parts of France had been barbaric. After World War I, moreover, other European powers had disqualified Germany from possessing a colonial empire due to its agressiveness in war. For both reasons, in 1940, Hitler's regime was deeply concerned about countering the notion that German soldiers were barbarians. This concern was demonstrated concretely, when the major National Socialist welfare organisation, the NSV, was sent to France to assist civilian victims of war, and in a more abstract way, through Germans' interactions with French cultural and historical monuments. In both cases, the regime sought to depict National Socialist occupation as fundamentally different from the vengeful occupations of the past.

German assistance to French (and Belgian) civilians was surprisingly extensive. Based at first in major cities of the French northeast and in Belgium, the Nazi Party's social welfare wing, the NSV, established camps to collect displaced civilians, and took over existing centres set up by the Wehrmacht.[72] By mid-June, the NSV claimed to be running

---

[72] *Der Durchbruch*, a newspaper prepared for soldiers in the West made by Propaganda Company 612, published images of Wehrmacht members feeding French refugees several times in June 1940 (BArch: RHD 69/18). On the NSV in France, see Daniel Hadwiger, "Austausch auf Augenhöhe? Deutsch-französische Begegnungen von Wohlfahrtsorganisationen während der Besatzungszeit in Deutschland und Frankreich (1940–1949)" in *Zum Phänomen des Austauschs in den Geistwissenschaften/Les phénomènes de l'échange dans les sciences humaines*, ed. Silvia Richter and Maude Williams (Frankfurt am Main: Peter Lang, 2016), 110–30; Julia S. Torrie, "The Many Aims of Assistance: The Nationalsozialistische Volkswohlfahrt and Aid to French Civilians in 1940," *War & Society* 26, no. 1 (May 2007): 27–38.

100 soup kitchens in France, organised by 283 staff members.[73] Over the summer, it handed out 27 million portions of cold food, over 15 million hot meals, 8.5 million servings of milk for children and mothers, and 3 million loaves of bread. It took credit for having delivered 700 babies, and looked after 103,000 sick individuals.[74] At the end of August, NSV personnel began heading home to Germany, and by the time French organisations were once again functioning in the occupied zone in early September, the NSV was gone.[75]

Naturally, this German assistance was not intended to be particularly altruistic; rather, it had practical and propagandistic goals. Assisting civilian victims of war favoured the security of the German troops and limited the spread of disease. The NSV's activities also enabled the occupiers to monitor refugees' movements, sort through the population, and identify undesirable or potentially dangerous elements. Finally, NSV and Wehrmacht handouts encouraged refugees' loyalty and promoted the idea that the Nazis were generous and benevolent victors. As Hans Klumpp, the soldier quoted at this chapter's outset put it, "they now found the horror stories they had heard about us turned upside-down. They obtained food from us, yes, the population had the best impression of us German soldiers."[76] NSV district leader Folkers, for his part, understood that civilian aid was being instrumentalised "to make it clear to these people that we Germans have a different understanding of human life than these gentlemen sometimes believe."[77] The occupiers bent over backwards to assure not only the French, but also themselves, that they were acting chivalrously this time around.

Dispensing aid and ideology together, the NSV worked to tie the local population more closely to the new regime.[78] NSV press releases

---

[73] NSV press agency report on "Mit der NSV. in Belgien und Frankreich," *Nationalsozialistische Partei-Korrespondenz*, 6 July 1940 (BArch: NS 26/258). The *Hilfszug Bayern*, a special train that provided emergency services, was also used in Belgium and France in the summer of 1940 (Politisches Archiv des Auswärtigen Amts: Paris 1288; AN: 40 AJ/41 and AN: 40 AJ/52).

[74] The NSV's perhaps exaggerated figures are the only ones to survive. The majority of the food came from French and Belgian stocks, as the NSV itself emphasised. Herwart Vorländer, Die NSV, 130, n. 5 Herwart Vorländer, *Die NSV: Darstellung und Dokumentation einer nationalsozialistichen Organisation* (Boppard am Rhein: Harald Boldt, 1988), 130, n. 5. and Hans Bernsee, *Aufgaben der NS-Volkswohlfahrt im Kriege* (Berlin: Zentralverlag der NSDAP, 1941), 22–6, 38.

[75] The group based at Vernon, in the department of Eure, for instance, left on 25 August 1940. See Folkers, report on his experiences in France, 27 November 1940 (BArch: NS 37/2065).

[76] Klumpp, diary, 3 July 1940 (DTA: 1942).

[77] Folkers, report on his experiences in France, 27 November 1940 (BA: NS 37/2065).

[78] The previous autumn, the NSV had accompanied the Wehrmacht's advance into Poland. Before that, it had expanded into Austria after the *Anschluß*, and into the

emphasised cooperation, and noted that *French* nurses and other staff helped run NSV camps and soup kitchens. However, French reactions to the NSV varied. *Le Moniteur*, in Clermont-Ferrand, published an admiring report that echoed the Germans' own rhetoric about the organisation's contributions.[79] This was reprinted in the pro-German newspaper, *L'Oeuvre*, where politician Marcel Déat soon called for a French agency to imitate the NSV.[80] For his part, however, prefect Villey of the department of the Seine (Paris) seems to have understood the larger implications of German war relief. He complained to the occupiers about the camera teams filming civilians receiving soup from the Wehrmacht. Perhaps as a result of his and other French officials' protests, such filming grew increasingly rare, and then ceased entirely.[81]

At the same time, the Germans' own attitude about war relief in France was ambiguous. By the end of August, NSV groups were withdrawing from occupied areas. The decision may have been linked to French disapproval, but in July, a German commentator wrote that it probably did not make sense to waste energy on France, for, "NSV care is certainly very humane and nice, but one should be allowed to doubt whether we make friends this way and awaken the impression that we are the victors and therefore the lords of the land."[82] In late August, NSV head Erich Hilgenfeldt told representatives of the American press that the NSV's work in France was done, and, "It would now be necessary for the French authorities, from 1 September, to take responsibility for

---

Sudetenland when that area was annexed by Germany. NSV actions in Belgium and France were supposed to help bring those areas, too, into line with the Reich. "Deutscher Sozialismus in Frankreich," *NSV-Helfer: Nachrichtenblatt des Gauamtes der NSV, Düsseldorf*, July/August 1940; NSV press agency report on "Mit der NSV. in Belgien und Frankreich (Schluß)," *Nationalsozialistische Partei-Korrespondenz*, 14 July 1940 (BArch: NS 26/258).

[79] "L'aide allemande en faveur du retour des réfugiés," *Le Moniteur* (Clermont-Ferrand), ca. 6 September 1940 (AN: 2 AG 613).

[80] "Comment l'armée allemande a organisé le retour des réfugiés," *L'Oeuvre*, 5 October 1940. See also Marcel Déat, "Solidaires dans l'épreuve," *L'Oeuvre*, 20 October 1940.

[81] Report of prefect of Seine, 13 September 1940 (Archives Départementales de Paris [ADP]: 1012/57/1 art. 3). On the depictions of German benevolence in the *Deutsche Wochenschau*, see Paul Maine, "L'image de Paris et de la France occupée dans les actualités allemande (Deutsche Wochenschau) de mai 1940 à novembre 1942" in *La France et l'Allemagne en guerre: septembre 1939 - novembre 1942*, ed. Claude Carlier and Stefan Martens (Paris: Fondation pour les études de Défense nationale; Institut d'histoire des conflits contemporains; Bundesministerium für Forschung und Technologie; Deutsches Historisches Institut Paris, 1990), 393–5. The German-diffused *Actualités mondiales* also included segments about German help to French civilians of the "exodus." See, for instance, Vidéothèque, Paris (VDP): 4684 (August 1940) and VDP: 4686 (November 1940).

[82] Essay by German Foreign office representative Frauenfeld, "Das Leben ist stärker!" ca. 17 July 1940 (Politisches Archiv des Auswärtigen Amtes [AA]: Paris 1289).

helping the refugees. This was, in the long-term, not the responsibility of a conqueror."[83] As the occupation became more established, the occupiers looked for less resource-intensive ways to reinforce their dominance.

In the first weeks after the armistice, as they sought to establish a new, model occupation, the precedents to avoid were in some cases German, but they might also be French. Alongside World War I, another recent event was at the top of occupiers' minds – the French occupation of the Rhineland. Germans insisted that their conception of occupation and their treatment of the French differed fundamentally from the way they themselves had been treated during the "humiliation" of the Rhineland after World War I. At that time, German propagandists had played up the fact that French African troops were deployed in Germany, their presence having been viewed as particularly degrading.[84] Now, an early July 1940 edition of the soldiers' newspaper *Der Vormarsch* resurrected this theme, claiming that during the interwar French occupation, the city of Mainz had received a list of required quarters with a note that if these were not provided, "Senegalneger" ("Senegalese negroes") would be used to clear the houses.[85] Playing up both racial and sexual aspects of this "humiliation," the article went on to describe how Rhineland communities had been required to pay for bordellos to be set up for "brown and black men," to be serviced by women belonging to the nations defeated in World War I. Surrounded by hunger and distress, "French officers and administrators showed off their excessive dissipation at Germany's expense."[86] The article was meant to remind Germans of the humiliations they had suffered at the hands of the French and by implication to suggest that German treatment of the French was comparatively generous and mild.

The idea that 1940 represented the dawn of a new kind of occupation, with occupiers who were not barbarians, was also reinforced through Germans' interactions with French cultural and historical monuments.

---

[83] "Keine deutsche Aufgabe," *Deutsche Zeitung* [Norway], 31 August 1940 (BA: R 4902/10294).

[84] On German propaganda about black occupation soldiers, see among others Peter Collar, *The Propaganda War in the Rhineland: Weimar Germany, Race and Occupation after World War I* (London: I.B. Tauris, 2013); Christian Koller, *"Von Wilden aller Rassen niedergemetzelt". Die Diskussion um die Verwendung von Kolonialtruppen in Europa zwischen Rassismus, Kolonial- und Militärpolitik (1914–1930)* (Stuttgart: Franz Steiner, 2001). Julia Roos has written articles on the subject, including "Racist Hysteria to Pragmatic Rapprochement? The German Debate about Rhenish 'Occupation Children', 1920–30," *Contemporary European History* 22, no. 02 (May 2013): 155–180.

[85] "Das bleibt unvergessen," *Der Vormarsch*, 14, 2 July 1940, 3 (BArch: RHD 69/50).

[86] "Das bleibt unvergessen," 3.

A commemorative volume written in September 1940 made this connection explicitly, noting that it was not always easy to know what the French "man on the street" expected of German invaders, but he probably believed that "a raggedy and drunken band of soldiers would plunder every shop, break all the window-panes, defecate on the church altars and kill all the men, in order to crown the whole by raping all the women." "And," the volume asked rhetorically, "what did the Parisians see when the first groups of German soldiers spent their free time in Paris? The first thing these terrifying soldiers did was to storm the churches and national monuments, not in order to desecrate them, but to gaze at them piously with big eyes."[87] Immediately after the occupation had ended, its former chief economic administrator, Elmar Michel, described Germans' attention to French monuments as a conscious effort to return France to normality and show the French they had nothing to fear.[88] Michel's rhetoric aside, it was also part of Germans' attempt to present themselves as civilised men, rather than barbarians, a theme that ran deeply through their occupation projects from beginning to end.

The new occupation was thus given continuity by linking it to occupations past, and at the same time it was consciously framed in opposition to specific facets of the way these occupations were recalled. Just as National Socialism had transformed Germany itself, National Socialist Germany sought to transform the notion of military occupation, claiming a moral high ground and espousing notions of partnership and benevolence rather than domination and humiliation. Especially in the first half of the occupation, Germans drew on gendered metaphors to style themselves not as dominators, but as chivalrous, "fatherly protector[s]" of a feminised and infantilised French nation.[89] Such rhetoric carried particular resonance in a foreign policy context in which, since World War I, conflicts were seen in terms of the victimisation of women and children, rather than in more traditional terms, such as treaty violation.[90]

---

[87] Hans Joachim Kitzing, *Wir liegen in Paris*, Berlin: Mittler & Sohn, 1941), 18–19. On occupier tourism, see Chapter 3.

[88] Elmar Michel, "Allgemeiner Rückblick," undated final report [1944], 16 (BArch: RW 35/244).

[89] A poster distributed in France showed "a soldier with no weapon, his helmet hanging discreetly from his belt, carrying in his left arm a smiling little boy, happily munching a slice of bread and jam. His right arm is around two little girls who appear to be reassured by his protective gesture." Fabrice Virgili, "Enfants de Boches: The War Children of France" in *Children of World War II the Hidden Enemy Legacy*, ed. Kjersti Ericsson and Eva Simonsen (Oxford: Berg, 2005), 139.

[90] See, notably, Susan R. Grayzel, *Women's Identities at War: Gender, Motherhood and Politics in Britain and France during the First World War* (Chapel Hill, N.C.: University of North Carolina Press, 1999); Ruth Harris, "The Child of the Barbarian: Rape, Race and Nationalism in France during the First World War," *Past & Present*, no. 141

Instead of grinding France into submission, Germans argued that they were subjecting the country to a subtler form of discipline and tutelage. This had its expression in occupation administrator Werner Best's theories about *Aufsichtsverwaltung* (oversight), discussed later in this chapter: a typology of occupation that positioned each nation according to the kind of surveillance it required in order to contribute positively to the National Socialist war economy. It also derived in part from the paternalistic attitudes that permeated Sieburg's work and other literature about France in the period. Given just a little German-style rigour, such texts seemed to say, the French too could become productive and industrious contributers to a German-dominated Europe.

Although it is difficult to be certain, the persistent recollection on the French side that, for the most part, German behaviour during the occupation was "correct" may have had its roots in these themes from 1940. At the occupation's outset, occupiers were told to follow the Hague Convention, and were reminded that "the best propagandist for the German cause is the disciplined, correct appearance of the German soldier."[91] The desire to combat the notion that they were barbarians fostered cordial relations with the French at a person-to-person level, and the perceived need for tutelage encouraged contact and cooperation between occupiers and occupied people in everyday life. It is possible, of course, that some Germans really did behave "correctly," though many did not. Still, despite the unequal power relations that underlay every exchange, and the very real brutality exercised by occupation troops, many encounters between German and French individuals were cordial, even warm. At the same time, the persistent theme of "correctness" obscures the occupation's underlying violence and remains, ironically, a legacy of the Third Reich's own "anti-barbarian" propaganda, echoing down through the years.

The "barbarian problem" that occupiers faced underlines the contested nature of memory. In some respects, Germans and French people had very different remembered "versions" of World War I, which inevitably influenced their renewed interactions. Occupiers' attempts to show they were not barbarians were an effort to smooth over tensions arising out of this divergence. Yet some memories of World War One did not diverge. The front-line soldiers' experience of technologised combat had been similar on all sides. Stationed in France in the early 1940s, Heinrich Böll, who became a well-known postwar West German

(November 1993): 170. On the popularisation of this discourse in the 1920s, see Roos, "Racist Hysteria," 177.
[91] Laub, *After the Fall*, 15.

novelist, wrote to his family that he enjoyed talking to older Frenchmen about war – this war, the previous war, and the fact that "a soldier's life is shit."[92] From the point of view of the occupation authorities, however, universal experiences and shared recollections were problematic. A common recognition of war's brutality lay at the root of the so-called "Spirit of Locarno," the desire for Franco-German rapprochement and peace that became a powerful force in Europe from the mid-1920s. Viewed from this angle, recollections of World War I, particularly if they were shared with the French in the way that Böll's remarks imply, might become deeply worrisome for National Socialists. Such shared memories helped ease soldiers' transition to becoming occupiers, but the regime could not permit them to become wide bridges between occupier and occupied civilians.

Instead, the German authorities tried to control shared memories in two ways. First, they exploited a kind of linguistic slippage that had already taken place regarding the term rapprochement in the interwar period. Second, they used symbolic and ceremonial means to manage the universal aspects of these recollections. In the 1920s, rapprochement was first understood in German as *Annäherung* (nearing), and implied reconciliation with former enemies based on a shared recognition of the horrors of war. In this sense, the word emphasised peace, and meant acceptance of the status quo. However, scholar Hermann Hagspiel has pointed out that in the 1930s, Germans increasingly employed a second meaning of rapprochement, *Verständigung* (understanding). This version of rapprochement was based on the same notion of shared horror. However, it expressed not the desire for reconciliation based on acceptance of the status quo, but an effort to use negotiation (as opposed to war) to revise or, from a German perspective, to equalise, the outcomes of World War I.[93] The Franco-German cultural collaboration centred around Germans Otto Abetz and Karl Epting in the 1930s and then, during the occupation, was an extension of this second notion of rapprochement, emphasising as it did communication and interaction between the parties. Soon, however, it moved beyond equalising the outcomes of World War I to reinforcing German dominance. Shared memories of World War I passed into the background, serving only as a

---

[92] Böll, vol. 1, 10 May 1942, 324.

[93] Hermann Hagspiel, *Verständigung zwischen Deutschland und Frankreich? Die deutsch-französische Außenpolitik der zwanziger Jahre im innenpolitischen Kräftefeld beider Länder* (Bonn: Rohrscheid, 1987), 350–77 and Christiane Tichy, "Ein protestantischer Sieburg: Pfarrer Hans-Helmut Peters in Frankreich zwischen 1930–1944," *Francia* 24.3 (1997): 67–89.

Figure 1.2 Soldiers at the Tomb of the Unknown Soldier.
Gefreiter Strohbach, Album 2, author's collection.

vague foundation upon which to build a unified, German-lead Europe for the future.

The second method of "domesticating" the shared memory of World War I was symbolic and ceremonial. In occupied Warsaw, German soldiers did not salute Poland's Unknown Soldier, but in Paris, they were required to show their respect at the Arc de Triomphe.[94] Even before the armistice was signed, journalist William Shirer had noted that "thousands of German soldiers congregate all day long at the Tomb of the Unknown Soldier, where the flame still burns under the Arc. They bare their blond heads and stand there gazing."[95] The army organised tours of Paris that stopped at the Arc, and soldiers photographed themselves and their comrades at the site (Figure 1.2).[96] In one of the few surviving accounts of such a Paris

[94] Copy of telex, OKH Heerwesen Abteilung to Militärbefehlshaber in Frankreich Ic, 5 November 1940 (AN: AJ 40/451); Gordon, "Warfare and Tourism," 628.
[95] William Shirer, *"This Is Berlin": Radio Broadcasts from Nazi Germany, 1938–40* (Woodstock, NY: Overlook Press, 1999), 17 June 1940, 328. The soldiers in Figure 1.2 have retained their head coverings, in contrast to what Shirer had observed.
[96] Hans-Peter Eckener and Peter Wolter *Lieber Vater – mein lieber Per: Briefwechsel mit zu Hause 1940–1944* (Selbstverlag: 1998) 25 October 1941, 125–7. Propagandists and other occupiers produced images of the site: see BArch: Bild 146–1978-053-30 / Jäger, Sepp.

tour, occupier Hans-Peter Eckener wrote that the Tomb of the Unknown Soldier had been the group's first stop. Acquitting themselves of their duty of respect allowed individual occupiers and the military authorities to acknowledge shared war memories, and move on. Men like Heinrich Böll, a reluctant soldier at best, may have understood war experiences as a bridge between himself and the occupied population, but many occupiers simply offered up a vague sign of respect for the fighters of the past and pursued occupation projects unchanged.

Rather than spending too much time on the kinds of universal battle experiences that might encourage dangerous fraternisation, the National Socialist regime preferred to allow the present to erase inconvenient aspects of the past. World War I must no longer be recalled as a sad embarrassment, nor should it become a lesson in peace and brotherhood, for despite lip-service to those concepts, German dominance was clear. The invocation and instrumentalisation of World War I and, more generally, of the past among Germans in France after 1940 exemplifies the shifting nature of memory and commemoration. It highlights various ways that individuals and states use memory and selective forgetting in a wartime context, and suggests how radically readings of the past can influence self-perceptions in the present day.

Taking memories and historical precedents into consideration, then, how should German soldiers begin a new occupation on a practical level? They might admire France's monuments and treat its population chivalrously, but how did that align with their overall task, and what were they hoping to achieve in France? Within the larger context of the war, the Germans' first objective was to maintain "peace" and ensure the security of troops stationed in the West. Their second goal was to exploit French resources, including manpower, as much as possible for the war effort. As background for what is to follow, this chapter concludes with a brief overview of the German position on France in summer 1940, the form of hegemony elaborated notably by occupation administrator Werner Best, and the organisation of the occupation apparatus.[97]

The Germans' first and foremost preoccupation was security. Sketching out the Third Reich's overall position on France to occupiers on the ground, an article in the soldiers' newspaper *Der Durchbruch* explained in mid-July 1940 that, "[t]he central aspect of the German attitude toward France is the requirement that France willingly recognize Germany's leading role in Europe and that it must cease to pursue thoughts of

---

[97] The most recent overview of German policy in France is Laub, *After the Fall*. See also Mitchell, *Nazi Paris* and the classic Umbreit, *Militärbefehlshaber*. Talbot Imlay reviews the relevant literature skillfully in "German Side."

revenge or hegemony."[98] Since observers doubted that the preconditions for such a "willing" recognition existed in France, at least for the time being, it was important "that the German Reich be afforded all guarantees that will rule out a repetition of [hostile] French policies toward the Reich."[99] France remained an enemy whose activities must be monitored for the security of the Reich, and despite rhetoric about cordial relations, clear dominance was required.

Beyond security, Germany's second concern was the orderly exploitation of land and resources. Even before invading the Soviet Union, planners saw the Reich as the core of a single, massive production unit (*Großraum*) that Germans had won the right to dominate and control. As occupation bureaucrat Werner Best explained in a 1941 essay, "in the hierarchy of peoples the stronger peoples impose their will on the weaker ones. And the order of the greater space [*Großraum-Ordnung*] will be shaped by the people that is strong enough to extend its own people's space [*Volksraum*] to create a greater space [*Großraum*]."[100] Within the European Großraum, the needs of each occupied or allied land must be subordinated to the whole, its riches turned to feed the Reich and its expansionist projects.

Exactly how exploitation was undertaken in each area depended in large part on the value that planners gave to the various parts of the Reich, and judgements of value were typically based on *völkisch* or racial conceptions.[101] As Best put it, "peoples within the Großraum who possess a highly developed, productive people's order [*Volks-Ordnung*] must be governed differently than those whose people's order is at a more primitive, predominantly survival-based level..."[102] In eastern Europe, which was seen as a less "advanced" region, selection, deportation and elimination of some elements of the population were integral aspects of the exploitation of labour and other resources. In western Europe, the occupation authorities rather pursued a policy of *Aufsichtsverwaltung*.[103]

---

[98] "Deutschland und Frankreich,"*Der Durchbruch*, 16 July 1940, 1.

[99] "Deutschland und Frankreich," 1.

[100] Werner Best, "Grundfragen einer deutschen Großraum-Verwaltung" in *Festgabe für Heinrich Himmler*, Darmstadt, 1941, 35, cited in Meyer, "Grossraumpolitik," 33.

[101] Ahlrich Meyer notes that *völkisch* and racial are not direct equivalents. Werner Best's *völkisch* conception of the state, for instance, repudiated the liberal focus on individual rights and constitutionalism that had emerged from the Enlightenment. The task of government, for Best, was not to express the collective will of individuals, but rather to protect and further the interests of the *Volk* (community). Racial-biological ideas, *per se*, were relatively unimportant in Best's conception; the repudiation of individual rights all the more. Meyer, 30. On Best, see the landmark study by Ulrich Herbert, *Best: biographische Studien über Radikalismus, Weltanschauung und Vernunft, 1903–1989* (Bonn: J.H.W. Dietz, 1996).

[102] Best, "Grundfragen," 45, cited in Meyer, "Grossraumpolitik," 34.

[103] Meyer, "Grossraumpolitik," 43.

"Fundamentally," noted Best, "the German military government must exercise oversight over the whole local administration of the occupied French area."[104] All legislation and regulations for the occupied areas must be approved by the occupation authorities, whose role it was to forestall any hindrance to the occupation's "military, political and economic goals."[105] In addition, in specific cases, the military authorities might "advise" the French to pass legislation that was in German interests, for example because it facilitated their exploitation of French resources for the war effort. If the French authorities refused to pass these laws or regulations, "the corresponding regulations [would be imposed] through orders by the military governor in France."[106] This method of "oversight" applied throughout the occupied areas – when French factories, administrations, and other instances could do the work themselves, they were encouraged to do so, the occupiers serving primarily in a supervisory capacity.[107] When the French refused, the Reich imposed its will.

As much as possible, then, the Germans preferred to oversee existing French structures, rather than administering France themselves. This economised manpower while still meeting the occupation's two main goals of security and exploitation. In the southern, "non-occupied" zone, World War I hero Maréchal Pétain headed a satellite French government from the spa town of Vichy. The Germans monitored the activities of this satellite government carefully, though it retained considerable latitude in domestic affairs until the late fall of 1942. At this point, concerned about the threat represented by the Allied activities in the Mediterranean, Germany occupied the lower half of France as well, extending the system of field commands to encompass the whole territory. Even before that, however, historian Ulrich Herbert explains, "Since the Vichy government held to the principle of a unified administration for the entire country and applied laws and regulations promulgated in occupied France to the unoccupied region, the influence of the Paris military command extended in practice into the southern part of the country."[108]

---

[104] "Der Stand der Verwaltungsreform in Frankreich (Mitte Nov. 1941)," summary of presentation by Werner Best, 14 November 1941 (BArch: RH 36/606).
[105] " Stand der Verwaltungsreform," 14 November 1941 (BArch: RH 36/606).
[106] " Stand der Verwaltungsreform," 14 November 1941 (BArch: RH 36/606).
[107] On "oversight" in the economic realm, see Arne Radtke-Delacor, "Die 'gelenkte Wirtschaft' in Frankreich: Versuch einer vergleichenden Untersuchung der technokratischen Strukturen der NS-Besatzungsmacht und des Vichy-Regimes (1940–1944)," *Pariser historische Studien* 72 (2006): 235–54.
[108] Ulrich Herbert, "The German Military Command in Paris and the Deportation of the French Jews" in *National Socialist Extermination Policies: Contemporary German*

In contrast to the southern zone, German troops occupied the northern and western parts of France, including the entire English Channel and Atlantic coastline directly from late spring 1940 through summer 1944. The military occupation was run from Paris by German staff who oversaw and directed local French administrators. During the first half of the occupation, three clusters of power vied with one another in the French capital – the two strongest were the German military authorities, led by *Militärbefehlshaber* (Military Governor in France, or MBH) Otto von Stülpnagel, and the German embassy under Otto Abetz, which represented the Foreign Office. Initially less significant was the "Representative of the Security Police and Security Service" (*Beauftragten der Sicherheitspolizei und des SD*, or BdS), Helmut Knochen, who was the local deputy of Reinhard Heydrich's Reich Security Main Office. Staff involved in policing became more independent and powerful in the occupation's latter half.

The Militärbefehlshaber was responsible for military security and overall administration. His personnel were divided into two sections, a command staff (*Kommandostab*), headed by Hans Speidel, in charge of security and the occupation troops themselves, and an administrative staff (*Verwaltungsstab*), which also had two parts. The first of these, the administrative branch, was responsible for overseeing the French administration, and dealt notably with justice and policing matters. It was led by Werner Best. Alongside Best, Elmar Michel led the economic branch, which oversaw and exploited French industry. When Best moved on to a new position midway through 1942, Michel became overall head of administrative staff.

Most men in both groups represented Germany's conservative, professional elite. They had known each other before the war, and formed a kind of old boys' network, "a relatively homogenous group of conservative elitists who, out of intellectual contempt, social arrogance, and political enmity maintained a distance from Hitler and the 'party people.'"[109] According to historian Herbert, "[t]the group was characterized by German-nationalist patriotism and was rarely disturbed by outsiders."[110] One outsider who did manage to enter the innermost circle was Best, who combined administrative talent and experience with strong National Socialist convictions and status as a high-ranking SS

Perspectives and Controversies, ed. Ulrich Herbert (New York: Berghahn Books, 2000), 131. My overview of the military command in Paris draws primarily on Herbert's summary in the cited article, and on Laub, *After the Fall*; Umbreit, *Militärbefehlshaber*.

[109] Herbert, "German Military Command," 131.
[110] Herbert, "German Military Command," 131.

officer. Initially, Best seemed a poor fit for Paris, but an air of restrained, flexible "rationality" tempered his ideological fervour and enabled him to work effectively with the rest of the military leadership. At the same time, Best made no secret of his views about the German domination of Europe and the need to either drive out or destroy racial elements that might stand in the way of this project.[111] Working with the Militärbefehlshaber, the German embassy was responsible for the rather vaguely delineated area of "political questions." Both the embassy staff of Abetz and the military men under Otto von Stülpnagel followed similar lines in terms of occupation praxis, though the embassy staff were more overtly political in their view, objectives, and actions.

Especially during the first half of the occupation, Heydrich's police representatives under Knochen played a less significant role in France than in other occupied areas. This was partly because after conflicts over leadership responsibilities in Poland, the army had managed to prevent *Einsatzgruppen*, or task forces of the Reich Security Main Office, from being established in France.[112] This changed in 1942 after conflicts over security policy discussed in Chapter 5, when the office of a Superior SS- and Police leader (*Höherer SS- und Polizeiführer*) was created in France under the control of Karl Oberg. Of the three instances, the Militärbefehlshaber was the most powerful initially, a position it retained easily at first, then with increasing difficulty as the situation on the ground in France became more polarised, the war turned against Germany, and Hitler ordered increasingly radical policies from Berlin.

In addition to dividing France into two major zones, the eastern departments of Haut-Rhin, Bas-Rhin, and Moselle were attached to Germany in what Hitler considered a just revision of the terms of the Treaty of Versailles. A significant swath of northeastern France, moreover, was separated and attached to Belgium, forming a distinct administrative area that is not the focus here. Other, smaller pieces of French territory, including coastal areas vulnerable to invasion, were closed to all but local inhabitants until December 1941, and the Germans also demarcated a "Reserved" or "Forbidden" zone with the so-called Northeastern Line, discussed above [See map].

Through the four years of occupation, the Wehrmacht rotated formations in and out of France to control the territory, prepare further military operations, and defend German interests from resistance attacks. The number of personnel in western Europe varied significantly over time, reaching a low point in May 1941 of about 320,000 men in occupied

---

[111] Herbert, "German Military Command," 131–2.
[112] Herbert, "German Military Command," 132.

France, Northern France and Belgium, and the Netherlands, combined.[113] In early summer 1942, there were 35,000 men under the
command of the Militärbefehlshaber in France, specifically. On the eve
of the Allied Landing on 6 June 1944, there were as many as 1.5 million
troops under the orders of the Oberbefehlshaber West (Supreme Commander West), of whom about 100,000 were under the command of the
Militärbefehlshaber in France.[114] Initially, the soldiers in France
belonged to combat units that stayed in the country after the invasion
to fortify and defend the Channel coast and to prepare for Operation
Sealion, the planned invasion of England. From winter 1941, front-line
troops returned to Germany to prepare for the invasion of the Soviet
Union. After that point, France was used increasingly for rest, convalescence, training and regrouping of combat units that had been decimated
in brutal fighting in eastern Europe. Security concerns were minor
compared to other areas, and France offered material prosperity and
other attractions to assist in soldiers' recovery. At the same time, from
1942 and especially 1943, occupation administrators faced rising pressure to comb through their staffs to identify and free up younger,
combat-worthy soldiers for front-line duty. In the course of various
deployments as well as home leaves, both active troops and military
administrators moved back and forth across Europe repeatedly. This
mobility, which formed an integral, if rarely acknowledged, element of
their experience, is discussed at greater length in subsequent chapters.

Over time, resistance activity grew and this, alongside the expected
Allied invasion of the continent, meant that fresher units began once
again to be deployed to France. Until the invasion actually occurred, in
June 1944, and even well beyond that, France continued to be used as an
indispensable area for rest and relaxation. Alongside the well-known
exploitation of French agricultural, economic, and cultural resources,
this additional form of exploitation represented an essential involuntary
French contribution to the German war effort.

Young male occupiers, most of whom were between 18 and 35 years of
age, were typically accommodated either in requisitioned facilities, or
billetted on the population, dispersed across the country, though in
significantly greater concentrations along the English Channel and
Atlantic coasts. At the local level, administrative matters were dealt
with by a series of rather stable Feldkommandanturen (Field Commands) and their staffs in major towns, with Ortskommandanturen

---

[113] Lieb and Paxton, "Maintenir l'ordre," 116.
[114] Lieb, *Konventioneller*, 98. See detailed discussion of numbers in Lieb and Paxton,
"Maintenir l'ordre."

(Local Commands) in smaller centres. These men represented the Militärbefehlshaber in their areas. Generally older and high-ranking career soldiers or reservists, they shared elements of the group profile of the top-level occupiers described above. With their staffs, they comprised the segment of occupiers with whom the French authorities, though not necessarily French people, interacted most closely on a daily basis.

Through the occupation, the lower-ranking soldiers, the troops responsible for defending German interests in France, spent much of their time simply watching and waiting. At first, they prepared for the invasion of England that never came. Thereafter, their time was taken up with standing watches, drill, exercises, and further training. Entering France as conquerors who saw their presence as justified in the context of the historical long-term as well as the more recent 1914–18 conflict and its outcomes, they now settled in. Chapter 2 explores how the regime tried to manage these soldiers at the occupation's outset, and highlights the roles of, notably, leisure and consumption in this project. It also explores soldiers' reactions to French space, and to their own roles as occupiers in a land that they enjoyed but also had to defend, monitor, and control.

2   Consuming the Tastes and Pleasures of France

"Dear Gerda," wrote twenty-eight year-old Bernhard Schulz, just back in Normandy after a home leave in March 1941, "I'm on watch again on the coast for the first time, and it's four in the morning. The Tommies just flew over Cherbourg, and the flak hammered away until the white-wash came crumbling off the walls. Imagine a big, white room with flagstone floors and a feeble lightbulb dangling from a long wire, rows of bunk-beds with snoring soldiers, and me, on watch, sitting at a thick oak table the French wasted three times more wood than necessary to build."[1] Schulz set the scene, and then went on to detail some less immediately military aspects of his life. He especially wanted to tell Gerda, his girl-friend in westfalian Osnabrück, about the shopping he had done for her. "While hunting for socks (which you can only get with points now in France!) I made off with a piece of soap," he wrote, "and beyond that, all kinds of French things, Paris scent and such, for your dressing-table. The parcel will take longer to arrive than the letter. Then you'll be able to 'amuse' (amüsieren) yourself with it. Our Irmgard already smells more like Paris than Osnabrück."[2] Three days later, Schulz regretted that during a short trip to receive a writing prize, he had looked for something nice for Gerda, "but you know, no matter how thick my wallet is, there's nothing reasonable to be had."[3] Still, he assured her, "when I find something that's good and not too tasteless, I'll buy it."[4] A few months later, Schulz wrote that he was sending a bottle of Lucien Lelong, one of the best French perfumes, and confessed that, "I plundered it directly,

---

[1] Bernhard Schulz, letters to Gerda Schulz 1941–45, 18 March 1941 (DTA: 2033). Schulz served in the infantry and became a journalist and writer after the war. Gerda was his girlfriend, fiancée from the fall of 1941, and later wife.

[2] Irmgard was probably Schulz's sister. In this letter, Schulz seems to use the term *erbeuten* (seize, make off with) figuratively to describe his purchase of soap. In other letters, the word is used literally, to indicate more direct appropriation of French goods (see, e.g. letter 31 August 1941). Schulz, letter, 15 March 1941 (DTA: 2033).

[3] Schulz, letter, 18 March 1941 (DTA: 2033).

[4] Schulz, letter, 18 March 1941 (DTA: 2033).

for the French don't give over such delicacies willingly. With that, [I'm sending] lavender water ... and a pound of butter (so that the parcel's full). I want to send you and my mother butter regularly so you'll grow big and strong. I hope that I can always get some. It comes via a 'black' route, and I have to smile once in a while at Jeannette, that's the butter maid's name, so that then suddenly the smile weighs a kilo more."[5] In November, he sent butter again, telling Gerda not to worry about the dirty colour, which tended to rub off from the newspaper wrapping. Truly, he assured her, "the people I get [the butter] from are very clean. Moreover, it's certainly the best butter in the world, without additives, from the richest meadows of Europe, in Normandy. Enjoy it!"[6]

Schulz's rich descriptions of French delights, the mixture of military and mundane, and the combination of both admiration and disdain for the local people, all point to themes in other occupiers' letters, too. His account, which outlines the contours of one individual's experiences in France, also suggests the extent to which Germans' desire to consume and enjoy themselves shaped the occupation overall. As French civilians returned home in the summer of 1940 and a semblance of "normal" life resumed, men like Schulz found that France offered much to experience and enjoy. Alongside more stereotypically "military" activities, they went shopping, sought leisure and entertainment opportunities, and interacted with the local population. If the desire to counter their image as barbarians meant that Germans' treatment of most French civilians was above reproach initially, their attitude towards French goods left much to be desired. From clothing to soap and perfume, along with "the best butter in the world," they bought up countless items to send home to their families. While other occupied areas later became, in historian Götz Aly's words, "the Reich's flea market," a place to exchange German junk for local produce, France was the Reich's department store, even its shopping mall.[7] For a time, you could get almost anything there, and shopping was, as it had long been, one of the country's greatest attractions.

In 1940, Parisians were surprised to find that their conquerors actually paid for most of what they wanted, but it was clear that, with an exchange rate so favourable, they could afford to do so.[8] Kenneth Mouré explains

---

[5] Schulz, letter, 31 August 1941 (DTA: 2033). On the couturier Lucien Lelong's interactions with the Germans, see Dominique Veillon, *La mode sous l'Occupation: débrouillardise et coquetterie dans la France en guerre, 1939–1945* (Paris: Payot, 1990), 163–6, 207.

[6] Schulz, letter, 17 November 1941 (DTA: 2033).

[7] Quotations are from the English edition, *Hitler's Beneficiaries*, 113. Cf. Aly, *Volksstaat*.

[8] Perrault and Azema, *Paris*, 12.

that "German purchasing benefited from a deliberate undervaluation of the franc (twenty francs per mark when its purchasing parity was twelve) and charging tribute as 'occupation costs' – initially four hundred million francs (twenty million marks) per day."[9] An astonishing volume of products left France either by mail, or carried home by soldiers on leave.[10] In a clear understatement, administrator Haase, at Lille in the Northern French and Belgian occupied zone, noted in his 1944 final report that "it was not seen as undesirable when Germans bought up food or clothing on the Black Market to provide for their families in Germany."[11] Indeed, as Haase's positive framing of black marketeering in terms of "providing for one's family" suggests, the authorities encouraged this practice.[12]

According to Aly, "[p]rivate purchases in the month of August 1943 in occupied France totalled 125 million Reichsmarks. Even allowing for the devaluation of the franc, the equivalent would be hundreds of millions of dollars today." He added that, "[p]rivate purchases drove up inflation, disrupted occupation authorities' attempts to control the market, and undermined all forms of economic stability."[13] Aly's formulation highlighted occupiers' rampant consumption, and the tension between allowing such activity and attempting to limit its destructive economic impacts. Aly also raised a central question about Germans' acquisition of goods in France – was it shopping, or was it plunder? Ultimately, he argued that the extent of German soldiers' shopping and its far-reaching consequences made it plunder. More generally, Aly used soldiers' consumption in occupied Europe to support his contention that popular consent for Hitler's regime derived in large part from its ability to satisfy Germans' appetite to consume.

Aly's critics, such as Adam Tooze, have contended that, in reducing Germans' consent to a kind of bribery, Aly underestimated the very real sacrifices that ordinary people, not just oppressed minorities such as Jews and foreign workers, made to support war and genocide. They argue that Germans were not nearly as prosperous during the war as Aly claims, and

---

[9] "La Capitale de La Faim: Black Market Restaurants in Paris, 1940–1944," *French Historical Studies* 38, no. 2 (April 2015): 316–17.

[10] Aly, *Volksstaat*, 114–32; Latzel, *Deutsche Soldaten*, 137.

[11] Haase noted that almost anything had been available on the black market throughout the occupation. Regierungsrat Haase, Beitrag zum Abschlußbericht des Militärbefehlshabers für Belgien und Nordfrankreich, n.d. [autumn 1944] (BArch: RH 36/518). See additional discussion of black market later in this chapter.

[12] The original reads "zur Versorgung ihrer Angehörigen in Deutschland." Regierungsrat Haase, Beitrag zum Abschlußbericht des Militärbefehlshabers für Belgien und Nordfrankreich, n.d. [autumn 1944] (BArch: RH 36/518).

[13] *Hitler's Beneficiaries*, 103–4.

that inequalities of distribution caused considerable tension among citizens.[14] Moving beyond these poles, Birthe Kundrus has suggested that scholars might learn more by looking at the role of German citizens themselves as consumers, and their reactions to Nazi policies. Building on the research of historians such as Shelley Baranowski and S. Jonathan Wiesen, Kundrus argues for increasing our attention to the features of "a specific Nazi model of a modern consumer culture" and to the behaviour of Germans as consumers who did not always do what the regime wanted them to do.[15]

Looking at consumption in occupied France contributes to these debates in several ways. On the whole, and making allowances for the polemical quality of Aly's argument, soldiers' rampant acquisitiveness supports the German historian's contention that satisfying people's desire to consume helped ensure political stability in Hitler's Reich. It could even be argued that the greater the sacrifices Germans made at home, the more important compensations such as the ability to consume in the occupied territories became. Early on, material goods were the real draw, but the situation in France also confirms that, as Baranowski has underlined, consumption must be understood in its broadest sense, with attention to the consumption of experiences, and in particular to tourism, as modes of consuming that satisfied many of the same impulses as shopping but did not rely on the purchase of material goods.[16] One of the reasons that tourism persisted until the very end of the occupation, long after material goods became scarce, was precisely that it had become such a useful form of displaced consumption. Soldiers' consuming behaviour in France is also worth exploring, moreover, because it points up the deep-rooted conflict between the popular desire to consume and the state's efforts to control and manipulate consumption so that it supported, rather than undermined, larger goals.[17] As a population subjected to formal military discipline, soldiers' behaviour should have been easy to regulate, yet the official decision to open a *Soldatenkaufhaus* (soldiers' department store) to canalise military shopping is just one sign of the fact that occupiers' consumption proved far from straightforward to manage.

---

[14] See discussion in the Introduction, and notably Buchheim, "Der Mythos vom "Wohlleben""; Tooze, *The Wages of Destruction*. Aly's response to critics can be found in *Volksstaat*, 365–97. Kundrus summarises the debate in Kundrus, "Greasing the Palm," 159–60.

[15] Kundrus, "Greasing the Palm," 161.

[16] Baranowski, *Strength*. Occupiers' tourism is the subject of Chapter 3.

[17] On this conflict, see Kundrus, "Greasing the Palm," 161–6.

Above all, to view occupying soldiers' consumption in France simply from the perspective of plunder, as many accounts do, shuts off avenues of analysis.[18] If occupiers' shopping was plunder, it can be read in the context of spoliation and war, yet characterising it this way removes it from the broader history of consumption and leisure. Even if the line between shopping and plunder was fine, sometimes non-existent in an occupation context, it is nonetheless useful to examine occupiers' activities not only in the framework of war, i.e. as plunder, but also, as Kundrus urges, as part of a longer history of consumption and leisure, i.e. as shopping.[19]

Fundamentally, for example, the fact that occupiers' shopping was so widespread not only underlines Hitler's determination to despoil France, but also brings out the popularity of shopping as a leisure activity among not only women, but also men by the 1940s, even in, or despite, wartime. The occupation of such a potentially fruitful land as France, combined with the beginnings of war-induced austerity at home, turned men into shoppers – shoppers, moreover, who purchased soap, textiles and perfume, items they would only occasionally have purchased at home. Wartime led to a significant, albeit temporary, shift in the traditional gendering of shopping habits.

Molly Loberg has emphasised the need to read wartime consumption patterns as distinct, while embedding them in longer historical processes. As she has pointed out, "[h]istorians have treated the postwar instability, the Depression and the Second World War as precursors to future abundance and causes of developmental lags, rather than as distinct periods in which habits and expectations established in previous moments of greater prosperity contracted or collapsed across broad segments of society."[20] While Loberg rightly stresses the long-term context of wartime consumption, occupiers' large-scale acquisitiveness suggests a need to nuance her reading of wartime as a period in which prosperity straightforwardly "contracted or collapsed" across broad segments of society. For German soldiers who had just won the Western campaign, and for their families at home, the war temporarily expanded consuming opportunities. This expansion may not have mitigated the overall austerity of wartime for long, but it serves as a reminder that wars

---

[18] Gilles Perrault and Pierre Azema, for example, reprinted images of Germans shopping in France and noted, as Aly and also Klaus Latzel have, that because of the exchange rate and price controls, this shopping was tantamount to plunder. Latzel, *Deutsche Soldaten*, 136–8; Perrault and Azema, *Paris*, 74–5.

[19] Kundrus, "Greasing the Palm," 161.

[20] Molly Loberg, "The Streetscape of Economic Crisis: Commerce, Politics, and Urban Space in Interwar Berlin," *Journal of Modern History* 85, no. 2 (June 2013): 366.

do not inevitably limit consumption for all.[21] Including wartime as part of longer consumption patterns while remaining alert to its distinctiveness, particularly the ways in which it altered the interaction of gender and shopping habits, individuals and the state at war, refines our understanding of consumer practices.[22] Although it would be going too far to say that opportunities to consume alone ensured popular compliance, occupiers' buying frenzy supports Aly's argument that consumption in the occupied territories was an important crutch of consent for the Nazi regime. Read broadly and with sensitivity to soldiers' agency and to their interactions with military authorities and the state, shopping during the occupation also demonstrates the extent to which leisure-based models of interaction persisted despite (and were in fact facilitated by) war.

This chapter looks at consumption "writ large," first shopping and eating, then leisure and the consumption of experiences, including amorous and sexual experiences with French women. In an occupation context, soldiers' relationships with local women were situated along a continuum between leisure and consumption, and exploitation. Acknowledged or not, the unequal power relations between occupiers and civilians underlay all such relationships, which were, to a lesser or greater degree, transactional in nature.[23] Like shopping, which was always also plunder, sexual fraternisation was always also exploitation.

German attitudes towards consumption of all kinds were Janus-faced. On the one hand, the regime recognised that even in wartime, France was an attractive destination. There were advantages in allowing soldiers to profit from the ready access to French goods and services (of all kinds) that occupation allowed. Discounted shopping and open contact with

---

[21] Pamela Swett underlines that "day-to-day buying and selling remained integral to life in Germany during the war," *Selling under the Swastika: Advertising and Commercial Culture in Nazi Germany* (Stanford, CA: Stanford University Press, 2014), 186.

[22] The early focus on women in the historiography of gender and consumption is slowly shifting. Dingel, "Consumption in Nineteenth- and Twentieth-Century Germany," 248. On gender and shopping, see Hartmut Berghoff and Thomas Kühne, *Globalizing Beauty: Consumerism and Body Aesthetics in the Twentieth Century* (New York: Palgrave Macmillan, 2013); Victoria De Grazia and Ellen Furlough, *The Sex of Things: Gender and Consumption in Historical Perspective* (Berkeley: University of California Press, 1996). On consumption in National Socialist Germany, see Baranowski, *Strength*; Hartmut Berghoff, "Enticement and Deprivation: The Regulation of Consumption in Pre-War Nazi Germany" in *The Politics of Consumption: Material Culture and Citizenship in Europe and America*, ed. Martin Daunton and Matthew Hilton (Oxford: Berg, 2001), 165–84; S. Jonathan Wiesen, *Creating the Nazi Marketplace: Commerce and Consumption in the Third Reich* (Cambridge University Press, 2010).

[23] Imlay, "German Side," 208–9; Paul Sanders, *The British Channel Islands under German Occupation 1940–45* (St. Helier: Jersey Heritage Trust, 2005), 170–71. Birgit Beck notes that soldiers were well aware of their powerful position vis à vis occupied populations, and exploited it in their relations with women. *Wehrmacht und sexuelle Gewalt*, 221.

French women became modern variants of the traditional conqueror's prerogatives: pillage and rape. At the same time, military authorities and party officials worried about the impact of unrestrained consumption and fraternisation on military discipline, the running of the occupation, and the war overall. In an often contradictory way, they sought both to allow and to monitor consumption, to encourage and to restrain soldiers' desire to experience and possess everything French. Exemplifying the National Socialist regime's larger tendency not to forbid outright, but to manage and direct through propaganda any potentially threatening signs of individuality, the management of leisure and consumption reflected ambiguities that underlay its entire approach to occupying France, a country it both admired and sought to control.[24]

After outlining the basic parameters of German soldiers' shopping, this chapter examines contradictory official attempts to both encourage and control this activity. Later in the chapter, it considers food and restaurants, the consumption of experiences, and finally soldiers' intimate fraternisation with French women. The chapter concludes by exploring contemporary reactions to German soldiers' acquisitiveness, which came to serve as a marker of their vulgarity. Understanding more about soldiers' acquisitive and leisure activities, including intimate fraternisation, contributes to writing the history of consumption not only in so-called "ordinary" times of prosperity and peace, but also those characterised as "extraordinary" times of scarcity and war. It underlines the significance of these activities as tools of power in a war and occupation context.

Wartime shopping, like other forms of interaction with the occupied land and its population, had to be managed. One persistent problem was that men used to front-line fighting found the line between shopping and plunder difficult to discern, and easy to cross when the overall attitude towards France was that it was a fruit ripe for the picking. As Hans K's diary cited at the beginning of Chapter 1 suggests, plunder, which soldiers euphemistically called "organising," was commonplace during the 1940 campaign. In July 1941, the Field Commander at Besançon had to remind his men that all booty must be turned over to the local

---

[24] Attitudes towards consumption paralleled those regarding soldiers' amateur photography, which the Wehrmacht permitted (unlike the Red Army), but tried both to regulate formally and to steer informally through publications and exhibitions. Peter Jahn, "Vorwort" in *Foto-Feldpost: geknipste Kriegserlebnisse 1939–1945*, ed. Peter Jahn and Ulrike Schmiegelt (Berlin: Elephanten Press, 2000), 7. On tensions between mass consumption and popular mobilisation in fascist Italy, cf. Victoria De Grazia, "Nationalizing Women: The Competition between Fascist and Commercial Cultural Models in Mussolini's Italy" in *The Sex of Things: Gender and Consumption in Historical Perspective*, ed. Ellen Furlough and Victoria De Grazia (Berkeley: University of California Press, 1996), 337–58.

Commander, and that they were not allowed to threaten or punish civilians or representatives of the French authorities unless the Field Commander had ordered this.[25] A few months later, the Amiens Field Commander clarified pointedly that "occupied France is not currently an operations area! Since war operations are completed, it is not commensurate with the reputation of the German Forces for troops to carry out confiscations and requisitions on their own initiative, thereby contravening the orders of . . . the Militärbefehlshaber, which are known to the local population."[26] Despite efforts to control plundering, notably for logistical reasons, the troops continued to view French goods, especially the furniture in their quarters, as their own. Again summarising his experiences in the Lille area, administrator Haase deplored that "[t]he greatest annoyance in the quartering domain was the appropriation of furnishings by units that were leaving the area."[27] Sometimes units could be forced to give back stolen items, but if they were headed to the Eastern Front, this was next to impossible. In the overall context of Germany's systematic plunder of France, soldiers failed to see why such appropriation was problematic.[28]

The line between shopping and plunder was all the more difficult to make out because the German authorities enthusiastically encouraged shopping. According to rules established by the Wehrmacht in September 1940, occupiers in France could receive money from their salaries up to the equivalent of fifty Reichsmarks per month, an amount that was soon raised to one hundred Reichsmarks.[29] To avoid transferring German currency abroad, these funds were paid out in French francs

[25] Feldkommandantur 550, "Merkblatt für die Truppe über den Aufbau und die Aufgaben der Militärverwaltung," 15 July 1941, 1, 10 (BArch: RH 36/205).

[26] "Merkblatt der Feldkommandatur 580," October 1941 (BArch: RH 36/225). The timing of these instructions suggests that problems may have grown more severe when units moved west after brutal fighting during the invasion of the Soviet Union. See Chapter 6.

[27] Regierungsrat Haase, Beitrag zum Abschlußbericht des Militärbefehlshabers für Belgien und Nordfrankreich, n.d. [autumn 1944] (BArch: RH 36/518).

[28] On the economic exploitation of France, see, e.g. Alan S. Milward, *The New Order and the French Economy* (Oxford: Clarendon Press, 1970); Arne Radtke-Delacor, "Produire pour le Reich: Les commandes allemandes à l'industrie française (1940–1944)," *Vingtième Siècle*, no. 70 (April 2001): 99–115; Philippe Verheyde, *Les mauvais comptes de Vichy: l'aryanisation des entreprises juives* (Paris: Perrin, 1999).

[29] O.K.W., Auszug aus Heeresverordnungsblatt vom 27 Sept. 1940 S. 387 ff., No. 562 "Zahlungsregelung für die Wehrmacht in Belgien und Frankreich," 19 September 1940 (AN: AJ 40/451). The change to 100 RM had been made by 4 March 1941. Der Militärbefehlshaber in Frankreich, Kommandostab Abt. Ia Br. B.Nr. Ia 150/41 "Merkblatt über den Ankauf von Lebensmitteln und Marketenderwaren, die Geld- und Zahlungsregelung sowie die Benutzung von Kraftfahrzeugen im besetzten französischen Gebiet," 4 March 1941 (AN: AJ 40/451).

at the very favourable rate of one franc for five pfennigs.[30] The result was that an individual soldier might have a monthly sum of up to 2,000 francs at his disposal. Since the army looked after his basic needs, this money was available for personal items, shopping and entertainment. It was about the equivalent of a modest monthly income for a French family of four.[31]

The regime encouraged occupiers' shopping for various reasons. It satisfied soldiers' desire to acquire and helped keep them busy and happy. The army may have hoped it would avert more open forms of plunder, although these continued to occur. Private purchasing also redistributed food and other valuable goods from the occupied lands to the Reich. From late September 1940 in France, except in the case of rationed goods, the Wehrmacht decided that "the individual member of the military may purchase whatever he likes."[32] Perishable and non-perishable goods alike were shipped by field post, and the soldier headed home on leave with rucksack bulging and parcels dangling around his neck became a familiar sight (Figure 2.1).[33] His welcome arrival made the soldier himself feel like a magnanimous hero, helped off-set shortages in Germany, and bolstered popular support for Hitler's continued occupation of much of Europe. As recounted by scholars Andrew Bergerson and Maria Stehle, soldier Rudi Mosaner described in his memoirs "his return home [from France] like the arrival of Santa Claus. By the time he got to Kaufbeuren, he was carrying so many groceries he had to transport them with a sleigh to his family. During his four days of leave they could not eat up all the foods, many of which were luxuries."[34] Soldiers and their families competed to see who was sending the most goods, and for some, like Mosaner, "providing such a feast to his family must have made him feel like he had finally climbed out of poverty into the bourgeoisie."[35]

---

[30] O.K.W., Auszug aus Heeresverordnungsblatt vom 27 Sept. 1940 S. 387 ff., No. 562 "Zahlungsregelung für die Wehrmacht in Belgien und Frankreich" 19 September 1940 (AN: AJ 40/451).

[31] In 1942, a Parisian family of four with an income of less than 2,350 francs per month qualified for French state evacuation assistance. Direction des réfugies, circulaire 115, 3 April 1942 (AD Seine-Maritime: 51 W/0339).

[32] Kommandantur-Befehl Nr. 127, Kommandantur Paris, 6 December 1940 (AN: AJ 40/451).

[33] Aly, *Volksstaat*, 116, 118–19.

[34] Andrew Bergerson and Maria Stehle, "Rudolph Mosaner's 'Wanderjahre': Irony and Impunity in Nazi Europe" in *War, Exile, Justice, and Everyday Life, 1936–1946*, ed. Sandra Ott, Center for Basque Studies Conference Papers Series; No. 7 (Reno: Center for Basque Studies Press, University of Nevada, 2011), 293.

[35] Bergerson and Stehle, *Rudolph Mosaner*, 293.

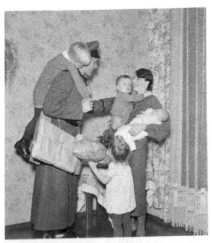

Figure 2.1 Propaganda image of a soldier bearing parcels returning home to his family for Christmas, 1940.
pbk Bildagentur/Stiftung preussischer Kulturbesitz : Or 04852–01 / Liselotte Purpur / Art Resource

While reinforcing men's traditional role as breadwinner and benefactor, soldiers' desire to impress and offer luxuries to their loved ones caused a marked, albeit temporary, shift in traditionally gendered patterns of consumption. Not only did men engage in extensive shopping, itself a more typically "female" activity, but they also shopped for items they would not normally have bought, including clothing and housewares for female relatives. Regulations from April 1941 mentioned that in addition to their salaries, soldiers could bring the equivalent of 300 Reichsmarks with them to France. In an appendix, the document listed the many products that could still be procured without ration tickets. Silk and rubber items were available and, alongside ties, handkerchiefs and suspenders, the document also listed brassieres, girdles and corsets. Clearly, the soldiers were not expected to wear these items themselves; rather, they were intended to bring or send them home to their relations.[36]

---

[36] Militärbefehlshaber in Frankreich, Kommandostab Abt. Ia/Iva Verwaltungsstab Wi, Merkblatt über den Ankauf von Lebens-, Genussmitteln und Marketenderwaren, sowie über die Geld- und Zahlungsregelung in Bereich des Militärbefehlshabers in Frankreich, 9 April 1941 (BArch: RH 36/205). Some women came to France as Wehrmacht auxiliaries, but it is clear that German shoppers from 1940 to 1944 were mainly male. On female auxiliaries, see Franka Maubach, *Die Stellung halten:*

Alongside the very loose distinctions occupiers made between shopping and plunder, this shift in buying practices can be seen in the letters of Bernhard Schulz, quoted at the beginning of this chapter. For Gerda, he bought perfume, soap, and "all kinds of French things … for your dressing-table."[37] Later, he sent angora yarn to make a sweater, but underestimated the quantity required. Gerda must have complained, for he assured her that French women wore their sweaters short, and said he would ask a comrade going to the Norman town of Vire to pick up some more yarn in the right colour. From Schulz's inability to estimate yarn quantities through his reassuring comments about fashion and the recruitment of a comrade to assist with yarn shopping, this vignette underlines how soldiers' shopping stretched traditional patterns of consumption.[38]

In its mixing of shopping and plunder, consumption in occupied areas also challenged traditional moral norms. Bernhard Schulz felt no compunction about having seized perfume and bought butter under the table, for he confessed to both crimes readily. To do so, he must have believed that Gerda would not object; indeed that she would condone his acquisitive activities.[39] Her support for, and even collusion in, his "shopping" is highlighted by the fact that the second shipment of butter mentioned above was mailed to her after a home leave in which the two became engaged. Around the same time, Schulz reported that he would see if he could find the gloves Gerda had requested for her sister.[40] From butter through perfume to women's gloves, soldiers like Schulz crisscrossed occupied France looking for appropriate items to send home. Relatives and friends supported their activities, more concerned about getting exactly the right products than about the precise origin of these wares.[41]

Despoiling Europe of food, clothing and housewares made "ordinary" Germans' lives easier in concrete ways. When aerial bombing grew severe in Germany from 1943 onwards, enlisted men scoured occupied areas urgently, looking for basic household goods to send home to their

---

Kriegserfahrungen und Lebensgeschichten von Wehrmachthelferinnen (Göttingen: Vandenhoeck & Ruprecht, 2009).

[37] Schulz, letter, 15 March 1941 (DTA: 2033).

[38] Schulz, letter, 25 November 1941 (DTA: 2033).

[39] Cf. Aly, *Volksstaat*, 114–20. In 2003, when Aly asked readers of German newspaper *Die Zeit* to write about their experiences with field post parcels, women remembered and described these in detail while "the men, without exception, denied ever having sent a single package home." Aly, *Hitler's Beneficiaries*, 97.

[40] Schulz, letter, 25 November 1941 (DTA: 2033).   [41] Aly, *Volksstaat*, 114–20.

bombed-out families.[42] The shortage of housewares was serious enough that in the fall of 1943, Reich Marshall Hermann Göring proposed that West Europeans be stripped of their nonessential furniture so that the excess could be given to bombed-out German civilians. The German military authorities in France objected to this scheme, however, citing the absence of army units available for such an undertaking, and its potentially disastrous political consequences. It was much less controversial simply to ensure that soldiers kept shopping. Occupiers' shopping thus continued to serve as a substitute for, and a supplement to, more open forms of despoilment.[43]

Consumption was one of the real benefits that France offered to soldiers; yet, there was a deep tension between the desire to encourage it because it nourished consent for the National Socialist system, and the need to manage it as part of the larger war economy. Occupiers asked their relatives to send money so that they could purchase more goods, while the authorities responsible for economic matters tried in vain to expose the dangers of unrestricted buying.[44] A document from March 1941 reminded occupiers that in order to steer consumption they must present ration tickets when purchasing basic foods, coffee, tea, chocolate, soap and other products, but soldiers often disregarded such regulations.[45] A further clarifying document later reinforced the rules, noting for instance that "in principle, wine and spirits may only be purchased in retail establishments and for personal use," but soldiers engaged in dubious buying practices nonetheless.[46]

---

[42] Sometimes, French collaborators did the scouring for them. See Sandra Ott, "The Informer, the Lover and the Gift Giver: Female Collaborators in Pau 1940–1946," *French History* 22, no. 1 (March 2008): 105–7.

[43] The collaborationist organisation Comité Ouvrier de Secours Immédiat was set up in large part in order to transfer resources and furniture stolen from French Jews to bombed-out French and German families. Torrie, *For Their Own Good*, 135–6. See also Jean-Pierre Le Crom, *Au secours, Maréchal !: l'instrumentalisation de l'humanitaire, 1940–1944* (Paris: Presses universitaires de France, 2013), 199–228.

[44] Fearing inflation, officers responsible for military finances, rather than the welfare of the troops, requested that limits be set on currency transfers. Aly, *Volksstaat*, 115.

[45] Most soldiers' basic needs were provided for directly through their unit. Some members of the military, so-called "Selbstverpfleger," were issued ration tickets because their responsibilities required that they travel, or they needed more flexibility than normal group provisioning allowed. Der Militärbefehlshaber in Frankreich, Kommandostab Abt. Ia Br. B. Nr. Ia 150/41 "Merkblatt über den Ankauf von Lebensmitteln und Marketenderwaren, die Geld- und Zahlungsregelung sowie die Benutzung von Kraftfahrzeugen im besetzten französischen Gebiet," 4 March 1941 (AN: AJ 40/451).

[46] Der Militärbefehlshaber in Frankreich, Kommandostab Abt. Ia/IV a Verwaltungsstab Wi Br. B. Nr. Ia 178/41 "Merkblatt über den Ankauf von Lebens-, Genußmitteln und Marketenderwaren, sowie über die Geld- und Zahlungsregelung im Bereich des Militärbefehlshabers in Frankreich," 9 April 1941 (AN: AJ 40/451).

Moreover, the official limits on the amount of currency a soldier might receive from home, while generous, did not seem generous enough to some soldiers. To get around the rules, men had goods sent from Germany, which they then traded or bartered for other goods in France. In early November 1942, in a longer note about lax discipline, the High Command reported that field post censors had uncovered letters from soldiers of all ranks who had been asking their relatives to send sewing needles, cigarette lighters, sweeteners, pocket knives, watches and costume jewelry so that they could trade these with the French. In some cases, the letters recounted the considerable profits soldiers had made on these exchanges.[47] Such behaviour undermined discipline and the reputation of the Wehrmacht, and the High Command had specifically forbidden it in a regulation from 30 May 1941. Troops were to be reminded of the rules, and infractions punished through the military courts.[48]

The complexities of managing occupiers' consumption are also suggested by an anonymous French letter received by the German embassy in Paris in May 1943. The letter-writer stated that he (or she) was "for German-French collaboration," and then recounted the experiences of a friend who owned a lingerie shop, and who had been offered 250 grams of chocolate by a German soldier for the same number of francs. The letter-writer remarked that "until that point [the shop-owner] had always thought that only Frenchmen were involved in the black market."[49] This was, of course, not the case. There was an extensive black market in France, and Germans were key players.[50]

The regime's attempts to rein in the black market and to regulate consumption underline the conundrum it faced. On the one hand, soldiers had a generous disposable income and France offered goods they wanted to buy. Consuming these goods themselves, or sending them home to their families gave a boost to morale, and as Aly has pointed out, it served as an important compensation for the sacrifices of war. The regime's ability to

---

[47] Oberkommando des Heeres, General z.b.V. beim OKH/Heerwesen-Abt. Az. FP.-Prüf. Nr. 70/10.42 geh. Betr.: Feldpostprüfberichte, 7 November 42 (AN: AJ 40/451).

[48] Oberkommando des Heeres, General z.b.V. beim OKH/Heerwesen-Abt. Az. III Nr. 236/10.42 geh. Betr. Tauschhandel mit der Zivilbevölkerung, 7 November 1942 (AN: AJ 40/451).

[49] The "friend" may have been the letter's author. The letter went on to complain about German trucks carrying food away from the fourteenth arrondissement of Paris, SS soldiers quartered in a private home who stole fruit while the owner was away, and other misdemeanours. Letter sent from NSDAP A-O Propaganda Amt to German Embassy Paris staff member Schwendemann, 14 May 1943 (AAN: DBP 1119c).

[50] See Kenneth Mouré, "Food Rationing and the Black Market in France (1940–1944)," *French History* 24, no. 2 (June 1, 2010): 262–82; Paul Sanders, *Histoire du marché noir: 1940–1944* (Paris: Perrin, 2000). Black market restaurants are discussed later in this chapter.

offer soldiers, and through them civilians, access to consumer goods, surely fostered its longevity.[51] From the point of view of the German authorities in France, therefore, private consumption was essential, yet at the same time, it was difficult to control. The war economy required careful husbandry of all resources, and the individuality of shopping behaviour itself threatened a regime that sought to manage as many aspects of its citizens' lives as possible. Incentives to control consumption worked at cross-purposes with those enabling soldiers to consume.

One attempt to address this conundrum lay in the opening of a so-called *Soldatenkaufhaus*, or soldiers' department store. This establishment, apparently set up with the cooperation of the French department store "Au Printemps," was located at 25, Ave. des Ternes.[52] In a letter from mid-November 1940, military bureaucrat Dr. Franz Albrecht Medicus explained that he had recently helped to establish a soldiers' department store in Paris. The store's objective, he noted, was to "catch" (abfangen) the thousands of Wehrmacht members arriving daily for sightseeing, and in order not to disturb the control of the economy "to keep them away from Paris shops." At the same time, the letter continued, "these members of the military, some of whom come from the smallest communities of our provinces, should be given the chance, by shopping for their family members, to take advantage of the opportunities for export that present themselves."[53] Referring to the "thousands" of soldiers visiting Paris daily, Medicus alluded somewhat patronisingly to the desire of soldiers from small communities to experience big-city French shopping. He clearly understood that through these men,

---

[51] Aly, *Volksstaat*, 360–61. A critique of Aly's interpretation is offered earlier in this chapter and in the Introduction.

[52] Although notably the Galeries Lafayette department store was "aryanised" by the occupation authorities, this does not seem to have been the case with Au Printemps. The occupation authorities sometimes claimed that the *Soldatenkaufhaus* had been set up by Au Printemps, but they were heavily involved themselves. Kriegsverwaltungsrat Hartmann to Chef des Militärverwaltungsbezirks Paris, Verwaltungsstab, Wi/II/Tex/20109/8, 31 December 1940 (AN: 40 AJ/774). An internal military administration document of 20 October 1940 mentioned a contract between "Fam. Laguioni & Matyas," [sic] who ran the Printemps company, and the German authorities in Paris. See Intendurrat Niecke, "Vermerk zum Vertrag betr. Soldatenkaufhaus der Kommandantur Paris" (AN: 40 AJ/878). On the Galeries Lafayette and other department stores during the occupation, see Verheyde, *Les mauvais comptes*, 131–49; 351–3.

[53] Letter from Chef des Militärverwaltungsbezirks Paris, Verwaltungsstab Wi/gew. an den Militärbefehlshaber in Frankreich, Verwaltungsstab, Wirtschaftsabteilung, z.H. von Herrn Min. Rat Burandt, Betr. Soldatenkaufhaus der Kommandantur Paris, 18 November 1940 (AN: AJ 40 /774). Fifty percent of earnings from the *Soldatenkaufhaus* were meant to go towards troop care. Note regarding the contract for the *Soldatenkaufhaus* of the Paris command, 20 October 1940 (AN: AJ 40/878).

Germany could "export" vast quantities of goods home. From its inception, the *Soldatenkaufhaus* was intended to both facilitate the despoilment of France and to control soldiers' consumption. It was easier and more profitable to canalise soldiers' shopping than to forbid it outright.

A report from 10 October 1940 gives a sense of the *Soldatenkaufhaus*'s significance in its early days. In the seven hours it was open, 33 groups representing a total of 2,261 soldiers had stopped by the establishment, and the total earnings were 125,100 francs.[54] After socks and stockings (9,600 francs), the next largest sellers were stationary (7,200 francs) and perfume (5,450 francs), followed closely by leather goods (5,100 francs). Occupiers also purchased 21,150 francs worth of food and baked goods in the store's restaurant, and spent 57,000 francs in an area called the "Special section Printemps," which may have been either a special area with luxury goods for officers, or an associated operation that retained the company's French name.[55] The *Soldatenkaufhaus* was so popular that it quickly sold out of the most attractive items. At the end of his letter about the department store, Medicus complained that its objectives of managing consumption could only be met if the establishment received sufficient supplies of goods, particularly textiles and soap, the two most popular items. To reinforce his point, he noted that if sufficient goods were not available through official channels, then soldiers "have a tendency to acquire the desired objects on their own."[56] Clearly, soldiers were not satisfied with the controlled consumption the *Soldatenkaufhaus* offered, especially if it was short of highly-coveted items. One official Paris group leader for Germans was actually fired in late fall 1940 because he had had the temerity to suggest that soldiers might find better goods more cheaply outside the *Soldatenkaufhaus*.[57]

Regardless of the success, or lack thereof, of the *Soldatenkaufhaus*, there was disagreement among German representatives about the extent to which soldiers should be encouraged to shop. When the *Soldatenkaufhaus* requested more generous deliveries of textiles and clothing in December 1940, a member of the military administration commented

---

[54] The same day, 4,000 soldiers were listed as participating in official tours of Paris, so about half of the total went to the *Soldatenkaufhaus*. Kommandant von Paris (Abt. Ic Besichtigungen) to Abt. Ic "Meldung," 9 October 1940 (AN: 40 AJ/878).

[55] Soldatenkaufhaus der Kommandantur Paris, Bericht Nr. 22, 10 October 1940 (AN: 40 AJ/878).

[56] Chef des Militärverwaltungsbezirks Paris, Verwaltungsstab Wi/gew. an den Militärbefehlshaber in Frankreich, Verwaltungsstab, Wirtschaftsabteilung, z.H. von Herrn Min. Rat Burandt, Betr. Soldatenkaufhaus der Kommandantur Paris, 18 November 1940 (AN: 40 AJ/774).

[57] Correspondence about guide R. Krell, October 1940 (AN: AJ 40/878) and Gordon, "Warfare and Tourism," 623.

critically that occupiers bought not only essentials but many luxury goods there. "It's obvious," he wrote, "that these soldier purchases benefit only one segment of the German population."[58] Rather than encouraging private consumption by better-off occupiers, this author argued that it was time to restrict individual purchasing in favour of stronger controls to exploit French production systematically for Germany's overall needs.[59] He drew attention, again, to the potentially destructive effects that poorly-managed shopping might have on the war economy.

Despite such criticism, the *Soldatenkaufhaus* continued to exist until the very end of the occupation.[60] It was not the only such establishment, either, for similar stores were set up in provincial towns like Granville, Morlaix and Rennes.[61] By canalising shopping through a *Soldatenkaufhaus*, the regime tried to enable, while also carefully steering, soldiers' consumption. Ultimately, the authorities were caught in their own conundrum, for it was impossible both to encourage and to control individual consuming behaviour. Official attempts to manage occupiers' consumption support Kundrus's and others' contention that consumers' own agency imposed limits on the National Socialist regime's ability to manage consumption in its own interest.[62] Consumption represents one of the many small ways that individuals pushed back against the authoritarianism of the Nazi regime. In the context of occupied France, examining shopping underlines that managing soldiers posed almost as many challenges as managing the French.

The Paris *Soldatenkaufhaus* was developed to address the contradictory way in which incentives to consume worked at cross-purposes with the desire to control the economy. Similar contradictions were also evident in other forms of consumption and leisure in occupied France. Several historians have pointed out that consuming experiences, undertaking tourist visits, and advertising the promise of future tourism all served the Third Reich as displaced forms of consumption, satisfying citizens'

---

[58] Kriegsverwaltungsrat Hartmann to Chef des Militärverwaltungsbezirks Paris, Verwaltungsstab, Wi/II/Tex/20109/8, 31 December 1940 (AN: 40 AJ/774).

[59] Kriegsverwaltungsrat Hartmann to Chef des Militärverwaltungsbezirks Paris, Verwaltungsstab, Wi/II/Tex/20109/8, 31 December 1940 (AN: 40 AJ/774). Individual purchasing was restricted in the Reich itself through the war. Wiesen, *Creating the Nazi Marketplace*, 192–7.

[60] The *Soldatenkaufhaus* was among amenities for soldiers listed in the last issue of *Der deutsche Wegleiter für Paris* 103, 12–26 August 1944, 7.

[61] Sanders, *The British Channel Islands Under German Occupation 1940–45*, 33.

[62] Rather than agency, Kundrus uses the more specific term *Eigensinn* to describe the way that individual consumption behaviour and the population's own ideas limited the regime's ability to act. Kundrus, "Greasing the Palm," 166. See also Wiesen, *Creating the Nazi Marketplace*, 214–16.

desire to consume without actually requiring much in the way of goods.[63] What was true of the general population was also true of soldiers – living in France as an occupier became an opportunity to collect not only goods but also experiences. Soldiers gained gastronomic pleasure from eating at fine restaurants, awe and joy at swimming in the ocean for the first time, and a sense of cultural enrichment from touring major historical sites. Bertram Gordon's pioneering work on occupier tourism in France confirms that the thousands of tourists administrator Medicus had alluded to in Paris were no exaggeration. The regime organised tours of the capital that were intended to offer a once-in-a-lifetime visit to the famed City of Light. Such tours, discussed at greater length in Chapter 3, reinforced to both the Germans and the French the notion that the conquerors were civilised: able to appreciate French historical and cultural monuments, not just to destroy them.

When he first visited Paris, Hans Klumpp, who we followed in Chapter 1 as he invaded France and discovered its pleasures and perils, was clearly impressed by the size of the city and by its modern amenities. "We took a look at the subway," he wrote in his diary on 9 July 1940, "and rode the escalator back up to the top. A funny feeling, for it was the first time."[64] Soon after, on Bastille day, he and a friend snuck into the city-centre without permission. Although it took 45 minutes and "lots of sweat" they climbed 1800 steps up the Eiffel Tower to stand at the top, next to the *Reichskriegsflagge* (Reich war flag).[65] Later in the day, they visited Montmartre, where they talked briefly with a prostitute from "a French colony in central America," perhaps Guadeloupe or Martinique, and then visited a cabaret show, where "the women were doing their dances half-naked." "Simply amazing," Klumpp concluded, "When you have the chance to be in Paris for once, you've just got to have seen it!"[66] Klumpp was from Karlsruhe, a provincial city by comparison, and from its famed monuments through the mixed population and seething underworld, Paris offered wonders beyond anything he had ever experienced.[67] Yet, as we will see, even an occupier rather more sophisticated

---

[63] Baranowski, *Strength*, Ch. 6; Berghoff, "Enticement and Deprivation," 175.

[64] Klumpp, diary, 9 July 1940 (DTA: 1942). A few days later, on 14 July 1940, Klumpp remarked on how nice it was that soldiers could travel on the subway free, but this first time he clearly had not climbed aboard.

[65] The symbolism of such a gesture, especially on Bastille Day, was unmistakable. On occupier photography, conquest and the Eiffel Tower, see Chapter 4.

[66] Klumpp, diary, 14 July 1940 (DTA: 1942).

[67] As Allan Mitchell emphasises, "many of the occupying troops were young boys far from home who were dazzled by the big city and who harbored no hostile or haughty attitude toward its citizens." Mitchell, *Nazi Paris*, 17.

than Klumpp, Hans-Peter Eckener, remarked after his own whirlwind visit to Paris, that "the impression is ... *big* and *lasting*, and despite certain challenges, I count these days among the finest I have yet enjoyed."[68]

Letters home allowed occupiers' families, too, to share in their adventures vicariously. Taking in some of France's other well-known pleasures, this time not in Paris, but at the seaside, an aviator stationed on the Channel coast confided to his parents that, "I don't want to and I am not allowed to write about what's happening here in military terms. Yesterday we swam again in the Channel. It was delightful! As proof, I'm sending two seashells."[69] Soldiers both described and often photographed themselves bathing and engaging in other forms of leisure or consumption that would have been difficult or impossible at home. Letters, photographs and souvenirs confirmed that they had "been there" and "done that," broadened their horizons, and become men of the world.

Beyond sightseeing and shopping, occupiers were particularly attracted by French food. They found the abundance and variety of edibles eye-opening, and even basics like eggs, fresh meat, fish, cheese, and especially butter, became prized commodities because their consumption was already limited in Germany itself.[70] More accustomed to army rations, men like Klumpp became ill after gorging themselves on plundered delicacies.[71] Consuming French food and beverages represented more than thoughtless hedonism, of course, for food was a spoil of war. Rationing, more severe than in any other West European occupied land, subjected French citizens to penury while agricultural products were carried off to support the German war effort.[72] Though a great deal

---

[68] Emphasis in the original. "Der Eindruck ist doch groß und *bleibend*, und trotz gewisser Strapazen – ich rechne diese Tage zu den schönsten, die ich je gehabt habe." See also Chapter 3. Hans-Peter Eckener, letter 25 October 1941 in Hans-Peter Eckener and Peter Wolter, *Lieber Vater – mein lieber Per: Briefwechsel mit zu Hause 1940–1944* (Self-published, 1998), 127.

[69] Herbert K., "Melde mich in aller Frische," letter 29 September 1940, 42 (Kempowski-Archiv: BIO/3885).

[70] Food was rationed in Germany from the war's outset. On the attraction of butter for occupiers, see below, and Kenneth Mouré, "La Capitale de la Faim: Black Market Restaurants in Paris, 1940–1944," *French Historical Studies* 38, No. 2 (April 2015): 328. Aly wrote that Hitler's soldiers had become "armed couriers of butter." Aly, *Hitler's Beneficiaries*, 324. For more on food in the Third Reich generally, see Lizzie Collingham, *The Taste of War: World War II and the Battle for Food* (London: Penguin, 2012); Gustavo Corni, *Hitler and the Peasants: Agrarian Policy of the Third Reich, 1930–1939* (New York: Berg, 1990); Gesine Gerhard, *Nazi Hunger Politics: A History of Food in the Third Reich* (Lanham: Rowman & Littlefield, 2015).

[71] Klumpp, diary, 8 June 1940 (DTA: 1942). See Chapter 1.

[72] Mouré, "Food Rationing," 263. Food shortages are examined in Eric Alary, Bénédicte Vergez-Chaignon, and Gilles Gauvin, *Les Français au quotidien : 1939–1949* (Paris:

of food was delivered by the French directly, to fulfil formal contracts with the conqueror, occupiers' daily appropriation of foodstuffs contributed to the country's economic exploitation.[73]

Even as requisitioned French food supplies offered material benefits to Germany as a whole, eating well reinforced Germans' dominance on an individual level. Like imperial representatives in the colonies, occupiers lived to a higher standard in France than they could have afforded at home. Those well up the chain of command were accommodated in fine hotels and elegant manor houses, and they ate sumptuously.[74] Even ordinary soldiers enjoyed soft beds in comfortable quarters while often eating better food than they would have had in Germany. The pleasurable aspects of this situation deserve attention because they represented a distraction from, and a form of compensation for, the hardships of war. Living well, moreover, allowed occupiers to project their power, and it reinforced their position.[75]

Young occupiers like Kurt F. were thrilled by opportunities to sample new foods and drink to their heart's content. F. informed his parents excitedly that, "[w]we've already tried oysters, mussels and shrimp; I haven't managed to acquire a particular taste for the first two. Everywhere you can drink good red wine ... Good sparkling wine – we've already drunk a few bottles – costs ... one Reichsmark fifty at the pub."[76] Johannes Gutschmidt, an older officer who commanded a prisoner of war camp near the western French city of Le Mans, described in his diary many of the meals he had enjoyed, typically noting their reasonable price. In early August 1940, for example, he magnanimously invited twenty-six members of his unit "for coffee, cake, wine and beer" in the town of Olivet, near Orléans on the Loire river. The whole outing cost just

Perrin, 2009), 209–36; Kenneth Mouré and Paula Schwartz, "On vit mal," *Food, Culture & Society* 10, no. 2 (Summer 2007): 261–95; Dominique Veillon, *Vivre et survivre en France, 1939–1947* (Paris: Payot, 1995).

[73] On German exploitation of food in France see Milward, *New Order*; Mouré, "Food Rationing"; Julia S. Torrie, "Frozen Food and National Socialist Expansionism," *Global Food History* 2, no. 1 (March 2016): 51–73.

[74] For example, Johannes Gutschmidt visited Spain in 1941 with a fellow officer whose son was stationed on the border at Hendaye. Alongside the excellent food, Gutschmidt noted that the son had "the villa of a former film star all to himself," 28 February 1941, 'Kriegstagebuch,' 28 February 1941 (BArch: Msg. 1/257).

[75] Food's function as a marker of power in imperial contexts is explored notably in E. M. Collingham, *Curry: A Tale of Cooks and Conquerors* (Oxford; New York: Oxford University Press, 2006), especially 111; Rachel Laudan, *Cuisine and Empire* (Berkeley, CA: University of California Press, 2013); Cecilia Leong-Salobir, *Food Culture in Colonial Asia: A Taste of Empire* (Milton Park, Abingdon, Oxon; New York: Routledge, 2011).

[76] Kurt F., 13 February 1941 (DTA: 270/I).

twenty-seven Reichsmarks fifty. In Olivet, Gutschmidt liked the wine so much that he bought a case, which came to just two Reichsmarks twenty-five.[77] A few months later, he and his men prepared a "giant feast," including a mushroom omelette with white bread and butter, two huge carp with lemon and melted butter, tender pea pods and potatoes, followed by an excellent soft cheese with more bread and butter and two oranges. They washed the whole thing down first with a white Bordeaux then with a very good red Bordeaux.[78]

The relatively high standing France enjoyed, and the fact that a good number of Germans had some prior knowledge of the country, meant that occupiers tended to be less cautious about enjoying food and drink than they might have been in other regions. The men had to be warned repeatedly not to buy ice cream from street vendors, nor to drink raw milk. Alongside wine and beer, the quintessentially French aperitif Pernod caused particular problems, as soldiers apparently did not realise how strong it was. In Besançon, they were forbidden to drink it without thinning it to a ratio of one to twenty with water.[79]

Nowhere was occupiers' position more obviously reinforced through food and drink than in Paris, where the highest German officers moved into the city's best hotels and took advantage of everything the capital had to offer. The French reputation for fine dining, burnished with the rise of the restaurant through the eighteenth and nineteenth centuries, remained intact during the occupation.[80] Occupiers stationed in Paris and those who circulated through the city as visitors were drawn to its dining establishments, which stayed open to serve whatever paying clientele came to the door.[81] As finding adequate food supplies became a challenge, many restaurants, particularly elegant ones with menus as fine as their reputations to maintain, had recourse to the burgeoning black market. "In a Paris that was for most citizens 'the capital of hunger,'" according to Mouré, "black market restaurants allowed a privileged elite to eat very well. This elite included not just the Germans but the rich, the nouveaux riches, and the influential, including French officials,

---

[77] Johannes Gutschmidt, 'Kriegstagebuch,' 4 August 1940 (BArch: Msg. 1/257).

[78] Johannes Gutschmidt, 'Kriegstagebuch,' 12 February 1941, (BArch: Msg. 1/257).

[79] Feldkommandantur 550, "Merkblatt für die Truppe über den Aufbau und die Aufgaben der Militärverwaltung", 15 July 1941, p. 5 (BArch: RH 36–205).

[80] On Paris and the rise of the restaurant, see Rebecca L. Spang, *The Invention of the Restaurant: Paris and Modern Gastronomic Culture* (Harvard University Press, 2001).

[81] In May 1941, restaurants were divided into categories from A through D in order to regulate the quality, content and cost of meals they offered. An extra category "E" (exceptional) was soon added, and a small number of select restaurants was designated "hors catégorie" (HC). Mouré, "Capitale de la faim," 317.

collaborators, and black market profiteers."[82] To the occupiers, it did not much matter that the restaurants were supplied by the black market and that food consumption in these contexts undermined Germany's own efforts to combat illicit trade.[83] The authorities tried to limit the most obvious excesses, but ultimately allowed high-class restaurants to stay open because while the inequality they symbolised led to discontent among the French, this discontent was never enough to threaten the existing order.[84] Above all, fine restaurants' value as vectors of power outweighed the risks inherent in keeping them afloat.

Ernst Jünger, the well-known author, military administrator and aesthete who lived in Paris through much of the occupation, wrote about a dinner he had enjoyed at one of Paris's best-known restaurants in July 1942.[85] At the Tour d'Argent ("silver tower") overlooking the Seine, "[o]ne has the impression that the people at table up there, devouring their eels and famous ducks, look out with diabolical relish, like gargoyles, over the grey sea of rooftops to see the hungry eking out a miserable existence below their feet. In times like these eating, eating well and plentifully, gives a feeling of power."[86] Mouré notes that unlike some occupiers, Jünger's comments show he understood the "inequities in access to food," to which the French were subjected.[87] This may be true, but at the same time and more importantly, Jünger also grasped that for many occupiers, consciousness of these inequities was in fact part of the attraction. One of Paris's oldest and most noble restaurants, the Tour d'Argent was on an upper floor of a corner building "from which you can look out over the Seine and its islands as if from the dining-room of a big aeroplane."[88] Modern visions of flight before his eyes, Jünger described the view, with its implications of dominance, as a specific part of the attraction.[89] Such a view, impressive to begin with, gained an added "frisson" from the knowledge that only a privileged few could enjoy it. Eating in such a context underlined the Germans' power to the French. It also reinforced awareness of this power to the Germans themselves.

---

[82] Mouré, "Capitale de la faim," 338.   [83] Mouré, "Capitale de la faim," 314.

[84] On Franco-German negotiations about restaurant surveillance, see Mouré, "Capitale de la faim," especially 317–24.

[85] For more on Jünger in Paris, see Allan Mitchell, *The Devil's Captain: Ernst Jünger in Nazi Paris, 1941–1944* (New York: Berghahn Books, 2011).

[86] Entry for 4 July 1942 Ernst Jünger, *Strahlungen* (Tübingen: Heliopolis-Verlag, 1949), 130. Also cited in Mitchell, *The Devil's Captain*, 27; Mouré, "Capitale de la faim," 313.

[87] Mouré, "Capitale de la faim," 313.

[88] Entry for 4 July 1942, Jünger, *Strahlungen*, 130.

[89] Peter Fritzsche has analysed the particularly German fascination with flight, which reached a high point during the Third Reich. Peter Fritzsche, *A Nation of Fliers: German Aviation and the Popular Imagination* (Cambridge, MA: Harvard University Press, 1992).

Such reinforcement may have seemed especially necessary because of the awkward fact that the Germans and the French were in many ways quite similar. On the Eastern Front, Germans' perceived superiority appeared obvious, but in France, the hierarchy was less clear-cut, which was problematic for a regime built on a foundation of supposed racial distinctions. Throughout the occupation, the military authorities fought a losing battle to shore up social and cultural distinctions that they perceived through racial-national lenses. Although the regime considered some local populations, like the Normans, racially kindred to the German Volk, and admired others, like the Bretons, for their independent spirit, the official line was that most of the French (unlike Austrians, Danes, the Dutch, or even Belgians) were too foreign, and not entirely worthy of joining the new Volk and Reich. Aligning with the views of the Westforscher discussed in Chapter 1, who saw most of the French population as degenerate, NSV district leader Folkers, who worked at Vernon in 1940, remarked for instance that "[t]he population of this area was not as racially perfect as that further north on the Channel coast."[90]

The problem was that many occupiers do not seem to have cared. For them, France was a delightful, enticing place with tasty food, cheap wine, and many other social and cultural attractions. Attempts to monitor interactions between soldiers and the local population confirm that the occupiers did not automatically perceive the French to be different, let alone inferior. Soldiers had evidently seen nothing wrong with attending French church services, because this had to be forbidden in 1941.[91] Germans had tried to donate to French charities, for they had to be ordered not to have anything to do with the French war relief organisation *Secours National*. Recognising the impossibility of keeping soldiers out of French cinemas, the authorities specifically permitted this, but the films were censored anyway, and the military argued that a German presence would keep order in the theatres.[92] Attempting to counter the

---

[90] Report of NSV district leader Folkers, Norden (Gau Weser-Ems), on his experiences in Belgium and France, 27 November 1940 (BArch: NS 37/2065). Werner Best's racial views on France followed the pattern described above. See BArch: N 1023/1; Herbert, *Best*, 295.

[91] Feldkommandantur 550, "Merkblatt für die Truppe über den Aufbau und die Aufgaben der Militärverwaltung," 15 July 1941, p. 10 (BArch: RH 36–205). See also Mitchell, *Nazi Paris*, 17. Special services for military personnel were developed as an alternative, and advertised regularly in Paris and elsewhere.

[92] Anti-German demonstrations had taken place during newsreels from October 1940 onwards. The French Prefect of Police in Paris, Langeron, complained about how hard it was to keep order in a darkened theatre, so German soldiers who attended French cinemas were encouraged to feel responsible for helping to quell any

attractiveness of existing French amenities, the occupation regime set up a large number of *Soldatenkinos* (soldiers' cinemas) to show German-language films. It also developed an extensive array of social and cultural activities for soldiers.

The need to manage French leisure and entertainment opportunities, and to develop sanctioned alternatives to counter the attractiveness of existing "amenities" was nowhere more apparent than in the context of occupiers' interactions with French women. Recognising that being able to see a striptease show or visit a prostitute had long been important Parisian attractions, the occupation regime made sure that the city's nightlife continued undisturbed.[93] To fulfil what even in wartime were seen as men's sexual "needs," while limiting the potential risks involved, the army set up brothels across the occupied zone.[94] As Insa Meinen has explained, German propaganda depicted France as a hive of prostitution and *Mädchenhandel* (maiden-trafficking)."[95] Wehrmacht leaders took it as a given that the French authorities were incapable of controlling and monitoring the country's prostitutes, who they believed were contaminated by disease. For this reason, the army requisitioned the majority of preexisting bordellos outside Paris for military use. In the capital, they ran some thirty houses out of a total of about 180 in the city in 1941.[96] The health of the *Kartenmädchen* or *femmes de carte* was overseen by the local military doctor, and the army sought out and forcibly hospitalised women suspected of infecting soldiers with sexually transmitted diseases.[97] It acted aggressively to identify suspected prostitutes, notably

demonstrations that took place. Feldkommandantur 550, "Merkblatt für die Truppe über den Aufbau und die Aufgaben der Militärverwaltung," 15 July 1941, p. 10 (BArch: RH 36–205); Perrault and Azema, *Paris*, 16; Mitchell, *Nazi Paris*, 17.

[93] Perrault and Azema, *Paris*, 79. After an initial crackdown on vice in Berlin in 1933, a similar decision had been made there as well. In both capitals, the National Socialists found it profitable to allow tourists to enjoy the nightlife they expected of a large city. See Chapter 4 on Montmartre and Koshar, *German Travel Cultures*, 130.

[94] Prostitution is addressed only briefly here – for more, see Insa Meinen, "Wehrmacht und Prostitution: Zur Reglementierung der Geschichterbeziehungen durch die deutsche Militärverwaltung im besetzten Frankreich 1940–1944," *1999: Zeitschrift für Sozialgeschichte des 20. und 21. Jahrhunderts* 14, no. 2 (1999): 35–55; Insa Meinen, *Wehrmacht und Prostitution im besetzten Frankreich* (Bremen: Edition Temmen, 2001); Max Plassmann, "Wehrmachtbordelle: Anmerkungen zu einem Quellenfund im Universitätsarchiv Düsseldorf," *Militärgeschichtliche Zeitschrift* 62, no. 1 (2003): 157–73. On prostitution and soldiers' intimacy with local women in occupied Europe more generally, see Beck, *Wehrmacht und sexuelle Gewalt*, 105–16; Regina Mühlhäuser, *Eroberungen: Sexuelle Gewalttaten und intime Beziehungen deutscher Soldaten in der Sowjetunion 1941–1945* (Hamburg: Hamburger Edition, 2012).

[95] Meinen, *Wehrmacht und Prostitution*, 49–50.   [96] Meinen, 200–201.

[97] Rules regarding visits to prostitutes in the Besançon area, for instance, are summarised in Feldkommandantur 550, "Merkblatt für die Truppe über den Aufbau und die Aufgaben der Militärverwaltung", 15 July 1941, p. 5 (BArch: RH 36–205). See also BArch:

among perceived or actually vulnerable groups like French prisoner of war wives, minors and French women who worked in various capacities for the occupying authorities.[98] To contain the threat of illness, soldiers were reminded about the dangers represented by non-regulated women, who were assumed to be infected by disease.[99]

Though forbidden in public, prostitution was deemed an acceptable outlet for male energies. The opportunity to enjoy sex freely in a military brothel fostered a "feeling of superiority vis à vis local civilian women"[100] and was easier to regulate than other types of sexual interaction. Access to regulated prostitution was intended partly to guard against illness, partly as a bulwark against homosexuality, and allowing prostitution was also thought to curtail rape.[101] Rapes certainly did occur, however, though their overall extent is difficult to determine.[102] In World War I, Germans were widely accused of having raped French and Belgian women.[103] Sexual violence of this kind also took place during the 1940 campaign, and to a greater extent as part of reprisal actions against the resistance from 1943 and during the retreat in 1944.[104] Rape was not confined to the immediate context of fighting, for between July 1940 and April 1941, nine members of the 253rd Infantry Division were brought before a military court on sex crimes charges.[105] Birgit Beck has traced incidences of rape across occupied Europe, as well as the army's attempts to punish the perpetrators. Of the 232 convictions contained in the records she examined, 46 involved rapes in France. Of these, over half were from 1940, and the majority of these concerned crimes that had taken place between May and August. Only two men were convicted of rape in 1944, but as Beck points out, this result may well be due to military courts' diminishing vigour in pursuing such crimes, rather than a

RH 36/188; Plassmann, "Wehrmachtbordelle: Anmerkungen zu einem Quellenfund im Universitätsarchiv Düsseldorf."

[98] Meinen, *Wehrmacht und Prostitution*, 100–105.

[99] Flyer "Deutscher Soldat," ca. 29 July 1940 (AN: 40 AJ/451); Meinen, 56.

[100] Beck, *Wehrmacht und sexuelle Gewalt*, 116. See also François Rouquet, Fabrice Virgili, and Danièle Voldman, *Sexes, Genre et Guerres* (Payot, 2010).

[101] Beck, *Wehrmacht und sexuelle Gewalt*, 105.

[102] Fabrice Virgili, "Les viols commis par l'armée allemande en France (1940–1944)," *Vingtième Siècle*, no. 130 (April 2016): 104.

[103] Beck, *Wehrmacht und sexuelle Gewalt*, 43; Lisa M. Todd, *Sexual Treason in Germany during the First World War*, Genders and Sexualities in History (London: Palgrave Macmillan, 2017), 42–4. Cf. Raphaëlle Branche and Fabrice Virgili, *Rape in Wartime* (New York: Palgrave Macmillan, 2012). On German soldiers' sexuality in World War I, see also Jason Crouthamel, *An Intimate History of the Front: Masculinity, Sexuality, and German Soldiers in the First World War* (New York: Palgrave Macmillan, 2014).

[104] Beck, *Wehrmacht und sexuelle Gewalt*, 79–80; Virgili, "Les viols," 104.

[105] Beck, *Wehrmacht und sexuelle Gewalt*, 80.

decrease in the crimes themselves.[106] More recently, using postwar French documents, Fabrice Virgili has identified 86 cases of rape or attempted rape in Brittany alone, and emphasised the "systematic" deployment of sexual violence as a method of torture against members of the French resistance from 1943 onwards.[107]

Alongside prostitution and rape, soldier-civilian relationships of a superficially less coercive nature also existed, despite being officially forbidden. More than two million French men were absent as POWs, as deportees, as both voluntary and forced labourers in Germany, and increasingly, as members of the Resistance. Germans belonged to the same age cohort as these missing men, and since many were accommodated in private households for weeks and months at a time, it was easy for intimacy to develop.[108] Marriage between Germans and the French was officially forbidden, though occasionally special permission was granted, notably to SS men, provided that their fiancées met National Socialist racial criteria.[109] Even without marriage, long-term relationships arose, sometimes broken off hastily when the soldier received orders for redeployment elsewhere.[110] Although it may be tempting to romanticise such relationships, the literature on so-called "horizontal collaborators" and their humiliation after the war demonstrates that soldiers' interaction with local women was deeply problematic for all parties.[111] Furthermore, given the unequal power relations involved, Talbot Imlay suggests that "[r]rather than romance, a more pertinent framework for considering the relations between the French and Germans might be a transactional one."[112] Benefits for women ranged

---

[106] Other reasons for the low numbers in 1944 include the radicalisation of occupation policy, the paucity of surviving sources and the idiosyncracies of Beck's sample, as she notes. 98–9, 256.

[107] Virgili, "Les viols," 104, 111.

[108] Virgili, "Enfants de boches," 139. On the attractions of the German soldier and for a rather sensationalist take on sexuality during the occupation, see Patrick Buisson, *1940–1945, années érotiques : Vichy ou les infortunes de la vertu* (Paris: Editions Albin Michel, 2008).

[109] Virgili, "Enfants de boches," 140.   [110] Virgili, "Enfants de boches," 140.

[111] See notably Fabrice Virgili, *Shorn Women: Gender and Punishment in Liberation France*, trans. John Flower (Oxford: Berg, 2002). A comparison of attitudes in different occupied lands is provided by Anette Warring, "Intimate and Sexual Relations" in *Surviving Hitler and Mussolini: Daily Life in Occupied Europe*, ed. Robert Gildea, Olivier Wieviorka, and Anette Warring (Oxford: Berg, 2006), 88–128. Cf. Sexual fraternisation by American soldiers in France, analysed in Mary Louise Roberts, *What Soldiers Do: Sex and the American GI in World War II France* (Chicago: University of Chicago Press, 2013).

[112] Imlay, "German Side," 208. Virgili underlines that while the children of such relationships attributed their conception to romantic attachments, "if such love stories indeed existed, they were rather the exception to the rule." "Enfants de boches," 140.

from protection through material advantages, which had to be balanced against the opprobrium that such relationships won them among their fellow citizens. Occasionally, in France as elsewhere in occupied Europe, children were born of these unions, and these "children of the Boches" suffered stigmatisation in the postwar era.[113] Although such children were not particularly numerous, making up some 5 per cent of all births, German authorities were concerned about intimate fraternisation, whether it led to children or not.[114] They tried to address it not only by making military bordellos available, but also by issuing regulations that amounted to "an elaborate new public etiquette" that, for example, forbade men from walking arm in arm with French women, and barred female passengers from military vehicles.[115] Intimacy between soldiers and French women also became the subject of propaganda – newspapers and books for occupiers included stories about "acceptable" romances in which, for example, a soldier falls in love with his French teacher, who turns out to be a German civilian working at the embassy.[116]

On an emotional level, some soldiers felt their lack of female companionship keenly. The more perceptive among them were deeply bothered by the limitations that being an occupying soldier placed on their behaviour. While enjoying strawberries and cream in a café in June 1941, Bernhard Schulz wrote to his girlfriend Gerda that "in a quarter of an hour I saw so many young, elegant women, that I could have wished to be back in the dunes [like last winter], where there's no life. I slunk back to my quarters, wet with sweat in my heavy boots and my thick gray rags, like someone who's been terribly beaten. The French women wore flowered summer dresses and big straw hats. They walk[ed] past us soldiers as if we were a wall."[117] These comments offer a glimpse not only of Schulz's embarrassment, even his feelings of inadequacy and vulnerability, but also of the way that some French women responded to the occupiers' presence by refusing even to look at them.

On the unequal power relations involved in wartime sexual encounters, see Beck, *Wehrmacht und sexuelle Gewalt*, 75.

[113] Fabrice Virgili, *Naître ennemi : Les enfants de couples franco-allemands nés pendant la Seconde Guerre mondiale* (Paris: Payot, 2009).

[114] Virgili, 155. In an earlier publication, Virgili uses the figure of 8–12 per cent of births in the occupied zone. Virgili, "Enfants de boches," 144. See Imlay, "German Side," 208.

[115] Mitchell, *Nazi Paris*, 14. Merkblatt für den Aufenthalt in Paris, n.d. [ca. March 1944] (BArch RH 36/42). On tension arising from fraternisation, see also Chapter 5.

[116] Gordon, "Ist Gott Französisch? Germans, Tourism and Occupied France 1940–1944," 294.

[117] Schulz, letter, 21 June 1941 (DTA: 2033).

Collectively, Germans called Paris "die Stadt ohne Blick," the city without a glance.[118]

Clearly, occupation complicated the interaction of men and women, blurring the lines between love and exploitation just as it had blurred those between shopping and plunder. Our exploration of these issues concludes by considering how both French and Germans reacted to soldiers' consumption, whether of foods, products, or even women. Although many French enterprises and individuals profited from the arrival of free-spending Germans and worked hard to attract their business, responses ran the gamut from acceptance and collusion, through passivity, to rejection. Germans' desire to consume, moreover, easily became a subject of scorn and ridicule, while mocking their preposterous shopping served to draw attention to the indignity of occupation itself.

Among the earliest French publications after the Liberation was a volume of photographs by Roger Schall called *A Paris sous la botte des Nazis*. Schall's brother Raymond, who provided the text for the volume, claimed that the photographer, who had worked for the Germans, had been preparing this book for some time. According to his brother, Roger Schall had captured numerous shots during the occupation "à l'insu de l'ennemi" ("without the enemy's knowledge.")[119] Published in November 1944, the book both attested to the extent of German consumption and gave insight into French attitudes towards it at the Liberation. A full-page spread in the middle of the volume depicted uniformed soldiers purchasing cloth, perfume, gloves and garments. One image showed a mature officer before a shop window full of women's shoes. The caption noted that "[t]hanks to the advantageous exchange rate they'd made for themselves, with the utmost 'correction,' they pillaged our shops."[120] A second caption, next to a photograph of two young sailors buying cloth from a well-dressed shop assistant, commented that "[i]n this consciously organized pillage ... lacking all critical sense, accustomed to junk, many were amazed by our oldest white elephants."[121] Rather ironically, both captions echoed administrator Medicus's snobbish

---

[118] Pierre Audiat, *Paris pendant la guerre* (Paris: Hachette, 1946), 30. See also Drake, *Paris at War*, 105.

[119] Jean Eparvier, *A Paris sous la botte des Nazis* (Paris: Editions Raymond Schall, 1944), frontispiece. Catherine Clark rightly doubts the extent to which these images were "secret," "Capturing the Moment, Picturing History: Photographs of the Liberation of Paris," *The American Historical Review* 121, no. 3 (June 1, 2016): 854–5. See additional discussion of Roger Schall in Chapter 4.

[120] Eparvier, *A Paris sous la botte des Nazis*, 66.

[121] Eparvier, *A Paris sous la botte des Nazis*, 66.

remarks about small-town soldiers having the opportunity to take advantage of Parisian shopping. Drawing on gender stereotypes to underline the sense of a world upside down, both images depicted men presumably out of their depth purchasing items more commonly associated with women. Targetting consumption, the publication sought to undermine German masculinity as well as occupiers' claims to rectitude, taste and discernment while reinforcing French notions that their own culture remained superior despite defeat. A third caption, next to a picture of two occupiers buying perfume, pointed out that "German women loved French perfumes, which would have done honour to their taste, had they possessed any" (Figure 2.2).[122] Throughout the book of Schall's photographs, images and captions reinforced the idea that the Germans had profited from France, yet were incapable of truly appreciating the refinements it offered.

It is perhaps unremarkable that in the immediate post-Liberation period, Schall should frame images of shopping as pillage and evidence of occupiers' greed and lack of good taste. This likely reflected the views of many French people, and it underlines the close link between consumption, self-perception, and notions of one's own and others' identity. Yet criticism of occupiers' rampant consumption was not the exclusive preserve of the French. Perhaps more surprisingly, occupiers themselves sometimes also expressed distaste about their fellow soldiers' buying habits. As early as August 1940, Kurt F. wrote home that he regretted not being able to send his parents a parcel, "but when I see the rear echelon swine [Etappenschweine] thronging the shops in Dijon and Auxerre to fulfill their wives' and family members' requirements for silk stockings and lingerie for years to come while exploiting the favourable exchange rates, I lose my appetite to get anything; moreover, in the occupied part of France, the best things have long since sold out."[123]

Kurt F. was not alone. In a *Sicherheitsdienst* (security service) report on the popular mood in Germany from 29 November 1943, "shopping trips in the occupied territories" were specifically mentioned in a litany of popular complaints about inequalities in the Wehrmacht.[124] Citizens criticised rabid consumption, and a more serious problem stemmed from the fact that consumption was seen as a perk, a privilege that, despite all

[122] Eparvier, 67.   [123] Kurt F., 7 August 1940 (DTA: 270/I).
[124] SD Report to the Party Chancellery on "Basic Questions Regarding the Mood and Attitude of the German People" (November 29, 1943), in German and English translation at German History in Documents and Images, http://germanhistorydocs.ghi-dc.org/docpage.cfm?docpage_id=3047&language=english, accessed 9 May 2017.

Figure 2.2 Image by French photographer Roger Schall of soldiers
in a perfume shop. The original caption reads "German women loved
French perfumes, which would have done honour to their taste, had they
possessed any. The occupiers cleaned out the shops for them."
Jean Eparvier, *A Paris sous la botte des Nazis* (Paris: Editions Raymond
Schall, 1944).

its claims to equality and "socialism," the regime had not managed
to distribute fairly. If enabling consumption helped support Hitler's
regime, unfair distribution of its fruits also threatened to destabilize the
popular mood.[125] This helps to explain why the regime spent so much

---

[125] Wiesen, *Creating the Nazi Marketplace*, 212–16. Cf. Kundrus, "Greasing the Palm,"
166–70.

energy trying to define the fine line between permissiveness and control of pleasures like shopping, eating, and intimate fraternisation.

Yet the question remains, how did soldiers' pleasure-seeking and consumption in France fit into longer, broader patterns of consumption? Also, to what extent can the French experience be used to support Aly's claim that the Third Reich relied on satisfying popular acquisitiveness for its strength? Certainly, the occupation offered unprecedented opportunities for shopping, eating, and enjoyment, and German soldiers took eager advantage of them. The Wehrmacht exploited France consciously as a rear area, notably for regrouping units after harsh combat in the East, and soldiers' letters demonstrate that for some men, at least, the chance to shop, sightsee, and enjoy the country's charms helped compensate for the rigours of war. On one level, therefore, the regime's policy of both encouraging and carefully managing consumption seems to have worked.

At the same time, an intriguing contemporary account from a rather different source helps to contextualise the issue. Alice Moats was an American journalist who spent the war years in Spain, and travelled into France secretly in the last months of the occupation to write about it for *Collier's*, the *New York Herald Tribune* and CBS.[126] Despite being fully aware of the downtrodden and impoverished state of France, not to mention her own perilous situation as an undercover Allied agent, Moats too, took advantage of her visit to the country to do some shopping. In a 1945 book about her experiences, she described occupied Paris as a dead city, comparing the Germans' position to that of "a man who has struggled and fought to possess a woman only to have her die on their wedding night."[127] Despite being upset by the appearance of the capital, Moats managed to purchase three pairs of silk stockings, three slips and a nightgown, all for (as she noted) 10,500 francs, or the equivalent of 26 dollars.[128] She took a friend to Maxim's for a delicious lunch of "pâté de foie gras, boeuf à la mode, salad, and wild strawberries" accompanied by a 1934 Nuits-Saint-Georges, all of which cost 2,000 francs. After lunch, Moats headed for the fashion house Molyneux next door, thinking that in view of the chilly spring weather, she might buy a fur jacket.[129] "It seemed to me," Moats wrote, as if echoing the German occupiers,

[126] Alice-Leone Moats, *No Passport for Paris* (New York: G.P.Putnam's Sons, 1945), 4.
[127] Moats, *No Passport*, 224–5.   [128] Moats, *No Passport*, 225.
[129] It appears that Edward Molyneux himself moved to London in 1940, but a shop bearing his name continued to exist in Paris. See: www.vam.ac.uk/vastatic/microsites/1486_couture/media/explore/index.php; Veillon, *La mode sous l'Occupation*, 177.

"that at the rate of exchange, it might be a good opportunity to pick up a bargain." In the end, because of the prices (250,000 francs for the cheapest Persian lamb coat), she decided she did not need a fur coat so very much after all.[130]

If Moats's admittedly exceptional account can be taken at face value, the Germans were not alone in finding occupied France an appealing shopping destination. They were also not alone in exhibiting consumer behaviour commonly associated with peacetime during a war. The fact that both cases of consumption seem to us quite jarring may speak more to our own misunderstanding of wartime's ongoing normality, than to the strangeness of the behaviour itself.

Yet perhaps there *was* a difference between Moats's consumption and that of the occupying soldiers, and one final anecdote may help to pinpoint its nature. On her way back to her accommodation, Moats stopped in at the perfumery Guerlain, but was thwarted in her desire to buy scent because she had not brought along her own refillable Guerlain bottles. While she was arguing with the saleswoman, "a German colonel came in and purchased three large bottles of L'Heure Bleue. They were sold to him with no talk about bringing his own containers. He went off carrying his parcel wrapped in pale pink paper. That parcel looked so incongruous with his uniform that, in spite of my anger, I burst out laughing."[131] Moats was struck by the odd portrait the military man made with his tiny pink parcel, but she also astutely observed the power dynamics at work. Moats, disguised as an ordinary French customer, needed to bring her own refillable bottles – a German officer did not. The fact that both Moats and the officer were shopping in France, but only one of them had to follow the rules, underlines that it was not wartime consumption itself that was the distinguishing and problematic feature of occupiers' behaviour. Rather, it was in the high-handed manner of that consumption – or should we say plunder – and in the unequal power relations it exposed, that the difficulty lay.

---

[130] Moats, *No Passport*, 226.   [131] Moats, *No Passport*, 227.

3   Touring and Writing about Occupied Land

In July 1940, World War I veteran Johannes Gutschmidt came to France to command a POW camp near Le Mans. In his diary, he documented a relaxed and agreeable stay until he was ordered back to Germany before deployment on the Eastern Front.[1] Rather than the unease one might associate with implementing a military occupation on foreign soil, Gutschmidt's diary records genteel conversations with the local Countess Bonvouloir, delicious meals available for next to nothing (in German terms), and visits to historical and cultural sites. Gutschmidt's overall attitude resembles that of a tourist as much as a conqueror. Between July and November 1940, Gutschmidt toured Paris, Sèvres, Chartres, Fourchambault, the Chateaux of the Loire Valley, Mont Saint-Michel, Saint-Malo, and Orleans. Before returning to Germany in early 1941, he noted "my men want to take a trip to Mont Saint-Michel and Saint-Malo." Some had already gone to Brest and Rouen, returning home "thrilled." Others were due back from Spain the following day, and soon after, Gutschmidt himself undertook a three-day trip to Spain with four colleagues, stopping at Tours, Bordeaux, Hendaye, Bayonne, Biarritz, Irun, and San Sebastián.

Though sightseeing during a military occupation may seem surprising, Gutschmidt's experience was not exceptional. Unlike their comrades on the Eastern Front after June 1941, German occupiers in the West spent most of their time holding terrain, building defensive structures, and policing the local citizenry. Like the shopping and other leisure activities discussed in Chapter 2, German tourism was most prominent in the early years of the occupation, but it remained significant throughout the period. Letters, diaries, and photo albums confirm that being in France

---

[1] Johannes Gutschmidt, 'Kriegstagebuch,' 24, 27, 28 February 1941 (BArch: Msg. 1/257). On Gutschmidt and POWs in the Soviet Union see Christian Hartmann, "Massensterben oder Massenvernichtung? Sowjetische Kriegsgefangene im 'Unternehmen Barbarossa.' Aus dem Tagebuch eines deutschen Lagerkommandanten," *Vierteljahreshefte für Zeitgeschichte* 49, no. 1 (2001): 97–158.

was a welcome respite from battle elsewhere, and most occupiers displayed an openness and curiosity normally associated with peacetime. Soldiers and military administrators alternated between the roles of occupiers and tourists, sometimes taking on both simultaneously.

John Urry defines tourism as an activity in which people leave their normal residence and workplace briefly, consuming goods and services "which are in some sense unnecessary." Tourism generates "pleasurable experiences which are different from those typically encountered in everyday life," and enables people to "view a set of different scenes, landscapes or townscapes which are out of the ordinary." The activity presupposes a conscious desire to use one's free time to explore a new environment.[2] As Peter Brenner has underlined, soldiers did not become tourists simply by leaving their native country to fight.[3] Rather, tourism occurred when occupiers left their places of deployment in France for short periods to visit nearby towns with no other objective than seeing the sights. Such tourism was exceptionally widespread, and perceptions and experiences of France as a tourist destination shaped occupiers' approach to the country and to the project of occupation overall.

Although war and tourism are typically thought of as being opposite, even mutually exclusive, they are linked in many ways. German soldiers' tourism in France illuminates the affinities and points of contact between tourism and war, and tourism and military occupation specifically. Soldier tourism occurred among Germans on all fronts, but France's previous reputation as a cultured land and an attractive destination, not to mention the fact that the occupation was long and comparatively peaceful in the beginning, helped tourism flourish. Evidence from soldiers' letters, diaries, and photographs confirms this, as does the publication under German auspices of numerous guides to Paris and the French regions between 1940 and 1944.

Ground-breaking articles by Bertram Gordon have revealed the extent of German tourism in occupied France, explored it as a window into German attitudes, and suggested links between Germans' appreciation of France as tourists and their unwillingness to destroy it in 1940 and

---

[2] John Urry, *The Tourist Gaze: Leisure and Travel in Contemporary Societies* (London: Sage, 2002), 1. Although Urry's definition applies to a majority of cases, some types of tourism (for instance to battlefields or memorial sites) are not intended to be pleasurable. Richard Sharpley and Philip R. Stone, eds., *The Darker Side of Travel: The Theory and Practice of Dark Tourism* (Bristol, UK: Channel View Publications, 2009).

[3] Peter J. Brenner, "Schwierige Reisen: Wandlungen des Reiseberichts in Deutschland 1918–1945" in *Reisekultur in Deutschland: Von der Weimarer Republik zum "Dritten Reich,"* ed. Peter J. Brenner (Tübingen: Max Niemeyer, 1997), 143.

during the 1944 retreat.[4] The phenomenon has also been discussed by Alon Confino in the context of *Vergangenheitsbewältigung* (coming to terms with the past) in West Germany, and by Rudy Koshar in *German Travel Cultures*.[5] Histories of Paris under the occupation mention tourism, but their focus on the capital may leave the impression that this activity was restricted to the City of Light alone.[6]

Using documents produced by soldiers themselves alongside published sources that reflect the regime's attempts to instrumentalise tourism, this chapter builds on existing research and takes it in new directions. Soldier-generated sources show that touristic attitudes were common from the occupation's earliest days, bubbling up from below as they were being promoted from above. Although existing research concentrates on Paris, German tourism occurred throughout the occupied zone. Occupiers with longer-term postings and military administrators had more opportunities for this form of leisure than others, but tourism was an integral part of occupiers' experience wherever they were stationed, regardless of rank. Beyond the well-known diaries and memoirs of the Paris elite – literary figures like Ernst Jünger and Gerhard Heller, or administrator Werner Best – sampling soldiers' letters and diaries reveals a tourism so widespread that it formed a constituent element of German attitudes towards France.[7]

Throughout the occupation, soldiers' desire to experience the country as tourists required careful management, for it was both useful to the regime, and potentially dangerous. Alongside tourism within the Reich proper, opportunities to explore subjugated Europe boosted morale and lubricated popular consent for the National Socialist regime.[8] Valuable

---

[4] Gordon, "Ist Gott Französisch? Germans, Tourism and Occupied France 1940–1944"; Gordon, "Warfare and Tourism."

[5] Confino, "Traveling," 108–10; Koshar, *German Travel Cultures*, 127. See also Baranowski, *Strength*, Ch. 6; Semmens, *Seeing Hitler's Germany: Tourism in the Third Reich*, 172. Klaus Latzel uses tourism as a metaphor for the way the Third Reich's soldiers "saw" Eastern Europe, but does not deal with tourism as such, nor the French case in "Tourismus und Gewalt: Kriegswahrnehmungen in Feldpostbriefen," *Vernichtungskrieg: Verbrechen der Wehrmacht 1941–1944*, ed. Hannes Heer and Klaus Naumann (Hamburg: Hamburger Edition, 1995), 447–59.

[6] E.g. Drake, *Paris at War*, 98 ff.; Mitchell, *Nazi Paris*; Perrault and Azema, *Paris*.

[7] For Jünger see notably Jünger, *Strahlungen* and Mitchell, *The Devil's Captain*. Other often-cited memoirs of members of the military administration include Walter Bargatzky, *Hotel Majestic: ein Deutscher im besetzten Frankreich* (Freiburg im Breisgau: Herder, 1987); Felix Hartlaub, *Kriegsaufzeichnungen aus Paris* (Berlin: Suhrkamp, 2011); Gerhard Heller, *In einem besetzten Land: NS-Kulturpolitik in Frankreich: Erinnerungen 1940–1944* (Cologne: Kiepenheuer & Witsch, 1982). On Best, see Werner Best, "Erinnerungen aus dem besetzten Frankreich 1940 bis 1942," 27 (BArch: N 1023/1) and Herbert, *Best*.

[8] On tourism as a vehicle for consent and a substitute for diminishing access to consumer goods, see Chapter 2 and Baranowski, *Strength*.

notably as a form of rest and relaxation for soldiers, tourism also had to be controlled to keep soldiers from becoming undisciplined or going "soft." Construing France as pleasurable, rather than contemptible or threatening, risked undermining the security interests and exploitative goals of the regime.

Perceiving war as travel and describing war in the form of travel-writing have long traditions. Both tourism and war involve journeys outside one's homeland that occasion cultural confrontations, and as such they bear similarities. Perhaps because it is easier and more accept-able to write of the sights one sees than the enemies one kills, tourist metaphors come easily to soldiers, who may be travelling outside their home countries for the first time.[9] In occupied France, affinities went beyond the metaphorical, for soldiers both wrote about France as if they were tourists, and undertook extensive tourism while they were there.

In the specific context of military occupation, tourism served several purposes. After an unexpectedly rapid victory, tourism provided soldiers with a ready-made framework for behaving in a foreign country. Distancing themselves from the harsh occupation of Belgium and North-ern France in World War I, occupiers aligned their comportment using stereotypes of Paris and France as centres of leisure and consumption, as Chapter 2 shows, and interpreted the country and their position in it through tourism and its visual accompaniment, photography. Given that war in France had "ended" with the armistice, belligerent hostility no longer seemed appropriate, and tourism gave soldiers a substitute code of

---

[9] Konrad Köstlin, "Erzählen vom Krieg: Krieg als Reise," *BIOS: Zeitschrift für Biographieforschung, Oral History, und Lebensverlaufsanalysen* 2 (1989): 179–81. Other explorations of the war/tourism nexus include Brenner, "Schwierige Reisen: Wandlungen des Reiseberichts in Deutschland 1918–1945," 144–5; Burckhard Dücker, "Reisen in die UdSSR 1933–1945" in *Reisekultur in Deutschland: Von der Weimarer Republik zum "Dritten Reich,"* ed. Peter J. Brenner (Tübingen: Max Niemeyer, 1997), 273–4; David Farber and Beth Bailey, "The Fighting Man as Tourist: The Politics of Tourist Culture in Hawaii during World War II," *The Pacific Historical Review* 65, no. 4 (November 1996): 641–60; Gordon, "Ist Gott Französisch? Germans, Tourism and Occupied France 1940–1944," 287–98; Gordon, "Warfare and Tourism," 616–38; James Kitchen, "'Khaki Crusaders': Crusading Rhetoric and the British Imperial Soldier during the Egypt and Palestine Campaigns, 1916–18," *First World War Studies* 1, no. 2 (2010): 153–7; Melanie Gordon Krob, "Paris Through Enemy Eyes: The Wehrmacht in Paris 1940–1944," *Journal of European Studies* 31 (2001): 3–28; Latzel, "Tourismus und Gewalt," 447–59; Richard White, "The Soldier as Tourist: The Australian Experience of the Great War," *War & Society* 5, no. 1 (1987): 63–77; Kerstin Wölki, *Krieg als Reise: Die Wahrnehmung Frankreichs durch deutsche Soldaten im zweiten Weltkrieg,* M. A. Thesis, Albert-Ludwigs-Universität, 2007; Bart Ziino, "A Kind of Round Trip: Australian Soldiers and the Tourist Analogy, 1914–1918," *War & Society* 25, no. 2 (2006): 39–52.

conduct, a way to behave and to interact with the land. Historians David Farber and Beth Bailey have argued that among American soldiers stationed in Hawaii in World War II, tourism was deployed to help men feel at home on "foreign" (if in fact American) soil. Following sociologist Dean MacCannell, Farber and Bailey suggest that, "the paradigm of the fighting-man-as-tourist enabled wartime visitors to consume the 'otherness' ... without risking a loss of primary identity and without needing to directly confront or reject the other."[10] Although Germans were not just stationed in France on their way to another war front, but actually holding hostile terrain, a similar dynamic was at work. Tourism satisfied soldiers' curiosity about France without, the regime hoped, allowing them to lose their identity as Germans, or the critical distance necessary for effective control.

Tourism thus served occupiers as a kind of coping mechanism, smoothing the transition from combat to surveillance and administration, from home to residence in a foreign land. After a strenuous campaign, sightseeing and outings to Paris also offered rest and relaxation, a reward for soldiers that allowed them to return refreshed to combat. In World War I, historian Richard White has found, Australian infantry joined the army for "five bob a day and the chance of seeing the world."[11] The later German experience likewise suggests that some men viewed the opportunity to explore new parts of Europe as a side-benefit that might make risking one's neck worthwhile. Tourism helped soldiers forget that exposing themselves to violent acts, not to mention committing them, was part of the job. White goes on to argue that World War I's tourism set up "a protective barrier between the observer and the observed" and that the "detachment" it engendered "might have been a crucial respite in war."[12]

At the same time, "seeing the sights" allowed German soldiers to project an image of themselves as civilised that contrasted with French popular memories of "Hun" barbarity in World War I. Especially in the early months of the occupation, when the exact place of France in Hitler's plans for Europe was unclear, the Wehrmacht emphasised civility and good relations with the French. Over the longer term, Bertram Gordon contends that German tourism in France was meant to suggest that everything was "business as usual" in the conquered territories.

[10] Farber and Bailey, "Fighting Man," 641; Dean MacCannell, *The Tourist: A New Theory of the Leisure Class* (New York: Shocken Books, 1976).
[11] White, "Soldier," 66.   [12] White, "Soldier," 71.

Tourism helped hide the dark side of the occupation: exploitation, repression, and the round-ups of Jews.[13] On a practical level, excursions in the area of their posting enabled officers and men to understand the terrain, become acquainted with the topography, and prepare for battle.[14] Equally significantly, during an increasingly contested occupation, tourism reinforced dominance. As Rudy Koshar has noted with regard to Eastern Europe, "[t]ravel was a way of getting to know the domain of Nazi conquest," and it underlined the unequal power relationship between the tourist and the toured land's inhabitants.[15] Even in peacetime, large-scale tourism is sometimes experienced by the local population as a kind of occupation. In wartime France, conquest was the necessary precondition for occupiers' tourism. Like imperial travel in the colonies, German tourism reminded the conquerors, and the peoples they controlled, of the power relations in play.[16]

Despite its various uses, tourism was a double-edged sword. Balancing soldiers' desire to explore and enjoy France with the demands of defence and occupation became a challenge that contemporaries, including some within the military administration, felt the occupiers failed to master. As detailed in Chapter 5 and 6, belated attempts to tighten policies failed, and soldiers, notably on the Eastern Front, criticised Western occupiers' *Etappengeist* (rear area attitude, or softness). This perception had a direct impact on manpower decisions, especially from 1943. The occupation's top-level administrators fought to retain experienced personnel against a crescendo of calls to pare down their operations so more men could be shifted to the fighting forces on the Eastern Front.

Tourism in France thus went well beyond maintaining a sense of normalcy in the face of resistance attacks. It became an indispensable lens through which Germans saw and interpreted their role. Tourism smoothed over feelings of unease in a foreign land, reinforced dominance, compensated occupiers' hard work, and helped them forget the war. Carefully managed, tourism benefited the occupation regime but, as

---

[13] Gordon, "Ist Gott Französisch? Germans, Tourism and Occupied France 1940–1944," 288.

[14] Hans Erich Bödeker, Arnd Bauernkämper, and Bernhard Struck, "Einleitung: Reisen als kulturelle Praxis" in *Die Welt erfahren: Reisen als kulturelle Begegnung von 1780 bis heute*, ed. Arnd Bauernkämper, Hans E. Bödeker, and Bernhard Struck (Frankfurt am Main: Campus Verlag, 2004), 17.

[15] Koshar cites Christopher Endy, who has argued with regard to Americans in Europe that "travel in another country ... represented an assertion of national strength" in the modern era. Koshar, *German Travel Cultures*, 152.

[16] Cf. Ellen Furlough, "Une leçon des choses: Tourism, Empire, and the Nation in Interwar France," *French Historical Studies* 25, no. 3 (Summer 2002): 453.

the situation in France grew more tense, it became a liability. Fatefully, having encouraged occupier tourism since 1940, the authorities in Paris later found it impossible to change course, even in the face of resistance and Allied reconquest. This story is taken up in later chapters, but tourism and war coexisted uncomfortably, and to focus on combat alone would ignore the fact that war also involves occupation, mundane cohabitation, boredom and even tourism.[17] None of the latter necessarily preclude the former, and particularly during the occupation of France, seemingly peripheral activities influenced policy-making and came to define war experience as much as, if not more than, fighting itself.

Helping to construct a narrative of occupiers as tourists, the National Socialist regime published a substantial number of tour guides, commemorative volumes, and "scholarly" treatises on France and its sights. The second half of this chapter focuses on material of this kind, which constitutes a significant and virtually untapped historical source.[18] Often sponsored by the Wehrmacht or Nazi organisations, and always approved by official censors, occupation-era publications were designed consciously for the future. They justified the invasion and memorialised Germans as culturally-sensitive conquerors who appreciated France's treasures. Like books about Germany's former colonies, such as the Africa books (Afrikabücher) historian Britta Schilling has analysed, these publications offered soldiers and their families a kind of blueprint, or set of frames, through which to interpret French experiences. Entertaining and educative on the surface, they carried political messages and outlined specific approaches to France and the project of occupation. Through a process of mutual influence and exchange, such books both shaped and were shaped by occupiers' own written and photographic documents. Together, official literature and occupier-generated sources formed soldiers' perceptions at the time, and constructed future memories of the occupation.[19]

From the moment they entered France in 1940, Germans saw it with the eyes of tourists as well as conquerors. Tourism made the country seem familiar and provided soldiers with reference points as they

---

[17] Ziino, "Round Trip," 52.

[18] This chapter draws on publications from the occupation period, though books about the 1940 invasion of France also appeared. Historians have used these books individually for illustrative purposes. They have not read them as a corpus of sources for analysing occupiers' attitudes to France and the project of occupation, as well as official attempts to influence these attitudes.

[19] A parallel might also be drawn with post-1945 books that commemorated lost German communities in Eastern Europe. Cf. Peter Fritzsche, "The Archive and the Case of the German Nation" in Archive Stories: Facts, Fictions, and the Writing of History, ed. Antoinette M. Burton (Durham, N.C.: Duke University Press, 2005), 202.

improvised an occupation. Their descriptions mix appreciation of the countryside with images of military defeat, suggesting that a touristic outlook served as a coping mechanism at this early stage. By helping men "rationalise," in some sense, their presence in France, it aided in the transition from battle to peaceful interaction with the land and its people. After a difficult night at an advanced post during the June campaign, Dr. Hansjörg P. described moving towards Reims. "On the way there," he wrote, "we perceived ... in the twilight the silhouette of the famous Reims cathedral ..." Like peacetime travellers, P. and his comrades viewed the structure's familiar "silhouette" in the "twilight," and P. recorded the "famous" sight in his diary. In the same sentence, his conqueror's role came to the fore when he remarked that his unit saw "the French airfield burning and clouds of smoke climbing skyward over the city."[20] P. saw no contradiction in recording symbols of French glory and signs of French defeat, his own responses to France as tourist and conqueror, side by side. His linkage of conquest and tourism underlines Germans' discomfort with an exclusively conqueror's perspective in a country that, while foreign, had until recently been viewed as a virtual equal and a desirable travel destination. Imagining themselves in the role of tourists allowed Germans to feel at ease, and helped culturally sophisticated conquerors like Dr. P. maintain their self-image by advertising their capacity to appreciate French civilisation, not simply destroy it. Equally, the juxtaposition of glory and defeat rendered victory all the sweeter.

Soldiers' initial impressions of the war-torn landscape sometimes reveal disappointment that it had not, immediately, lived up to its reputation for beauty. Young Hans-Peter Eckener of Stuttgart, on his way into occupied France in March 1941, wrote to his parents that new snow had just fallen, and "the landscape looked drab. In fact, I did not see any particularly attractive landscape or city on the whole [train] trip." Settlements appeared run down and abandoned, but Eckener conceded "it was not exactly the prettiest part of France that we had passed through."[21] Although he had probably never visited France before, Eckener responded to its unfamiliarity by drawing on preconceived notions about what the country should look like. Glossing over

---

[20] Dr. Hansjörg P., *Frankreich Tagebuch 1940*, entry for 11 June 1940 (DTA: 812).

[21] "...[D]ie Landschaft sah eintönig aus. Überhaupt habe ich auf der ganzen Fahrt keine besonders anziehende Landschaft oder Stadt gesehen. Alles macht für unsere Augen einen verwahrlosten und ungepflegten Eindruck. Aber freilich war das nicht gerade der schönste Teil von Frankreich, durch den wir gekommen sind." Eckener and Wolter, *Lieber Vater*, 7 March 1941, 81.

destruction, he addressed its aesthetic qualities primarily, as if writing a travelogue for home-bound relatives.[22]

Upon reaching his destination, Eckener noted that although the landscape remained rather melancholy, it was "[n]ot without appeal, especially because the atmospheric light conditions [northeast of Saint-Nazaire] are similar to those on the North Sea."[23] Clearly, Eckener's satisfaction with his location was based on physical attributes as much as practical aspects, and Eckener, who came from an artistic family, saw deployment in France as an opportunity to appreciate its landscapes as well as carry out his duties. The comparison he made with familiar German scenery was typical of other soldiers' descriptions too, serving partly to aid family members in imagining their relatives' situations, partly as a back-handed and politically acceptable complement to France – pretty because it resembled this or that part of Germany. Like tourists, soldiers came to France expecting it to be pleasing. They were satisfied when their experiences confirmed preconceived notions about the country.

Eckener was visiting France for the first time, but other men's attitudes were informed by past visits. As noted in Chapter 1, some occupiers had travelled or studied in France, and others knew the country because they had fought there in World War I. Remembering the previous conflict made Germany's recent victory sweeter, a notion that was reinforced by tourism to World War I battlefields and memorials.[24] The interwar forts of the Maginot Line drew many visitors, who were impressed by their technological modernity. Apparently, Luftwaffe officers "wept openly" to see how little damage their bombs had done to the structures.[25] At the same time, seeing French defences virtually untouched by battle emphasised for the Germans the notion that France's internal decay had caused its defeat.

As the occupation became established, sightseeing in the French regions continued, but the strongest magnet for occupiers' tourism was Paris. Hitler visited on 30 June, followed by Goebbels, and most of the Third Reich's other major figures. Well before them, soldiers had begun exploring and taking photographic possession of the capital.[26] Within

---

[22] Köstlin, "Erzählen," 179–80.

[23] "Nicht ohne Reiz, besonders da hier ähnliche atmospherische Lichtverhältnisse sind wie an der Nordsee." Eckener and Wolter, *Lieber Vater*, 7 March 1941, 82.

[24] In May 1941, for example, a member of the 98th Infantry Regiment wrote home happily that he had just been given the role of tour guide for the battlefields at Verdun. Wm. Ernst von K., 4 May 1941 (BfZ SS).

[25] Anthony Kemp, *The Maginot Line: Myth and Reality* (Military Heritage Press, 1988), 101, cited in Gordon, "Warfare and Tourism," 625–6.

[26] Susan Sontag has suggested parallels between tourism and photography, war and conquest, commenting that all tourists' photography is a "way of taking possession of

three days of the city's conquest, as mentioned in Chapter 1, American journalist William Shirer saw Germans "photographing Notre-Dame, the Arc de Triomphe, the Invalides," and noted that "thousands of German soldiers congregate all day long at the Tomb of the Unknown Soldier, where the flame still burns under the Arc. They bare their blond heads and stand there gazing." To Shirer, the soldiers resembled "naïve tourists."[27]

Luxuriously accommodated in Paris's major hotels, quintessential tourist spaces, the occupation's highest authorities set about organising the administration of France.[28] In their off-duty hours, they and lower-ranking occupiers took photographs, admired monuments, and enjoyed the capital's pleasures after a rigorous campaign. Visitors with time on their hands could pick up a copy of *Der deutsche Wegleiter* (*The German Guidebook*), also called *Wohin in Paris?* (*Where to go in Paris*), a compendium of upcoming German and French entertainment and sporting events. Published every fifteen days from mid-July 1940 through mid-August 1944, the *Wegleiter* became the major guide to leisure activities for Germans in the city. It was distributed free or for a small fee, and included restaurant and entertainment reviews, articles on museum collections open despite the occupation, and suggestions for day trips in the Paris area (Figure 3.2).[29]

From the outset, occupiers' longing to get to know and "consume" France had to be reconciled with the need to control the country and its population. Little more than a month after the Wehrmacht took the city, the Commander issued a stern warning about appropriate behaviour. In Paris, of all places, occupiers' bearing should be exemplary, but "the nastiest dance clubs with French whores of the worst sort in Montmartre and elsewhere are over-filled with German soldiers, whose behaviour is often fully consistent with the environment. Officers, even older officers, can be found there in no fewer numbers and they appear to take no offence at the goings-on." Occupiers' behaviour flew in the face of national honour, and contradicted the Führer's own wish that Paris should not become a tawdry rear area city, an *Etappenstadt*.[30]

---

the places they visited." Susan Sontag, *On Photography* (New York: Doubleday, 1990), 65. In France, the photography that accompanied war and occupation became an essential part of "capturing" the land in both a figurative and a literal sense.

[27] Shirer, 17 June 1940, 328. Also cited in Gordon, "Warfare and Tourism," 621. Cf. Confino, "Traveling," 109.

[28] Mitchell, *Nazi Paris*, 14.

[29] The French Bibliothèque Nationale houses a collection of *Wegleiter* (8-JO-4976).

[30] Kommandant der Stadt Paris, 16 July 1940 (AN: AJ 40/451). Montmartre was already among the "must-see" destinations in Paris by the turn of the century, its dens of iniquity

Nonetheless, on-going reminders about discipline throughout the occupation suggest that both officers and regular soldiers continued to act inappropriately in the capital.[31]

Recognising Paris's inexorable attraction and the need to control soldiers' interactions with the city, its population and economy, German authorities organised bus and subway tours that shepherded as many as 6,500 soldiers a day through the capital.[32] Run from a special department of the Paris Command, *Ic Besichtigungen* (Ic, Visits), these tours were offered as rewards to soldiers invited to Paris for the weekend. They were also available to units passing through or stationed in the city, and sources suggest that close to a million soldiers had taken part by May 1941.[33] The Deutsche Arbeitsfront (German Labour Front, DAF), too, offered tours through the Paris office of the Kraft durch Freude (Strength through Joy) programme.[34] A late November 1943 issue of *Der deutsche Wegleiter*, for example, listed daily DAF visits through "old Paris" in the morning and "modern Paris" in the afternoon, plus a rotating cycle of Saturday tours of "Paris from the 16th to the 18th century," the city's catacombs and cemeteries, and its observatories. On Sundays, Germans in the French capital could join excursions to Meaux and the valley of the Chevreuse, the castles of the Loire, Reims and the World War I battlefields, or Versailles and Malmaison.[35] Finally, an organisation called Jeder einmal in Paris (Everyone to Paris once) even arranged visits to Paris for soldiers stationed as far afield as Greece and the Ukraine.[36] This vast array of curated opportunities, which continued throughout the occupation, enabled men (and some women) of all social levels to engage

---

reinforcing Germans' ideas about French decadence. Nolan, *The Inverted Mirror: Mythologizing the Enemy in France and Germany 1898–1914*, 56.

[31] Kommandant von Gross-Paris, Kommandeur der Gruppe Heeresstreifendienst, 17 March 1941 (AN: AJ 40/873); Kommandant von Gross-Paris Ia to Militärbefehlshaber in Frankreich, 6 January 1942 (AN: AJ 40/451); Militärbefehlshaber in Frankreich Ia, 16 October 1943 (AN: AJ 40/451). See also Mitchell, *Nazi Paris*, 14–15.

[32] Kommandantur Paris, Erste Generalstabsoffizier to Deutsche Rote Kreuz, Beauftragter für Frankreich, 5 February 1941 (AN: 40 AJ/873). This figure represents a high point for the period, while a fragmentary accounting of participants that survives for the period from 10 October 1940 to 30 December 1940 (AN: AJ 40/878), shows that around 3,000 men per day took part in tours at that time. See Gordon, "Warfare and Tourism," 621. On 'capturing' consumption through tourism in the Third Reich, see Baranowski, *Strength*; Shelley Baranowski, "Family Vacation for Workers: The Strength through Joy Resort at Prora," *German History* 25, no. 4 (2007): 540, 545.

[33] Gordon, "Warfare and Tourism," 621.   [34] Gordon, 621–2.

[35] "DAF-Veranstaltungen," *Der deutsche Wegleiter*, no. 84 (November 20, 1943): 48.

[36] Confino, "Traveling," 109; Gordon, "Ist Gott Französisch? Germans, Tourism and Occupied France 1940–1944," 289; Perrault and Azema, *Paris*, 17.

in tourism to a greater extent than would otherwise have been possible.[37] Soldier-tourism built on preexisting ideas about France as a quintessential destination, and prefigured the development of mass tourism in the post-war period.[38]

Tourism in France also tempted civilians, and anyone with a reasonably good excuse to go there seems to have made a trip. There were so many visiting bureaucrats that Werner Best and his colleagues in the military government came to resent them deeply. Speaking ironically of "Organisation JEIP" (for Jeder Einmal in Paris), they compared them to the sprawling Organisation Todt, responsible for building the fortifications of the Atlantic Wall. Best seemed particularly offended by visitors who thought a brief sojourn enough to comprehend a whole country in all its complexity. Defending his own experience and expertise against mere tourists, he recalled that, "based on such a visit, some of them believed that they could write reports about the occupied area and influence occupation policy."[39] Best contrasted the superficial "tourist's" understanding of France, with his own, deeper knowledge based on years working as part of the military government.

For tours organised by the armed forces, the Paris Command furnished one tour guide per hundred men. Units could hire additional guides at a cost of five Reichsmarks per tour.[40] Guides, at least some of whom were German citizens, were selected for their knowledge of the city, political reliability and willingness to pass on the right messages about France to the soldiers. Group tours became occasions to remind soldiers that France's glory lay in the past, while today's nation was old-fashioned, weak and individualistic, no match for the German Volk community united behind the Führer.

For soldiers visiting Paris, strict discipline was the order of the day. The men were warned not to stray from their group, or smoke in public, or wear their uniform collars open. To limit fraternisation and ensure they would not be seen dallying in local cafés and restaurants, meals were provided. Supervised stands sold authorised

---

[37] The occupation staff included increasing numbers of female auxiliaries, especially in Paris. See AN: 40 AJ/456.

[38] Confino, "Traveling," 108; Farber and Bailey, "Fighting Man," 657–9; White, "Soldier," 65.

[39] Werner Best, "Erinnerungen", 21 (BArch: N 1023–1).

[40] Kommandant Paris, Ic Besichtigungen, instructions regarding visits of the city of Paris, 18 November 1940 (AN: AJ 40/878).

souvenirs, while other French goods could be purchased at the officially sanctioned *Soldatenkaufhaus* (soldiers' department store) examined in Chapter 2.[41]

In late October 1941, Hans-Peter Eckener, then serving on the Atlantic coast, recorded a typical Paris tour in a letter to his parents.[42] This letter, which provides a rare participant's view of such a trip, also illustrates the authorities' attempts to control tourism. It points to the wide gap between official guidelines for visitors, and soldiers' own expectations of leisure and pleasure in Paris.

Given his artistic background, Eckener was initially "quite sceptical" about touring Paris with "a herd of soldiers" that included a "driver, a smithy and a cobbler" from his unit. But, aided by his respect for the visiting group's commanding officer, an educated man who appreciated Parisian history and art, he came to enjoy the sightseeing.[43] Eckener's experience contrasted with that of his comrades who, eager to enjoy Paris pleasures "complained in every key that they were 'dragged from one church to another' and the like."[44]

In many ways, the tour resembled a route march past Paris's major historical and cultural attractions. After an overnight train ride from their coastal stations, the soldiers first took the subway to pay their respects at the Tomb of the Unknown Soldier (Figure 1.2). Then, they crossed the Seine to Napoleon's tomb, where Eckener commented on the linkage of religion and nationalism. The men viewed the Eiffel Tower and Trocadéro, then rode into the city centre to admire the Eglise de la Madeleine, the Place Vendôme and the Opéra Garnier, a "pompous building that [they] unfortunately did not visit from the inside."[45] After lunch at one of Paris's many *Soldatenheime* (army-run "clubs" for rest and relaxation), the tour proceeded from the Place de la Concorde through the Tuileries to the Hôtel de Ville and Notre-Dame. Following dinner at the same *Soldatenheim* where they had had lunch, the men took in a variety show called *Paris plage* (Paris Beach),

---

[41] Kommandant Paris, Ic Besichtigungen, instructions regarding visits of the city of Paris, 18 November 1940 (AN: AJ 40/878).

[42] Eckener and Wolter, *Lieber Vater*, 25 October 1941, 124–7.

[43] Eckener noted of the three other men sent to Paris that one was "Fahrer, einer Schmied, und einer Schuster." He added that, "Ich gestehe, daß ich anfangs einer solchen Stadtbesichtigung mit einer Herde Soldaten recht skeptisch gegenüber stand." Eckener and Wolter, *Lieber Vater*, 25 October 1941, 124.

[44] "Sie [die anderen Soldaten] schimpften in allen Tonarten, daß sie 'von einer Kirche zur anderen geschleppt werden' und dergl." Eckener and Wolter, 25 October 1941, 124.

[45] The opera was "einem pompösen Gebäude, das wir leider innen nicht besichtigten." Eckener and Wolter, *Lieber Vater*, 25 October 1941, 125.

in the area west of Montmartre. According to Eckener, "[m]ost of us came alive here for the first time, for the day had brought them more strains than edification."[46]

On Sunday, Eckener observed strolling Parisians who "show themselves as elegantly clothed as the times allow – and endeavour as much as possible to behave as if the Germans were not there."[47] After visiting the Luxembourg gardens, viewing the Pantheon and several other sites, he and the others went up the Eiffel Tower to a height of 105 metres, where Eckener was impressed by the view. In the evening, the group was taken to the Moulin Rouge where, Eckener conceded, "presentation, costumes, and set showed taste and a certain artistic niveau."[48]

On Monday, the programme continued with a trip to Versailles and an hour's free time for shopping. Finally, the soldiers visited Sacré-Coeur, took a quick tour of Montmartre, and hurried to the train. "The others," Eckener noted, "would have loved to remain hanging in the countless bars of dubious reputation and appearance that we passed."[49] They found it unfair that, at the last minute, their guide should take them to Montmartre, where they could find "the precise thing … that alone in Paris seriously interested them," but had no time to enjoy it. Eckener closed his letter by saying that although his tour of Paris had not been without trials and tribulations, "the impression is nonetheless *big* and *lasting*" and he would count these days among the finest he had yet enjoyed.[50]

While Eckener evaluated the tour positively overall, his account also highlights the regime's desire to control soldiers' experiences of Paris. It was not just that the timetable was so packed there was no time to wander around, or that the men were taken past Montmartre's bars only when

---

[46] "Die meisten von uns lebten erst hier auf, da der Tag ihnen mehr Strapazen als Erbauung gebracht hatte." Eckener and Wolter, *Lieber Vater*, 25 October 1941, 126.
[47] "Die Pariser zeigen sich so elegant gekleidet als die Zeit erlaubt — und bemühen sich so gut wie möglich, zu tun, als ob die Deutschen nicht da wären." Eckener and Wolter, *Lieber Vater*, 25 October 1941, 127.
[48] "Aufmachung, Kostüme, Dekorationen, zeigen Geschmack und ein gewisses künstlerisches Niveau." Eckener and Wolter, 25 October 1941, 127.
[49] "Die anderen wären am liebsten kleben geblieben in den zahllosen Kneipen von zweifelhaften Ruf und Aussehen, an denen wir vorbeikamen. — Daß der Leutnant sie jetzt, ausgerechnet jetzt, in letzter Stunde, wo man sich nicht mehr aufhalten konnte, — hierherführte, wo sie grade das fanden, was sie allein in Paris ernstlich interessierte, — das werden sie ihm nie verzeihen!" Eckener and Wolter, *Lieber Vater*, 25 October 1941, 127.
[50] Emphasis in the original. "Der Eindruck ist doch *groß* und *bleibend*, und trotz gewisser Strapazen — ich rechne diese Tage zu den schönsten, die ich je gehabt habe." See also Chapter 3. Hans-Peter Eckener, letter 25 October 1941 in Eckener and Wolter, *Lieber Vater*, 127.

they were about to leave the city. More generally, the trip included only sanctioned attractions, drawn from the canon of prewar tourism, certainly, but also echoing the visits of Adolf Hitler and the other National Socialist bigwigs who toured soon after the conquest.[51] It opened with the Tomb of the Unknown Soldier, an especially fitting site for martial visitors, to underline German chivalry in the face of a conquered foe. We have seen that German soldiers in Warsaw were forbidden to show signs of respect at monuments to Polish war dead, but visiting the Paris Tomb of the Unknown Soldier was a required stop (Figure 1.2).[52] The essential climb up the Eiffel Tower took on new resonance, enabling men to experience a feeling of awe and power as they overlooked the city their forces controlled (Figure 4.4). Since Hitler rather admired Napoleon, a visit to his tomb at the Invalides was included in the programme, whereas the Pantheon, burying-place of other French heroes, was admired only from the outside. Group visits canalised tourism, reinforced National Socialist ideas about Paris and France, and enabled the regime to take credit for having offered even such an aesthete as Eckener some of the finest days of his life. Eckener's letter home encouraged his parents, too, to appreciate the generosity of the regime.

Echoes of the standard occupiers' tour of Paris survive not only in accounts like Eckener's, but also in soldiers' photo albums, which reproduce Paris sites with remarkable uniformity. Confinement to an organised tour ensured that the men would photograph certain sites, not others, and there was also a trickle-down effect, in which soldiers duplicated, independently, photos they had seen in newspapers and books.[53] Wehrmacht Propaganda Companies documented conquest and occupation with shots of soldiers standing before the Eiffel Tower, buying cake from street vendors, resting in a café, or posed in front of the Moulin Rouge (Figure 4.15).[54] Occupiers who had seen these images reproduced them themselves, much the way today's tourists inevitably

---

[51] Gordon, "Warfare and Tourism," 620–21. Interwar visitors to Paris would have seen many of the same sights, but not in the same order, likely beginning with Notre Dame or the Louvre rather than the Tomb of the Unknown Soldier. See emphemera in Historischen Archiv zum Tourismus, Berlin: F 06/xx/-45; Baedeker, *Paris und Umgebung.*

[52] Gordon, "Warfare and Tourism," 628. See Chapter 1.

[53] Cf. Robert Moeller's exploration of "war stories" in Robert G. Moeller, *War Stories: The Search for a Usable Past in the Federal Republic of Germany* (Berkeley: University of California Press, 2001).

[54] BArch Bild 101I–129–0482–32 / Heinz Bösig ; Bild 101I – 129–0480–05A / Bösig ; Bild 101I – 247–0775–09 / Langhaus; Bild 101I – 129–0480–26 / Bösig.

photograph sunny beaches when they visit the Caribbean, or take snapshots of the Acropolis in Greece.[55]
Historians' accounts of German soldier-tourism focus on Paris, a city
to which the men were drawn by a mixture of envy and admiration
difficult to reconcile with their role as occupying forces. A look at
regional and local sightseeing, notably in Normandy and Brittany, gives
a fuller sense of tourism's extent, its importance for soldiers' worldview,
and the ways in which the occupation regime both fostered tourism and
tried to control its impact. It also allows us to consider how soldiers
themselves tried to reconcile the contradictory calls of leisure and pleasure, and of duty.

Wherever they were stationed, regardless of rank, soldiers used their
spare time for tourism. In letters home and diaries, they described what
they had seen, perhaps partly because it was a break in their routine that
censorship allowed them to document. In May 1941, Hans W., a Luftwaffe official stationed near Brest in Brittany, wrote to his wife that, "last
Sunday our whole administration went on a rest and relaxation excursion
[*Wehrbetreuungsfahrt*] and visited the rocky cliffs on the coast . . . [Despite
the rain], it was a nice change."[56] Some visits, like this one, were
organised by military units for rest and relaxation, and to encourage
group cohesion. Others were spontaneous and undertaken at quieter
moments by individuals or groups of friends.

Outside the capital, Mont Saint-Michel was one of the most popular
sites. Both its atmospheric location, on a sea-bound isle between Normandy and Brittany, and its past made it an ideal destination for the
many units stationed along the nearby coast.[57] The site was linked to the
history of the Bretons and Normans, two peoples who the National

---

[55] Urry, *The Tourist Gaze: Leisure and Travel in Contemporary Societies*, 129. See, for
instance, Friedrich Siebert, photo album "La Rochelle 1940–41," 1 July 1940–26
March 1941 (BArch: N 586/9); Friedrich Kittel, photo album, 16–24 June 1940
(BArch: Msg. 1/1353). Occupiers' photography is the subject of Chapter 4.
[56] Hans W, letter 27 May 1941, No. 176 (DTA: 1960).
[57] A survey of three soldiers' newspapers in France uncovered five articles on the site
between August 1940 and October 1941 alone. Chomton, 'Mont Saint-Michel: Die
ruhmvolle Geschichte eines französischen Nationalheiligtums: Der Schicksalsfelsen an
der normannischen Küste', *Der Durchbruch*, 16 March 1941, 4; M. Dey, 'Aus der PK.
Unserer Armee: 3 Tage Sonderurlaub auf dem Mont St. Michel', *Wacht Am Kanal*,
15 October 1941, 4; H. Hesse, 'Bei Normannen und Bretonen', *Der Durchbruch*,
24 August 1940, 3; K. Lea, 'Soldaten unserer Armee auf dem Mont St. Michel: Eine
Gralsburg steigt aus dem Meer', *Westfront*, 25 May 1941, 3; H. Wiebe, 'Eine Winterfahrt
durch die Normandie: Le Mans, St. Malo, Caen und das Wunder von St. Michel', *Der
Durchbruch*, 8 February 1941, 6. See also Fedor von Bock, 'Tagebuchnotizen', entry for
August 2, 1940 (BArch: N 22/5); Gutschmidt, 'Kriegstagebuch', entry for September
22, 1940 (BArch: Msg. 1/257).

Socialists viewed as racially distinct from, and superior to, the French masses. Tourism in Normandy, more generally, was justified through the notion that the Normans were northerners, Vikings by origin, and thus racially "acceptable" descendants of Germanic tribes. Rather than being obnubilated by foreign treasures, Germans could learn something about their own history by admiring Norman churches and monuments, and travellers would be able to confirm that "we still encounter blond-haired, blue-eyed people with oblong head shapes here, the last traces of Germanic blood."[58] As in other parts of Europe, sightseeing in France was used to reinforce a racialist worldview, as certain sites' propagandistic value added to their aesthetic and historical interest.

Tourism supported the National Socialist war effort in other ways as well. On regime-sanctioned regional outings, occupiers' desire to "see the sights'" was sometimes elevated into a kind of obligation – soldiers should not just hold the land, but get to know it while they were there.[59] The foreword to a book about Normandy, for example, argued that, "[a]s much as his duty allows, the German soldier should look around in this foreign land."[60] Lest readers worry that soldiers might come to love France more than their own homeland, the book explained that getting to know the particularities of another country served above all as a way to understand more fully the value of one's own: "The more keenly he can then perceive foreign lands, the more strongly love for his German homeland, its beauty and its never-ending richness, will seize him. We want to see what is foreign as foreign, so that the image of our homeland that we all carry in our hearts may grow yet more alive."[61] Like Hans-Peter Eckener, who complimented the light in France because it reminded him of the North Sea, occupiers were supposed to view France through a filter of comparison with Germany. Comparison would keep memories of the *Heimat* fresh, and protect men from "going native" in an occupied land.

Absolved of guilt about finding France attractive, occupiers nonetheless felt varying degrees of unease about enjoying themselves while other men worked, fought and died. They often insisted that tourism did not get in the way of their military obligations. Werner Best, one of the top German military administrators in France, recalled that during his two

---

[58] Hugo Wiebe, "Eine Winterfahrt durch die Normandie," 6

[59] For more on tourism in Eastern occupied areas, see Dücker, "Reisen in die UdSSR 1933–1945," 253–83; Koshar, *German Travel Cultures*, 152–5 and later in this chapter.

[60] Meinhold, *Die Normandie*, ed. Befehlshaber Sicherung West (n.p., 1940), foreword.

[61] Meinhold, *Die Normandie*, foreword.

years stationed there he "had not missed the chance to combine [his] official visits to our field commands with exhaustive touring of the land, its characteristic scenery, its cultural documents and monuments."[62] Best did not deny that he had acted as a tourist in France; rather, he suggested that he would have been wasting a precious opportunity if he had not taken advantage of the chance to tour France while fulfilling his obligations as an occupier.

In his diary, POW camp Commander Gutschmidt, stationed north of the Loire river halfway between Paris and the Atlantic coast, similarly stressed that sightseeing was linked to the fulfilment of his duties, or at least did not interfere with his job. In February 1941, for example, he reported that he did not have much to do, so he "drove ... first today to the field command on business and then visited the ruins of the old Abbaye de l'Epau outside Le Mans."[63] Equally, in other sections of his diary, Gutschmidt documented independent "Ausflüge" (excursions) to various locations, and the three-day trip to Spain mentioned at the beginning of this chapter evidently had little to do with his formal responsibilities. In the early period of the occupation, at any rate, and when facing transfer back to Germany to prepare for deployment to the Eastern Front, Gutschmidt felt it was his right to travel and relax for a few days. Others too saw France's pleasures as a reward for hard work, and when individual occupiers broke travel regulations, their superiors defended them with arguments about their long hours, including over-time, and the rarity of vacations in wartime.[64]

Striking a balance between duty and pleasure, and coming to terms with the desirability of France as a site of enjoyment during, and even despite, wartime was an ongoing problem. War may have mitigated the pleasures of tourism, but Germans' desire to discover and experience France persisted, and the tension between this and the need to control the country grew. In addition to channelling tourism through propaganda and endeavours like the guided tours of Paris for soldiers, the regime responded by imposing limits on the fun.

As early as December 1940, Oberbefehlshaber West Gerd von Rundstedt ordered a reduction in requests for accommodation in Paris, for billets were no longer available for those with business in the city,

---

[62] Werner Best, "Erinnerungen," 27 (BArch: N 1023/1).

[63] Johannes Gutschmidt, 'Kriegstagebuch,' entry for 21 February 1941, (BArch: Msg. 1/ 257). Literary censor Gerhard Heller, for his part, recalled that he had admired the Mediterranean coast when he crossed the demarcation line on business in 1942 Heller, *Besetzten Land*, 151, 156, 226 ff.

[64] Cf. case involving ROGES, below.

let alone "those on leave, visitors and shoppers."[65] From spring 1941, the Militärbefehlshaber clamped down more generally on unofficial travel accompanied by "wild" consumption – independent shopping for rationed goods by Wehrmacht members acting individually or on behalf of their units. In March, he announced that "trips taken for shopping, pleasure and out of laziness are to be punished as disobedience regardless of individual standing."[66] Still, these restrictions were justified primarily on economic grounds, confirming that although the Militärbefehlshaber wished to discourage profligate use of resources, he did not consider tourism as such to be inappropriate for occupiers. A further sign of change was that, while Gutschmidt described his late February 1941 trip to Spain in vivid detail, in early April, the Spanish border was closed to all travellers, including Germans.[67] Wehrmacht members continued to cross, however, because nearly a month later, the Militärbefehlshaber noted drily that, "[t]here is reason to underline that the ban extends to German citizens including all members of the military regardless of rank."[68]

By July 1941, Germans required a permit to enter the occupied zone south of the Loire river, and in spring 1942, excursions extending more than 100 km. from one's post were forbidden.[69] Despite these efforts to limit tourism, an incident involving three female staff members at the Rohstoff-Handelsgesellschaft (ROGES), a raw materials purchasing

---

[65] *Oberbefehlshaber West (Heeresgruppe A) Ia to Militärbefehlshaber Frankreich*, 1 December 1940 (AN: AJ 40/451).

[66] Militärbefehlshaber in Frankreich, Kommandostab Abt. Ia, 4 Mar. 1941 (AN: AJ 40/451).

[67] Reasons for this border closure included on-going Spanish-German tensions, security concerns associated with the Wehrmacht's advance into Yugoslavia and Greece ahead of Operation Barbarossa, and perhaps above all the need to limit the traffic of refugees and goods across the French-Spanish border. Militärbefehlshaber in Frankreich, Kommandostab Abt. Ic, 10 April 1941 (AN: AJ 40/451). On trafficking across this border see Sandra Ott's research, notably *Living with the Enemy: German Occupation, Collaboration and Justice in the Western Pyrenees, 1940–1948* (Cambridge, UK: Cambridge University Press, 2017).

[68] Militärbefehlshaber in Frankreich, Kommandostab Abt. Ic/4, 7 May 1941 (AN: AJ 40/451).

[69] Verwaltungsstab Abt. Z to Kommandostab Abt. IIa (Z), 8 June 1942 (AN: AJ 40/450). To clarify, until July 1941, Germans were free to visit areas of the occupied zone that were both north and south of the Loire. On the other hand, travel to the non-occupied zone, where Pétain's government was based at Vichy, was exceptional. Indeed, tourists became so rare in non-occupied areas after 1940 that the Vichy authorities closed the office of the high commissioner of tourism. Harvey Levenstein, *We'll Always Have Paris: American Tourists in France since 1930* (Chicago, IL: Univ. of Chicago Press, 2004), 73. By the time Germany took over France's southern zone in November 1942, soldiers' movements were more restricted generally, and there is no evidence of the blooming tourism that can be found in the older occupied areas.

agency linked to the military administration, suggests that the right to travel in France continued to be taken for granted. Equipped with holiday passes issued by their employer, the ROGES staff members travelled to Biarritz for Easter 1942, but were turned back by the field command because Biarritz was closed to vacationers. Frustrated at having to return to Paris, one of the women, Hildegard Schindel, stayed overnight in Royan, and was stopped again because she was more than 100 km. from Paris and had sought accommodation independently of the field command. Statements taken in the context of disciplinary action indicate that the women had little idea (or at least, they claimed to have little idea) that they were doing anything wrong. Their employer ROGES seemed to be unaware that the travel regulations had changed. In the end, the affair was settled with a slap on the wrist for ROGES, and a reminder of the policies in force. Perhaps ROGES was particularly ignorant, but the incident as a whole suggests that some occupation staff were (perhaps deliberately) blind to the regulations, seeing it as self-evident that they would be able to travel wherever they liked.[70]

Whether genuine or not, the ignorance of the ROGES staff underlines the fact that travelling seemed natural to occupiers. Even if their range of activities grew progressively smaller, and the perimeter within which a soldier or officer might journey shrank, tourism was allowed to continue. The regime tried to address the conflict between duty and pleasure through regulating and organising occupiers' tourism, like their shopping and leisure activities. Guidebooks, commemorative volumes and coffee-table books were used as tools to shape appropriate occupier behaviour, and to define how France should be perceived, understood and remembered. These publications normalised occupiers' tourism, making it seem a natural form of interaction with the land and its people.

Nevertheless, unease about soldier tourism remained, not just at official levels. It affected individual occupiers, some of whom pondered privately the strange juxtaposition of pleasure, beauty, and war that marked their time in France. This more contemplative approach was exemplified by the future novelist Heinrich Böll. Like his fellow soldiers, Böll took advantage of the chance to visit France while he was stationed there during the war. After rising at six am and spending six hours on the train to have a brief sojourn in Paris in January 1942, Böll wrote glowingly to his fiancée, "I really believe that Paris is the height of everything human and the deepest depths of mankind; and I experienced all of that

---

[70] The incident may have been treated more leniently because the perpetrators were women, assumed to be less "responsible" for their actions (AN: AJ 40/450).

in four hours!"[71] At the end of his letter, Böll told his fiancée with conviction that their first destination together after the war could only be Paris.[72]

Like other occupiers, Böll saw the beauty of French land- and sea-scapes as important compensation for having to spend his youth in the army. But he was subtle enough to understand that his "tourism" in France was not quite the real thing. In late September 1942, after two years as an occupier, he wrote home about how he longed to return to civilian life, "and to take a trip, experience the beauty and unsettling foreign-ness of other lands and peoples, . . . these are all human pleasures that are granted to thousands and thousands, but our generation, it seems, will know no Sundays, not to mention the pleasure of going abroad in peacetime."[73] The delight of discovering new lands and peoples was spoiled for Böll by the simple fact of being at war. In war, beauty seemed false, and the foreign quality of other lands became more than pleasantly unsettling – it was threatening, a feeling no amount of false "tourism" could dispel.

Partly to address the unease that Böll expressed, partly to remind Germans that their presence was justified and to set their tourism in context, the regime produced many books to accompany the occupation of France. There were city guides notably to Paris, Dijon, and Rouen, regional works on Normandy, Brittany, and the Southwest, and lavishly illustrated publications about France's landscape and architecture, particularly its palaces and cathedrals.[74] Some books had existed before the war and were simply translated and updated for the occupying forces; others were written specifically with occupying soldiers in mind. On one level, such publications entertained and informed readers, offering them accessible accounts of regional history and geographical features.

---

[71] Heinrich Böll, *Briefe aus dem Krieg, 1939–1945*, vol. 1 (Cologne: Kiepenheuer & Witsch, 2001), 2 January 1942, 283. Böll's opinion reflected contemporary views about French degeneracy as well as cultural splendor. See discussion of "France books" later in this chapter.

[72] In interviews with veterans and their families, Alon Confino found that a desire to revisit the places they had lived during the war was common. Confino, "Traveling," 109–10.

[73] Böll, *Briefe*, 1:25 September 1942, 484. Like Böll, German administrator Gerhard Heller expressed unease about how occupiers' pleasure and leisure intersected with war and destruction, though in his case it was in postwar memoirs that sought to downplay his role in the regime's oppression of France. Heller, *Besetzten Land*, 244–5.

[74] See, e.g. Armee Oberkommando Bordeaux, *Kleiner Wegweiser für die Soldaten der deutschen Südwestarmee an der Atlantikküste* (Bordeaux: Delmas, 1940); Franz Albrecht Medicus and Hans Hörmann, *Kathedralen in Frankreich unter deutschem Schutz* (Paris: Wegleiter Verlag, 1942); Franz Albrecht Medicus and Hans Hörmann, *Schlösser in Frankreich* (Paris: Wegleiter Verlag, 1944). Individual guides are cited where necessary and all those consulted can be found in the bibliography.

For troops stationed in each area, they suggested suitable leisure-time destinations, illuminated local idiosyncrasies, and recommended particular foods and beverages to try. On a second level, these books constituted a literature of the occupation that was carefully designed to transmit regime-sanctioned ideas and perspectives to its readers. Third, the texts were part of a conscious drive to commemorate the occupation, constructing memories for the future from the experiences of the present day.

An analysis of more than thirty books produced during the German occupation of France reveals a spectrum ranging from tour guides in the narrowest sense, in which a majority of the information was geared towards sightseeing, through volumes detailing regional features that were written as memoirs by occupiers stationed in the area, to "educational" treatises intended to convey to their readers "scholarly" information about historical monuments located in France.[75] With varying degrees of subtlety, these publications projected specific images of France and its people to German readers. They might include an ostensibly objective account of French history, for instance, that emphasised the aggressions of the Anglo-Saxon enemy, highlighted the flaws of past French regimes, and lingered lovingly over previous periods of German domination and occupation. Treating French culture with a mixture of admiration for anything that could be linked to a shared Classical, Medieval or "Nordic" heritage, and stark denigration of the rest, such guides were meant to shape how occupying soldiers perceived France and experienced their time there. They imparted cultural literacy, thus helping to "create" occupying soldiers as informed tourists, while also encouraging positive memories of war. Such books might easily be dismissed as ephemeral and propagandistic, but like tourism itself, they helped render occupation palatable, even enjoyable, to those who undertook it. By underlining concepts such as French degeneracy and German cultural superiority, moreover, these publications justified conquest and reinforced occupiers' confidence in their mission.

Books about France published during the occupation shared many attributes with a similar genre of popular literature that predated the National Socialist rise to power. As part of a larger study of postcolonial memory, Britta Schilling has analysed "Africa books" produced between 1915 and 1925 to commemorate Germany's colonial experiences.[76]

---

[75] These categories were not distinct. France books that contained primarily images are covered in Chapter 4.
[76] Schilling, *Postcolonial Germany*, 22.

The publications examined here, which might be called "France books," functioned in a similar way, although they were produced while the expansionist activity was actually going on. They formed part of a broader literature about Germany's World War II conquests that was aesthetically appealing and provided entertainment, yet also conveyed political messages that were valued by their audience.[77] Africa books lamented the loss of Germany's colonies through the Treaty of Versailles, justified Germans' former presence in Africa, and sought to counter notably British arguments that German rule in Africa had been particularly cruel.[78] With this recent history as backdrop, France books celebrated the reversal of the Versailles treaty through armed conquest, justified Germany's presence on foreign soil, and argued for occupiers' status as noble and fair warriors. Authors who might well have read Africa books as children were primed to see their French experiences in a similar "world historical" vein, and they wrote in an equally grand-iloquent, self-justifying style.[79] Without seeking to draw a direct line from Germany's past colonial experiences to its expansionism in World War II, historian Birthe Kundrus has argued that colonial references influenced attitudes and policy-making in World War II indirectly, through a series of "productive, imaginative transfers."[80] Kundrus focuses mainly on Eastern Europe, but books about France suggest one of the ways that these types of transfer affected Western occupied areas as well.

In texts about France, which echoed the themes and rhetorical style of Africa books, German soldiers came across as heroes. They stood guard valiantly on the Atlantic coast, chivalrously protected the French population, and vindicated past injustices against Germany through their presence on foreign soil. The regime's success in making members of the *Volksgemeinschaft*, whether at home or abroad, feel that they were participating in important national projects that vindicated

---

[77] My focus is on France, where there was a profusion of this literature. Guides and commemorative volumes about other occupied areas like Norway, Belgium, Italy, Ukraine and Poland were also published, mainly from 1940 through 1942, though a few appeared later. See Hans-Eugen Bühler, *Der Frontbuchhandel 1939–1945: Organisationen, Kompetenzen, Verlage, Bücher – Eine Dokumentation* (Walter de Gruyter, 2002), 219–31.

[78] Schilling, *Postcolonial Germany*, 22.

[79] Africa books were valued as educative literature and widely disseminated in the interwar period. Schilling, 17–22.

[80] Birthe Kundrus, "Colonialism, Imperialism, National Socialism: How Imperial Was the Third Reich?" in *German Colonialism in a Global Age*, ed. Bradley Naranch and Geoff Eley (Durham: Duke University Press Books, 2015), 340–41.

the Reich's "honour" constituted a valuable "smokescreen" that worked to maintain consent.[81]

Audiences accustomed to "educative" literature about Germany's former colonial possessions made a ready market for books about Germany's new conquests. While Africa books aimed to "explain ... the meaning of the Heimat (home) abroad, or zweite Heimat (second home), to those who had never experienced it ...," books about France strove to transmit information about the occupied land, and also to convey something of the experience of being an occupier to their readers. For readers who were themselves occupiers, these books crystallised impressions into words, much the way that a photograph might seem to capture a moment and fix it as a ready-made memory for eternity.[82] Just as, we will see, even occupiers who did not own a camera bought and traded images they believed represented what they themselves had seen and done, occupiers purchased France books because the texts seemed to distill their own experiences and offered ready-made descriptions of them to men who perhaps did not have the literary skills to set these down themselves. Individual experiences became universalised, even as these books offered approaches and subject matter soldiers could use to elaborate their own narratives and recollections.

The similarities between Africa books and France books underline that commemorative literature was a well-established genre that formed and reinforced private and public memories in Germany over generations.[83] In an era better-known for radio and film propaganda, mass-market books remained an important medium for the transmission of political messages. Such books offer evidence of how official propaganda, individual book authors, and audience expectations worked together in the Third Reich to construct and diffuse ideas both immediately and in the longer term.

---

[81] The term "smokescreen" comes from Kundrus, who has highlighted the role the Nazi regime's "smokescreen of solicitude" for ordinary citizens played in ensuring their consent. "Greasing the Palm," 166–9.

[82] Schilling, *Postcolonial Germany*, 22.

[83] Drawing on Jan and Aleida Assmann's research into "communicative" and "cultural" memory, Schilling suggests that "The Assmanns' definitions of communicative and cultural memory can be extended and renamed in order to reflect their location in 'public' or 'private' spaces." She also emphasises the fluidity of the boundaries between these two types of memory, and the position of *Africabücher* "at the intersection of oral and written forms of culture." Schilling, *Postcolonial Germany*, 7, 15. Cf. Jan Assmann, "Communicative and Cultural Memory" in *Cultural Memory Studies: An International and Interdisciplinary Handbook*, ed. Astrid Erll and Ansgar Nünning (New York: de Gruyter, 2008), 109–18.

The first "France books" were guides for German soldiers that appeared almost as soon as the occupation began. Among them was the glossy biweekly magazine *Der deutsche Wegleiter*, already mentioned earlier in the chapter, which was printed from 15 July 1940.[84] Sold for just six francs, it listed up-to-date entertainment and attractions, and included short articles and stories about Paris events and sites. Alongside advertisements for regime-sanctioned theatre productions, cabarets, and shopping opportunities, the *Wegleiter* printed a convenient map and instructions for using the Metro. Specifically designed for soldiers new to the city and for visitors, the guide's practical information helped Germans navigate unfamiliar urban spaces. It also included sample prices so that soldiers could determine whether they were being charged fairly for food and beverages.[85] Like peacetime tour guides, the *Wegleiter*'s curated offerings directed tourism as visitors undertook it, and the publication offered a German gloss on Paris for the specific audience of occupiers. In 1943, staff at the German embassy in Paris described it as the "quasi-official organ of the city commander and the local group of the [National Socialist Party's] foreign organisation." The embassy considered the 1943 print run of 6,000 copies, limited by paper restrictions, to be "not nearly sufficient."[86]

The *Wegleiter* was an up-to-the-minute guide that focused primarily on leisure and entertainment options. By 1 August 1940, the Stadtkommandant in Paris had sanctioned publication of a more formal guidebook called the *Kleiner Führer durch Paris für deutsche Soldaten: Erinnerung an Paris 1940* (*Short guide to Paris for German Soldiers: Memento of Paris*

[84] It was published by Wegleiter Verlag, owned by a Swiss citizen named Locher. In November 1943, staff at the German embassy in Paris spoke in favour of purchasing the firm, of which Locher apparently sought to divest himself. Major Heinz Lorenz, formerly on the staff of the Paris Commander and author of two publications for soldiers discussed later in this chapter, comanaged the firm. Within the military administration, Franz Albrecht Medicus, head of the Abteilung Verwaltung, was a particular patron and Wegleiter Verlag printed both of Medicus' co-edited works, *Kathedralen in Frankreich unter deutschem Schutz* and *Schlösser in Frankreich* in 1944 (when he was stationed in Athens). File note Pr. Nr. 6829/43, Schwendemann for Generalkonsul Gerlach and Gesandten Schleier, German Embassy in Paris, 27 November 1943; G. Hibbelen, "Aufzeichnung für Herrn Gesandten Schleier," 20 November 1943 (AA: DBP/1141b). See also Geiger, *L'image*, 379–80; Krob, "Paris Through Enemy Eyes: The Wehrmacht in Paris 1940–1944."

[85] See, for instance, list of cabarets and prices in *Der deutsche Wegleiter* 32, 16–20 November 1941, 58.

[86] At 96 pages per issue, the *Wegleiter* generated a monthly revenue of between 80,000 and 100,000 francs, probably mainly from advertising. Embassy staff noted that this amount had been twice as high before paper allotments were cut. G. Hibbelen, "Aufzeichnung für Herrn Gesandten Schleier," 20 November 1943 (AA: DBP/1141b).

Figure 3.1 A 1940 guide to Paris for German soldiers. On the left-hand side, note the "Deutsches Haus" (German Pavilion) from the 1937 Paris Exposition.
Anon., *Kleiner Führer durch Paris für deutsche Soldaten: Erinnerung* an *Paris 1940* (Paris: Dompol's Editions, 1940): 6–7.

1940).[87] The clumsy German text of this tour book suggested that it had been translated hastily from an earlier French text, possibly produced for the 1937 Paris World Fair. This new edition was issued to take advantage of new "visitors" in 1940, and printed in multiple copies with the specific sanction of the department responsible for visits at the Paris command. The guide noted that the most imposing building at the World Fair had been the Deutsches Haus (German pavilion), and that "German arts and sciences and the immense progress in various domains of human activity were widely admired here" (Figure 3.1).[88] Apart from occasional flattering comments about Germany such as this one, the depiction of Paris in the *Kleiner Führer* seems little different from a non-occupation-era book. In describing the city, it commented favourably on "the treasures and marvels that Paris possesses, as well as its magnetic attraction, that makes

[87] *Kleiner Führer durch Paris für deutsche Soldaten: Erinnerung an Paris 1940* (Paris: Dompol's Editions, 1940).
[88] A depiction of the German pavilion at the 1937 Paris Exposition was, unlike the rest of the pen and ink images, captioned in German (not French), and in a slightly different font. *Kleiner Führer*, 6.

Paris the centre of world tourism."[89] The fact that Germany now controlled Parisian treasures made it acceptable to underline their value. The guide mentioned the American embassy on the Place de la Concorde, and alluded to a "Jewish quarter" in passing, stating that Saint Paul's church was located there, and that there were many other interesting sights nearby.

Other similar guides listed major sites and provided a brief commentary on each, or proposed walking tours and itineraries for visiting soldiers. There were also "special interest" publications, such as a guide called *Pariser Nächte*, that focused on Paris nightlife.[90] While such books might appear to be poor vehicles for propaganda, their choice of sites and entertainment to either recommend or omit, as well as their wording, reinforced messages the authorities sought to convey to readers.

Alongside offering practical advice, these books also had an avowedly commemorative purpose, as the *Kleiner Führer's* subtitle "memento of Paris 1940" suggests. Soldiers were meant to keep such a book, to read it over, and to share it with their families. Indeed, many such books have survived until today because soldiers mailed or carried them home, and used them to record their experiences, sometimes checking off the specific sights they had visited as a kind of occupiers' "bucket list" (Figure 3.2). Like Africa books, publications about France helped to develop and maintain a private, individual and familial memory of the war that lasted well beyond 1945, when it was no longer possible to depict the German occupation of France in a positive light in the public sphere.[91]

Through these material objects, tourist memories became interlaced with, even as they reinforced, awareness of the conquest that had made such tourism possible. Guides did not need to be overtly propagandistic to achieve this effect. Indeed, even after 1940, books were published that were either neutral, or openly admiring of French achievements. However, their tonal shading emerges best though a brief comparison with three non-French guides, all of which deal with East European areas. This is not the place for an exhaustive analysis of World War I and II guides on both Eastern and Western Fronts, but a glance at guides from other times and places illuminates two key aspects of the World War II publications dealing with France. The first is their racialist tone. While this tone is, unsurprisingly, more pronounced in guides to Eastern

---

[89] *Kleiner Führer*, 1.   [90] Doré Ogrizek, ed., *Pariser Nächte* (Paris: Odé Verlag, 1941).
[91] Schilling writes that "every time *Afrikabücher* were read, every time children and adults leafed through the illustrated pages or gazed at the colourful covers, the memory of the German colonial past was 'recharged' through the cultural framework of the present, and the memory of colonialism kept alive." Schilling, *Postcolonial Germany*, 40.

Figure 3.2 *Der deutsche Wegleiter*, bi-weekly guide for Germans in Paris.
Cover and a page with French museum listings including marginal
notation by a reader.
Der deutsche Wegleiter no. 15, 1–15 March 1941, cover and 12.

Europe, the more subtly shaded deployment of race in French guides
deserves notice as well. Second, as suggested above, the World War II
era guides had an avowedly commemorative purpose. They were written
in a heavily-laden, portentous style that encouraged soldiers and occupiers to see themselves as protagonists on a world-historical stage, participants in a grand endeavour for the German fatherland that must be
remembered and documented for posterity.

The first guide for comparison, *Ich weiss Bescheid: kleiner Soldatenführer
durch Wilna* (*I Know What's What: Short Soldiers' Guide through Vilnius*),
was published in 1918 for German soldiers in what is now Lithuania.[92]
This guide focused primarily on practical advice. A soldier arriving at
Vilnius's main train station learned where to make a phone call, how to

---

[92] Zeitung der 10. Armee, ed., *Ich weiss Bescheid: kleiner Soldatenführer durch Wilna*
(Hamburg: Hanseatische Druck- und Verlags-Anstalt, 1918).

find his unit, and where to seek appropriate accommodation. Having covered these basics, the guide accompanied him on two walking tours of the Vilnius downtown, admonishing him not to make hasty judgements about the city. "Avoid premature ridicule!" it insisted, "the foreign land seeks to be understood. Pay attention to the local customs and habits; seek to understand them. It's always worth keeping your eyes open."[93] Vilnius had a sizable Jewish population, a fact that was apparent when a walking tour took soldiers past "Judengasse" (Jews' lane). Soldiers were informed that this street offered a "striking view," and they were encouraged to take a step or two down it to view the synagogue, located across from the rag market. "The images of this street that are foreign (fremd) to your eyes seem strange (seltsam) to you," the guide commented.[94] Vilnius's Jewish population may have been described as foreign and strange but, on the whole, the tone of the guide was relatively open. This may have been partly due to the fact that the Germans hoped to win the favour of a local population that had until recently been occupied by Russians. The guide avoided setting up an overt hierarchy between soldiers and locals and instead offered an overview of the city's main landmarks, gave soldiers practical information, and reminded them to maintain soldierly discipline and a suitable bearing because the German nation as a whole would be judged by their actions.

World War II guides also talked about appropriate bearing and encouraged soldiers to keep their eyes open while abroad, but there was little or no mention of avoiding hasty judgements or seeking to understand foreign peoples. A German-published guide to the Ukraine in World War II underlines the more ideologically and racially-charged nature of Nazi-era guides.[95] As in Vilnius in the previous conflict, Germans had entered an area that had recently been under Russian influence. The guide described admiringly Ukrainians' ability to persist in the same territorial area for centuries and to retain their "ethnic type" despite pressures from "foreign racial groups."[96] Even if positively

---

[93] Zeitung der 10. Armee, *Ich weiss Bescheid*, 6.
[94] Zeitung der 10. Armee, *Ich weiss Bescheid*, 18.
[95] Cf. Klaus Latzel's conclusions regarding the more ideologically and racially charged nature of Wehrmacht soldiers' letters from World War II's Eastern Front, compared to that of the previous world war. Latzel, "Tourismus und Gewalt."
[96] Zeno Kuziela and R. Dyminskyj, *Die Ukraine*, ed. Luftwaffenführungsstab Ic/VIII (Stuttgart: Alemannen-Verlag, n.d.), 5. A favourable account of the Ukrainian people is also given in Bohdan Schemet, *Die Ukraine einst und jetzt: kurzer Überblick der ukrainischen Geschichte* (Berlin: Verlag der Ukrainischen Wirklichkeit, 1941). For more on tourism and tour guides in Eastern occupied areas, see Jane Caplan, *"Jetzt judenfrei." Writing Tourism in Nazi-Occupied Poland* (London: German Historical Inst., 2013); Dücker, "Reisen in die UdSSR 1933–1945," 253–83.

turned in this case, the racialised language of this guide marked a tonal difference from earlier publications.

This difference in tone was even clearer in guides dealing with other East European areas, like Poland, where there was no pretence of good relations with the locals. The texts were replete with pejorative statements and the 1940 Woehrl guide to Posen, for instance, noted that Poles in the area "never developed a notable culture ... but rather lived apathetically and without spiritual striving."[97] Rudy Koshar has pointed out that guides to many East European areas gave local people no positive traits.[98] French guides exhibited a similar tendency, albeit more muted. For example, while German guides typically ascribed no favourable characteristics at all to East European populations, they might praise past French cultural and technological accomplishments even if the overall tone of a guide was scornful of French decadence and decay.[99]

Still, it was not positive or negative judgements per se, but a racialised tone overall that most clearly distinguished World War II guides from earlier publications. The racial dimension of guides to France was evident in their treatment of French regional populations. Examples can be found in guides about Normandy and Brittany, two regions that, because they were adjacent to England, were densely occupied throughout the occupation. Guides to both emphasised distinctiveness and identified fundamental differences between Normans and Bretons, on the one hand, and the remaining French population on the other. As discussed earlier in the chapter, occupiers' touristic interest in Normandy, specifically, was justified though the notion that the Normans were descendants of the Vikings and thus racially "superior" to the remaining French population. Apparently on their own initiative, Lieutenant Andreas Reindl and Sergeant Karl Gossner produced a guide to lower Normandy's attractions for their fellow-soldiers. "Comrade standing guard on lower Norman soil," the book began, "open your eyes wide ... and enjoy the beauty and uniqueness of this land that is considered the jewel in the crown of French provinces."[100] Necessarily vague on areas the authors had not visited due to the demands of their service, the guide focused on sights in and around the city of Caen, lauded as the capital of William the Conqueror, victor over the English in 1066. In the occupation's early years, at any rate, publications about France propagated the notion that

---

[97] Cited in Koshar, *German Travel Cultures*, 152.
[98] Koshar, *German Travel Cultures*, 152.
[99] Koshar, *German Travel Cultures*, 153. See also Caplan, *Jetzt judenfrei*.
[100] Andreas Reindl, *Die Nieder-Normandie: Führer für deutsche Soldaten* (Caen: Imprimerie centrale de Basse-Normandie, Caron et Cie., 1941), 5. Gossner illustrated the volume. I am grateful to Valentin Schneider for a copy of this publication.

Germans and at least some French might profitably work together to conquer their common enemy, England.

Admiration for Normandy and its people also comes across clearly in *Die Normandie* (*Normandy*), a detailed narrative guide compiled by Navy chaplain Professor Dr. Meinhold and published by the Befehlshaber Sicherung West. Meinhold admired the Normans for their putative independence and racial purity, qualities that they had struggled (and continued to struggle, he wrote) to retain in the face of "softening" influences leeching in from the rest of France. After William the Conqueror's celebrated victory in England, moreover, Norman policies provided a model for occupation that, the book implied, Germans would do well to follow in France. According to Meinhold, the Normans under William had understood how to meld Norman and English customs, while always retaining the upper hand. William's leadership had led "not through violence, but cleverly and gradually, to a full transformation of English life."[101] To reinforce this message for Hitler's occupiers, *Die Normandie*'s historical segment concluded with an overview of previous German presence in the area, going back to 1815, at the end of the Napoleonic wars. The reader was intended to gain an appreciation of Normans as "different" from, and superior to, other Frenchmen, to learn about their successful conquest and occupation techniques, and to gain awareness of himself as a victor who belonged to a long line of German occupiers whose role it was to get along with the locals while making the hierarchy of power clear.

Guides like these had Breton counterparts as well. *Bretagne: ein Buch für die deutsche Kriegsmarine* (*Brittany: A Book for the German Navy*), was less a tour guide per se than a compilation of essays by members of the occupying forces in Brittany. Put together by Navy Propaganda Department West, it included vignettes about various port cities, including one on the city of St Nazaire written by Lothar-Günther Buchheim, later the author of the post-war novel that became a well-known film, *Das Boot*.[102] Buchheim described Saint-Nazaire's rapid rise from obscurity to an industrial port, and concluded with a lyrical and somewhat underhandedly positive verdict on the city. "She is without adornment and without riches to hide the nakedness of her poverty," he wrote. "Her face is not beautiful, it is black, dark, tormented by difficult and arduous work, and

---

[101] Meinhold, *Die Normandie*, 15.
[102] *Bretagne: ein Buch für die deutsche Kriegsmarine*, ed. Heinrich Droege (Marine Propaganda Abteilung West, 1941); Wolfgang Petersen, *Das Boot* (Bavaria Film, 1982).

still it grabs you with its unvarnished truth."[103] Although Buchheim apparently saw beauty in Saint-Nazaire's rough industrial affect, the overall message of *Bretagne* was that, although the region's "racial" attributes made it distinct from France and it showed more promise than other areas, it still had a long way to go before being fully worthy of German praise.[104]

While these books about Normandy and Brittany were relatively subtle in transmitting their messages, some guides to France presented a National Socialist worldview more openly and brutally. A particularly striking example was a 1941 pocket guide called *Paris: deutsch gesehen* (*Paris: As Germans See It*), published under the auspices of the Kraft durch Freude organisation with the approval of the Paris Commander. This work was handed out free of charge to visiting soldiers, and offered a Hitlerian rendering of Paris history, culture and contemporary sights. It included, for example, a section on the nature of the French people, which expounded at length, predictably, about topics such as the difference between French "amour" and German "Liebe" (the former defined as a shallow, rationalistic, and physical attraction; the latter deep, mystical, blindly soulful love).[105] Especially notable in this book were segments referring to a rampant Jewish "problem" that the French had been unable to master alone. Recognition of this issue, the guide contended, "led during the occupation by the German army to the first far-reaching measures of racial protection [des Rassenschutzes]. The usual instruments of police power did not allow for drastic measures. As a result, a sharper crack-down was undertaken by means of legislation from spring 1941. Non-French Jews were sent to French concentration camps."[106] The guide underlines that a racialising worldview influenced not only depictions of Eastern occupied areas, but Western ones as well. This publication argued that it had been fortunate that the Germans had been

---

[103] Lothar-Günther Buchheim, "St. Nazaire" in *Bretagne: ein Buch für die deutsche Kriegsmarine*, ed. Heinrich Droege (Marine Propaganda Abteilung West, 1941), 18.

[104] A section on the town of Saint Mathieu, for example, described a small bar that German sailors had established to provide a spot of Heimat-like cheer. The author contended that this endeavour had been essential for "[a]nyone who has been in a French village bar – here they call anything a bar that looks like a counter with a curly black-haired Mademoiselle behind it – and [anyone who] has sat in the slovenliness and grime of such a place, ... will understand why, out here at a lonely command post on the Atlantic, we built a pub out of a rough old stone hut. It's the oasis at the end of the earth [Finis Terrae]." *Finis Terrae* is an allusion to the Latin-derived French name for the tip of the peninsula, Finistère. Heinrich Droege, "St. Mathieu" in Droege, 32.

[105] Paul Arnold Schulz-Wilmersdorf, *Paris: deutsch gesehen* (Berlin: Hermann Hillger, 1941), 94.

[106] Schulz-Wilmersdorf, *Paris: deutsch gesehen*, 53; Petra Bopp, *Fremde im Visier: Fotoalben aus dem zweiten Weltkrieg* (Bielefeld: Kerber, 2009), 28.

able to step in in France, passing laws that worked decisively to address the Jewish "problem" by sending foreign Jews to French concentration camps. Armed with such a gloss on how to "see" France and its Jewish inhabitants, not to mention German policies towards them, a soldier could, in the words of the guide's foreword signed by Paris Commander Ernst Schaumburg, "shape" his many impressions of Paris into "a lasting memory."[107]

Guides to other areas, including the French Southwest, were more restrained in their tone with regard to race, but they echoed Schaumburg's words about memory. They encouraged soldiers to see themselves as witnesses to, and participants in, a glorious historical moment that required commemoration. Alongside the treatment of race, this is the second feature that stands out in the World War II guides, which linked seeing as a tourist, to assigning meaning to what one saw, and then to remembering it over the longer term. Such volumes offered information about a region's historical and geographical specificities to introduce soldiers to a particular area and to serve as a souvenir, and they also commemorated the experience of occupying the territory and reinforced soldiers' sense of themselves as historical actors. In this way, such books made occupiers feel important, and gave them the sense that what they were doing was valuable to the national community.[108]

Superficially, these publications presented themselves as pleasant leisure-time reading, a souvenir that occupiers might take or send home and leaf through in later years. They typically included a foreword written either by the author or by an important local military commander who served as patron. The foreword introduced the book and distilled the messages it was intended to convey. Often, as in Schaumburg's statement, there was an overt appeal to memory, even to history itself and the need to document today's glory for the future. A typical foreword read: "May this book be a joy to all comrades and in later years a book that recalls the time when we carried out our duty for the Führer and Volk bravely and proudly on Europe's Western Front."[109] In these books, Germans were presented not as invaders and conquerors, but as

---

[107] The whole foreword read "[t]he German soldier takes in a wealth of big impressions during his visit to Paris. This book seeks to assist him in shaping the most important of these into a lasting memory." Ernst Schaumburg, "Foreword" in Schulz-Wilmersdorf, *Paris: deutsch gesehen.*

[108] This was also true of the small number of photographic memoirs, books that attempted to capture occupiers' experiences through images rather than words, mentioned in Chapter 4.

[109] Droege, *Bretagne*, Geleitwort.

righteous and noble warriors, as the publications themselves were consciously understood as tools of memory production.[110]

Beyond gaining a sense of his own historical importance, a soldier reader might inform himself about the area he occupied, and also learn something about French history. History was seen less as intrinsically interesting than as a way to comprehend more fully the significance of German power in the present. As one guide to the Bordeaux area put it, readers should grasp the "fact" that "[f]or its final liberation from being patronized by the French ... the German people must thank Adolf Hitler."[111] Such statements reinforced soldiers' sense of superiority and reminded them that their victories under Hitler's leadership had removed the "stain" of Versailles and redressed the European balance of power after centuries of French domination.

Building on the practical guides and commemorative books, but with scholarly pretensions and a more educated audience in mind, the occupiers also produced a third type of book. This comprised a set of lavishly illustrated works on France's landscape and architecture, particularly its palaces and cathedrals, that were part of a conscious policy to create a "cultural" literature of the occupation and counter the notion that German occupiers were barbarians. An important member of the Paris military administration, Franz Albrecht Medicus, co-edited two such books, called *Kathedralen in Frankreich unter deutschem Schutz* (*Cathedrals in France under German Protection*), and *Schlösser in Frankreich* (*Palaces in France*).[112] For his part, Major Heinz Lorenz, responsible for troop care in Paris, prepared two publications to accompany exhibitions of soldiers' art and photography that took place in Paris in 1941 and 1942, respectively.[113] Like the exhibitions upon which they drew, *Frankreich, ein Erlebnis des deutschen Soldaten* (*France, a German Soldier's Experience*) and *Soldaten fotografieren Frankreich* (*Soldiers photograph France*) brought together visual depictions of France, its people and sights. They documented soldiers' ongoing fascination with the aesthetic aspects of France, and underlined that sightseeing was not only an acceptable

---

[110] Cf. Robert Darnton's comment that "books do not merely recount history; they make it.' Robert Darnton, "What Is the History of Books?," *Daedalus* 111, no. 3: 81.

[111] Armee Oberkommando Bordeaux, *Kleiner Wegweiser*, 7.

[112] Medicus and Hörmann, *Kathedralen in Frankreich unter deutschem Schutz*; Medicus and Hörmann, *Schlösser in Frankreich*. Medicus was head of the military administration in Angers from 1941, moved to Paris in 1942, and was transferred to Athens in 1944. Dr. Hans Hörmann, who wrote the text of both books, was in charge of the "protection" of art treasures in northwestern France.

[113] H. Lorenz, *Frankreich, ein Erlebnis des deutschen Soldaten* (Paris: Odé Verlag, 1942); H. Lorenz, *Soldaten fotografieren Frankreich, ein Bilderbuch mit Erzählungen* (Paris: Wegleiter Verlag, 1943).

activity for occupying soldiers, but also strongly encouraged by the regime. At the same time, they constituted the occupation as culturally constructive, rather than destructive, and created whitewashed memories of it for the future.

Perhaps unsurprisingly, given the tenor of these works, and notwithstanding their longer-term objectives, some voices began to express concern about Germans' fascination with French monuments and sights. In a file note about the rather positive tone of books like *Soldaten fotografieren Frankreich* and *Kathedralen in Frankreich*, German embassy staff in Paris commented that, "[t]hese publications certainly have their value for the German soldier and his relatives, yet on the other hand they represent cultural propaganda for France."[114] In the future, the publication of books, "that engage in one-sided French cultural propaganda" should cease.[115]

It is not clear whether these remarks led to a change in policy. After *Kathedralen in Frankreich* (1942), Medicus's second volume, on palaces, was published as late as 1944, when its editor had already been transferred to Athens. The fact that this volume appeared at all suggests that fundamentally, the occupation authorities continued to approve of such books, or at least that they felt the advantages of publishing them outweighed the risks.

The objective of all these volumes, from the most basic guides through the detailed regional and high-class cultural works, was threefold. First, these texts informed occupiers' perceptions of France and directed their tourism as they planned and undertook it. Posing as factual manuals, they offered practical advice while propagating a racialised vision of France to a greater or lesser degree, and reinforcing soldiers' sense of themselves as significant actors on a world-historical stage. Second, the vividly illustrated guidebooks and coffee-table volumes became mementos for soldiers to share with their families, ensuring that the Home Front participated in Germans' conquest and enjoyment of France vicariously. Finally, such publications created meaning and shaped memory. In a similar way to the *Africabücher* examined by Schilling, they offered models of how to perceive France in the present, and how to remember it in the future.

---

[114] Both works were published by Wegleiter Verlag, which also published *Der deutsche Wegleiter*, discussed above. File note Pr. Nr. 6829/43, Schwendemann for Generalkonsul Gerlach and Gesandten Schleier, German Embassy in Paris, 27 November 1943 (AA: DBP/1141b). Cf. Geiger, *L'image*, 379–80.

[115] File note Pr. Nr. 6829/43, Schwendemann for Generalkonsul Gerlach and Gesandten Schleier, German Embassy in Paris, 27 November 1943 (AA: DBP/1141b).

The relatively peaceful nature of the early occupation years and Hitler's exultation about having overturned Versailles meant that the National Socialist regime invested especially heavily in documenting conquest and occupation in France, and in determining, at least provisionally, how these events would be recalled in the future. Even very late in the occupation, as criticisms were voiced against them, tour guides, commemorative volumes and "scholarly" treatises continued to appear. And, like the books that continued to be published despite concerns about their messages and apparent frivolity, tourism itself persisted, although it might at first glance appear to have had little to do with occupation. Officially part of a military rest and relaxation program, it was justified as a desirable and even necessary companion to duty. Both tourism and the books that accompanied it helped soldiers become oriented and make sense of what they were doing in France. As such, these tools rendered occupation palatable, enabled it to persist, and fostered popular consent in the Third Reich at war.

Consciously deployed by the regime, both tourism and the France books it spawned were also shaped by individual occupiers. The American Shirer had, after all, seen soldiers behaving as tourists immediately after they entered Paris. German authorities' attempts to organise and direct this conduct underlines the reactive quality of their endeavours. Measures to control tourism, like those to control leisure and consumption, became necessary because occupiers' participation in these activities was unavoidable. Although the authorities preferred to see themselves as being in complete control, often the best the regime could do was to direct and steer occupiers' tourism as they undertook it, using it and the books that accompanied it as vehicles to transmit specific messages about France, the French, and soldiers' place in the country. Taken up and used in this way, occupiers' tourism became, for a time, a valuable tool to bolster consent and further the pursuit of the war.

As time passed, however, the deployment of tourism and publications that presented a relatively benign view of the occupation became a double-edged sword. As this book's later chapters demonstrate, the occupation regime proved slow to shift its policies and too weak, or unwilling, to crack down on "softer" interactions with France even when they undermined its ability to respond to rising insecurity. Before attending to the breakdown of order and the growing tensions between pleasure and violence, however, we turn first to photography, the ubiquitous accompaniment to tourism that functioned alongside it to construct, this time visually, the way that occupiers "saw" and experienced France.

4 Capturing Experiences
Photography and Photo Books

In 1942, an exhibition of occupiers' amateur photography called *Soldiers photograph and film* was held in Paris. Its self-proclaimed objective was to bring together the best photographs taken by members of the German military stationed in France. "Of course everyone would like to hold onto what he has experienced in what is surely the most meaningful segment of his life, and to take it home as a visible memento for later," wrote Heinz Lorenz, an administrator responsible for military support services and the editor of the exhibition's companion volume.[1] The vast numbers of soldiers' photographs that have survived from France suggest that Lorenz was right. Many occupiers did want to hold on to what they had experienced, to take it home as a "visible memento," or perhaps more aptly, a visible trophy of war. Hitler's regime encouraged photography in France, seeing it as a leisure activity for soldiers that perpetuated images of the country that aligned with National Socialist goals.

The resulting photographs raise various questions. Their most striking feature is their apparent banality (Figure 4.1).[2] Images of landscapes, soldiers' leisure activities, and historical monuments predominate

---

[1] Lorenz, *Soldaten fotografieren*, preface. See also Chapter 3 and Krob, "Paris Through Enemy Eyes: The Wehrmacht in Paris 1940–1944," 14 ff.

[2] Frances Guerin points out that "banality" in this context does not, as in Hannah Arendt's formulation, describe a bureaucratic, routine approach to genocide. Rather, it refers to a kind of "bourgeois normality" visible in soldiers' photos "that framed the stress of war." *Through Amateur Eyes: Film and Photography in Nazi Germany* (Minneapolis: University of Minnesota Press, 2011), 69. Maiken Umbach has noted that amateur photographs from the Third Reich more generally often "resemble similar scenes photographed in the decades before and after the Nazi period, as well as comparable photographs in British and American albums of the same era." "Selfhood, Place, and Ideology in German Photo Albums, 1933–1945," *Central European History* 48, no. Special Issue 03 (September 2015): 336. Historiographical issues are summarised later in this chapter. See also Julia Torrie, "Visible Trophies of War: German Occupiers' Photographic Perceptions of France, 1940–44" in *The Ethics of Seeing: 20th Century German Documentary Photography Reconsidered*, eds. Jennifer Evans, Paul Betts, and Stefan-Ludwig Hoffmann (New York: Berghahn, 2018).

Figure 4.1 Domestic scene from an anonymous soldier's photo album.
Anonymous Album, 35, Deutsch-Russisches Museum Berlin-Karlshorst,
KH 203442_35-3.

among the tens of thousands of photographs taken by occupying soldiers, while photographs that refer openly to war, let alone show violence or atrocities, are rare.[3] No doubt partly because of this,
photographs from France have not received the same scholarly attention
as those taken on the Eastern Front.[4] Yet snapshots from France
are worth examining for several reasons. The fact that soldiers took
so many pictures invites us to consider the purposes of photography
in the context of a military occupation. Although the French occupation seemed "strange" and "peaceful" compared to German fighting

---

[3] The focus here is on images of the occupation itself, rather than the invasion of France in
spring 1940. Photographs from the campaign and the period immediately following it show
greater evidence of brutality, including destroyed and burning structures, and
propaganda-influenced images, notably of African prisoners of war. See Bopp, *Fremde
im Visier*, 2009, 53–67.

[4] For instance, Peter Jahn indicated that the exhibit *Fotofeldpost* focused on images from the
Eastern not Western Front because the former highlighted the "tension between the
extreme war situation and a photographic habitus that was shaped by private life." Jahn,
"Vorwort," 7. This tension was also present in photographs from the West, though
perhaps less obviously so.

elsewhere, the discordance between what soldiers were actually doing – occupying a neighbouring country militarily and oppressing the popula- tion – and the ways they represented their role through photography was stark. What motifs did occupiers favour, and why? Beyond the question of what they actually photographed, what made photography so appealing to these soldiers? Once taken, how did their images work together with other materials to shape ideas about, and memories of, the German experience in France?

Occupiers' photographs suggest that photography played an import- ant role in occupiers' attempts to come to terms with their position. Amateur photography and official publications interacted to sketch the contours of the occupation for contemporaries, and to shape memories of it for the future. For individual men, photography filled spare time, documented interesting life experiences, smoothed over the transition from soldier to occupier, and may have offered a way to distance oneself from violence. For the regime, it was a means of teaching soldiers how to see occupied France, and it planted the seeds of memories for the future. Identifying key themes, and probing the alignments and divergences between the photographs occupiers were encouraged to take, and the images they actually recorded, offers new opportunities to understand not only how official views were propa- gated, but also how German soldiers constructed themselves as occu- pying men. With this goal in mind, this chapter first establishes major themes for discussion, surveys historiographical and methodological issues briefly, and outlines the basic parameters for occupiers' photog- raphy. Then it examines photography from the perspective of the individual and moves on to explore published images and the regime's attempts to exploit and influence amateur photography. It concludes with discussion of the complex interplay between amateur and official, and between German and French photographic visions of the occupa- tion of France.

The German occupation of France was characterised by a curious contradiction between the superficially "pleasant" aspects of occupying a country with so many opportunities for leisure and pleasure, and the violence and oppression inherent in a military takeover. This contradic- tion manifested itself in soldiers' letters and diaries, and was particularly obvious in photographs. The predominance of photographs of seemingly "harmless" occupier activities, like sightseeing, confirms that the leisure, consumption and tourism discussed in previous chapters were key parts of occupiers' experience. When soldiers' photographs documented leis- ure activities, the putative "truth-telling" function of the medium made these images particularly effective in creating and disseminating the illusion that Germans' presence in France was harmless; that they were guests or tourists rather than warring men.[5]

At the same time, occupiers' photographs demonstrate how intimately the leisure they enjoyed was linked to everyday systematic oppression. A happy group of soldiers such as that depicted in Figure 4.1 was sitting around a French table, having displaced a local family from its requisitioned home. Table, chairs and refreshments had doubtless either been requisitioned, or plundered outright. On the same album pages, two other images show the front of a manor house with a German pillbox, and its rear gardens. On one level, an occupier had simply documented where he was staying and recorded a celebration with his comrades. On another, he had exposed the fundamental indignity and brutality of being occupied, laid bare the takeover of domestic space and preserved images of a stranger's home for all eternity in his own album of souvenirs.

Not only did photographs record the intimate details of occupation, but photography itself extended possession and exercised dominance. Each time a soldier admired, then snapped a picture of, a French landscape, he exercised both the privilege of looking at conquered land, and a freedom to photograph out of doors that had been denied the French population since mid-September 1940.[6] Photographs also served as an important way to see and come to terms with France as a foreign country and oneself as an occupier. Amateur photographers imitated and disseminated visual themes drawn from official sources; in turn, these amateur images were picked up and reused by the regime, which thus exploited the perceived "veracity" of soldiers' photographic productions. Photography functioned during the occupation (and continued to function after 1944) as a delivery system for a sanitised occupation story that deliberately occluded the period's darker aspects. Exploring how photography was used in this context speaks to broader debates about the power of images and the interaction of leisure and violence as well as occupying soldiers' perceptions and wartime mentalities.

Although some images may have been shared privately, the albums and boxes containing German soldiers' amateur photographs often lay in attic storage rooms, untouched for decades. In the 1970s, social historians began to contemplate these images as historical sources, but it took

---

[5] Susan Sontag, *Regarding the Pain of Others* (New York: Picador, 2003), 47.

[6] A law of 16 September 1940 forbade photography out of doors except by professional photographers and members of the German occupation forces. Françoise Denoyelle, "Walter Dreizner, un amateur sous influence: des télécommunications à la photographie," *Francia* 33, no. 3 (2006): 89. Catherine Clark has explored French attempts to reclaim the visual representation of France at the Liberation in "Capturing the Moment."

until the 1990s and the rise of a new interest in how photography participates in processes of remembering and memory-formation for a public discussion of images, including those of amateur photographers, to take place.[7] Perhaps because photographs are artifacts at the frontier between material history and written texts, much of the initial research addressing them came from outside "traditional" scholarly history, and some of the most thorough explorations of soldiers' photographs have taken the form of museum exhibits.[8] Most notably, photo historian Petra Bopp assembled a significant collection of soldiers' albums in *Fremde im Visier (Focus on Strangers: Photo Albums of World War II)*, an exhibit that explored how soldiers formulated their war experiences in photographs and photo albums, and looked at the role that amateur images played and continue to play in the shaping of memories.[9] Bopp emphasised that soldiers' private images can be used primarily to understand "how war was seen – not how it was," and she used interviews to learn more about the context of soldiers' photographs, recovering important background details that would otherwise have been lost.[10]

---

[7] An important early contribution was Sybil Milton, "The Camera as Weapon: Documentary Photography and the Holocaust," *Simon Wiesenthal Center Annual* 1 (January 1984): 45–68. See Peter Burke, *Eyewitnessing: The Uses of Images as Historical Evidence* (Ithaca: Cornell University Press, 2001). For a brief overview of the development of visual history, Gerhard Paul, *Visual History: ein Studienbuch* (Göttingen: Vandenhoeck & Ruprecht, 2006), 13.

[8] Bopp, *Fremde im Visier*, 2009, 7. The controversial *Verbrechen der Wehrmacht (Crimes of the Wehrmacht)* exhibit in Germany brought discussions about the authenticity and uses of amateur photographs as historical sources into the public domain. Hannes Heer and Klaus Naumann, eds., *Vernichtungskrieg: Verbrechen der Wehrmacht 1941–1944* (Hamburg: Hamburger Edition, 1995); Christian Hartmann, Johannes Hürter, and Ulrike Jureit, eds., *Verbrechen der Wehrmacht: Bilanz einer Debatte* (München: Beck, 2005); Guerin, *Amateur Eyes*, 41–5; 85–91. Later, the Deutsch-Russisches Museum Berlin-Karlshorst developed exhibits on wartime photography, including one about amateurs called *Foto-Feldpost: geknipste Kriegserlebnisse 1939–1945* (Photo Field Post: Snapshots of War Experiences, 1939–1945). Contributors to the accompanying catalogue addressed key questions about how images might be used to understand soldiers' attitudes and perceptions. Peter Jahn and Ulrike Schmiegelt, eds., *Foto-Feldpost: geknipste Kriegserlebnisse 1939–1945* (Berlin: Elephanten Press, 2000). Amateur photography in the long twentieth century was the subject of "Knipser." Timm Starl, *Knipser: die Bildgeschichte der privaten Fotografie in Deutschland und Österreich von 1880 bis 1980* (München: Koehler & Amelang, 1995).

[9] *Fremde im Visier* opened in June 2009 in Oldenburg. It was shown in the German cities of Munich, Frankfurt am Main, Jena, Peine, in Graz and Vienna in Austria, and in Delft in the Netherlands. See www.fremde-im-visier.de.

[10] Bopp, *Fremde im Visier*, 2009, 10. The roughly 150 amateur albums in *Fremde im Visier* were all scrupulously documented. My own investigation of occupiers' photography focuses on broad mentalities and perceptions, using anonymous, as well as well-documented, albums. The former are used to confirm, for example, that themes identified in the latter were widespread rather than simply representative of individual tastes.

Bopp's focus was on perceptions and mentalities, and the exhibit's richest moments juxtaposed images of violence and brutality with superficially banal photographs of leisure pursuits and the everyday lives of soldiers. The most striking single element was a probing examination of a treacherously beautiful image that actually showed a local woman being driven across a river as a human mine-sweeper. This image highlighted the ambiguity of soldiers' photographs, their openness to (mis)interpretation, and the way that their meanings change depending on the context.[11]

If early studies used photographs as evidence of the past, and scholars subsequently discussed images as reflections of attitudes and perceptions, today experts are increasingly aware that, as Gerhard Paul has put it, "[i]mages are not simply reflections of reality, but also influence the historical process."[12] This chapter develops Bopp's inquiries about mentalities and perceptions, examining not only how photography was used as a tool to exercise power, but also how individuals deployed it to construct their experiences visually. It highlights the specific problems of apparently "harmless" images from the occupation which, because of their immediacy and the familiarity of their form, and because they were often taken by amateurs, worked particularly effectively to disseminate a "whitewashed" vision of the occupation of France. The act of photography and the images that emerged shaped occupiers' understanding of their role, influenced the tenor of the occupation, and formed memories of it to the present day.

By 1939, amateur photography was widespread in Germany, and perhaps particularly so among soldiers. Cameras and photography had become standard tools for viewing and understanding new places, as well as preserving memories of one's experiences for later. In World War II, a significant number of soldiers, not only officers, went to the Front with the tourist's talisman – a camera. Since, according to photo historian Timm Starl, some seven million Germans had cameras at the beginning of World War II and young men were among the most enthusiastic photographers, historian Bernd Boll estimates that more than 10 per cent of soldiers probably had a camera. Those who did not

---

[11] Bopp, *Fremde im Visier*, 100–106.
[12] Gerhard Paul, following Heike Talkenberger, *Visual History*, 9. In this sense, photographs do not simply "recount" but also "make" history in the same way that Robert Darnton argued books do, as noted in Chapter 3. Darnton, "What Is the History of Books?," 81.

initially own one often acquired such a device through plunder in the occupied territories.[13] On the day the French asked for an armistice, American journalist William Shirer commented that "most of the German troops act like naive tourists … it seems funny, but every German soldier carries a camera."[14] If, as Susan Sontag contends, "to photograph is to appropriate the thing photographed," what were the implications of such widespread photography by soldiers beginning an occupation?[15] For these occupiers, photography became an essential part of seeing the land, and of "capturing" it in the figurative and in the literal sense.[16]

Despite the ubiquity of photography and photographs, historians of the occupation, uneasy about the distinctive aspects of visual sources, have neither analysed them consistently, nor used them as a window into how Germans saw (and were encouraged to see) occupied Europe. They are in this sense a virtually untapped source.[17] Basic questions about authenticity complicate analysis, and often the subject, photographer, location and date of a photograph are unknown. Certainly, many soldiers went to the front with a camera, and even more ordered photographs from their friends or from the Propaganda Companies, which had so many requests for reprints of their shots that, as early as the end of 1939, they were allowed to claim ten pfennigs per picture to cover their costs. Soon, the ten pfennigs became twenty pfennigs, and by spring 1940, distributing photos had become such a big part of Propaganda Companies' job that the OKW had three photo labs in Berlin working exclusively to fill soldiers' orders for prints.[18] Another sign of photography's ongoing popularity was that the authorities set up a special photo house for the

---

[13] Starl, *Knipser*, 98 cited in Bernd Boll, "Vom Album ins Archiv: zur Überlieferung privater Fotografien aus dem Zweiten Weltkrieg" in *Mit der Kamera bewaffnet: Krieg und Fotografie*, ed. Anton Holzer (Marburg: Jonas, 2003), 167.

[14] Shirer, 17 June 1940, 328; Confino, "Traveling," 109.

[15] Sontag, *On Photography*, 4.

[16] Susan Sontag remarked on the overlapping vocabulary of fighting and photography: "shoot," "aim," "capture." Sontag, *On Photography*, 44.

[17] Bernd Boll has commented that, "[s]ince place, time, context and photographer have been passed down for only a fraction of photographs, historians quickly reach the limits of their usual methodology and therefore often downplay the usefulness of amateur photography as an historical source." Bernd Boll, "Das Adlerauge des Soldaten: Zur Fotopraxis deutscher Amateure im Zweiten Weltkrieg," *Fotogeschichte* 22, no. 85/86 (2002): 75. Despite such concerns, the potential of photography as a source is apparent, for example, in Elissa Mailänder, "Making Sense of a Rape Photograph: Sexual Violence as Social Performance on the Eastern Front, 1939–1944," *Journal of the History of Sexuality* 26, no. 3 (September 2017): 489–520. See also the special issue edited by Elizabeth Harvey and Maiken Umbach, "Photography and Twentieth-Century German History" *Central European History* 48, no. 3 (September 2015).

[18] Boll, "Vom Album," 169–70.

German forces (Fotohaus für die deutsche Wehrmacht) in Paris in late 1942. This establishment developed negatives, produced prints, distributed film, took soldiers' portraits and offered an apparently well-patronised "support and advice centre for the photographing soldier."[19] Photography was nearly as much a part of occupiers' experience as writing letters, and may in fact allow us to glimpse a broader range of perspectives than traditional written media.

Equally, because photographing and album-compilation were separate acts, and the photographs present in soldiers' albums not necessarily taken by the men in whose collections they appear, reading these images requires sensitivity to their mobility and to the ways their meanings and purposes changed depending on context. Even when they were not direct duplicates, soldiers' photographs often repeated themselves, with similar themes and compositions appearing across dozens of shots. The insistence with which particular themes and tropes appeared and reappeared invites attention, as does photographers' decision to omit other possible subjects. Even in anonymous and repetitive albums with few titles or explanations, the choice of images to preserve is significant, as is the thematic or chronological organisation of the shots.[20] Given the ubiquity of photographs and the role they played in how World War II's soldiers perceived and interpreted foreign lands, photographs are key sources for understanding soldiers' attitudes and perceptions, and the regime's attempts to influence both.[21]

Unsurprisingly, there were rules about what a German soldier could and could not photograph. Briefly summarised, it was forbidden to photograph anything directly related to fighting or defence, and anything at all in areas controlled by the navy, including bridges, locks and ports. Photographs that would damage the "reputation" of the Wehrmacht were not allowed, nor were those depicting executions.[22] There were not supposed to be any amateur photographs of accidents and war

---

[19] "Ein Jahr Fotohaus für die deutsche Wehrmacht," *Der deutsche Wegleiter*, no. 84 (November 20, 1943): 28.

[20] Historians working with such photographs seek what Helmut Lethen has called the order "of the private memory warehouse," trying to determine how this order functioned and what it may indicate about soldiers' attitudes and perceptions. Helmut Lethen, "Der Text der Historiographie und der Wunsch nach einer physikalischen Spur: das Problem der Fotografie in den beiden Wehrmachtsausstellungen," *Zeitgeschichte* 29, no. 2 (2002): 84.

[21] Soldiers' letters raise similar questions. See Klaus Latzel, "Wehrmachtssoldaten zwischen 'Normalität' und NS-Ideologie, oder Was sucht die Forschung in der Feldpost?," ed. Rolf-Dieter Müller and Hans-Erich Volkmann, *Die Wehrmacht: Zwischen Mythos und Realität* (Munich: Oldenbourg, 1999), 573–88.

[22] Punishments included destruction of the offending negatives. Ulrike Schmiegelt, "Macht Euch um mich keine Sorgen...," in *Foto-Feldpost: geknipste Kriegserlebnisse*

damage on the German side, and the Paris Commander issued a specific prohibition in March 1942 against photographing bomb-damaged parts of the city.[23] These rules notwithstanding, both the images soldiers took and scholarly interviews with veterans suggest that Wehrmacht members were poorly informed about the regulations, and that these were not heavily enforced.[24]

The lack of enforcement was indicative of the Third Reich's larger desire to encourage and exploit, rather than discourage soldiers' photography. In theory, anyone could pick up a camera, and any subject might thereby be captured. Aware of the inherent freedom in photography, British poet W.H. Auden viewed "amateur snapshots" as "the only decent photographs" and praised photography as "the democratic art."[25] Particularly in the context of an occupation, when it was easy for a German to acquire a camera, photography became remarkably accessible and widespread. Yet the very "democracy" of the photographic medium was problematic for an authoritarian state, a circumstance underlined by the fact that the Soviet Union forbade photography by individual soldiers (though it used many propaganda photographers).[26] Instead of forbidding amateur photography, the National Socialists preferred to intervene in and direct photographic practice, exploiting amateur photography as a leisure activity, a documentary medium, and a way to exercise power.

It is clear, then, that individual German occupiers photographed extensively while in France. Apart from the ready availability of cameras and the men's own fascination with technology, why did they do so? What purposes did photography serve? Regrettably, soldiers only rarely explained why they took photographs. In the case of most anonymous

---

1939–1945, ed. Peter Jahn and Ulrike Schmiegelt (Berlin: Elephanten Press, 2000), 25, 74–5.

[23] This regulation was likely prompted by the destructive bombing of the Renault plant in Paris suburb Boulogne-Billancourt in early March. Notice from Commander of greater Paris to units in the city, 11 March 1942 (AN: 40 AJ/451).

[24] Schmiegelt, "Macht Euch," 25.

[25] W. H. Auden, letter to Erika Mann Auden, in W. H. Auden and L. MacNeice, *Letters from Iceland* (London: Faber and Faber, 1937), 137, cited in Lara Feigel, "'The Photograph My Scull Might Take': Bombs, Time and Photography in British and German Second World War Literature" in *Bombing, States and Peoples in Western Europe, 1940–1945*, ed. Claudia Baldoli, Andrew Knapp, and Richard Overy (New York: Continuum, 2011), 122.

[26] Jahn, "Vorwort," 7. This rule too appears to have been widely disregarded. Amateur photographs survive from the latter part of the war, once Red Army soldiers entered German territory and obtained cameras through plunder. Stefan-Ludwig Hoffmann, "Gazing at Ruins: German Defeat as Visual Experience," *Journal of Modern History* 9, no. 3 (2011): 339.

and undocumented albums, moreover, there is no way to evaluate whether soldiers took more (or different) photographs as occupiers than they might have taken in civilian life. Still, by drawing on the consciously composed photographs themselves in the context of other contemporary sources, we can begin to unravel not only why soldiers recorded specific images, but also what photography in general "gave" soldiers and the occupation regime.[27]

First, and most obviously, photography was a form of leisure, a hobby and a type of entertainment. As in peacetime, it took men's thoughts away from their obligations, offered a distraction and made them members of a "club" with its own technical expertise and arcane knowledge of apertures and shutter speeds. Photography opened up a fraternal world of exchange and camaraderie to which not only those who owned a camera, but also those who purchased and collected others' snapshots, might belong.[28] At home on leave, compiling photographs into albums filled a soldier's time, maintained a link with fighting comrades, and fostered a sense of satisfaction about the things one had seen and done.[29] Soldiers on active duty could not carry large numbers of photos with them, yet they sought to preserve these keepsakes and memories for later. They sent exposed films home to their (often female) relatives with specific instructions to have these developed and to save or return the prints. In this way, women too shared in men's experiences, and participated in the production of war memory through photography.

---

[27] While recognising the specificity of these visual sources, this chapter places occupiers' amateur photography alongside other "ego-documents" like letters and diaries, and contextualises them further using contemporary publications and ephemera.

[28] The strongly masculine make-up of the occupying forces, combined with the fact that most amateur and professional photographers of the 1930s and 1940s were already men, meant that most photographers in France were also men. *Soldaten fotografieren Frankreich* included two photographs by "DRK-Wachführerin von Koehl," but women photographers were likely a very small minority. Lorenz, *Soldaten fotografieren*. Among professional propaganda photographers there were some women, like Liselotte Purpur. Elizabeth Harvey, "'Ich war überall': Die NS-Propagandaphotographin Liselotte Purpur" in *Volksgenossinnen: Frauen in der NS-Volksgemeinschaft*, ed. Sybille Steinbacher (Göttingen: Wallstein Verlag, 2007), 138.

[29] Guerin claims that "when [amateur soldiers' photos] were placed in albums and captioned, it was usually done in retrospect at the war's end." *Amateur Eyes*, 38. This may have been true of images from the Eastern Front, but the context-specific sarcasm of captions in some albums from France, and other evidence, suggests that soldiers put these together during the war, perhaps during home leaves. See album of Friedrich Siebert, discussed over the next few pages, and the album of Johann Wetjen in Bopp, *Fremde im Visier*, 2009, 15. Boll, "Vom Album," 174. Petra Bopp, "'...ich habe ja nun aus Russland genug Bilder': Soldatenalltag im Sucher eines Amateurfotografen im Zweiten Weltkrieg" in *Der engagierte Blick. Fotoamateure und Autorenfotografen dokumentieren den Alltag*, ed. Irene Ziehe and Ulrich Haegele (Berlin: LIT Verlag, 2007), 73–4; Bopp, *Fremde im Visier*, 2009.

Not only was photography itself a leisure activity, but a good number of the soldiers' photographs also document leisure time. Men photographed themselves sitting around with friends relaxing, celebrating a birthday, promotion, or other event. Sometimes, the photos depict a prank or joke that reflects a certain kind of jocular enlisted man's humour. In many ways, these photos are no different from those young men might have taken at home in peacetime. They draw on a repertoire of image types and conceptual frames that predated 1939, and even 1933, raising questions about the degree to which the Nazi regime was able to change representational paradigms given soldiers' familiarity with other conventions.[30] For Peter Jahn, the soldiers' ongoing need to feel connected to "normal" civilian life motivated these images, making it "not surprising that the largest part of the photos looks like the continuation of the family album in military life."[31] Ordinary and embedded in convention as they may seem, these photographs show the value soldiers placed on leisure time, even in the service, an effort Jahn is surely right to connect with the desire to retain a sense of normalcy in the face of war.

Photography was, however, not only a leisure activity. It also served to document. Satisfying a collector's urge, photographers accumulated snapshots as records of their activities, testaments to their exploits. As suggested, the many images of men enjoying a good meal are, on the one hand, reminiscent of "normal" peacetime depictions of family or other celebrations. On the other hand, they confirm that plundering France of food, drink and other goods was part of an occupier's experience, even his duty.[32] A remarkable photograph in the *Fremde im Visier* exhibit shows a quiet lake, captioned "Peacefully rests the lake" (Still ruht der See) (Figure 4.2). Only an interview by Bopp with the album's owner revealed that this lake hid goods occupiers had stolen while searching houses in a nearby village. Their unit commander had apparently got wind of the theft, and the men jettisoned the items in the lake before they could be caught red-handed.[33] The photograph served to remember the occasion and perhaps also as a kind of "treasure map" indicating the location of the loot.

The theme of plunder is likewise present in photographs of damaged weaponry, an obvious allusion to the French defeat, and at the same time a

---

[30] Cf. Umbach, "Selfhood," 336–7, 364.
[31] Peter Jahn, "Bilder im Kopf – Bilder auf dem Papier" in *Foto-Feldpost: geknipste Kriegserlebnisse 1939–1945*, ed. Peter Jahn and Ulrike Schmiegelt (Berlin: Elephanten Press Verlag, 2000), 9.
[32] The exchange rate of 20 francs to one Reichsmark in France favoured German consumption and exploitation. Cf. Aly, *Volksstaat*, 114–32. See Chapter 2.
[33] Bopp, *Fremde im Visier*, 2009, 15–16.

Figure 4.2 An apparently pastoral photograph captioned "Peacefully rests the lake" (Still ruht der See). In fact, the lake hid goods occupiers had stolen from a nearby village.
Johann Wetjen, Album 1, Frankreich 1940, Wetjen family.

celebration of German victory. Soldiers' photographs depict individual French defences and military hardware, and they show whole fields full of captured tanks or other vehicles. The mood of some of these shots is documentary, while others evince a spirit of triumphalism, for instance depicting satisfied and confident members of the German forces standing next to damaged equipment, with the title caption "booty" (Beute) (Figure 4.3).[34]

Still, images with directly war-related themes do not make up the bulk of the snapshots taken by occupiers once France had fallen. Rather, the leisure-time photos already described, and a sub-category of what might be called "sightseeing" photographs, predominate. These images are present in albums from other theatres of war as well, but they seem especially prevalent in the albums from France.[35] The duration of the occupation, its relative "peacefulness," and France's position, even before the war, as a desirable tourist destination, helped to ensure that

[34] Friedrich Siebert, "Bilder zum Westfeldzug 1940" (BArch: N 586/8).
[35] Albums from other occupied areas with "Aryan" populations, like Norway and Holland, show greater similarities with those from France. Petra Bopp, personal communication, 12 December 2016.

Beute.

Figure 4.3 Photographs with faded caption "booty" (Beute), 1940.
Album of Friedrich Siebert, "Bilder zum Westfeldzug 1940" (Images
of the Western campaign, 1940) (BArch: N 586/8).

this was so. The predominance of non-violent images from France also
points to the unique aspects of this occupation, including the relatively
high standing at least initially accorded the French among occupied
peoples, the rhetoric and real efforts towards collaboration with them,
and the desire on the Germans' part to characterise the status quo in
France after 1940 as "permanent." Together, these elements fostered a
freer and more open relationship with France and the French than was
characteristic of other occupied areas. The "sightseeing" images, moreover, illustrate the deepening rift between the apparent tranquillity of the

French occupation (a vision that these photographs themselves helped create and perpetuate) and its increasing brutality as time went on.

On one level, soldiers' photographs of historical monuments simply signalled their curiosity about the foreign areas they "visited" during their service. At the same time, through these images, one can observe a kind of transposition of the soldier to tourist. Shirer made his comments about Germans seeming like "naïve tourists" at the very start of the occupation, but soldiers' tendency to behave like tourists persisted as time went on. As we have seen, the regime encouraged it, for it provided soldiers with a convenient framework for perceiving themselves and relating to a foreign environment. With a camera in hand instead of a gun, they could imagine themselves welcome visitors rather than hostile invaders. Sontag has noted that for tourists, "[t]he very activity of taking pictures is soothing and assuages general feelings of disorientation that are likely to be exacerbated by travel." "Unsure of other responses," she comments, "they take a picture."[36] Sontag's assertions about the comforting value of photography ring true for anyone abroad, including occupying soldiers, who may, ironically, have felt rather vulnerable. Taking pictures was a way to disguise this unease, part of a transformation from perceiving oneself as a soldier to imagining oneself as a tourist.[37] In most images, France came across not as a recent battleground or hostile enemy land, but as a pastoral and even peaceful place, full of quaint peasants and stately historical monuments. Seeing themselves as tourists and France as an object of aesthetic consumption helped to define both in ways that rendered occupation easier. Soldiers could distance themselves from the inherent violation and violence of their presence on foreign soil. They photographed less what was actually happening than what they wanted to see; less what they may actually have been doing, than what they wanted to imagine they were doing.[38] Occupiers' photographs were thus more than signs of curiosity – they postulated an alternate interpretation of the German presence in France and perhaps served, like tourism itself, as a coping mechanism for men facing and trying to come to terms with "foreignness" and unease.

The "touristic" photographs taken by occupying soldiers also expressed their dominance. Bernd Hüppauf has pointed out that, "[i]n principle, the photographer finds himself in a privileged position of power vis à vis his target." Hüppauf draws attention to the way photographs of victims of German brutality in the East underlined the inequality inherent in these power relations and increased the privileged position

---

[36] Sontag, *On Photography*, 10.   [37] See Chapter 3.
[38] Cf. Sontag, *On Photography*, 6.

Figure 4.4 Sightseeing occupiers on the Eiffel Tower.
Anonymous, Album 3, author's collection.

of the photographer.[39] A similar phenomenon was at work in the superficially more benign photographs from the Western occupation. Each time they pressed their shutter releases, occupying soldiers "captured" France and its inhabitants anew, reinforcing the power relations inherent in a military takeover. A favourite theme, for instance, was that of soldiers standing on the Eiffel Tower or other high point, defeated Paris literally at their feet (Figure 4.4).[40] Being able to photograph out of doors, when the French were not allowed to do so, was itself a mark of occupiers' dominance.[41] Each photographic event created or reinforced a relationship of subjugation between the photographer and his subject. The French

[39] Bernd Hüppauf, "Der entleerte Blick hinter der Kamera" in *Vernichtungskrieg: Verbrechen der Wehrmacht 1941–1944*, eds. Hannes Heer and Klaus Naumann (Hamburg: Hamburger Edition, 1995), 515. Cf. Guerin, *Amateur Eyes*, 72.
[40] See, e.g. Konvolut Walter Gerloff, Einzelfoto, "Zwei deutsche Offiziere auf dem Arc de Triomphe," Paris 1940, in Bopp, *Fremde im Visier*, 2009, 26.
[41] French citizens who tried to photograph outdoors were viewed with suspicion. In October 1941, a young French brother and sister, apparently on holiday from Paris, were apprehended by the Feldkommandant for taking photographs in the reserved coastal zone of Calvados. They were held for questioning, fined 50 francs and let go. Letter from Préfet du Calvados to M. de Brinon, Délégué Général du Gouvernement

were not at liberty to remove themselves from Germans' photographs any more than the land itself was able to avoid being claimed.[42] Only the conditions of war had brought these men to France, and each image they captured was a form of tribute paid by the defeated. Through photography, Germans created themselves as occupiers, and the French people, landscape, and historical structures as objects of occupation.

Photography, then, assisted soldiers in positioning themselves as conquerors. As a leisure activity, it fostered a sense of normalcy and connected them to civilian life. Taking its value as a coping mechanism, a way to remove the "disorientation" of travel one step further, photography surely also offered a way for soldiers to distance themselves from the violence inherent in their position. In the context of perpetrators' photos of German violence in the East, Hüppauf has established the concept of an "emptied gaze" (entleerten Blick) behind the camera, arguing that soldiers tried to create a world on the other side of the lens from which they could imagine they were separate, to which they did not belong.[43] In seemingly benign pictures of France, in contrast, occupying soldiers sought to create an alternate reality, behind the camera, to which they imagined they did belong.[44] This was a fabricated peaceful world of sunlit landscapes and friendly peasants, in which Germans were welcome tourists and neighbours, not invaders.

When it came to overt violence, putting themselves behind the camera may have allowed soldiers to believe that they were merely observers, rather than participants in oppression. Even as it expressed dominance,

Français dans les Territoires Occupés, 14 October 1941 (Archives Départementales du Calvados: 5 W 8/3).

[42] Sybil Milton noted that, "even the private photographs [of Propaganda Company members] had compliant subjects, vulnerable to the whims of the Nazi photographer." Milton, "Camera as Weapon," 51. Occasionally, images documented their subjects' reluctance to be photographed, as when they showed art sellers in Montmartre with their berets pulled down to cover their faces. Petra Bopp, "Fremde im Visier: Private Fotografien von Wehrmachtssoldaten" in *Mit der Kamera bewaffnet: Krieg und Fotografie*, ed. Anton Holzer (Marburg: Jonas Verlag, 2003), 28, 34.

[43] Hüppauf writes that,"[i]mages taken from the perspective of no-where [i.e. with an emptied gaze] are an expression of the hope of duplicating, with the camera, a reality from which the photographer is distanced by a clear line of separation and upon which his camera can therefore impose its own order. The desire to maintain a space for the self that remains unaffected by the documented horrors creates the necessity of emptying the gaze by desensitizing and de-corporealizing it." Bernd Hüppauf, "Emptying the Gaze: Framing Violence through the Viewfinder," *New German Critique*, no. 72 (Fall 1997): 32.

[44] In this sense, occupiers' photographs functioned like travel narratives, which as Mark Hewitson notes (following Samuel Hynes), seek to make their readers feel at home in a foreign land. The difference in this case is that the reader of these images was also their photographer, who sought to make both himself and his "readers" feel at home. Hewitson M, "'I Witnesses,'" 313.

therefore, photography may also have revealed soldiers' longing for a less hostile environment. This longing was occasionally expressed in writing, as we have seen in the letters of Heinrich Böll, who regretted losing his "Sundays" and yearned for the "pleasure of going abroad in peacetime."[45] Admittedly, the literary Böll may not have represented a typical occupier, but his words suggest that at some level, soldiers' photography was not just an expression of dominance. It may also have reflected a deep desire to return to a peacetime existence.

Perhaps, at the same time, the peaceful, apparently "harmless" quality of most soldiers' photographs from France was simply due to the way amateur photographers practise photography. Amateurs typically are not interested in realistic or dispassionate documentation. They photograph what is striking, shocking or beautiful, what stands out, and often what they are supposed to see, rather than what may actually be there. In Eastern Europe, which the National Socialists did not consider merited touristic interest, some Wehrmacht members claimed that there was nothing worth photographing. When they did take pictures, these images reflected and reinforced their racist worldview. They sometimes also documented shocking scenes of violence in snapshots that circulated privately or were kept hidden for decades at war's end.[46] In France, probably because the real violence of the occupation was less apparent to many occupiers at least initially, and because this oddly peaceful-seeming occupation seemed less distant from their everyday civilian lives, soldier-photographers readily fell back on standard forms. Although the violence inherent in occupiers' position emerges in other ways, photographs of outright violence are rare to non-existent in amateur photo albums from France once the period of the invasion had ended. These albums were shaped by the fact that, between the armistice and mid-1941, open violence in France was relatively unusual; by the time the deportations on the one hand, the aerial bombings and resistance attacks on the other, grew difficult to ignore, many amateur photographers were probably out of film. Finally, in the same way that letters from the field were not only censored by the military authorities, but also self-censored by soldiers who did not consider it appropriate to share the full horrors of war with their families, photographs intended for broader viewing depicted only the pleasant aspects of the men's military service.[47] Instead

---

[45] See Chapter 3. Böll, *Briefe*, 1:25 September 1942, 484.
[46] Elissa Mailänder analyses one such image in "Making Sense." On occupiers' attitudes towards photography in Eastern Europe, see also Chapter 6.
[47] On self-censorship, see Bopp, "Soldatenalltag im Sucher," 83, 90; Mailänder, "Making Sense," 407–8.

Figure 4.5 Propaganda image of soldiers clearing the "Vieux Port" neighbourhood of Marseilles, soon to be razed.
BArch: Bild 101I-027–1480–02 / Wolfgang Vennemann.

of depicting open violence, these images abstracted war's brutality to the level of a gravestone, a dead friend's portrait, or a funeral notice from the newspaper.

When violence did appear, its treatment in occupiers' photographs was often quite oblique. For example, many pictures taken by Propaganda Company member Wolfgang Vennemann during the razing of the Vieux Port district of Marseilles depict how the population was evacuated and household goods were removed before the area was levelled (Figure 4.5).[48] The images aimed to document and justify the destruction of a neighbourhood that the occupiers perceived as a haven for dangerous elements. Deliberately restrained, these propaganda photos centred on German soldiers and the orderly removal of household furnishings, not on individual French faces and fates. Photographs of internment camps in France also survive, but those that do not stem

[48] A series of photos taken by Wolfgang Vennemann (PK 649) is available online. See BArch: Bild 101I-027–1477–04; Bild 101I-027–1480–02; Bild 101I-027–1480–11; Bild 101I-027–1480–15, etc. at www.bild.bundesarchiv.de and also Ahlrich Meyer, *Der Blick des Besatzers: Propagandaphotographie der Wehrmacht aus Marseille, 1942–1944* (Bremen: Edition Temmen, 1999).

from official German photographers were most likely made by sympathetic French bystanders, or perhaps the internees themselves, rather than individual occupiers.[49]

Hints of a darker story sometimes do emerge from amateur soldiers' photographs, especially when we consider the occupiers' own comments on their snapshots. Major-general Friedrich Siebert, for example, revelled in Germany's victory in 1940 with mocking photos of "French 'obstacles'" ("Französische 'Hindernisse'") composed of old farm equipment. Undisguised racism emerged in Siebert's use of ironic captions like "France's fighters" ("Frankreichs Kämpfer") and "Frenchmen" ("Franzosen") for pictures of French Africans, seemingly disempowered and purposeless as prisoners gazing hesitantly into the camera. The word "Soldiers" ("Soldaten") was reserved for Germans (Figures 4.6 and 4.7), uniformed and busy, keenly planning their next moves.[50] Later in the same album, an apparently pastoral image showed a group of Frenchmen relaxing on a grassy knoll next to a shelter surmounted by a kind of windmill (Figure 4.8). The subsequent shot depicted one of them cracking open an oyster with his pocket-knife, and a sign above the men read "Moulin du Bon Heure [sic]" (Mill of the Happy Hour or, punning in French, of happiness). Without the caption added by the occupier who snapped these images, there would be no way to discern their full import, but Siebert noted that the men were "Frenchmen on cable watch" ("Franzosen auf Kabelwache,") in other words, the locals had been requisitioned to guard German communications cables against sabotage. This was no "happy hour," but dangerous work – the men, like the cables, constantly vulnerable to resistance attack.[51]

The deceptively "harmless" quality of some of Siebert's photographs serves as a reminder of the darker story underlying many occupiers' apparently "innocent" images. What did it mean to take such a photograph, and to add it to an album as if this were just another picturesque "sight" to see? Once captured, such an image was domesticated, rendered in black and white, in a way that enabled the viewer to overlook, literally, its underlying violence. The whole problem of being an occupier could be simplified; made manageable and liveable. In later years, it was easy to forget that anything brutal had ever been going on.

---

[49] Milton, "Camera as Weapon," 59. Photos by propaganda photographer Dieck giving a sanitised view of the internment camp at Beaune-la-Rolande are available online at the Bundesarchiv-Bildarchiv. See Bild 101I-250–0939–28A; Bild 101I-250–0939–26A, etc. at: www.bild.bundesarchiv.de.

[50] Friedrich Siebert, "Bilder zum Westfeldzug 1940" (BArch: N 586/8). Cf. Bopp, "Soldatenalltag im Sucher," 81–3; Bopp, "Fremde im Visier," 2003, 102.

[51] Friedrich Siebert, "La Rochelle 1940–41" (BArch: N 586/9).

Figure 4.6 "France's fighters" (Frankreichs Kämpfer).
Friedrich Siebert, Album "Bilder zum Westfeldzug 1940" (BArch: N 586/8).

This kind of selective forgetting was encouraged by the National Socialist regime, which constructed the occupation of France deliberately as a visual experience that would nourish memories. As occupiers recorded images for themselves, their relatives, and the nation as a whole, photography became self-consciously constitutive of the memory of the occupation, and also of its history. Rolf Sachsse has explored the ways that the National Socialists used photography more generally to create positive memories for Germans.[52] In France, the preservation of

---

[52] Rolf Sachsse, *Die Erziehung zum Wegsehen: Fotografie im NS-Staat* (Dresden: Philo Fine Arts, 2003); David Crew, "What Can We Learn from a Visual Turn? Photography, Nazi Germany and the Holocaust," *H-German Forum: German History after the Visual Turn*, September 18, 2006, http://h-net.msu.edu/cgi-bin/logbrowse.pl?trx.

Soldaten.

Figure 4.7 "Soldiers" (Soldaten).
Friedrich Siebert, Album "Bilder zum Westfeldzug 1940" (BArch: N 586/8).

personal memories was linked to the larger project of constructing a glorious history of the occupation era. Rather than relying on someone else's version, soldiers were to write, and "capture" through photography, their wartime history themselves. Only this way, the regime contended, would the "true" story be told. Photographs of Wehrmacht members admiring French historical monuments, for example, not only reminded people that Germans in uniform had been "everywhere" in France. Such images were also deployed as evidence of the culture, discernment and education of the aggressors, to counter the long-standing notion, amplified by propaganda during World War I, that Germans were barbarians.[53] Photographing each other in front of the

---

[53] In 1940, National Socialist publications often made reference to the fact that German soldiers had not behaved like "barbarians" the way the French supposedly expected. The occupation regime was at pains to demonstrate at least superficial civility. See, for instance, Franz Goetz, "Deutsche Truppenparade," *Der Vormarsch* 2, 18 June 1940, 3 (BArch: RHD 69/50). See also Chapter 1.

Figure 4.8 Photographs with faded caption "Frenchmen on 'cable watch'" (Franzosen auf "Kabelwache").
Friedrich Siebert, Album "La Rochelle 1940–41" (BArch: N 586/9).

Tomb of the Unknown Soldier at the Arc de Triomphe (Figure 1.2) reinforced Germans' victory, and allowed them to demonstrate their chivalrousness before the conquered enemy.[54]

---

[54] Bopp, *Fremde im Visier*, 2009, 28.

As in the France books that memorialised the occupation in writing, there was a reciprocal relationship between published and casual amateur photography, between books modelling how to see France and the ways that soldiers actually saw it.[55] In 1942, Imprimerie Défossés-Néogravure produced a compilation of photographs by Sergeant Norbert Windfelder called *An der Kanalküste: Foto-Erinnerung* (*On the English Channel Coast: Photo-memento*). According to the introduction, Windfelder's work aimed to offer "a lively remembrance of German soldiers' service on the Channel coast."[56] Beginning with photographs of captured weaponry, the book told the story of the German invasion and occupation of France. In a depiction of war-damaged Dunkirk, the caption drew the reader's eye to a large church tower, where "the German flag flies." Subsequent photos alluded to the tragedies of war by showing the burial of a British corpse and a makeshift cemetery for British military personnel. Later, the theme of Franco-German collaboration emerged from an image of German soldiers at the graves of unknown German and French soldiers. A lighter section followed, with pristine dune and beach landscapes, one showing a French woman knee-deep in seawater while fishing for shrimp under the watchful eye of a uniformed soldier (Figure 4.9). Close to the end of the book, images of German defensive positions on the Channel coast suggested the "true" reason for the German presence on French soil: defending it against the British. The book exemplified the standard themes of such works – German dominance, French submission, "unavoidable" war damage and an uneasy admiration of selected French landscapes and historical monuments. The overall message was clear: Germans had fought a hard battle in 1940 that had also, unavoidably, killed enemy soldiers and damaged France. Now, they were chivalrously protecting the country, working together with it to defeat the "hereditary enemy," Britain.[57] Books like this one provided templates for soldiers who snapped their own shots of France, while also giving those who did not take photographs a way to remember their "own" experiences visually.

The regime exploited soldiers' desire to document their experiences through photography. It solicited their contributions through photo contests, and then reused them as propaganda. Frances Guerin has pointed

---

[55] See Chapter 3 on France books.
[56] Norbert Windfelder, *An der Kanalküste: Foto-Erinnerungen* (Paris: Imprimerie E. Desfossés-Néogravure, 1942), 1. Given the quality of the photos, Windfelder (perhaps a pseudonym) was either a very skilled amateur, or a propaganda photographer who chose to publish a solo collection of images. An "Uffz.[Sergeant] Windfelder" contributed one photograph to the volume *Soldaten fotografieren Frankreich*, which claimed to contain only amateurs' snapshots. Lorenz, *Soldaten fotografieren*, 95.
[57] Windfelder, *An der Kanalküste*, 9–10; 12; 36; 46; 49–51.

Krabbenfischerin.

Figure 4.9 Fishing for shrimp under an occupier's watchful eye.
Norbert Windfelder, *An der Kanalküste: Foto-Erinnerungen* (Paris: Imprimerie
E. Desfossés-Néogravure, 1942).

out that "when amateur photographs demonstrated a commitment
to [the] ideals [of National Socialism] through their depictions of idyllic
landscapes and industrious, productive workers, it was common for
the unofficial image to be appropriated, manipulated, and reproduced
as official propaganda."[58] A process of collecting, digesting and
then regurgitating amateur images reinforced the official German view
of the situation in occupied France, particularly as it grew more tense
in 1941.

  In autumn that year, as the full barbarity of the regime became evident
on the Eastern Front and resisters in France stepped up their attacks on
the occupation forces, the Wehrmacht sponsored an exhibition of soldiers' paintings in Paris. This was followed in the spring by a show of
occupiers' photographs and films. The Paris Commander Ernst
Schaumburg defined the art exhibition in a companion volume as,
"nothing other . . . than the visible expression of the thoughts and feelings
of every German soldier who has served on French soil since the signing

---

[58] Guerin, *Amateur Eyes*, 75.

of the armistice at Compiègne."[59] As noted at the head of this chapter, Heinz Lorenz, who edited the companion books for both exhibitions, wrote in the preface to the work on photography that, "everyone would like to hold onto what he has experienced . . . and take it home as a visible memento for later."[60] For Schaumburg and Lorenz, photography represented an essential documentary tool for everyman. The exhibitions and their accompanying catalogues were intended to unify and bring soldiers' individual experiences of the occupation into focus, and to shape how they and their families would look back on them in the future. In assembling amateur photographs by occupiers of all ranks (including one woman), these events rewarded the "right" sort of photograph, and helped disseminate appropriate motifs.

Both the 1941 "Kunstausstellung der deutschen Wehrmacht in Paris," and the 1942 photography exhibition were intended to underline that Germans were civilised beings who appreciated fine art and were capable of producing it themselves using both traditional and highly modern techniques. The regime used these events to harness the potentially threatening individuality of photography, ensuring that a few selected images would stand in for the experience of the whole. The exhibitions filled the leisure time of soldiers on weekend trips to Paris and implanted the "right" kinds of images in their minds.

Soldiers' photographic choices were also steered by regime-sponsored tour guides and glossy coffee-table volumes in which the regime's professional photographers laid down the visual rules of the game.[61] Having seen well-publicised portraits of Hitler visiting Paris, for example, occupiers readily photographed themselves in the same, or similar poses, hands folded to the front, looking intently into the distance, with the Eiffel Tower behind them (Figures 4.10 and 4.11). Their self-assured stance and raised central position in relation to modern France's most famous monument underlined their confident authority, as did the vast scale and near-emptiness of the geometric scene behind. The visual resonance of such images was heightened for contemporaries by the fact that the Palais Chaillot, where the soldiers were standing, had been built as the centrepiece of the 1937 Paris Exposition. Many viewers would have been familiar with what Karen Fiss has called "the most reproduced

---

[59] Lorenz, *Frankreich, ein Erlebnis des deutschen Soldaten*, preface.
[60] Lorenz, *Soldaten fotografieren*, preface. See also Krob, "Paris Through Enemy Eyes: The Wehrmacht in Paris 1940–1944," 14 ff.
[61] At the peak in 1941–2, there were some 12,000 PK members active on all war fronts. Milton, "Camera as Weapon," 50.

Figure 4.10 "Mit Hitler im Westen" (With Hitler in the West), cover
of a commemorative book of images by Hitler's official photographer,
Heinrich Hoffmann.
Heinrich Hoffmann, *Mit Hitler im Westen* (Munich: Zeitgeschichte Verlag, 1940)

and the most infamous image of the exposition," a photograph taken
from the same vantage point that depicted the Soviet and German
pavilions facing one another below the great tower.[62] Now, the Soviet
pavilion was gone and the Germans were in charge of not only Paris, but
of France and much of Europe as well.

Shots in front of and atop the Eiffel Tower exemplify the way in which,
rather than demonstrating an eclectic individuality, occupiers depicted
similar themes over and over again – if they took one shot of themselves at
the beach, in front of the Paris Opéra or at the Tomb of the Unknown
Soldier, they took hundreds. Part of the reason had to do with older habits of
photographing "events seen as significant, either because they are mile-
stones in a life narrative . . . or because they open up new experiences and
perspectives, such as a trip away from home."[63] Another reason, however,
was that guidebooks sponsored by the regime encouraged soldiers to think

---

[62] Karen Fiss, *Grand Illusion: The Third Reich, the Paris Exposition, and the Cultural Seduction
of France* (Chicago: University of Chicago Press, 2010), 3.
[63] Umbach, "Selfhood," 349.

Figure 4.11 Soldiers standing in front of the Eiffel Tower.
Anonymous Album "Ehren-Chronik" (Deutsch-Russisches Museum Berlin-
Karlshorst, KH 206542_03-1).

of themselves as tourists and to take advantage of their remarkable opportunity to admire France's grand historical monuments. Primed with such
guidebooks, or as participants in one of the sightseeing trips organised by
their unit or the central military administration, soldiers readily included
among their photographs the French castles and cathedrals to which they
were steered. Together, books, guided tours and exhibitions contributed to
a kind of "Gleichschaltung" of the eye and mind that helped propagate
regime-sanctioned views of occupied lands.[64]

---

[64] See Chapter 3. Jane Caplan has also explored the way that tour guides (in particular the
1943 Baedeker guide to the Generalgouvernment) function to create and support the
Third Reich's official story on occupied areas. Caplan, *Jetzt judenfrei*.

Still, the German perspective on occupied France did not go unchallenged. French contemporaries, like the Germans, made a link between experiencing France visually, and remembering it through images. In 1942, a volume of photographs from the prewar period by well-known French photographer Roger Schall, entitled *Reflets de France*, was reprinted.[65] Soon after, it was published in a German version called *Frankreich: ein Bilderbuch*.[66] The foreword to the German edition, written by Jean Baugé, drew a direct connection between experiencing France visually and remembering it through images. As Baugé noted, "[f]ew of the many foreigners who visit this land will forget how grand the view up the broad Champs-Elysées to the Etoile is, ... or how powerfully for example the structure of the Louvre stays in his memory."[67] Like the comments of Heinz Lorenz cited earlier, Baugé's foreword reinforced the link between seeing and remembering through photographs. Schall and Baugé's book, however, sought to help visitors retain French-made images of France and to take these depictions home in the form of memories (Figure 4.12).

Clearly, the French themselves had an interest in presenting France to their occupiers visually, and this example points to a deeper conflict over photographic depictions of the land.[68] In fact, though it is difficult to be certain, the publication of Schall's photographs in 1942 may have been intended as a salvo in a kind of proxy war between occupiers and the occupied population over who controlled the image (and the images) of occupied France. Apart from the high quality of the images, the most remarkable feature of *Frankreich: ein Bilderbuch* was the complete absence of war. Referring only to "visitors," the work neither mentioned nor depicted occupiers.[69] Doubtless to accommodate the requirements of German censorship, it alluded to past conflicts between Germans and

---

[65] René Miquel and Roger Schall, *Reflets de France* (Paris: Imprimerie E. Desfossés-Néogravure, 1942). On Schall, see also Chapter 2 of this book.

[66] Roger Schall and Jean Baugé, *Frankreich: ein Bilderbuch* (Paris: Imprimerie E. Desfossés-Néogravure, 1942).

[67] Schall and Baugé, Foreword.

[68] The French side of this contestation has been explored by Abigail Lewis in the unpublished paper "Making Propaganda French: The Service Central Photographique and the Battle for Photography under Vichy" (Society for French Historical Studies, Washington, 2017). For the Liberation period, see Clark, "Capturing the Moment." Conflicts over the visual depiction of France during the occupation continue, as witnessed by the heated public debate surrounding a 2008 exhibition of French photographer André Zucca's images at the Paris city hall. See Clarisse Fabre, "L'exposition Zucca divise le public," *Le Monde.fr*, June 28, 2008, www.lemonde.fr/culture/article/2008/06/28/l-exposition-zucca-divise-le-public_1064053_3246.html.

[69] As noted, the images themselves were from the prewar period. The fact that they were published in 1942 underlines that the occupation regime saw no obstacle to publishing benign-seeming "peaceful" imagery of France, even by a French photographer – indeed, this may have been part of the attraction of these images.

Figure 4.12 "Landscape on the Orne [River]" – a pastoral image of
France by French photographer Roger Schall.
Roger Schall and Jean Baugé, *Frankreich: ein Bilderbuch* (Paris: Imprimerie
E. Desfossés-Néogravure, 1942), 75.

French only when commenting on how these had shaped the landscape
of Northeastern France.[70] The volume played up the notion of an eternal
France that existed outside specific contemporary conditions, and
readers leafing through it could have been forgiven for imagining France
to be a pastoral idyll, full of peaceful scenery, picturesque local costumes,
and impressive historical monuments.

Any analysis of this publication is complicated by the knowledge that
the photographer Schall continued to work professionally during the
occupation and sold his images to Vichy publications.[71] Still, Schall's
celebration of "timeless" French culture and historical monuments may
not only have been designed to get around censorship, but also to
suggest, even to German readers, an alternate vision of France that
would survive long after the occupation was over. This notion is
reinforced by the fact that in October 1944, Schall's brother Raymond
published a new collection of Roger Schall's images entitled *A Paris sous
la botte des Nazis*, discussed in the context of consumption in Chapter 2.
The brothers claimed to have conceived this work over the last four years,
and to have been working on it actively since May 1944. The German
soldiers so conspicuously absent from the 1942 volume now appeared in

[70] Schall and Baugé, *Frankreich*, 96.
[71] Denoyelle, "Dreizner," 90; Clark, "Capturing the Moment," 854.

full force.[72] It is tempting to discount the 1944 publication as a hasty attempt at whitewashing.[73] However, read in the context of the 1942 book, *Reflets de France*, it may speak more eloquently of the delicate and morally blurry balancing act that French citizens like Schall undertook in the occupation years, and their desire to retain a form of agency in the creation of images about France.

Reflets de France, as we have noted, appeared with German permission and was then translated specifically for the occupier market. Yet because it used French images that predated the occupation, even as it appeared to send a German-approved message, it subtly undermined German claims to control photographic representation of the country, offering a patriotic French, rather than strictly German, view of the land. For the French, a volume like Schall's may have presented a way to hold on to the notion of an ideal, eternal France, free of enemy occupiers. At the same time, Schall may have sought to implant that vision of the country in the minds of the German conquerors. The catch, however, was that any interpretation of the images remained in the eye of the beholder. The same photographs that spoke of an eternal, timeless France to a French photographer and audience also served occupying soldiers as visual hooks upon which to hang their own slippery and very different memories.[74] Occupiers without a camera or lacking the skill to capture such beautiful images could purchase a French-produced volume like *Frankreich: ein Bilderbuch* to send to their friends or relatives (Figure 4.13). Even though these occupiers saw the country very differently from Schall, nothing in his photographs got in the way of their version of the story. Whatever Schall and Baugé's own intentions, their book remained deeply problematic, for it propagated a pastoral, timeless and apolitical image of France that many occupiers were only too happy to embrace.

As the challenges that Germans faced in France grew, military administrators began to express concern about occupiers' fascination with French sights. In 1943, we have noted, German embassy staff in Paris complained about the "cultural propaganda" that they discerned in the

---

[72] Eparvier, *A Paris sous la botte des Nazis*. See Charles Chadwyck-Healey, "Literature of Liberation," *Parenthesis* 20, www.fpba.com/parenthesis/select-articles/p20_literature_of_liberation.html. *Reflets de France* was also published again after the war: Roger Schall, *Reflets de France* (Paris: Editions Raymond Schall, 1950).

[73] This is the approach of Clark, who depicts Schall as a confirmed collaborator and cites evidence that ambassador Otto Abetz had intervened personally in 1940 to have Schall released from a POW camp. "Capturing the Moment," 854–5.

[74] Writing about photographers' urge to document, Bernd Hüppauf points out that the desire to retain images as an aide-mémoire motivated soldiers even when their images would never be shown beyond their most intimate circle, as was the case with most images of racial persecution and terror in the East. Hüppauf, "Entleerte Blick," 511.

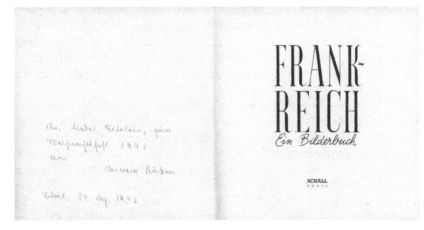

Figure 4.13 Title page and fly-leaf of a book of images by French
photographer Roger Schall. The fly-leaf bears a Christmas dedication
hand-written in German at Blois, France, 24 December 1942.
Roger Schall and Jean Baugé, *Frankreich: ein Bilderbuch* (Paris: Imprimerie
E. Desfossés-Néogravure, 1942).

rather positive depiction of France in books like Lorenz's *Soldaten fotografieren Frankreich*.[75] In fact, even as such books continued to be published, the effort to reshape Germans' visions of France more
aggressively had already begun, notably through tour guides like *Paris:
deutsch gesehen* discussed in Chapter 3.[76] These works offered propagandistic renderings of Paris history and contemporary sights that, with varying degrees of intensity, aimed to justify German attitudes and lend
legitimacy to occupation practices.

Clearly, the regime made concerted efforts to influence how soldiers
saw and photographed France. Yet a striking contrast sometimes
emerges when we compare amateur and "official" portrayals of similar
scenes. Indeed, amateur photos are among the few sources that allow us
to gauge the distance between officially-mandated views, and soldiers'
own versions of the story. For example, a photograph of Montmartre,
taken by an "ordinary" occupier, shows German soldiers meandering
without apparent purpose, perhaps simply curious or seeking the seamy
underside of Paris life (Figure 4.14). Another shot, captured by a

---

[75] See Chapter 3. File note Pr. No. 6829/43, Schwendemann for Generalkonsul Gerlach
and Gesandten Schleier, German Embassy in Paris, 27 November 1943 (Politisches
Archiv des Auswärtigen Amtes (AA): DBP/1141b); Geiger, *L'image*, 379–80.
[76] Schulz-Wilmersdorf, *Paris: deutsch gesehen*, 53; Bopp, *Fremde im Visier*, 2009, 28.

Figure 4.14 Paris 1940, Montmartre – image from an anonymous
soldier's private album.
Anon. album, author's collection.

propaganda photographer, shows the same district, soldiers conversing
with what are presumably respectable German women, rather than
French dancing girls (Figure 4.15). The first photo seems casual, dis-
ordered; the second depicts the daylight, cleaned-up version of Montmartre propagated by occupation officials.[77] Another album reflects the
distance between official and unofficial visions of the occupation by
separating, physically, photographs having to do with service and sanctioned leisure-time activities, from those involving French civilians, and
women in particular, that are collected at the back of the album.[78]

---

[77] "Paris (1940) Montmartre" from album in author's collection; Soldiers in front of the
Moulin Rouge, Paris, PK 689, summer 1940 (BArch: Bild 101I-129–0480–26 / Heinz
Bösig). Cf. Figure 4.16 and Konvolut Giesbert Witte, Einzelfoto, Moulin Rouge, Paris
1942 Bopp, *Fremde im Visier*, 2009, 33. Since at least the turn of the century, Germans
had considered Montmartre an essential Paris destination, its dubious reputation
confirming their notions of French decadence. Nolan, *The Inverted Mirror:
Mythologizing the Enemy in France and Germany 1898–1914*, 56.
[78] Three generations of French women; two men and two women at a table, Kfz. Uffz.
album, author's collection.

Figure 4.15 German soldiers with women in front of the
Moulin Rouge.
BArch: Bild 101I-129–0480–26 / Heinz Boesig.

The tension between official and "unofficial" visions of the occupation
is also evident in the photography of Lothar-Günther Buchheim. Buchheim, the author of the 1973 novel, and later film, *Das Boot*, served as a
Wehrmacht reporter and propagandist during the war. Although his
propaganda work primarily involved writing and sketching, he also took
many photographs.[79] Buchheim was not a trained photographer, but
since his role was that of a professional reporter, his photographs were
not exactly those of an amateur, either.[80] He photographed with an eye
for detail and aimed to document what he saw around himself.

Buchheim spent a considerable amount of time in occupied France,
and came back to his wartime photography several times in the postwar

[79] One of Buchheim's essays is discussed in Chapter 3.
[80] PK members used various media to capture a story. During the war, Buchheim
produced a collection of images documenting life aboard a U-Boot. The same
collection, published almost unchanged in 1976, depicted submariners as modern
knights of the sea, tragically misled by their commander, Karl Dönitz. Lothar-Günther
Buchheim, *U-Boot-Krieg* (München: Piper, 1976); Anton Holzer, "Die oben, wir unten:
Das Boot, der Krieg, die Fotografie: Der U-Boot-Krieg als deutsche Heldengeschichte?"
in *Mit der Kamera bewaffnet: Krieg und Fotografie*, ed. Anton Holzer (Marburg: Jonas
Verlag, 2003), 122, 136; Daniel Uziel, *The Propaganda Warriors: The "Wehrmacht" and
the Consolidation of the German Home Front* (New York: Peter Lang, 2008), 401–18.

era. In 1977, he published a book that reproduced a series of photographs he had taken in France in the 1940s. Buchheim explained in the book's preface that he had not enlarged these images or shown them to his comrades at the time because "[s]uch photos were not suited to the times: I ought to have photographed parades, the shine and glory of the occupiers and 'Les Monuments'."[81] In framing these photos as "hidden" or "unofficial," Buchheim both covered himself against accusations that he was simply reproducing National Socialist propaganda, and made a claim for the heightened "veracity" of these images, which thus purported to depict the "real" Paris, rather than an official occupiers' version of the city. Equally, Buchheim's comments underlined that propaganda reporters like himself had a very clear understanding of the kinds of stories and images they were expected to produce.[82]

Despite his claims to the contrary, however, Buchheim's photographs were not nearly as different from those of his contemporaries as he liked to think. Buchheim in fact did photograph major Paris monuments, perhaps from a more interesting angle than fellow soldiers with less artistic sense, and interspersed with more shots of everyday street life in Paris, but "Les Monuments" nevertheless. More tellingly, his 1977 volume constructed an occupied French capital almost without occupiers (Figure 4.16).[83] Buchheim's introduction to the photographs suggested that this simply reflected images as he captured them in the 1940s, for "[a]t that time, when the occupier came into the picture, I looked away – also with the camera."[84] Buchheim had photographed the "bombastic" military parades along the Champs-Elysées, he noted, but otherwise this volume of occupier photography contained very few occupiers, and only fleeting signs of war.

Buchheim made attempts, some of them in fiction, to explain, or justify, his wartime photographic activities. In addition to *Das Boot*, he

[81] Lother-Günther Buchheim, *Mein Paris: eine Stadt vor dreißig Jahren* (Munich: Piper, 1977), 10.

[82] Cf. Guerin, *Amateur Eyes*, 76.

[83] In this sense, Buchheim's images are reminiscent not only of those in the Schall and Baugé volume, but also the snapshots of many aesthetically-minded tourists, who fastidiously omit themselves and their ilk from their photography.

[84] Buchheim, *Mein Paris*, 13. There is a precedent for emptied street views in prewar photography of the French capital, for example that of Eugène Atget. Françoise Denoyelle draws attention to the work of another highly-skilled occupation-era German photographer, Walter Greizner, who created a contradictory vision of Paris in images that show, on the one hand, Parisians coming to terms with the challenges of daily life under duress, and on the other hand, like Buchheim's, omit the occupiers who were at the root of their oppression. Denoyelle, "Dreizner," 88, 91.

Figure 4.16 Lother-Günther Buchheim's occupied Paris almost
without Germans, though Buchheim wrote that "one who examines the
photo . . . carefully discovers behind the French Gendarme a motorcycle
courier of the German Wehrmacht in his steel helmet."
Lother-Günther Buchheim, *Mein Paris: eine Stadt vor dreißig Jahren* (Munich:
Piper, 1977), 122–3, Buchheim Stiftung.

published two other novels that revolved around his experiences in
occupied France. In the second of these, *Die Festung*, Buchheim
described his autobiographical protagonist wandering around the ruined
city of Rouen in 1944, haunted by the visible consequences of warfare,
taking photograph after photograph. Rather than sinking into passive
despair, Buchheim's character pushed himself onwards with the words,
"[s]o, continue, and take pictures of these streets of rubble! Document
what it looks like here! Capture for all time what the vandals have done
with a beautiful medieval city."[85] Here, Buchheim presented photography as a specifically documentary activity, a conscious recording of
war's horrors, even a statement about the nature of Hitler's regime. The
author turned occupiers' photography into recording, and that recording
into a political act, implying that his protagonist's photographs constituted a very limited form of opposition to war and the Nazi regime.

[85] Lother-Günther Buchheim, *Die Festung* (Hamburg: Hoffmann und Campe, 1995), 354.

How are we to interpret this statement, made (after all) after war's end, and in a work of fiction? At the very least, it appears that Buchheim used the camera in his novel, and perhaps used it in reality as well, to create a separation between the actions of "vandals" and the photographer's presumably civilised self. Returning to Hüppauf's point, Buchheim employed his camera to imagine himself a simple observer, or even a conscientious documenter, of a violent scene. The catch was of course that Buchheim was writing well after 1945, and perhaps above all seeking to justify having taken so many photos in a context where, in hindsight, photography itself might appear a callous act.[86] Like other occupation soldiers, Buchheim fell prey to the notion that he could simply be a tourist – a voyeur. His photographs remained remarkably blind to the war and his own role in it. He certainly did not go so far as to document German brutality per se.

Buchheim's photos include many tropes found in other occupiers' images. In fact, like the "war stories" Robert Moeller identified among survivors of World War II (and notably of the expulsion from Germany's former eastern territories), soldiers' photographs repeat themselves to the point that we might be tempted to question their ability to say very much at all about what the occupation was "really" like. Yet unlike the postwar oral accounts Moeller investigated, that were only as reliable as the fading memories they reflected, occupiers' photographs date from the period, and captured precise moments in time. In one sense, therefore, they may seem more reliable, but of course the occupiers considered only certain images to be worthy of capture, and a selection took place before the shutter was ever released. Some of this selection was mandated from on high, as in the prohibition against photographing anything that would damage the reputation of the Wehrmacht. In other cases, the selection may have been less conscious, yet it too was influenced by a nebulous set of "rules" or conventions about the kinds of photos a soldier ought to take.

Many images, we have noted, could have been drawn directly from peacetime albums – the photographs of men sitting around a festive table, for example, or those showing off youthful pranks. Photographs like these underline how engrained, already, was the sense of a "proper" moment to photograph, and how persistent such notions were, despite an extraordinary context. At the same time, they suggest how quickly war and occupation became "normal" for those who participated in them; or

---

[86] Sontag writes that, because the photographer has chosen to photograph, rather than to intervene, "photography is essentially an act of non-intervention." Sontag, *On Photography*, 11–12.

at least, how insistent the desire to assimilate the extraordinary into the ordinary remained.

Although today's "official" memory of the French occupation emphasises themes of German brutality, French collaboration, and resistance in the face of overwhelming oppression, the images taken by occupying soldiers hardly reflect this story at all. Hidden away in an attic, perhaps shown only decades later to curious grandchildren, they offer a far more benign picture. It would be easy to dismiss these photographs, eagerly captured by young men in uniform lured onwards by a regime that sought to use their images to write its own glorious history. Indeed, such evidence often has been dismissed on the grounds that it was not only unreliable and possibly unauthentic, but more importantly, could not possibly reflect the past in any objective way. These concerns are largely beside the point. These soldiers' amateur photographs do not reflect any "real" past; rather, they shed light on young men's attempts to capture, construct, and make sense of the experience of being occupiers. They also reveal how the National Socialist regime sought to direct occupiers' seeing, and through photography, encouraged soldiers to see themselves not as oppressors, but rather as sightseers; not as participants and actors, but simply as detached observers of what went on. Occupiers' amateur photographs do not illustrate the public, let alone the academic and scholarly histories of the occupation. However, they certainly do illustrate, and above all helped to create, a popular memory, recounted privately, which centres not on violence and war, but on the very real pleasures that German soldiers in France enjoyed. In other contexts, among victors who believe they have fought a "good war," photos that show the camaraderie and adventurous side of wartime get more play – but in Germany, the notion of soldier is too inextricably linked with that of perpetrator for such a "harmlessly" positive narrative to survive.

5   Rising Tensions

Just as he was headed to bed one Saturday night in October 1941, Bernhard Schulz was called out to duty. Although it was pitch dark and raining, he and other members of his unit were issued bicycles and sent to ride around the Norman countryside looking for a downed British flight crew. "We sealed off entire villages, searched them house to house, but found nothing," Schulz reported. "The French are keeping the fellows hidden despite orders that anyone in whose home a Tommy is found will be shot."[1] By the time Schulz wrote about the search, after it was over, he had not slept for two days. He was exhausted and hungry, but wanted to send a letter anyway so that his new fiancée, Gerda, would not worry. She responded by sending a parcel with Dextropur, a fruit sugar compound, to help him keep up his strength.

The way Schulz wrote about this incident suggests that it may have been the first challenging military action he had yet undertaken. He had stood sentry duty, watched the city of Cherbourg being bombed from a position on the coast, and lived for several weeks cut off and on short rations on the British Channel Island of Alderney. However, the war had not yet come as close to him as it did that night. As far as we can tell from his letters, Schulz's time as an occupier had been quiet. This was not unusual in France, but from the spring of 1941, the tone of the occupation shifted. Measures like the village search, and the deadly threat that hung over the French population as Schulz and his comrades cycled through the rain, were not new, but they gained a novel harshness and brutal certainty. The seeds of this change, which had existed from the outset, germinated and grew with the invasion of the Soviet Union in June, developing into a sinuous vine by the late summer when French resisters made their first direct attacks on German personnel. By the fall, the Militärbefehlshaber in Paris struggled to clear a path between Berlin's demands for retribution and circumstances on the ground that, to his

---

[1] Schulz, letter, 28 October 1941 (DTA: 2033).

mind, called for moderation to favour ongoing collaboration. To resolve his dilemna, Otto von Stülpnagel developed the brutal, not to mention futile, policy of substituting deported Jews for executed hostages. By February 1942, unable to satisfy Berlin and, it appears, his own conscience at the same time, Otto von Stülpnagel resigned. He was replaced by a distant cousin, Carl-Heinrich von Stülpnagel, while the administration of France was reworked to strengthen the role of policing and surveillance powers under Reinhard Heydrich, and to render them more independent of military control.[2]

While these changes were taking place at higher levels, occupiers on the ground like Schulz became accustomed to carrying out ruthless searches and contributing to, while also becoming the targets of, rising insecurity and violence. After the invasion of the Soviet Union, they were alternately frustrated by the fact that they were so far from the "real" action in the East, and relieved that they had not yet been called to a front rumoured to be more brutal than anything they had previously experienced.

Although the men in France felt safer than those elsewhere, events on other war fronts impinged on France directly. The Wehrmacht's failure to win a quick victory in the Soviet Union meant that by early 1942, the Reich was beginning to experience shortages of all kinds, from manpower to materiel and food supplies. Although the high command had originally intended to avoid drawing on Germany's own food stocks by feeding soldiers off the land in the Soviet Union, this proved only partly successful.[3] Civilian rations in Germany were reduced in April 1942, and though they were raised slightly in the autumn, they never returned to previous levels. The need to address the dirth of food and other supplies deepened the exploitation of occupied areas and created pressure to streamline the occupation apparatus. In France, resources for activities designed to foster cultural interactions and collaboration at the highest levels began to dry up, and there was less and less support for the notion that France should be treated comparatively well so that it might collaborate willingly in a German-run Europe. At lower levels, manpower shortages meant that, rather than leaving occupation personnel in place so that they could get to know local areas and work more effectively with their French counterparts, new rules limited the amount of time soldiers

[2] This chapter's summary of events in the summer and autumn of 1941 draws upon Eismann, *Hôtel Majestic*; Herbert, "German Military Command"; Imlay, "German Side"; Laub, *After the Fall*.

[3] Gustavo Corni and Horst Gies, *Brot, Butter, Kanonen: Die Ernährungswirtschaft in Deutschland unter der Diktatur Hitlers*, 1997, 532 ff.

and administrators spent in the West. The occupation administration was pared down to an absolute minimum so that more and more men could be freed up for front-line fighting. Together, these developments altered the character of the occupation, and gave form to its central contradiction. On the one hand, France remained a pleasant place to be, a desirable posting whose advantages became increasingly clear when contrasted with the horrors of the Eastern Front. Recognising this reality, the army played up French attractions, for it needed the country as a staging area to rest, regroup and retrain troops. On the other hand, as German exactions became harsher, French territory grew more difficult to control, and occupiers' security harder to guarantee. As the war drove on towards its endpoint, managing this contradiction became perhaps the greatest challenge facing occupiers in France.

Scholars have devoted considerable attention to the "turn" towards more openly brutal occupation policies beginning in 1941. They have investigated the roots of this change and weighed the responsibility of the army and the police apparatus in the transition. For many years, historians argued that representatives of the police under Reinhard Heydrich pushed for more radical repression, while the offices of the Militärbefehlshaber favoured restraint.[4] From the 1990s, however, scholars such as Ulrich Herbert and Ahlrich Meyer began, with differently shaded analyses, to reevaluate the involvement of the Militärbefehlshaber in laying the groundwork for repression.[5] They revised traditional pictures of Otto von Stülpnagel as a voice for conciliation with the French, a last and ultimately weak barricade against police and SS violence, or, alternately,

---

[4] See notably Umbreit, *Militärbefehlshaber*, 124–40. For an insightful summary of the scholarship on these issues, see Eismann, *Hôtel Majestic*, 53–91. Also, on recent contributions, Imlay, "German Side." In the three-way constellation of power in Paris, alongside the police and the military under von Stülpnagel, the German embassy's role seems to be the least clear, alternately pushing for collaboration and transmitting radical ideas from Berlin. In keeping with the main focus of this book, the following account attends to the military above all.

[5] Key works are Herbert, *Best*; Herbert, "German Military Command"; Herbert, "Militärverwaltung"; Ahlrich Meyer, *Die Besatzung*; Ahlrich Meyer, "'Kleistische Prosa oder Polizeibericht? Anmerkungen zu Ernst Jünger's Denkschrift zur Geiselfrage," *Vierteljahreshefte für Zeitgeschichte* 52, no. 2 (2004): 281–6. Divergences between the interpretations of Herbert and Meyer, especially with regard to the overall importance of the persecution of the Jews in German repression in France, are summarised in Eismann, *Hôtel Majestic*, 63–7. Other important contributions to the debate include Sven Olaf Berggötz, "Ernst Jünger und die Geiseln: Die Denkschrift von Ernst Jünger über die Geiselerschießungen in Frankreich 1941/42," *Vierteljahreshefte für Zeitgeschichte* 51, no. 3 (2003): 405–72; Regina M. Delacor, *Attentate und Repressionen: ausgewählte Dokumente zur zyklischen Eskalation des NS-Terrors im besetzten Frankreich 1941/42*, Instrumenta 4 (Stuttgart: Thorbecke, 2000); Delacor, "Weltanschauungskrieg"; Eismann, "Représailles"; Neumaier, "Escalation."

too much the patrician officer to really comprehend Hitler's ruthless intentions. In these newer accounts, von Stülpnagel emerged as a leader who, marked by his own anti-Communism and anti-Semitism, deliberately facilitated the deportation of French Jews. He did so in a misguided and tragic effort to retain control over the running of the occupation by deflecting Hitler's orders to execute French "hostages" onto a vulnerable population already viewed as unwelcome outsiders by most French. Representing the newest generation of scholars, Thomas Laub, while incorporating recent research on the Militärbefehlshaber's anti-Jewish policies, echoes the conclusions of earlier historians in describing Otto von Stülpnagel as a fundamentally honourable officer caught in an untenable situation.[6] Finally, Gaël Eismann's nuanced analysis of German security policy in France emphasises links and common ground between police and military instances while painting the war in the West neither as completely conventional, nor as violently genocidal as that of the East.[7] More generally, Eismann's and other recent publications form part of the reevaluation, since the 1990s, of the Wehrmacht's part in the atrocities of the Third Reich, the role of violent anti-Semitism in determining policy in occupied Europe, and the fundamental nature – either conventional or ideologically charged – of the war in the West.[8]

Rather than focusing on the top level of decision-making alone, while summarising choices made in Paris, the following account adds to the picture by highlighting how the need to maintain France's contributions to the war, including as a quiet rest area for the troops, exerted pressure to moderate reprisals. It also underlines the connections between various levels of the occupation apparatus, and the impact of rising insecurity on ground-level soldiers. Documents related to troop discipline and management, for example, reveal that at least initially, leaders in Paris suspected that their own soldiers' behaviour had helped to provoke resistance attacks. Clinging to the notion that theirs was a model occupation, they sought to control soldiers' comportment in order to diffuse the situation. As the gap widened between the "peaceful," leisure-, consumption-, and tourism-based vision of the occupation promoted by National Socialist authorities and the reality of rising tension, insecurity, and brutality, occupiers struggled to adjust to the new

---

[6] Laub, *After the Fall*, 163.

[7] Eismann emphasises the plurality of actors at work and suggests that similar ideas about how to respond to anti-German activity in France may have come from several directions at once. Eismann, *Hôtel Majestic*; Eismann, "Représailles," 110, 113.

[8] Eismann, *Hôtel Majestic*, 89; Eismann, "Représailles," 122, nn. 51, 52; Herbert, "Militärverwaltung." See also Imlay, "German Side."

climate. How did the need to navigate between the competing priorities of the occupation influence policy-making? This chapter and the two that follow it take up this question, first by surveying the period of the transition and tracing the growth of formal resistance activity and responses to this development in Paris. While summarising the interplay of policy-makers in Paris and Berlin, this chapter breaks through the artificial separation in many histories between these men's high-level actions and the pressures for either restraint or escalation coming from lower levels. In doing so, it highlights the breadth of factors to be taken into consideration in evolving responses to insecurity and violence. At the same time, it considers the impact of the changing atmosphere on both central administrators and "ordinary" occupiers. How did their duties and responsibilities evolve? How did the men themselves see the situation, and their own role in France at this time? Later chapters trace the interaction of Western and Eastern war experiences, the use of France as a "safe" area for rest, relaxation and regrouping combat units, and the effect on the occupation of efforts to rationalise manpower as the Reich fought to stave off defeat.

Before examining the transition from the early, relatively calm months of occupation to the later, more violent, exploitative and ruthless ones, it is important to emphasise that despite appearances and the regime's investment in shoring up these appearances, the occupation was never either peaceful or benign. From the very beginning, during the battle for France and shortly thereafter, suspected partisans were shot, soldiers raped local women, and notably French colonial soldiers were killed rather than being taken prisoner. Jewish citizens and non-citizens were singled out early on, for instance when those who had fled during the 1940 "Exodus" were refused permission to cross the demarcation line and return to their homes in the northwestern occupied zone.[9] Jewish families faced discrimination and the organised theft of their property, while Germany exploited French resources and reduced the local people to second-class status. The occupation authorities imposed collective punishments and took "hostages" from the general population in response to opposition activities.[10] As we have seen in earlier chapters, even seemingly harmless activities like shopping, tourism and photography reinforced the power imbalance between occupiers and occupied

[9] Risser, *France under Fire*, Ch. 7; Torrie, *For Their Own Good*, 131.
[10] Until 1941, hostage-taking corresponded to the traditional use of this practice by campaigning armies – hostages were not executed until 1941. Eismann, "Représailles," 109; Umbreit, *Militärbefehlshaber*, 135.

people, and created a web of interactions that constantly reminded both parties of their unequal positions.

The occupation was, therefore, cruel from the beginning, but in 1941 the hostility between Germans and the French became more apparent, resisters' attacks more overt, and violent reprisals more deadly. For the occupiers, questions arose about how to answer rising anti-German activity. On the one hand, a firm and rapid response to opposition might discourage future attacks. On the other, reacting too harshly might nourish hostility in the general population, endanger collaboration, and make holding French territory, which after all relied heavily on French cooperation or at least passivity, more difficult.

A mid-May 1941 report on the situation in Bordeaux illuminates the complexity of the situation. Asked about resistance activities in their area, the authorities there noted that these were typically limited to damage to communications cables. Commenting on the punishments that should be meted out in response to such events, the Field Commander warned that, "we can not be careful enough in imposing these punishments."[11] Pushing for moderation, he suggested that there was radicalising pressure coming from lower levels of the army itself, for when cables were damaged, "[t]he troops, influenced by their comprehensible immediate outrage about the act, often request harshest punishments following only minimal inquiries."[12] As we have seen, Bernhard Schulz was convinced the French in his area were hiding downed airmen regardless of the risks, and after two long, wet nights, he just wanted to get back to his quarters and sleep.[13] When a specific culprit could not be found, it was common for local people to be punished collectively, with measures such as cable surveillance duty and extended curfew. For his part, the Bordeaux Field Commander questioned whether collective punishments actually achieved their purpose. Sometimes, after the fact, it turned out that drunken soldiers themselves had been the perpetrators of putative "sabotage," or that "cables that appeared to have been cut were laid so badly and without following instructions that it was all too easy for accidental damage to occur."[14] He pointed out that collective punishments undermined the relationship between German and

---

[11] Chef der Militärverwaltungsbezirks Bordeaux, Chef des Verwaltungstabes I A 3232, "Lagebericht für die Zeit vom 16. März bis 15. Mai 1941," 14 May 1941 (AN: 40 AJ/ 448).
[12] Chef der Militärverwaltungsbezirks Bordeaux, "Lagebericht," 14 May 1941 (AN: 40 AJ/ 448).
[13] Schulz, letter, 28 October 1941 (DTA: 2033).
[14] Chef der Militärverwaltungsbezirks Bordeaux, "Lagebericht," 14 May 1941 (AN: 40 AJ/ 448).

French administrative offices, and argued that "the popular mood with regard to the German occupation is getting worse." When collective punishments were imposed, the affected communities tended to see themselves "as innocent and random victims."[15] Fines did not work, as local people simply assumed that the Germans were creating the "sabotage" themselves in order to fill their war chests. Assigning local men to cable surveillance duty perhaps increased the security of the cables, but it often took young workers away from projects that were in the German interest. The Commander ended by arguing that lengthening curfews and confining residents to their homes were the only really effective measures, and these should be preferred henceforth. He also suggested that security troops needed more information about the overall context for decision-making on how to punish acts of sabotage and resistance, for "up until now the troops have often thought that administrators were lacking both the necessary vigour and the will to deal with [these incidents] quickly."[16]

These statements summarised differences of opinion within the military administration about how to react to resistance activities. They also highlighted a central problem – when individual administrative officials argued for a more diplomatic, moderate approach, their security and policing counterparts tended to see this as "softness" or a failure of decisiveness and strength. This local divergence was overlaid by a corresponding difference of opinion between leaders in Paris, who typically favoured moderation, and both the military and party hierarchy in Berlin, which did not.

Operation Barbarossa, the Nazi invasion of the Soviet Union, began on 22 June 1941. Having been held in a kind of stasis by the Nazi-Soviet Non-Aggression Pact signed just before the war began, French Communists now stepped up their anti-German activities. At the same time, occupiers became more sensitive to resistance, and more inclined to react violently. The High Command saw Western occupied areas in the context of a much larger conflict, which was characterised by the sanctioned brutality of the "criminal orders" on the Eastern Front.[17]

---

[15] Chef der Militärverwaltungsbezirks Bordeaux, "Lagebericht," 14 May 1941 (AN: 40 AJ/448).
[16] Chef der Militärverwaltungsbezirks Bordeaux, "Lagebericht," 14 May 1941 (AN: 40 AJ/448).
[17] There is a vast historiography on the criminal orders and warfare on the Eastern Front. See the landmark works Omer Bartov, *The Eastern Front 1941–1945: German Troops and the Barbarisation of Warfare* (Basingstoke, Hampshire: Macmillan, 1985); Omer Bartov, *Hitler's Army: Soldiers, Nazis, and War in the Third Reich* (Oxford: Oxford University Press, 1992); Christopher R. Browning, *Ordinary Men: Reserve Police Battalion 101 and the Final Solution in Poland*, Reprint edition (New York: Harper Perennial, 1998). More

This context fed a dynamic of increasing violence across German-occupied areas. Although the war in the West had never been completely "clean," the fact that soldiers moved from West to East, North to South and back again across German-controlled Europe reinforced the ripple effects of violence in the East. As they changed postings, soldiers brought behaviours and habits learned in the West to the East and, more problematically, from the East to the West.[18]

Still, it would be a mistake to suggest that all violence in France came from the outside, or that it was the result of pressure from Berlin. Even before the invasion of the Soviet Union, the Militärbefehlshaber had initiated repression against Communists and other opponents. Notably, on 23 May 1941, he ordered the creation of an internment camp for Communists in the occupied zone.[19] Other camps already existed under French control in the southern, non-occupied zone, including the camp of Gurs, just north of the Pyrenees, which had opened to house refugees from the Spanish Civil War.[20] Anti-Nazi Germans who had taken refuge in France were later sent to Gurs, as were more than 6,000 Jews from Southwestern Germany in the first planned deportation of German Jews, 22 October 1940.[21] Scholars estimate that in February 1941, some

recent studies of the attitudes and actions of soldiers and policemen include Neitzel and Welzer, *Soldaten*; Hürter, "Kameraden, Foreword"; Michael Wildt, *Generation des Unbedingten: das Führungskorps des Reichssicherheitshauptamtes* (Hamburg: Hamburger Edition, 2002). On the controversy surrounding the Wehrmacht and extreme violence see Hartmann, Hürter, and Jureit, *Verbrechen der Wehrmacht*; Heer and Naumann, *Vernichtungskrieg*.

[18] Historians have typically dealt with one or two occupation zones and ignored flows of personnel, ideas and "habits" of occupation among zones. An innovative exploration of the impact of Eastern Front experience on soldiers in France is Lieb, *Konventioneller*. See also Virgili, "Les viols," 112.

[19] Eismann, "Représailles," 111.

[20] In all, there were some 400 internment camps in the southern zone. In a separate but parallel development, the concentration camp Natzweiler-Struthof, southwest of Strassbourg in (now-German) Alsace, had opened on 1 May 1941. The standard work on camps in France is Denis Peschanski, *La France des camps: l'internement, 1938–1946* (Gallimard, 2002).

[21] Most of these Jews, who were initally supposed to be shipped to Madagascar, were later sent to extermination camps in Germany. Christian Eggers, "Gurs – und die Anderen: Gedanken zur Erforschung der Französischen Internierungslager 1939–1945," *Francia* 21, No. 3 (September 1994): 171–9; Anne Grynberg, "Les camps du sud de la France: de l'internement à la déportation," *Annales. Histoire, Sciences Sociales* 48, No. 3 (1993): 563; Claude Laharie, *Le camp de Gurs, 1939–1945 : un aspect méconnu de l'histoire du Béarn* (Paris: J & D Editions, 1993); Jacob Toury, "Die Entstehungsgeschichte des Austreibungsbefehls gegen die Juden der Saarpfalz und Badens (22./23. Oktober 1940 – Camp De Gurs)," *Jahrbuch des Instituts für Deutsche Geschichte, Universität Tel-Aviv* 15 (January 1986): 431–64.

40,000 Jews were interned at Gurs and other camps in the southern, non-occupied zone.[22] There was a climate of escalating violence against perceived enemies in France from 1940 onward. Immediately after the invasion of the Soviet Union, Germans undertook a wave of arrests across occupied Europe. In France, more than 1,000 individuals were imprisoned. Through the summer, resistance activities became more overt, and the question of how to respond to them grew more pressing. One small sign of the rising insecurity was that occupiers were warned in July not to sign the guest book in restaurants, for this seemingly innocuous gesture might allow opponents to gain valuable information about the whereabouts of specific units and personnel.[23] On 31 August, clashes between young Communists and French and German security forces took place in Paris, and the occupiers responded by killing two of the agitators they had arrested.[24] Repression began to target Communists specifically, and von Stülpnagel warned the public on 15 August that anyone involved in Communist activities would be subject to capital punishment.[25]

Evidently, Communists were the primary target at this stage, but a closer examination of orders intended for ground-level troops shows that the occupation authorities were far from certain that their own personnel had not been exacerbating problems. Three days after von Stülpnagel's 15 August warning, the Paris Commander, Ernst Schaumburg, issued a general statement to German troops in the city explaining that, while the French police were responsible for combating what was specifically identified as Communist activity, German forces would step in if required. He emphasised, though, that soldiers should not get mixed up in any altercations on Paris streets, intervening only as a unit if ordered to do so. If they were threatened directly, they should use their weapons, and other Germans in the area were instructed to assist if necessary.[26] The commander went on to recommend that soldiers undertake late afternoon or evening outings in pairs or groups. He also reminded the men that, "It is unworthy of a soldier to enter the bars with prostitutes in the Montmartre neighbourhood. Visiting the bordellos

---

[22] Grynberg, "Les camps du sud de la France," 557.
[23] MBH Kommandostab Abt. Ic/III (6) Nr. 2732 u 2742/41, Re: "Eintragung in Gästebücher, Kundenlisten, usw.," 7 July 1941 (AN: 40 AJ/451).
[24] Berggötz, "Ernst Jünger," 409.
[25] Eismann points out that this was a month before Keitel's famous order (16 September 1941) to execute 50–100 communists for every German killed in a communist-initiated assassination in the occupied territoires. Eismann, "Représailles," 111.
[26] Kommandant von Gross-Paris Ia Nr. 460/41, 18 August 1941 (AN: 40 AJ/451).

there endangers your health, and in some cases, your life."[27] Finally, the men were informed that it was against the dictates of soldierly camaraderie to leave an intoxicated soldier by himself at night in the capital.

On the one hand, these regulations suggested that the occupation authorities may have been trying to use the growing insecurity to curtail soldiers' undisciplined behaviour. On the other hand, reading between the lines, they reveal that French resisters recognised and, perhaps to make a point about occupiers' excesses, deliberately preyed on soldiers who were vulnerable through drunkenness or because they had strayed into certain neighbourhoods. German leaders themselves vacillated between seeing assaults on their troops as the preventable result of personal disagreements and isolated provocations, and viewing them as political acts.[28] Apparently unwilling to recognise that simply being an occupier made each German soldier a target, the Paris Commander's orders implied that he thought some soldiers were reacting too quickly to perceived affronts and that, in other cases, occupiers' own laxity might have left them open to attack. Policy-makers like von Stülpnagel and Schaumburg felt their way forward, aiming to de-escalate tensions with a two-pronged strategy of limiting opportunities and ground-level German provocations while imposing harsh repression on French perpetrators. Thus, they asked soldiers to reexamine their own behaviour and advertised that they were pursuing a broad-based group of potential threats to security, while at the same time announcing on 19 August that cases involving suspected Communists should be referred to German military courts.[29] They also stepped up measures against Paris Jews, engaging in large-scale house searches and making arrests.[30]

Then, on 21 August, a naval adjutant was killed in the Paris Metro in what represented the first open attack on a member of the occupation forces in France. The following day, the German authorities announced in the newspaper that, "1) All French held in any kind of detention either by or for German entities in France will be considered hostages from 23 August onward. 2) On each further occasion [of violence against occupiers], a number of these hostages will be shot that corresponds to the severity of the act."[31] In early September, a further member of the occupation forces was shot, and three so-called hostages were executed. On 6, 10, 11, and 13 September, there were four additional attacks, and

[27] Kommandant von Gross-Paris Ia Nr. 460/41, 18 August 1941 (AN: 40 AJ/451).
[28] Cf. Eismann, "Représailles," 135.   [29] Eismann, "Représailles," 111.
[30] Berggötz, "Ernst Jünger," 409.
[31] "Abdruck aus 'Pariser Zeitung' v. 22.8.41 – Bekanntmachung!," 22 August 1941 (BArch: RW 35/1).

ten hostages were executed. An assassination on 16 September led to the execution of twelve hostages four days later. Another two hostages were executed on 24 September, this time in response to an attack on objects, rather than people, for the first time.[32] German reactions became increasingly harsh, though the desire to assuage tensions and moderate the impact of the attacks on German/French collaboration was still evident at this stage. Germany needed France to remain relatively quiet so that it could focus the bulk of its energies elsewhere.

Responding to the threatening situation with new rules for ground-level troops, Militärbefehlshaber von Stülpnagel now ordered, rather than simply recommending, that members of the occupying army go about in pairs. He also recommended (though did not order) men who had been issued a pistol to carry it with them, a measure that might discourage attacks, and above all made it easier to pursue and kill perpetrators on the spot. The same document informed occupiers that due to "specific incidents" they were forbidden from associating with, or going out with, French women.[33] Soldiers' interactions with local women, addressed in Chapter 2, continued even though this prohibition, like others mentioned earlier in the chapter, recognised that soldiers' behaviour might be seen as provocative, and implied that the men themselves should take some responsibility for helping to de-escalate tensions.

Information from Bordeaux around the same time also reflected restraint and a willingness to recognise that German actions might exacerbate an already tense situation. Reporting on the period from mid-July through mid-September 1941, staff in the Bordeaux military administrative district noted that Communist activities, notably the distribution of pamphlets, had been increasing since the beginning of the Russian campaign. At the same time, they concluded that overall "nothing unusual has happened."[34] Cooperation with French adminis-trative offices had continued to be smooth, and "the security of the German troops was not in danger at any point." The report writer added that "as far as we can predict, it will not be in danger for the next while."[35] Having been asked whether special measures against the

---

[32] Berggötz, "Ernst Jünger," 410.
[33] Der Militärbefehlshaber in Frankreich Kommandostab Abt. IIa Az. 14a12/41 Betr. Verhalten in der Öffentlichkeit, 10 September 1941 (AN: 40 AJ/451).
[34] Chef der Militärverwaltungsbezirks Bordeaux, Kommandostab, Abt. Ic Nr. 2780/41 g to MBH Kommandostab Abt. Ic, "Lagebericht des Ic der Militärverwaltungsbezirks Bordeaux für die Zeit vom 18.7.41 bis 23.9.41," 22 September 1941 (AN: 40 AJ/448).
[35] Chef der Militärverwaltungsbezirks Bordeaux, "Lagebericht," 22 September 1941 (AN: 40 AJ/448).

population were required in his region, he noted that while the value of such measures "might be weighed for other military administrative areas, they should not be contemplated for the Bordeaux area at present."[36] For now, attacks on German personnel remained localised, centred in Paris.

By early October, the situation seemed calmer even in the capital. Since no further assassination attempts had been made, the rules were relaxed. Rather than forbidding contact with French women outright, the Militärbefehshaber now suggested that "[i]f the situation again becomes more tense, I must demand restraint from every member of the military when together with, and when in public with, French female persons, in order to exclude any possibility of jealousy with French men and thus a further aggravation of the domestic situation in difficult times."[37] Von Stülpnagel again placed responsibility on soldiers themselves to maintain good relations with the French, notably by exercising judgement and restraint in their interactions with women in order not to escalate the uneasy situation.

The tone of these instructions signals the continuing vacillation in Paris in this period. Some occupiers clearly believed, or at any rate sought to interpret, resistance attacks as isolated, even justified responses to provocative behaviour on the part of individual soldiers. Read in this way, such actions called for a moderate response, marked by prevention and self-restraint rather than repression. It would be too bad, these relaxed rules seemed to say, to prohibit all German occupiers from enjoying France and its pleasures simply on account of a few isolated attacks. The relaxation of regulations in October also suggested that the Militärbefehshaber thought continuing "normal" life in France might demonstrate that a few incidents of what he viewed as "terrorism" would not impinge on Germans' strength and control of France.

At the same time, however, there was a growing conviction in some quarters, bolstered by radical rhetoric, that the violence in France was political in nature, part of a larger European pattern of anti-German activity with "Judeo-Communist" roots.[38] In the fall of 1941, the attempt to find a balance between these two points of view coloured not only discussions within France, but more significantly, exchanges between the Militärbefehshaber and his Paris staff, and their superiors in the Reich. The former preferred a relatively soft course, privileging the local

---

[36] Chef der Militärverwaltungsbezirks Bordeaux, "Lagebericht," 22 September 1941 (AN: 40 AJ/448).

[37] Militärbefehlshaber in Frankreich Kommandostab Abt. IIa Az. 14 a 12/41 Betr. Verhalten in der Öffentlichkeit, 10 October 1941 (AN: 40 AJ/451).

[38] Eismann, *Hôtel Majestic*, 358–63.

situation and seeking to diminish tensions that they viewed as counter-productive because they put German lives in danger and jeopardised the collaboration required for successful occupation.[39] The latter, with less knowledge of, interest in, and sensitivity towards, local conditions and more deeply convinced by the ruthless logic of European conquest, favoured a harsh course modelled on German treatment of resisters elsewhere.[40] Thus, on 16 September 1941, Field Marshall Keitel had ordered that between 50 and 100 Communists be shot for every German killed by what he insisted was "a mass movement under unified leadership from Moscow."[41] For Keitel, and the Führer whose orders he followed, Communists were at the root of every act against the occupying authorities, regardless of individual circumstances.[42] A few days later, Keitel recommended that military commanders in occupied areas always have "hostages" from various opposition circles available for execution.[43] Jails in France had been filling with political prisoners from the beginning of the occupation and these hostages now became guarantors for the good behaviour of the rest of the population. Three days after Keitel's 16 September order, moreover, the Paris Commander announced that any civilian who broke curfew "will be arrested and made a hostage."[44] Still, there remained a difference of scale between these local measures, which, Thomas Laub argues, aimed to defeat a resistance interpreted as a "political and military phenomenon," and Keitel's assimilation of all resistance to communist motives, accompanied by the all-encompassing order to execute 50–100 Communists each time German installations or people were attacked.[45] This difference was at the heart of tensions through the autumn among German agencies in Paris, and between Paris and Berlin.

On 20 October, news came through to Paris that Lieutenant-Colonel Karl Friedrich Hotz, Field Commander of the western city of Nantes, had been shot dead. The attack shocked not only the Germans, but also

---

[39] Laub, *After the Fall*, 128.   [40] Cf. Herbert, "German Military Command," 139–40.
[41] Keitel's order is reprinted in Jan Philipp Reemtsma and Ulrike Jureit, eds., *Verbrechen der Wehrmacht: Dimensiones des Vernichtungskrieges 1941–1944: Ausstellungskatalog* (Hamburg: Hamburger Edition, 2002), 515. In late June, Keitel had still expressed the somewhat more moderate viewpoint that security needs must be weighed against the pressure that "too rigorous an approach" would put on the German relationship with France. OKW Nr. 505/41 g Betr. Aussetzung der Vollstreckung von Todesurteilen gegen franz. Staatsangehörige, signed by Keitel, 30 June 1941 (BArch: RW 35/1).
[42] See Keitel's order in Reemtsma and Jureit, 515; Laub, *After the Fall*, 129.
[43] Keitel Anweisung an OKH and Wehrmachtbefehlshaber Südost betreffs Geiselnahme, 28 September 1941, Reemtsma and Jureit, *Verbrechen der Wehrmacht*, 514.
[44] Kommandant von Gross-Paris, Kommandantur-Befehl Nr. 129, 19 September 1941 (BArch: RH 36/34).
[45] Laub, *After the Fall*, 139.

the French community, for it targetted a senior member of the occupation hierarchy who was well liked and familiar to local people from before the war. As Robert Gildea has pointed out, the people of Nantes viewed the killing as misguided, for it eliminated a man in his sixties who was seen as a moderate and an ally. According to the German teacher Edmund Duméril, who served as a translator and liaison with the Germans on behalf of the French prefecture, Hotz was "a sure support vis à vis the Germans, an intelligent and fair man, in no sense a hitlerian, [and he was] a friend to the French."[46] Now, Duméril feared that the commander would be replaced by "some odious Prussian sabre-rattler."[47]

The Nantes population saw this attack not only as misguided, but also dangerous. Although it had been undertaken by an outsider, the Alsacian Communist Gilbert Brustlein, who had travelled to the city some days before, the Nantais were justifiably concerned that they would now become the target of German reprisals. When news of the attack reached Hitler, Field Marshall Keitel ordered the killing not of the 50 to 100 men his orders had forseen, but rather 100–150. Struggling to retain some control over the situation, von Stülpnagel parried by agreeing to execute 100 people, but only if Hotz's killer failed to turn up after three days. In the end, Hitler decided that 50 "hostages" were to be shot immediately, and 50 more two days later if the murderer was still at large.[48]

On 22 October 1941, a first group of forty-eight prisoners was shot, including sixteen local notables and World War I veterans who had been imprisoned earlier in the year for resistance activity, twenty-seven Communists held at the Choisel camp north of the city, and five prisoners from Nantes held in Paris. Then, however, a combination of French mobilisation and German intercession led to a reversal of the planned reprisals, and a stay of execution was obtained for the second group of prisoners. The city of Nantes and the French government offered generous rewards for information leading to the perpetrator's arrest while Nantes notables, and even a group of families of the first wave of "hostages" killed, petitioned for leniency and offered assurances of

---

[46] Edmond Duméril, extract of 1947 memoirs "Visions d'histoire" based on diary entry for 20 October 1941 in Duméril, *Journal*, 181. Duméril is cited in Robert Gildea, "Resistance, Reprisals and Community in Occupied France," *Transactions of the Royal Historical Society (Sixth Series)* 13 (December 2003): 165.

[47] Duméril, *Journal*, 20 October 1941, 181. Cited in Gildea, "Resistance," 165. This account of events in Nantes and local reactions follows Gildea's.

[48] Herbert, "German Military Command," 140. For more details, see Laub, *After the Fall*, 137 ff.

continuing loyalty.[49] Nonetheless, Hotz's assassination and the hostage executions that followed in its wake were "of particular importance," as author Ernst Jünger put it in a secret manuscript he prepared for Otto von Stülpnagel about the events of autumn 1941.[50] Jünger saw this assassination as a critical moment, because it was linked to "a drastic shift in methods."[51] These events raised the "fundamental question of whether it was advisable to insist on following this path, that would lead to both a profound change in the relationship between the occupiers and the occupied land, but also between the two peoples overall."[52]

The concern Jünger expressed in this report, framed to defend von Stülpnagel, was indicative of the debates at the centre of the occupation leadership, and especially between the Militärbefehlshaber and his superiors in Berlin. Not long after Hotz was killed, von Stülpnagel contacted Hitler's headquarters to warn the Führer against using what von Stülpnagel labelled as "Polish methods" in France.[53] Von Stülpnagel was not against taking prisoners as hostages, or executing them, but he found the scale of the new measures hard to stomach. He argued that harsh repression, such as that used in Poland, would simply provoke bitterness and jeopardise a future rapprochement with France. He added that Propaganda Minister Joseph Goebbels agreed with his point of view, as did the French Prime Minister (Vice-président du Conseil) Darlan. But, while von Stülpnagel hoped to maintain a relatively moderate course, resistance activity, like German exactions on France, persisted. The day after Hotz was shot walking to his office, a military administrator was killed in Bordeaux on his way home from work. The campaign against the German occupiers had moved well beyond Paris and threatened to destabilise the occupation regime as a whole.

The gap between Hitler, Keitel and other high-ranking National Socialists in Berlin, and Otto von Stülpnagel in Paris, grew. The former saw events in France in the context of occupied Europe as a whole.

[49] Gildea, "Resistance," 167. See also Jünger's account in Berggötz, "Ernst Jünger," 427 ff.
[50] A copy of this report, consciously prepared to record and justify von Stülpnagel's decision-making, survived at Jünger's home in southern Germany. After Jünger's death, it was published with scholarly apparatus by Sven Olaf Berggötz. Ernst Jünger, "Zur Geiselfrage: Schilderung der Fälle und ihrer Auswirkung" in Berggötz, "Ernst Jünger," 418 ff. Cf. Meyer, "'Kleistische Prosa." Allan Mitchell's otherwise comprehensive account of Jünger's life in Paris does not offer an analysis of this document. Mitchell, The Devil's Captain.
[51] Ernst Jünger, "Zur Geiselfrage" in Berggötz, "Ernst Jünger," 432.
[52] Ernst Jünger, "Zur Geiselfrage" in Berggötz, 432.
[53] Otto von Stülpnagel, Notes on telephone conversation with General Major Wagner on 22 October 1941, 23 October 1941 (BArch: RW 35/1).

For them, repressive measures were part of Germany's broader strategy to counter a Communist uprising Europe-wide, and no compromises could be made. Viewed from this angle, Stülpnagel's objections seemed dangerous, even ridiculous. As historian Ulrich Herbert has underlined, between September 1941 and January 1942, while reprisals in France were being debated at the highest levels, more than 20,000 people were murdered in reprisal actions in Serbia, and untold numbers in the Soviet Union.[54] Gaël Eismann, for her part, emphasises that there were fundamental political, economic, and ideological differences between the National Socialists' approach to war in the West and in the East. These two spaces nonetheless influenced each other, and in 1943–4, repressive methods sometimes moved from one to the other.[55]

For the occupation authorities on the ground in France in 1941, however, "precisely the political relations with the individual countries — more precisely, [Germans'] own political and cultural evaluation of those [occupied] countries," held considerable weight.[56] Quite apart from occupiers' widespread perception that French people were, if misguided and decadent, at least highly cultured and thus should not be subjected to "Polish methods," exercising brutal dominance in France also ran up against occupiers' own view of themselves as civilised, rather than barbaric men. Contemporary documents and postwar memoirs discussed later in the chapter suggest that to some occupiers who had not experienced the harsh realities of the Eastern Front, and instead had spent the war thus far enjoying French culture and cultivating good relations with French people on the ground, killing large numbers of hostages seemed extreme, and inappropriate. Worse, it risked jeopardising France's exploitation for the German war effort, for it might interrupt the easy flow of resources and above all, the country's use as a quiet staging area to rest and prepare troops.

This is not to say that occupiers in France were innocent bystanders, let alone valiant heroes trying to oppose Hitler's brutality. Von Stülpnagel and his close advisors viewed hostage-taking, and even executing small numbers of hostages as a warning to others as normal ways of doing military business.[57] Their goal in France, however, was

---

[54] Herbert, "German Military Command," 140.   [55] Eismann, Hôtel Majestic, 363.
[56] Herbert, "German Military Command," 140.
[57] Umbreit points out that other powers also employed this practice. For Eismann, however, von Stülpnagel had departed from conventional practices by expanding the group of potential (and real) hostages beyond local notables. See Umbreit, Militärbefehlshaber, 135; Eismann, "Représailles," 110.

"pacification" of the territory rather than "eradication" of an ideological enemy or the "cleansing" of a living space for Germans.[58] Considerable friction between Berlin and Paris arose from this fundamental difference in viewpoints and objectives. Supported by his administrative staff in particular, Otto von Stülpnagel fought for a more moderate response to the security problem. On the one hand, he tried to convince Hitler of the effectiveness of his policies to ensure the security of ground-level troops. He offered rewards to French people who gave information leading to the arrest of resisters and he intervened more decisively in the French judicial system.[59] On the other hand, he stepped up repression directed towards "outsiders," coming up with a kind of devil's bargain to satisfy Hitler's requirements as well as his own. Von Stülpnagel elected to slow the pace of hostage executions, and instead ramped up the persecution of France's resident Jews.[60]

Many Jews had arrived in the Republic during the interwar period, some having fled persecution in Germany. Alongside the German authorities, many French people viewed these newcomers, as well as Jews who were already French citizens, with suspicion. Local discrimination and anti-Semitism made them easy targets. Von Stülpnagel thought that measures against Jews might allow him to satisfy the demand for retribution from Berlin without, at the same time, exacerbating the domestic political situation by killing more non-Jews in France. When the next assassination took place on 28 November, instead of killing 300 "hostages" as Hitler requested, von Stülpnagel offered to have "50 Jews and Communists" executed, and to impose "a damages payment of one billion francs on the Jews of Paris."[61] Further, he proposed "interning Jews with records of criminal or anti-German activities for deportation to the East."[62] For these deportations, a figure of about 1,000 individuals was put forward. Assassinations continued in subsequent days, and Stülpnagel proposed a further 50 executions and 500 deportations. In the end, 95 people were executed, and 1,500 people pinpointed for deportation, most of them Jews, though due to "transport problems" they could not be shipped eastwards right away.[63]

---

[58] Eismann, *Hôtel Majestic*, 363.   [59] Eismann, *Hôtel Majestic*, 366.

[60] The following account is based on that of Herbert. See also the work of Ahlrich Meyer and the comparison of their interpretations in Eismann. Eismann, 63–5; Herbert, "German Military Command"; Ahlrich Meyer, *Die Besatzung*.

[61] MBH to OKH, 1 November 1941 in "Das Geiselverfahren im Bereich des Militärbefehlshabers in Frankreich vom August 1941 bis Mai 1942," 77 (BArch: RW 35/524) cited in Herbert, "German Military Command," 142.

[62] Herbert, "German Military Command,"142.

[63] Herbert, "German Military Command,"142.

By January 1942, a total of 264 "hostages" had been murdered, and Stülpnagel made one last attempt to halt the hostage-killings.[64] Mid-month, he wrote that, "[k]nowing as I do the general situation and the effects of such harsh measures on the whole population and on our relations with France, I can ... no longer reconcile mass shootings with my conscience, nor answer for them before the bar of history."[65] Imprisoning more Jews and Communists was not a viable solution either, for France's prisons and camps were over-full.[66] The only remaining response to attacks on German occupying forces, therefore, was "the incident-by-incident transporting to Germany or the East of a certain number of Communists or Jews who are *already* interned."[67] Hitler and Keitel disagreed, however, seeing deportations not as a replacement for, but as a supplement to, the execution of hostages as "vengeance" for resistance attacks. Understanding that he had lost Hitler's confidence, Otto von Stülpnagel resigned on 15 February 1942.[68]

Seen in this light, then, the deportation of Jews in France emerged as the military government's answer to the question of how to respond to rising numbers of attacks on the German occupation forces. Having hoped to use this method to appease voices calling for retribution, while at the same time smoothing over local tensions by halting hostage executions, von Stülpnagel in fact came up with a "solution" that not only failed to stop executions, but also ushered in a new, more radical phase of anti-Jewish measures in France. From this point forward, deportation became a regular part of the German response to resistance attacks, aligning with, and feeding, Hitler's overall plans to deport and murder Europe's Jews.[69] Far from being obliged to undertake radical measures by pressure from the police branch under Heydrich's authority, or by Nazi party representatives in Berlin, "[t]he military administration itself had authorized and arranged not only the detention first of foreign, then in August 1941, of French, Jews, but also the first mass deportations

[64] Herbert, "German Military Command,"142.
[65] MBH to OKW, 15 January 1942, (BArch: RW 35/543) cited in Herbert, "German Military Command," 142.
[66] As Herbert points out, this deliberate overfilling was used to "justify" deportation elsewhere too, including in Poland. Herbert, "German Military Command,"149.
[67] MBH to OKW, 15 January 1942 (BArch: RW 35/543) cited in Herbert, "German Military Command,"142–3.
[68] MBH to Keitel Nr. 11/42, 15 February 1942 (BArch: RW 35/1).
[69] Herbert, "German Military Command," 143, 151. The first deportations were actually carried out on 27 March 1942. Martin Jungius and Wolfgang Seibel, "The Citizen as Perpetrator: Kurt Blanke and Aryanization in France, 1940–1944," *Holocaust & Genocide Studies* 22, No. 3 (Winter 2008): 457.

'to the East.'"[70] This was possible, as Herbert has indicated, because in this war, "for the conservative military officers, the Jews, like criminals and Communists, were not recognized as honorable opponents."[71]

After Otto von Stülpnagel's departure, his position was filled by a cousin, Carl-Heinrich von Stülpnagel. The occupation administration in France was reorganised, and policing powers separated more clearly from the military government. An office of the Superior SS- and Police leader (Höherer SS- und Polizeiführer) was established in France under the control of Karl Oberg, and the occupying forces were split from this time forward, with police and military instances fighting ongoing battles over power and prestige. Simultaneously, the process that had begun with discrimination, spoliation of Jewish property, and persecution of individual Jews, became a generalised policy of round-ups and deportation to the East. Initiated by the German occupation forces, it met with approval and cooperation from French people, and culminated in the deportation of some 76,000 individuals.[72]

The change in leadership and the administrative restructuring of late 1941 and early 1942 represented a shift in the character of the occupation. Von Stülpnagel's immediate subordinates in the military administration had tended to support his point of view, and when they had been asked in mid-October 1941 what they thought should be done about the threats to German security, even those who saw hostage-taking as acceptable argued against mass executions.[73] Emphasising the importance of maintaining good relations with the population in order to exploit France to the fullest, including as a "peaceful" rest area for troops, von Stülpnagel underlined in his resignation letter, "that in the whole time I held office, calm and order were on the whole maintained and the land was exploited in the most useful and extensive way, even going well beyond the terms of the armistice agreement."[74] Stülpnagel's resignation signalled that from here on in, it would be increasingly difficult to reconcile occupiers' ongoing "softer" interactions with France with radicalising pressures stemming from Berlin and the war as a whole.

In hindsight, occupiers saw this as the fateful point at which they themselves became directly involved in Hitler's atrocities. Their retrospective accounts have contributed to the tendency to view this moment as a caesura, a complete break, rather than a phase in which existing

---

[70] Herbert, "German Military Command," 141.
[71] Herbert, "German Military Command," 151.
[72] Only about three percent returned. Michael R. Marrus and Robert O. Paxton, *Vichy France and the Jews* (Stanford: Stanford University Press, 1995), xv.
[73] Umbreit, *Militärbefehlshaber*; Laub, *After the Fall*, 161.
[74] MBH to Keitel Nr. 11/42, 15 February 1942 (BArch: RW 35/1).

practices were developed further and radicalised.[75] In his memoirs, Walter Bargatzky, a former member of the Militärbefehlshaber's legal staff in Paris, documented a growing awareness that the Third Reich's crimes now touched each individual.[76] "At the Majestic [Hotel]," he wrote, "faces are turning to stone. We had already lived through many of Hitler's atrocities, and now we see them crossing our desks every day."[77]

Bargatzky also indicated in his postwar account that Paris administrators were familiar with what was happening in other German-occupied areas, including to European Jews. However, it had not seemed very real up to this point.[78] Notably, the officer Georg Wilhelm Knoke had been transferred to the Militärbefehlhaber's staff in Paris in April 1942 after witnessing mass murders in Babi Yar. According to Bargatzky, Knoke spoke about these crimes to his colleagues.[79] Still, Bargatzky recalled that he himself had not been particularly affected by this information until July 1942, when the wife of a German-speaking pharmacist named Silberberg, who he and other occupiers had used for their prescriptions, was picked up by the French police and taken to an internment camp at Compiègne. Silberberg's white professional coat having given the pharmacist access to the administrative offices at the Majestic hotel, he came to plead for Bargatzky's help to liberate his spouse, or at very least, to make sure she received the warm blanket he held out hesitantly, wrapped in brown paper. After obtaining the permission of his superiors, making the rounds of the military administration, and telephoning Oberg's staff, only to be taken to task for interfering, Bargatzky came back to Silberberg with assurances – going against his own certain knowledge – that all would be well. Silberberg's wife was never heard from again and, within a few weeks, Silberberg himself was picked up too. Later, Bargatzky commented that it was "strange to say," but he had learned that in order to begin to grasp atrocities, "knowledge of a generalized horror is insufficient, we must also experience individual terror."[80]

---

[75] For a critique of these memoirs and their influence on the historiography of the occupation, see Eismann, *Hôtel Majestic*, 40 ff. Read with an awareness of their origins and context, the memoirs remain useful for reconstructing occupiers' attitudes and self-justifications.

[76] Bargatzky was linked to the 20 July 1944 plot on Hitler, though not one of its leaders. A lawyer, he later became a civil servant and rose to the position of State Secretary of Health in West Germany. After retirement, he became President of the German Red Cross from 1967 to 1982.

[77] Bargatzky, *Hotel Majestic*, 89.   [78] Bargatzky, *Hotel Majestic*, 102–9.

[79] Bargatzky, *Hotel Majestic*, 102–9; Jungius and Seibel, "The Citizen as Perpetrator," 458, ftnt. 130.

[80] Bargatzky, *Hotel Majestic*, 109.

With this knowledge of "individual terror," partial as it was, for Bargatzky was on the perpetrating side, came individual responsibility, and that was a more difficult suit to wear. Around the time of von Stülpnagel's resignation, according to Ernst Jünger's diary, published in 1949, Jünger met with the head of the command staff in Paris, Hans Speidel, who had just returned from the Führer's headquarters. Speidel shared some notes he had taken while visiting Hitler. Jünger claimed that he had been horrified by Speidel's description of the "tendencies toward destruction, the strivings to shoot, eradicate, and starve" that he had seen.[81] "There is no doubt," Jünger wrote, "that there are individuals who must be held responsible for the blood of millions. And they go after blood-letting like tigers." Jünger interpreted the regime's brutality as the work of Hitler and his henchmen, external to himself. Jünger also believed that many French people were willing and ready to participate in Hitler's projects, and that the German staff at the Majestic were the only individuals, "who are able to prevent, or at least delay, the union of these partners." "And yet," he continued, "this must occur with completely hidden cards – above all, it is important that any appearance of humanity be avoided. That would be like showing a red cloth to a bull."[82] For Jünger, publishing after the war, von Stülpnagel and his staff had served the role of brakes – they were the only people able to keep German leaders and French collaborators from working the bellows together to fan the flames of hatred. It had been essential that they act in secret, however, for any "appearance of humanity" would have given them away. Even after 1945, Jünger refused, or was unable, to see the extent to which von Stülpnagel, and by extension, he himself, were implicated in the crimes of the Nazi regime. Like Bargatzky, he realised that Hitler's atrocities were now moving across his own desk, but unlike Bargatzky, he had little sense that these atrocities might also be his own.[83]

Jünger's remarks go to the heart of the controversy that has surrounded the events of autumn 1941 and Stülpnagel's resignation ever since they occurred. Jünger, after all, was a member of the occupation administration and a close confidant of its most important men. Just after tendering his resignation, von Stülpnagel charged Jünger with documenting for posterity the Militärbefehlshaber's role in the escalation of violence in France.[84] Jünger argued that von Stülpnagel was acting with

---

[81] Jünger, *Strahlungen*, entry for 8 February 1942, 94.
[82] Jünger, *Strahlungen*, entry for 8 February 1942, 94.
[83] To be sure, Bargatzky's memoirs were published much later, not until 1987, in a different context of memory and reinterpretation of the Third Reich.
[84] Jünger described the meeting in his diary. Jünger, *Strahlungen*, entry for 23 February 1942, 94. Cf. Berggötz, "Ernst Jünger," 405.

the best of intentions, attempting to stem the tide of atrocities as much as he could without raising the suspicions of his superiors in Berlin. However, Jünger's own involvement in the high military administration makes these statements questionable, to say the least. Rather than the sole beacon of humanity, von Stülpnagel comes across as one among a number of actors, none of whom were innocent. Attempting to retain some measure of control over the situation and to hold his own position vis à vis various competitors both in France and in Berlin, he made decisions that, in the context of the Third Reich, inevitably led to more violence and destruction of life, not less.

One could write more about the roles of von Stülpnagel, Jünger and others in the events of 1941, but beyond the occupation's highest levels in Paris, how did the changing climate in France affect soldiers on the ground? What role did they play in this transition? We begin to examine this question here, and pursue it in subsequent chapters. As Peter Lieb and Robert Paxton have pointed out, it is impossible to know the extent to which any individual soldier participated in the repression of opponents and resisters in France.[85] Some men, like those assigned to coastal defence and surveillance, probably had little to do with it, while others were specifically ordered to search out resisters who had taken to the maquis. Police groups and especially Waffen-SS units may have been responsible for many of the worst excesses, but they were certainly not alone in exercising repression.[86]

Whether they were directly involved in reprisals or not, the growing instability was apparent both to soldiers on the ground, and to visitors. In October 1941, Bernhard Schulz was sent out to track down French householders harbouring downed airmen. By December 1942, according to an official report from Paris, French "animosity toward the occupying power [could] be felt in growing passive resistance that [was] expressed through unfriendly behaviour and difficulties purchasing wares, in delays executing orders, and through work slow-downs in factories and workshops."[87] Rather than an often quite relaxed cohabitation, mistrust and wariness now characterised relations between occupiers and local people. The dry tone of official reports notwithstanding, soldiers felt the tension in a visceral way. From Marseilles in early January 1943, an occupier identified only as Richard wrote that "[a]t the moment we're in a constant state of readiness because Marseilles is under a state of siege. There have already been exchanges of fire and a

[85] Lieb and Paxton, "Maintenir l'ordre," 118.
[86] Lieb, *Konventionneller*. For a critique of Lieb, see Eismann, *Hôtel Majestic*, 72.
[87] Lagebericht der Abteilung Ic Dez. 1942 (Paris), 1 January 1942 (AN: 40 AJ 89).

few bombs have been thrown into various buildings. There have been quite a few wounded ... At the moment we're not allowed into the city because it's too dangerous."[88] A few days later, on 22 January 1943, Richard might well have been among the German forces who carried out the notorious large-scale raid that destroyed the city's Vieux Port neighbourhood.[89]

Ground-level occupiers typically supported efforts to combat resistance, and in their letters sought to shore up and justify their own position as legitimate occupiers. In January 1943, Sergeant E. B., a veteran of World War I who had been called up for a second time six months earlier, claimed that the French were showing themselves just as untrustworthy now as then. Although he was part of a coastal battery, he wrote that he and his comrades were "not only watching the sea carefully, but also listening and preparing against the land here."[90] A few weeks later, Peter G., who belonged to a unit of mountain infantry, complained that although he had just completed an action "à la Chambéry," there had been no "big booty" this time.[91] Indeed, he compared the anti-partisan raid he had just undertaken to a mere "practice run" in Russia and lamented that, "instead of a large-scale battue, [mere] rabbits and foxes were caught. The partisans [Partisanski] had already fled long ago."[92] Lance Corporal Alex B., in his correspondence, reported that soldiers' mail had been stolen, but scoffed that it "was that kind of Communist gang that wants to get themselves noticed a bit. But they're still a little too stupid."[93] There was no question in these occupiers' minds that the French were untrustworthy, inferior, and should be put in their place once and for all.

A few months later, in Paris, Lance Corporal Alfred M. expressed a more nuanced viewpoint, commenting on the difficulty of knowing where the average French person stood with regard to the occupying soldiers: "It's really very hard to get a clear picture of people's real opinions. On the one hand, you hear more and more often the call for honest collaboration with Germany, and then on the other hand there are the assassinations."[94] As the atmosphere shifted, Germans adjusted their

---

[88] Richard, letter, 8 January 1943 (BfZ SS).   [89] See Chapter 4.
[90] E. B., letter, 26 January 1943 (BfZ SS).
[91] The reference to Chambéry, in French in the original, is not entirely clear – a prefect's report from December 1943 mentions information gleaned after the arrest of two resisters at Chambéry that fall and perhaps G. had been involved in rounding up such individuals. H. R. Kedward, *In Search of the Maquis: Rural Resistance in Southern France 1942–1944* (Oxford: Clarendon Press, 1993), 79 n. 24.
[92] Peter G, letter, 18 February 1943 (BfZ SS).   [93] Alex B., 19 April 1943 (BfZ SS).
[94] Alfred M., letter, 19 April 1943 (BfZ SS).

behavior and expectations to the new climate. In May 1943, Air Force sergeant Alfred N. wrote in an almost blasé way, "and apart from that, the city is again in a state of emergency because some act of sabotage or other has been carried out. Everything's closed early and the streetcars don't run as long. Through any number of things, in fact, you can see that you're living in half-hostile territory abroad. It's mostly Communist elements who do these things."[95] The sergeant described the recent attacks on his unnamed location as if such incidents had become routine, and repeated the propaganda line that the attackers were probably Communist agitators. He seemed almost surprised by the way that the curfew and early streetcar closures reminded him of something that should have been obvious – he was living in a "half-hostile" land abroad.

If, for Alfred N. and others just cited, attacks and curfews had become the new norm, to other soldiers, the changed atmosphere was not nearly as evident, or if it was, they chose not to write about it. In August 1943, an occupier identified only as Rudi reported home to his wife in Betzdorf, midway between Cologne and Frankfurt, that his unit was the first to occupy an unidentified area in southern France. He wrote that he was thrilled to consume fresh grapes every day, the swimming was delightful, and he hoped to be able to send some tasty food parcels home: "Things are pretty good here so far, just an awful lot of mosquitoes."[96] Only in 1944 did something of the war's violence slip through, when Rudi repeated, "I like it pretty well here so far," and then added, "but we're on alert all the time, day and night. Then we hop in the vehicles and again out into the countryside."[97]

The sense that France was now a lot more dangerous than occupiers expected shines through in a further example. In memoirs that were probably written in the early 1950s, training officer Wilhelm Schadt described his experiences from autumn 1943 onward. The officer had just spent twenty-six months in Russia, including a narrow escape during the Soviet offensive at Orel. When his decimated unit was rotated out to rest, he was sent to France and could not believe his luck that he had gotten out of Russia unscathed. France was not as safe as he might have imagined, however. Posted to Clermont-Ferrand in the early autumn of 1943, he was badly hurt in a truck accident while involved in a search operation near Vichy. By mid-winter 1944, Schadt was back on duty and noted that there were "continuous losses due to the increasingly strong guerrilla warfare [Kleinkrieg] in France. Our situation is becoming more

[95] Alfred N., letter, 24 May 1943 (BfZ SS).
[96] Rudi, letter to his wife and son, 13 August 1943 (BfZ SS).
[97] Rudi, letter to his wife and son, 10 May 1944 (BfZ SS).

and more serious from day to day, no nights without explosions, raids, etc."[98] Everyone around him grew increasingly nervous, with bombers flying overhead daily. After the Allied invasion in Normandy, two men from his unit deserted.

Earlier than that, in October 1943, Professor Friedrich Grimm, a propagandist and lawyer who often spoke to French collaborationist circles, visited Southern France on a lecture tour sponsored by the "Groupe Collaboration." He found the situation there alarming. Grimm may have been particularly sensitive to the unsettled atmosphere because he had recently arrived from Germany, where aerial bombing was a much greater threat than partisan activity. Grimm was also a civilian, and unlike occupying soldiers, he may not have expected to encounter such hostility. Grimm noted that although he was heartily welcomed by audiences that included, in Nîmes, members of the Milice as well as local dignitaries and youth associated with the Collaboration movement, "It was especially characteristic that the whole thing stood under the sign of attacks and acts of terror." Grimm himself and the organisers of his various speeches were targetted in a direct attempt to intimidate high-profile proponents of Collaboration on both the German and French sides. In Nîmes, there were plans to assassinate one of the meeting organisers, while in Lyon, at the last minute a plot was thwarted to throw hand grenades into the meeting room, and to put a time bomb in the car carrying Grimm and his French hosts. While Grimm was giving a speech in Clermont-Ferrand, the meeting rooms of the local Parti populaire français (PPF) were bombed. Two days after he spoke in Nîmes, "a serious attack was made on German troops marching past, with over twenty soldiers wounded and several killed."[99] Given his official role as a propagandist, Grimm was an obvious target, and he may also have sought to exaggerate the instability in France for political reasons. He did not, of course, consider Germany's responsibility for provoking these attacks. Still, his report confirms that the situation was degrading rapidly.

Clearly, then, the events of the late summer and autumn of 1941 signalled the beginning of a new, more deadly phase of the occupation. This change affected not only conditions on the ground, but also the ways occupiers thought about France, and perhaps about the project of occupation itself. Even foreign observers noticed the change.

[98] Wilhelm Schadt, "Die Erlebnisse von Wilhelm Schadt aus Legelshurst in den Jahren 1939–1950," 10 (DTA 1628).

[99] Professor Grimm, "Bericht über meine Vortragsreise in Südfrankreich vom 17. bis 23. Oktober 1943," 26 October 1943 (AA: DBP/1110a).

On 8 September, soon after the execution of the first three hostages, the *New York Times* wrote:

> The barbaric cruelty of the Nazi conquerors toward their vanquished, helpless victims is so widely known that a new crime of theirs against humanity occasions no surprise. That they who have perfected the science of making war have failed so completely in the art of [peaceful] conquest; that they can sometimes be so downright stupid, however, is difficult to understand."[100]

The *New York Times*'s remarks were blunt enough that Ernst Jünger included this commentary in his wartime report about the Militärbefehlshaber's role in 1941 in France, ostensibly to demonstrate how the Americans were trying to make propagandistic use of the events. Yet the *New York Times* had also put its finger on something essential – the Germans, so skilled at war, were failing at occupation. All the hard work they had put into convincing France and the world that they were not barbarians was coming unravelled. They could no longer pretend that they were developing a model occupation, and from now on, could only hold and exploit French territory as long as possible, at whatever the cost.

The change that became visible in 1941 must be understood in the context of the overall German war effort; for, having moved from victory to victory since 1939, Hitler's forces had failed to take Moscow in the late autumn of 1941, and faced the prospect of an extended war in the Soviet Union. Moving from a short-term war of conquest to a long, drawn-out conflict led to supply problems affecting everything from materiel and ammunition, through food, to manpower. Increasingly, Germany relied on its occupied territories to supply homeland needs and to support its troops. The repercussions of the situation in the East were felt across German-held lands, including in France.

The combination of rising insecurity, a new emphasis on policing and repression, and ever-growing exploitation of French industrial and food resources to feed the German war machine changed the character of the occupation. It had never been as gentle as the Germans liked to imagine, yet the first eighteen months have often been compared to a honeymoon, in which occupiers' behaviour was "correct" and their presence, while resented by many French, was tolerated in view of its likely brevity. Some French, of course, welcomed the Germans' arrival and shared willingly in their projects for France's future. After 1942, this stance was more difficult to maintain, though collaborationist circles persisted. The shift

---

[100] "A Crime and a Blunder," *The New York Times*, 8 September 1941, Evening edition, sec. C. quoted in Ernst Jünger, "Zur Geiselfrage" in Berggötz, "Ernst Jünger," 423.

in many French people's moods from cautious *attentisme* to increasing resentment and overt opposition is well documented. At least on the face of it, Germans too should have shifted their behaviour, ceasing to pretend that they were welcome guests – mere tourists, photographers, and consumers of French leisure and pleasures.

And yet they continued to pretend this – overall, as we will see, occupiers' actual behaviour changed relatively little after 1941; certainly, it changed less than even contemporary German observers thought it should have changed. France had been considered a desirable posting from the occupation's outset; now, as conditions steadily worsened both within France and on other battlefronts, especially in the East, the perception arose that occupiers in France were simply enjoying themselves, contributing little to the war effort while other men suffered. This resentment soon spilled over into policy-making with far-reaching effects, notably in the crucial area of manpower management.

6   *Westweich?* Perceptions of "Softness" among Soldiers in France

After taking part in the 1940 Blitzkrieg campaign and then being stationed in France for nearly a year, thirty-one year-old artillery man Kurt F. was transferred to East Prussia in spring 1941. His unit was preparing to invade the Soviet Union, and military life had begun to grate on F. Complaining that he was quartered in barracks, twelve men to a room, with even the latrines built for ten to use at once, he told his parents that, "I often think back longingly on my little house on the Atlantic."[1] Initially, and perhaps ironically, he described the campaign in the East as "comfortable" (gemütlich) compared to the 1940 French campaign, but it soon looked very different indeed.[2]

Pushing forwards into the Soviet Union, F.'s unit came within 400 km of Moscow by July, and then stalled. In October 1941, their train was hit near Orel and, although all the men escaped, their belongings were destroyed when 40 grenades they were carrying exploded. Lamenting the loss of his rifle, his camera with "over 200 war photos," 160 cigarettes, some tobacco and cigarillos, F. wrote that he was wearing rags for socks and was sleeping under two winter coats he had taken from Russian POWs.[3] The weather grew colder, and although he had been strolling among palm trees and laurel blossoms near Bordeaux the previous winter, in February 1942, F. could only dream of such delights.[4] He expressed frustration that his unit could not be taken out of combat because "the infantry divisions that came from France to relieve us, and for the most part had never been sent into action before, need more time to get used to this tough war than we had counted on."[5] The contrast between France and the Soviet Union was often on his mind, and when F. heard that a male relative was headed to Dijon, he remarked that if the situation in France had not worsened fundamentally, this posting should be greeted with pleasure. "I helped take Dijon on

---

[1] Kurt F., 26 April 1941 (DTA: 270/1).   [2] Kurt F., 26 June 1941 (DTA: 270/1).
[3] Kurt F., 6 October, 1941 (DTA: 270/1).   [4] Kurt F., 1 July 1940 (DTA: 270/I).
[5] Kurt F., 15 February 1942, (DTA: 270/1).

192

17 May 1940," he continued, "and after that often went shopping there from Auxerre. Once my shopping was done, I drank a quite few bottles of good Burgundy there. We still often sustain ourselves on our memories of France. Compared to this one, that campaign was pure child's play."[6]

At the end of twelve months of brutal combat, consuming the first real beer he and his comrades had seen since the invasion, F. summed up his experiences: "[T]he hardest year of our lives is ending," he wrote, "and we don't need to worry anymore that the men of the Great War achieved more at Verdun than we have [here]."[7] Just as the conquest of France had restored German honour by reversing the Treaty of Versailles, now German "achievements" in the East had vindicated a whole generation, showing that it need no longer live in the shadow of the heroes of Verdun.

Although this sense of vindication, combined with fond memories of France, may have "sustained" F. initially, the resurgence of warm memories was not always easy to manage. The contrast between a pleasurable "then" and the gruelling "now" fed F's growing disenchantment with the conflict. After harrowing rear-guard action at Kursk in 1943, his tone was harsher. He admitted in a letter home:

Yes, it's true that even on our side we were missing real *men* in some places; otherwise this complete foul-up [dieser Saustall] could not have taken place. Our rear area probably lived too well, and our French divisions have apparently partly forgotten what this war in the East is really about – about all the things that make life worth living, and that after all, it's worth laying your own life on the line for them.[8]

The pleasures of France were no longer a cherished memory – the contrast between life there and current hardships had become a thorn that rankled. If F.'s comrades were dying, it was because other men had failed to take the war seriously, and their continued failure to measure its true dimensions was a dangerous weakness.

F. was relatively fortunate, at least at first, for he got out of Russia with frostbitten fingers and the Iron Cross, First Class. Later, he was wounded in the Ukraine, and after a period of rest at home and his marriage, he was sent again to France. In spring 1944, he was stationed briefly in Hungary, and then transferred back to the West, where he died in Normandy two days after the Allied invasion.

F.'s mobility across Europe was typical of a member of Hitler's army, and the implicit and explicit comparisons he made between various war fronts, and especially between occupied France and the Soviet Union,

---

[6] Kurt F., 19 February 1942, (DTA: 270/1).   [7] Kurt F., 27 June 1942, (DTA: 270/1).
[8] Kurt F., 19 February 1943, (DTA: 270/1). Emphasis in the original.

offer insight into the mental world of these soldiers. Accounts of the occupation of France, which typically revolve around a small number of top German administrators in Paris, have left the impression that the occupiers were a relatively stable and static group, and that events in France took place in a kind of vacuum.[9] Such accounts take bilateral relations with Berlin into consideration, but often ignore the wider context of the war, and the fact that lower-level occupiers like F. rarely stayed in one place for more than a few months. Far from being tied to their positions, these soldiers spent time in France before, after, or between tours of duty elsewhere. Officers and men moved to and from the Reich for training, to meet with their superiors, or on home leave. Whole units were shifted in and out of France repeatedly, and from mid-1941, the country was used extensively as a rest and recuperation area for soldiers from the Eastern Front.[10] Although the French may have perceived one group of Germans to be much like another, mobility was a salient feature of the occupation. It led to little-recognised transfers of behaviours, attitudes, and practices between fronts. These transfers troubled policy-makers because they created tension between ideals of a "model occupation" in which Germans were not "barbarians," and practices on the ground.

Soldiers' mobility also matters because it underlines that, far from representing a totally separate and "softer" war, the occupation of France was an integral part of National Socialist warfare Europe-wide.[11] Certainly, war played out differently and was far less brutal overall in France than in, notably, the Soviet Union. Soldiers who had experienced several fronts perceived them as distinct, but the starting points and overall framework were the same, and especially in the summer of 1944, practices tended to converge. This in turn brings into sharper focus questions about how, why, and to what extent the occupation of France was different. To understand not only its distinctiveness, but also its alignment with, and contribution to, the war as a whole, the French occupation must be read beyond its specific national context, not only as a transnational event involving Germans and the French people, but as part and parcel of a European and global conflict.

The deep interconnectedness of East and West, North and South struck contemporaries as one of the novelties of this war. World War

---

[9] See discussion of historiography in the Introduction, p. 25–6.
[10] Lieb, *Konventionneller*, 37 ff.
[11] Eismann, among others, has pointed out that the image of the war in the West as "clean" survived the reevaluation, beginning in the 1990s, of the military's role in atrocities on the Eastern Front. Eismann, *Hôtel Majestic*, 89–90.

One had also increased individuals' mobility, but the extent of movement in World War II was unprecedented. F.'s letters and other first-person accounts confirm that participants understood the conflict to be an event that went well beyond their home nation. They were struck by the links that war made between far-flung places, and they recognised that it had brought remarkable exposure to foreign lands and peoples.

From the point of view of the occupiers, mobility had both advantages and disadvantages. Being able to move soldiers in and out of France and other Western occupied areas made it easier to keep men fresh, and the comparatively "peaceful" atmosphere, particularly of the early occupation years, afforded important opportunities for rest, relaxation, and training new recruits. By helping them to recover and prepare for renewed combat, the relatively pleasant lives that occupiers enjoyed in the West contributed to prolonging the war.

At the same time, as Kurt F.'s letters at the start of the chapter suggest, the idyllic atmosphere of France, in particular, could be problematic. Memories of France were both a comfort and a source of resentment among men stationed in the East. Soldiers transferred eastwards after basic training or a quiet period as an occupier were understandably ill prepared for the merciless conditions they now faced. Conversely, when soldiers from the East arrived in France after hard combat, they found the contrast with what they had just experienced jarring. Some units failed to make the shift, and instead transferred brutal practices that were current in the Soviet Union, such as routine pillaging and the harsh treatment of civilians, to the West. This gave rise to a kind of culture clash with other occupiers, often military administrators, who had been stationed in France longer and had different ideas about how to treat local people.

An important element of the East/West problem was that while men in the East had been fighting tooth and nail against a terrifying and brutal enemy, committing atrocities that at least some of them found difficult to digest, their comrades in France appeared to have been enjoying themselves. Partly as a result of the different conditions and agreeable lifestyle available to occupiers in France, and partly due to divergent war experiences and practices, the perception arose that occupiers in the West were going soft. Contemporaries referred to this phenomenon as becoming, *westweich* (literally, "West-soft," or unfit for combat after being too long in the West). Men in France were accused of exhibiting an *Etappengeist* (spirit of the rear), which was contrasted with *Kampfgeist* (fighting spirit). As German losses grew, the occupation regime in France became a kind of scapegoat. Referring to an *Etappengeist* was another way of saying that occupiers were too comfortable, too complacent, and were failing to make the sacrifices required to contribute adequately to the war effort.

To address perceived inequalities and counter the rumoured *Etappengeist*, there were repeated efforts to slim down and tighten the occupation apparatus. An across-the-board Wehrmacht ruling in March 1942 required forces in the West to be reduced by 25 per cent.[12] Later, a manpower efficiency commission lead by General Walther von Unruh travelled around the Reich and occupied territories, trimming superfluous positions in order to send a maximum number of able men to the front. Despite these efforts, the perception remained that France was not only a soft billet, but also a weak link in the German defensive armour. Perhaps this was inevitable, for conditions for Germans in France remained more comfortable than those elsewhere, at least until the Allied invasion in 1944, and in some cases well beyond. Still, this perception was problematic, for it both threatened to destabilise morale on the fighting fronts, and fed ongoing pressure to tighten things up and escalate violence in France.

This chapter begins with soldiers' mobility and their views of the differences between East and West. It then considers transfers between these two areas, their impact on the French situation, specifically, and the stereotypes that arose to express the variations in culture and practice between East and West. Finally, it examines efforts to pare down the occupation staff, and attempts to resolve the tension arising from the notion that occupiers in the West were enjoying themselves while other men suffered and died.

Even before Operation Barbarossa began, soldiers were aware that something significant was happening in the East. Occupiers in France were both eager to get in on the action and apprehensive about the idea of being transferred to a new front. In early May 1941, Wilhelm Ernst von K. expressed his "regret" (Leidwesen) that operations in the Balkans were going ahead without him and his unit.[13] Another soldier, already transferred from West to East, wrote about the long marches he had undertaken, commenting that "[t]his time, we'll be facing an enemy we know nothing about."[14] As the invasion got underway in late June, Bernard Schulz in France initially felt frustrated and restless, for he was

---

[12] Kommandostab Abteilung Ia, Aktennote, 24 March 1942 (AN: AJ 40/455).
[13] Wm. Ernst von K., 5 May 1941 (Württembergische Landesbibliothek, Bibliothek für Zeitgeschichte: Sammlung Sterz [BfZ SS]).
[14] Willi K., 11 May 1941 (BfZ SS).

tired of sitting around while combat proceeded elsewhere.[15] Once he had seen a newsreel about the war in the Soviet Union a couple of months later, however, his attitude changed to relief. He wrote home that he was delighted not to be in the East, and that he would "much rather" stay in France and "wait for the Tommies." "Sure, they didn't always fight fairly in the West," he continued, "but the partisan war in the East looks to be worst of all."[16] A couple of weeks later, Schulz again expressed relief that he was still in France, and then, in December, as his unit was about to be transferred eastwards, he speculated about the contrasts between France and what he was about to experience:

I believe that our division has been in the French 'paradise' longest, for that Normandy was a paradise compared to Russia is completely clear. We had such riches here: the landscape, the climate, the magical colours, the sea, the butter, the wine, the cognac, an endless chain of delights that was always offered to us anew. What will Russia give us[?] Lice, typhus, desolation, distance, mud, cold, rifle fire. Nothing good.[17]

Any occupier in his right mind would have wanted to stay in the West, yet soldiers were not given the choice. Apprehension about what to expect also affected author Ernst Jünger, who was far from eager to leave his comfortable administrative position in Paris. After receiving confirmation that he was about to be transferred to the East in 1942, he slept badly for several nights, and then had himself checked into the military hospital at Suresnes, just outside the capital, for a few days' rest before departure.[18]

Occupiers' anxiety was well justified, for war on the Eastern Front seemed different from the outset. Just five days after the invasion began, another former French occupier, the musically talented Hans Klumpp, described in his diary how burning villages turned the night sky red.[19] Hinting not only at the physical, but perhaps also the psychological impact of committing brutal violence, he commented that "[t]his campaign makes far greater demands on us, yes, the good times in France will probably never come back."[20] Over the next days, Klumpp reported

[15] Schulz, letter, 21 June 1941 (DTA: 2033).
[16] Schulz, letter, 8 August 1941 (DTA: 2033).
[17] Schulz, letter, 19 December 1941 (DTA: 2033). "Paradise" was frequently used to describe France and also, with irony, the Soviet Union – Stalin's "paradise for workers." See, e.g. Hans K., Tagebuch 1938–1948, 27 October 1941 (DTA: 1942).
[18] Jünger, *Strahlungen*, entries for 12 and 13 October 1942, 185.
[19] Klumpp, diary, 27 June 1941 (DTA: 1942).
[20] Klumpp, diary, 27 June 1941 (DTA: 1942).

both his excitement about the rapid German advance, and his dismay about watching two prisoners of war being shot "close up."[21]

The brutality that soldiers occasionally recorded in diaries and letters only provided glimpses of the real extent of such practices as village-burning and executing Soviet prisoners of war and civilians. Still, the way that Germans described landscapes and people as they moved eastwards also offered insight into the attitudes that underlay harsh warfare. Particularly when contrasted with depictions of France, comments on Poland and the Soviet Union show little ambiguity in soldiers' minds about the existence of a racial hierarchy with Germans at the top. This hierarchy influenced everything from the way battle was conducted to the forms of occupation and the treatment of local civilians. As they had done a year earlier in the West, soldiers observed the countryside and local people, but now their letters painted an almost unremitting picture of poverty, dirt and degeneration. Germans had come to France expecting to find beautiful landscapes inhabited by decadent individualists, and were satisfied when what they saw met their preconceptions. Moving eastwards, they expected to see derelict huts and impoverished peasants, and when they found these, they described them with an assurance bordering on satisfaction.[22]

A side effect of the German attitude towards Eastern landscapes and people was that photography, an essential instrument for capturing French experiences and exercising dominance in a context where German superiority seemed less self-evident, sometimes appeared superfluous here. POW camp Commander Johannes Gutschmidt, who had travelled extensively and taken many photographs in France, confided in his diary from Poland that, "I haven't taken any pictures here. There's nothing interesting."[23] Aviator Alfred Haas sent home images from Poland with the comment that "[w]hat I'm photographing here is certainly worth seeing, but only as an example to avoid. You can see more dirt, poverty and squalor here than you could ever have imagined."[24]

---

[21] Klumpp, diary, 3 July 1941 (DTA: 1942).

[22] On German perceptions of Eastern Europe, see Dücker, "Reisen in die UdSSR 1933–1945"; Latzel, "Tourismus und Gewalt"; Koshar, *German Travel Cultures*, 152–5. Occasionally, soldiers' comments show the disdain with which they viewed French as well as East European rural life. Crossing the Polish border, for example, Klaus Peter Suhrkamp noted that close to Germany, there were still attractive farms, but the further east one went, "[r]ather than the stylish farmers' houses there are primitive boxes like the ones that we got to know in France." Klaus Peter Suhrkamp, Kriegstagebuch 1940–1942, 4 June 1941 (DTA: 1900).

[23] Johannes Gutschmidt, "Kriegstagebuch," 5 May 1941 (BArch: MSG 1/257); also reprinted in Hartmann, "Massensterben," 139.

[24] Alfred Haas, Briefe an der Freundin 1940–1941, 16 May 1941 (DTA: 1818/I).

Both men visited Warsaw, and like many others, they took the opportunity to ride through the city's massive ghetto.[25] Although it was closed
off from the rest of the city, streets and streetcars still ran through the
ghetto, and despite official prohibitions, it became an important "attraction" for visitors (Figure 6.1). Appallingly crowded, disease-ridden and
deadly to the people confined there, the ghetto served the regime as a
kind of open-air exhibit of Jewish "depravity." Gutschmidt visited by car
in late May 1941, reporting on the "incredible faces ... caftans and long
beards" he observed, and on the vigorous parallel economy. Trying to
reconcile the official line on Jews with what he actually saw, he noted that
"[t]he Jews look very run-down and yet many of them are still supposed
to have a lot of money."[26] Here, Gutschmidt took many photographs,
concluding that "[c]ertainly the whole thing was very interesting, but
unpleasant."[27]

The aviator Haas also rode through the Warsaw ghetto, and found
what he had seen difficult to put into words. The ghetto was huge, yet
people were crowded together terribly, disease raged, and the morgue
was full every day. "I would find the idea more congenial that the whole
riff-raff be shot out of hand," Haas wrote, for "the outcome of the
measures used here won't be much different." The last time he had
visited, he had wanted nothing more than to leave as soon as possible.
The population viewed German soldiers with undisguised hatred and,
Haas added, "I can hardly begrudge them that, for their treatment is
so completely different from that in France." Here, the contrast between
West and East was clear, and the difference between German practices
in Poland and in France made Haas uneasy. Not all soldiers saw it quite
this way, however, for Klaus Peter Suhrkamp, who visited the same
ghetto a month later, described not Germany's repressive measures,
but the "powdered ladies in furs whose dresses reveal their knees, who
ride by in rickshaw-like vehicles ... while next to them, in the

---

[25] The ghetto was established on 12 October 1940, and had 442,337 registered residents
when Gutschmidt visited. He estimated the population to be 600,000. Johannes
Gutschmidt, "Kriegstagebuch," 25 May 1941, reprinted in Hartmann,
"Massensterben," 140–41. Although it was supposedly "off-limits," to soldiers, they
were allowed to ride through the ghetto on the streetcar; indeed, this was a popular
"sightseeing" opportunity in Warsaw. See Alfred Haas, Briefe an der Freundin
1940–1941 (DTA 1818/I); Klaus Peter Suhrkamp, Kriegstagebuch 1940–1942,
15 June 1941 (DTA: 1900); Rudolf Meier, *Soldatenführer durch Warschau*, ed.
Oberfeldkommandantur Warschau (Warsaw: Verlag der deutschen Buchhandlung,
1942), 35, 57.
[26] Johannes Gutschmidt, "Kriegstagebuch, " 25 May 1941, reprinted in Hartmann,
"Massensterben," 140–41.
[27] Johannes Gutschmidt, "Kriegstagebuch, " 25 May 1941, reprinted in Hartmann, 141.

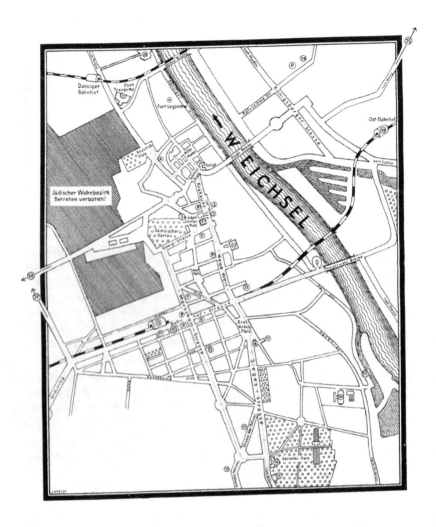

Figure 6.1 A 1942 sightseeing guide for soldiers described the Warsaw ghetto as having been established to protect the city's population from disease. An accompanying map showed the area (on the left) as off-limits to soldiers on foot, but many travelled through by car or on the tram.
Rudolf Meier, *Soldatenführer durch Warschau*, ed. Oberfeldkommandantur Warschau (Warsaw: Verlag der deutschen Buchhandlung, 1942), 57.

street, people are dying."[28] Gutschmidt recorded a similar thing, suggesting that a propaganda image of "shameless" Jewish women that had been planted in soldiers' minds became a trope soldiers expected to see when passing through the ghetto.[29] Moving from West to East, soldiers were confronted with new sights, sights that they assimilated and tried to contextualise with the help of the "information" they had been given.

In addition to the sights to be seen, the mobile quality of this war was itself a novelty. Certainly, in World War I, German soldiers had been transferred from East to West, but the scale and frequency of movement in World War II was considerably greater.[30] Hans W. wrote home to his wife in April 1942 that he had had no wristwatch for weeks because the glass of his old one had broken and there was no watchmaker available locally to install a new glass. Now, however, he had found an opportunity to send the watch with a man of his unit who was travelling to France on official business. "Isn't it interesting," W. wrote, "that to fix a watch, it will be sent marching from Russia to France. The war brings odd moments with it."[31] In this case, the watch became a metaphor for the men, who likewise were sent marching back and forth across the continent like goods.

A further sign of the strangeness of war's mobility was that a few months later, apparently unaware that there was any real difference between the dispersed parts of the bloated German Reich where he had been stationed, a soldier near Chalons-sur-Marne ran into trouble with the military police. He had paid for a haircut with Ukrainian money that he claimed was worth much more than was actually the case. When questioned, he insisted that he had not been aware that the money could not be used in France, and had thought that the hairdresser would be able to exchange it at the bank. The incident was referred to the military courts.[32]

The mobility that war engendered was both useful to the Germans and problematic. As the conflict on the Eastern Front grew ever more demanding, France developed into a critically important staging area

---

[28] Klaus Peter Suhrkamp, Kriegstagebuch 1940–1942, 15 June 1941 (DTA: 1900).
[29] According to Gutschmidt, "Many young wenches [Weiber] had painted lips, many rode out in horse carriages or pedaled carts." Johannes Gutschmidt, "Kriegstagebuch, " 25 May 1941, reprinted in Hartmann, "Massensterben," 141.
[30] Journalist Werner Stephan set World War Two's mobility in the context of that of 1914–18 in "Paradies für Ostsoldaten? Ablösung in der Normandie," *Das Reich*, May 16, 1943.
[31] Hans W., Briefwechsel 1942–48, 18 April 1942 (DTA: 1960, 5).
[32] Report of Feldgendarmerie Troop 706, 15 December 1942 (BArch: RH 36/188).

for training new recruits and regrouping units decimated at Stalingrad and other major engagements. Germany requisitioned increasing numbers of hospitals, hotels and rest homes, and exploited French food supplies to feed recuperating soldiers, whose presence at the same time helped reinforce the occupation's strength. After the Battle of Stalingrad, which he had been lucky to miss due to a leave, Helmut E. wrote that, "[a] roll-call was made of the remnants of the 6th Army, they were assembled and then transferred by divisions to France. Here we've already brought our former units up to strength."[33] Now, E. worried that he would be sent back to the East, convinced this would lead to the amputation of his feet, which were already so damaged by frostbite that he could not walk more than 3 km.

Even if they had been sent to France to rest and recuperate, being stationed in the West continued to make some soldiers impatient, especially if they were healthy and had just received bad news from the front. Upon learning that two more of his comrades had died in combat in early 1943, Alex B. wanted nothing more than to return to Russia. A specialist in mountain warfare who was positioned near the Italian border at Briançon, B. was involved in training new recruits. He admitted that he enjoyed passing on his front-line experience to the next group of fighters, "but as soon as there's an opportunity, . . . I'm headed back to the front." He was partly motivated by a sense of responsibility, even guilt, that he had survived while others had not, writing that "[i]t's particularly those of us who've already served out there and who were lucky who feel first that we need to go back out to help our comrades."[34]

Sentiments like these came to a head when the Wehrmacht experienced major losses, for example during the terrible battle of Stalingrad.[35] Two days after B. expressed his desire to return to the East, Winfried A., who had served in Serbia and was now stationed in France, wrote that he had never felt any real longing to go to Russia, but:

in the last few days I would have been happy to go, and the others here too, because when you hear about the awful fights to the death at Stalingrad daily and you're sitting here where you can't do anything, and you're even living peacefully and well while thousands are bleeding to death daily in the East . . . you have no peace anymore, and just want to take [a weapon] in your hand and throw yourself into the fray.[36]

---

[33] Helmut E., 29 March 1942 (BfZ SS).   [34] Alex B., 24 January 1943 (BfZ SS).
[35] On the impact of Stalingrad on German morale overall, see Stargardt, *German War*, 322 ff.
[36] Winfried A., 26 January 1943 (DTA: 1908).

A. found his enforced inactivity frustrating, a feeling that was aggravated by the very calm of his surroundings. Possessing such an expansive and comparatively peaceful rear area to rest troops favoured the war effort, but soldiers often had trouble adjusting to the very different atmosphere in the West.

However happy they may have been to have escaped the Eastern Front, even temporarily, newly arrived troops had difficulty understanding that circumstances in the two areas were not the same.[37] As early as October 1941, the Field Commander at Amiens felt obliged to issue a statement emphasising that Germany had signed an armistice with France that required military policies and procedures to be followed. Orderly interactions with local French authorities were essential, he insisted, and he reminded the troops that "requisitioning goods of any kind and interference in the economy by the troops are forbidden." Quartering must be undertaken through local German military administrators only, and "[f]urniture and other housewares may not be removed from the homes without the permission of the local Commander [Kreiskommandant]."[38] The Amiens Field Commander underlined that France was no longer an operations area, and he insisted that the reputation of the Wehrmacht did not permit pillage and unauthorised requisitions. In their final report, written in 1945, former Paris military administrators commented that their relationship with the active troops had often been difficult "especially when units coming from the eastern theatre of war were first deployed in France."[39] Unit leaders often failed to recognise that central organisation through the military administration, as opposed to "wild" requisitions, was the best way to ensure the most complete exploitation of French resources.[40]

The behaviour of troops coming from the East tended to get worse as time went on. Demonstrating their utter disregard for the sanctity of a religious structure, for example, one platoon of the Eleventh Panzer Division, recently transferred into France in spring 1944, "carved a drinks bar from the choir stalls of an old church in the

---

[37] Lieb refers to their sense of dislocation as a "positive culture-shock." *Konventionneller*, 38.
[38] "Merkblatt der Feldkommandatur 580," October 1941 (BArch: RH 36/225).
[39] Militärverwaltung in Frankreich, "Abschlussbericht der Verwaltung, Allgemeines und Gruppe 'Allgemeine und innere Verwaltung,'" 25 March 1945, 26–7 (AN: AJ 40/536).
[40] Regardless of their efforts to organise exploitation, unauthorised requisitions and pillage continued to occur. Militärverwaltung in Frankreich, "Abschlussbericht der Verwaltung, Allgemeines und Gruppe 'Allgemeine und innere Verwaltung,'" 25 March 1945, 27 (AN: AJ 40/536).

Dordogne."[41] Peter Lieb has suggested, moreover, that "it seems likely that many officers transferred from the East were not really acquainted with the details of the valid orders for the West and may have stuck to the old guidelines and methods with which they had been familiar in the East."[42] More generally, Lieb has shown that past deployment on the Eastern Front was part of the background to several incidents of extreme violence committed in France in 1944. Investigating connections between Eastern Front experiences and soldiers' treatment of resisters and civilians in France, Lieb argues that the worst abuses, hostage-killings and massacres were typically carried out by the SS, or by units arriving in the West after hard fighting during the Eastern retreat. Formations that had been in France for some time were only rarely involved.[43] Thus, members of the Second SS Panzer Division "Das Reich," for example, "pillaged a synagogue in Bordeaux and committed their first atrocities in anti-partisan warfare even before D-Day."[44] They went on to murder civilians at Tulle and became responsible for the worst atrocity on French soil, at Oradour-sur-Glane, where they killed the town's men and burned the church where women and children had sought protection.[45] After hanging ninety-nine men publicly along the main street of Tulle, the German officer who led the reprisal action reportedly responded to the French prefect's protestations about the action's cruelty by saying, "I am sorry, in Russia we took the habit of hanging, we killed more than one hundred thousand men at Kharkov and Kiev, this here is nothing for us."[46]

A combination of ideological indoctrination and frustrating battle experiences in the East, according to Lieb, explains some units' propensity for engaging in extreme violence in France. What Lieb fails to consider is the role played by a less tangible factor – the sense among soldiers in the East that occupiers in the West were having too good a time, enjoying themselves while others bore the burden of the war. The feeling that there was an *Etappengeist* in France, and the desire to eradicate it in others while not falling prey to it themselves, may well have

---

[41] Peter Lieb, "Repercussions of Eastern Front Experiences on Anti-Partisan Warfare in France 1943–1944," *The Journal of Strategic Studies* 31, No. 5 (2008): 816.

[42] Lieb, "Repercussions," 803.   [43] Lieb, *Konventioneller*, 506 ff.

[44] Lieb, "Repercussions," 817.

[45] In all, 642 people died at Oradour. Lieb, 818–19. For more on Oradour, see notably Sarah Farmer's research. Farmer noted the connection between the "Das Reich" Division's Eastern Front experiences and its brutality in France. Sarah Farmer, *Martyred Village: Commemorating the 1944 Massacre at Oradour-Sur-Glane* (Berkeley: University of California Press, 1999), 48.

[46] Pierre Trouillé, *Journal d'un préfet pendant l'occupation allemande* (Paris: Gallimard, 1964): 134 cited in Farmer, *Martyred Village*, 230 n. 63.

contributed to some groups' willingness to engage in brutal warfare once they arrived in France. The connection between Eastern Front experiences, the sense that there was an *Etappengeist* in France, and radical violence, is taken up again in Chapter 7. In the meantime, we turn to the broader impact of the notion that occupiers were going soft in the West, and in France specifically.

In order to understand how this notion influenced occupation policy, notably in the area of manpower management, it is important to get a sense of how France looked to soldiers just arriving from the East. Such men were typically astonished by the chasm between eastern hardships and western pleasures, and there was a significant clash of cultures between eastern fighters and western occupiers. If, as noted, occupiers already in France found it necessary to enforce a certain brand of civility upon exhausted and battle-hardened front-line troops, the sudden calm and confusing semblance of peace jarred the consciousness of soldiers transferred into France from elsewhere. Contrasting what they had just experienced with what they now saw easily led new arrivals to the conclusion that the French population was being treated too leniently, and worse, that living in France was eroding the military bearing of occupiers themselves. In February 1943, we have seen, Kurt F. blamed Germany's weaknesses on the fact that the army was missing "real men in some places."[47] "Our rear area probably lived too well," he added, pointing a finger at France, specifically.

F. was not the only one to suggest that French living had softened, perhaps even feminised soldiers, making them unfit for battle. After twenty-six months in Russia, training officer Wilhelm Schadt, whom we met in Chapter 5, travelled from Paris to Lyon in early September 1943. He then moved to Marseilles and was finally assigned to lead a course in Clermont-Ferrand. "Units in France very soft," he commented, "non-commissioned officers and men sleeping in beds with mosquito canopies. The mere implementation of daily morning exercises under my leadership met with little approval."[48] Rightly or wrongly, from at least 1941, the French occupation had become a byword for flaccid decadence, and soldiers there were described as *westweich*.

A May 1943 essay in the weekly publication *Das Reich* aimed to address precisely this problem by helping occupiers contextualise and

---

[47] Kurt F., 19 February 1943 (DTA: 270/I).
[48] That Schadt included these comments in postwar memoirs underlines the persistence of the idea that men in France were going soft. Wilhelm Schadt, *Die Erlebnisse von Wilhelm Schadt aus Legelshurst in den Jahren 1939–1950*, 9 (DTA: 1628)

better resist the temptations of France.[49] Titled "Paradise for Soldiers from the East?" it first described the country in idyllic terms, full of small villages and peaceful pastures, as a war-weary soldier on rotation might see it. The author then parsed the image. Eastern experiences might help Germans fully comprehend "the splendour of the thousand year-old miracle structure of Mont Saint-Michel," he wrote, but they must also see, "that the traditional two-wheeled Norman peasant's cart cannot continue to exist alongside the tractor of the Ukraine." Even now, France offered an enviable wealth of food and drink, and beds that were "the softest and most comfortable in the world," but a soldier would soon become impatient with the technologically backwards French people who fished all day and looked forwards to nothing with more eagerness than their evening's aperitif. Not France's eternal, peaceable habits, but Hitler's defensive structures were the real guarantors of civilisation, for "in the fourth year of the war, every German bunker, every armoured gun emplacement has more significance for French culture than the peace-time activity that resembles a stage set in the cities of the rear." If they did not want to succumb to superficial French charms and the putative *Etappengeist*, soldiers must understand that *la douce France* was a nation of backwards individualists whose decadent lifestyle was untenable in the face of the Bolshevik threat, and modern war itself. War was omnipresent even in France, notwithstanding its soft beds and other feminising attractions, and it could only be withstood by one "who takes it into his consciousness, and through it, lets himself be transformed into a new man."[50] Remasculinising, sharpening, and toughening the occupiers was Germany's only hope if the Reich was to be victorious.

The fear that soldiers were growing soft from spending too long in France was linked to longer-standing resentments between front-line and staging-area troops. The suspicion that men at the rear were inefficient, lazy, and enjoying special privileges was a constant of warfare, which, according to historian Bernd Kroener, was connected in the minds of Hitler and his closest associates to the legacy of World War I, when failures in this domain were seen to have weakened the military and its martial reputation at critical moments.[51] The word *Etappe*, originally a neutral term for staging areas behind the front, had been removed from the official military lexicon in 1939.[52] However, it remained in common

---

[49] Stephan, "Paradies," 4.   [50] Stephan, "Paradies," 4.

[51] Bernhard Kroener, "'General Heldenklau:' Die 'Unruh-Kommission' im Strudel polykratischer Desorganisation (1942–1944)" in *Politischer Wandel, organisierte Gewalt und nationale Sicherheit*, ed. Ernst Willi Hansen (München: R. Oldenbourg, 1995), 269–70.

[52] Kroener, "Heldenklau," 270.

use as a pejorative term to refer to bloated bureaucracy and decadent behaviour in staging areas. As the German army encountered increasing difficulty holding its positions, the feeling grew among front-line troops that they were bearing the brunt of the fighting while others failed to pull their weight.

To combat such notions, a newspaper for soldiers stationed in the Ukraine, for example, carried an article in early January 1943 that outlined the many important tasks carried out by the men behind the lines. Although a messenger travelling back and forth from front to rear might wonder why there were so many men living in enviably clean quarters behind the front, each trucker valiantly delivering supplies, each administrator organising clothing, food and armaments from behind his desk had an important role to play. Even if the article underlined that "the front soldier bears the greatest burden of the war," each man was a comrade, contributing to the combined war effort.[53]

The campaign to recognise all contributions and share the burdens of war equally reached the Home Front as well, for inequalities threatened to undermine German morale as a whole. In his famous speech at the Berlin Sportpalast in mid-February 1943, Joseph Goebbels, who served as a kind of public relations expert for the Reich, called on Hitler's followers to make ever-greater sacrifices in the name of total war. Among the ten questions to which his hand-picked audience responded with a resounding "yes" was one about whether Germans were ready to punish shirkers and war-profiteers, and those who "play peace in the midst of war."[54] Goebbels did not mention the French occupation specifically, but his words made it clear that the regime sought to root out perceived laziness and good living wherever they were found.

As well as redirecting any criticism away from Hitler and the Third Reich's leadership, Goebbels was also responding to broader muttering in the population. A few months on, in late November 1943, an SD report on the mood and attitude of the German population noted that although people generally had confidence in the quality and strength of the military:

the excesses in the bases and to some extent in the home garrisons have been the subject of growing criticism. This culminates in the statement that the

---

[53] "Front — Etappe," *Soldatenzeitung der Ukraine*, January 12, 1943, 4th edn. (BArch: RW 41/85).
[54] *Frankfurter Zeitung*, 20 February 1943, 7, published in Helmut Heiber, ed., *Goebbels Reden 1932–1945*. (Bindlach: Gondrom Verlag, 1991): 203–5 available at http://germanhistorydocs.ghi-dc.org/docpage.cfm?docpage_id=2428&language=english.

present-day situation surpasses First World War conditions. People make particular reference to the alleged growing gap between the officers and men, among the troops behind the front and at home (special provisions for the three [levels of] messes, use of spirits, shopping trips to the occupied territories, the inappropriate use of soldiers who are capable of front-line service in messes, offices etc.).[55]

Concerns about decadence among military personnel behind the front-lines and in occupied areas had reached home, and creeping bitterness about special treatment threatened morale.

For Hitler and party chancellery head Martin Bormann, one root of these problems lay in weak political leadership in the army. Seeking to tighten military attitudes and strengthen morale, they sought to reenergise military political education and deepen the Nazi Party's permeation of the Wehrmacht.[56] To this end, Hitler ordered an important change in terminology in late autumn 1943, turning what had hitherto been called rather generically "defensive leadership" (Wehrgeistige Führung) into the specifically political term "national socialist leadership" (Nationalsozialistische Führung). Existing officers responsible for soldiers' morale and welfare acquired a new title, *Nationalsozialistische Führungsoffizier* (National Socialist Leadership Officer or NSFO), and became responsible not only for the material welfare and morale of the troops, but also for their ideological "education." In practice, these officers' role involved spreading regime-sanctioned messages among the troops and reporting back to Reich authorities about soldiers' concerns.[57] In this context, morale expert Dr. Horstmann, based at Angers, toured Western France in December 1943 to get a sense of soldiers' attitudes and to intensify officers' leadership training in this domain. He told local staff that enemy propaganda was especially dangerous in the West, "where good living etc. lull to sleep many men's inner defensive strength."[58]

---

[55] SD Report to the Party Chancellery on "Basic Questions Regarding the Mood and Attitude of the German People" (November 29, 1943), English translation from http://germanhistorydocs.ghi-dc.org/sub_document.cfm?document_id=1585.

[56] Following Dieter Rebentisch, Kroener has pointed out that the power of the party chancellery grew in the second half of the war. Kroener, "Heldenklau," 272; Dieter Rebentisch, *Führerstaat und Verwaltung im Zweiten Weltkrieg: Verfassungsentwicklung und Verwaltungspolitik 1939–1945*, Frankfurter historische Abhandlungen, Bd. 29 (Stuttgart: F. Steiner Verlag Wiesbaden, 1989), 471.

[57] The NSFO role was officially established by Führer order on 22 December 1943 (BArch: NS 6/142), but the change in titles was already mentioned in an OKH letter 28 November 1943 (BArch: RH 36/552).

[58] Dr. Horstmann, speech delivered to soldiers in Angers and several cities of southern Brittany, 9–18 December 1943 (BArch RH 36/552).

In late January 1944, Horstmann and other NSFOs in France met at the Majestic Hotel in Paris to discuss how to maintain occupiers' fighting spirit. According to a colleague of Horstmann's, Maj. Dr. Weniger, soldiers in northwestern France were complaining about "frequent trips by some officers to Paris, others' passion for hunting, and in some cases also differences in provisioning."[59] Apparently, from one officers' mess, "a menu that was completely unsuited to the times was printed and mailed to families."[60]

Concerns about decadence, unfair treatment, and unsoldierly conduct in staging areas permeated the army, the Nazi Party, and the Home Front. This was dangerous since strong popular support not only from civilians but also among the army's foot soldiers was essential to continued fighting. A clear measure of the issue's significance is the fact that in early 1944, Propaganda Minister Goebbels published his own views about the notorious *Etappe* in the newspaper *Front und Heimat* (*Front and Homeland*). While the article cited above, which was directed at soldiers in the Ukraine, emphasised camaraderie and the importance of sharing the burdens of war, Goebbels' tone in addressing home and front a year later was much harsher, expressing nothing but scorn for niggling, rule-obsessed desk warriors. Rather than valourising their jobs and reminding front soldiers that the men in staging areas were part of a team effort, Goebbels downplayed the importance of administrative work and propounded a combative attitude for everyone. "You can not shoot with typewriters," he wrote, which explained why, when the army was occasionally required to pull back, it carried machine guns to safety before office equipment.[61] Goebbels' goal was to mobilise society as a whole, for "[t]here are no fixed work hours either at home or on the front today. One works and fights as long as it takes to get the job done."[62] Anyone who sought to evade duty was a traitor, and laziness and inefficiency should be swept away with an "iron broom."[63]

In fact, whether Goebbels wished to recognise it publicly or not, the iron broom had already been sweeping vigorously, at least since autumn 1941. Losses in the East and the failure to take Moscow made finding replacement troops a priority. At first, soldiers were shifted from West to East in the spirit of equalising burdens and making sure that younger

---

[59] Transcript of 29 January 1944 meeting of NSFOs, 8 February 1944 (BArch: RH 36/552).
[60] Transcript of 29 January 1944 meeting of NSFOs, 8 February 1944 (BArch: RH 36/552).
[61] Joseph Goebbels, "Ein Wort zu Etappe," *Front und Heimat: Die deutsche Soldatenzeitung*, May 1944, 7th edn. (BArch: RH 69/10).
[62] Goebbels, "Ein Wort zu Etappe" (BArch: RH 69/10).
[63] Goebbels, "Ein Wort zu Etappe" (BArch: RH 69/10).

military administrators, in particular, had opportunities to see active service that would help them earn promotions. With time, however, the Wehrmacht's losses, combined with the sentiment that occupiers were not pulling their weight translated, at higher levels, into aggressive efforts to trim the fat off occupation regimes. In France, these efforts targetted the administrative branch in particular.[64]

At its height, in the winter of 1941–2, the military administration included some 1,600 men, not counting low-level staff such as drivers, clerks, and translators. The average number of military administrators was around 1,200.[65] In October 1941, acting on orders from above, the Militärbefehlshaber had requested an inventory of men born in 1910 or later who had already seen active service.[66] Those young men who had not yet fought, and who possessed the rank of Wehrmacht officers, were pinpointed for front-line duty. In practice, this meant that mid-level administrators were selected first, for they were generally young, and many were employees of Reich Ministries, notably the Interior, who had been transferred into military administration after being mobilised.[67] Employees in lower-level positions had often seen active duty, did not hold the rank of officers, or had been rotated out of France already because their roles as drivers or clerks did not require specialised knowledge. High-ranking men such as Franz Albrecht Medicus, head of the administrative branch in district B (Southwestern France) and his closest assistants, were typically older and had already served in World War I. They were left in their positions for the time being.[68]

Although the idea of switching men from West to East sounded good in theory, almost immediately, two interrelated problems arose. The first

[64] Alongside France, other western occupied areas were also targetted, including the Netherlands, "where more administrative personnel than in France had apparently piled up." Hans Umbreit, "Die deutsche Herrschaft in den besetzten Gebieten 1942–1945" in *Organisation und Mobilisierung des deutschen Machtbereichs: Kriegsverwaltung, Wirtschaft und personelle Ressourcen 1939 bis 1941*, ed. Bernhard R. Kroener, Rolf-Dieter Müller, and Hans Umbreit, Das Deutsche Reich und der Zweite Weltkrieg, 5/2 (Stuttgart: Deutsche Verlags-Anstalt, 1988), 126.

[65] Laub, *After the Fall*, 45.

[66] Zentralabteilung Az. Tgb. No. 399/41 an den Militärverwaltungsbezirke, Betr. Personal in der Militärverwaltung, 7 October 1941 (AN: 40 AJ/455). On attempts to rationalise military staffing in the first part of the war, see Bernhard R. Kroener, "Die personelle Ressourcen des Dritten Reiches im Spannungsfeld zwischen Wehrmacht, Bürokratie und Kriegswirtschaft 1939–1942" in *Organisation und Mobilisierung*, 871 ff.

[67] Der Militärbefehlshaber in Belgien und Nordfrankreich, Militärverwaltungschef Gruppe Pers, Az. 182 No. 102/42 geh. an den MBH in Frankreich, Oberstleutnant Borgmann, 16 May 1942 (AN: 40 AJ/455). Cf. Kroener, "Heldenklau," 278.

[68] Chef des Militärverwaltungsbezirkes B Südwestfrankreich Verwaltungsstab an MBH, Verwaltungsstab, Betr. Personal in der Militärverwaltung, 21 October 1941 (AN: AJ 40/455).

was linked to the ongoing, and in some areas growing, demand for men in France with specialist knowledge and administrative experience.[69] The second stemmed from the modalities of deployment of former administrators from France. The first problem surfaced as soon as German offices in France began to receive requests to pinpoint employees available for front-line duty. Although, in statistical terms, the men whose names appeared on various lists drawn up appeared to be roughly identical, in fact, local superiors argued, many mid-level administrators in the right age cohort were actually highly-trained specialists whose expertise in legal, financial, and other administrative areas would be difficult to replace. Some had been sent to France by particular Reich ministries, others had expert knowledge of key industries such as iron and steel, or experience working on priority projects, such as the "Aryanisation" of French businesses. As the Reich's demand for workers grew, moreover, cutting down on administrators responsible for recruiting labour from France was out of the question.[70]

The second problem had to do with the way that former occupation administrators were deployed. Initially, at least, the Wehrmacht failed to take their previous positions and training into account, leading to complaints that skilled personnel was being "wasted" in low-level roles. A senior staff member in occupied Northern France and Belgium argued, for instance, that many of the men who had been drawn into military administration directly from Reich ministries in 1939 and 1940 were potential officer material. Since they had not had the opportunity to serve thus far, they had looked forward to a transfer to the East as a chance to make up for lost time. Combat duty was an essential precondition for rising in military rank, but it seemed that some were being sent directly into battle without proper preparation, let alone opportunities for accelerated training that would facilitate promotion.[71] In one particularly egregious case, former administrators were first sent to the central clearing-house for desk staff at Marburg on the Lahn in Germany, where they sat around for a month awaiting deployment, then transferred back to France to join a division that was just on its way to the Eastern Front.

[69] While the number of general administors decreased between January and October 1941, economic administrators went up. MBH Verwaltungsstab Abt. Z an Kommandostab, Abt. IIa/IIb Betr. Stärkemeldung, 25 April 1942 (AN: 40 AJ/455).
[70] See, e.g. MBH Wi VII/703a/42 an die Zentralabteilung im Hause Betr. Freigabe von Kriegsverwaltungsbeamten jüngerer Jahrgänge aus der Arbeitseinsatzverwaltung, 1 April 1942 (AN: 40 AJ/455).
[71] Der Militärbefehlshaber in Belgien und Nordfrankreich, Militärverwaltungschef Gruppe Pers, Az. 182 No. 102/42 geh. an den MBH in Frankreich, Oberstleutnant Borgmann, 16 May 1942 (AN: 40 AJ/455). Cf. Kroener, "Heldenklau," 271.

Once they arrived in the East, "[t]he upshot was that the administrators immediately had to join the forced marches [sic] through the Ukraine (over 600 km) without any preparation and training. The majority were completely overstrained and collapsed with very painful foot ailments."[72] It made no sense to redeploy poorly-trained former administrators only to see them become incapacitated and unable to fight.

Equally problematic was the fact that reports had started to come back from young administrators that suggested some former occupiers, instead of being directed towards combat, were being shifted into desk jobs behind the front.[73] Mild health problems might mean that some men were not suitable for fighting even though they could theoretically be deployed closer to the front-lines. However, it made little sense to remove competent and experienced administrators from France simply to have them assigned to push papers on the other side of Europe. Already in late 1941, administrators in France had expressed concern that if talented young staff were sent east, the men would be "claimed" for the administration of occupied areas there. Now, their fears appeared to be realised.[74] What was the point of freeing up more men for front-line duty if, in fact, they never saw combat?

Senior German administrators in France and those in occupied Belgium and Northern France worked together to bring these issues to the attention of the military hierarchy.[75] Redeploying administrators only made sense if the men received accelerated training to favour promotion, and if they were then sent into active combat as soon as possible. Moreover, if competent administrators were transferred out of France, suitable replacements must be provided immediately. Back in the Reich, however, there was little sympathy for these complaints. In early January 1942, the army High Command had written to Paris to say that although it recognised that notably the economic tasks undertaken in France were important and complex, across-the-board measures were necessary. Such measures must be undertaken to free up not more administrators, but more fighting men, and the need for replacement soldiers "obliges us to put off projects that are desirable and worthwhile in and of

---

[72] Der Militärbefehlshaber in Belgien und Nordfrankreich, personnel department, Az. 182 No. 167/42 geh. an den OKH Betr. Einberufung der MV-Beamten der Jahrgänge 1908 und jünger als Soldaten, 21 July 1942 (AN: 40 AJ/455).

[73] Der Militärbefehlshaber in Belgien und Nordfrankreich, Militärverwaltungschef Gruppe Pers, Az. 182 No. 102/42 geh. an den MBH in Frankreich, Oberstleutnant Borgmann, 16 May 1942 (AN: 40 AJ/455).

[74] Leiter der Wirtschaftsabteilung an die Zentralabteilung Betr. Freigabe von Militärverwaltungsbeamten für die Truppe, 2 December 1941 (AN: 40 AJ/455).

[75] See correspondence in AN: 40 AJ/455.

themselves ... if these projects do not need to be done *right away*."[76] Men who were available to fight should be deployed to the front by 1 March 1942.[77]

Within a few weeks, Hans Speidel, head of the command staff (Kommandostab) in France, issued a summary document that emphasised the need to make as many men as possible available for combat, and stated that henceforth, most administrative matters were to be looked after by occupiers who were not physically able to fight, or were over 34 years of age. In a new departure, Speidel also wrote that, "[a] widespread deployment of female auxiliaries is foreseen in all military administrative offices."[78] Women would now be employed in "clerical and filing work" brought together into "a female auxiliary corps [Stabshelferinnenschaft] that [would] be newly constructed."[79] Although female replacement staff were not available just yet, German offices should send their requests for auxiliaries immediately, with the proviso that such requests must free up men for combat duty. In addition to clerical work, women were to replace men as translators, and the use of female signals staff (Nachrichtenhelferinnen) must also increase. In fact, suggesting that female staff were new was disingenuous, as German women had been employed in France almost from the beginning of the occupation.[80] In early 1942, there were about 130 female staff members working under the authority of the administrative branch of the military government in Paris.[81] Using female auxiliaries was not unprecedented, therefore, but creating a corps of *Stabshelferinnen* formalised their status, making it easier to recruit, manage and deploy female employees by tying them more closely to the military apparatus.[82]

---

[76] Emphasis in the original. Oberkommando des Heeres, Abt. K Verw. (V) an MBH Fr., Verwaltungsstab, Betr. decreasing personnel, 9 January 1942 (AN: 40 AJ/455).

[77] Zentralabteilung Paris an Gruppenleiter der Abt. Wirtschaft, 20 January 1942 (AN: 40 AJ/455).

[78] Der Militärbefehlshaber in Frankreich, Kommandostab Abt. Ia/IIa, Betr. Personelle Verlagerung, 22 January 1942 (AN: 40 AJ/455).

[79] Der Militärbefehlshaber in Frankreich, Kommandostab Abt. Ia/IIa, Betr. Personelle Verlagerung, 22 January 1942 (AN: 40 AJ/455).

[80] Reich ministries such as Food and Agriculture sent female staff to France to help determine how French foods might best be exploited. An early attempt to regulate such women's behavior was MBH "Benutzung von Wehrmachtfahrzeugen durch weibliche Angestellte," 13 September 1940 (AN: 40 AJ/451).

[81] MBH Verwaltungsstab Abt. Z an Intendanten beim MBH Betr. OKH order Az. 986 No. I/7182/42, 18 March 1942 (AN: 40 AJ/456).

[82] On female Wehrmacht auxiliaries, see notably Ursula von Gersdorff, *Frauen im Kriegsdienst 1914–1945* (Stuttgart: Deutsche Verlags-Anstalt, 1969); Karen Hagemann, "Mobilizing Women for War: The History, Historiography, and Memory of German Women's War Service in the Two World Wars," *Journal of Military History* 75, No. 4 (October 2011): 1055–94; Birthe Kundrus, "Nur die halbe Geschichte: Frauen im

In the third week of February, the personnel branch in Paris informed the army high command that there were 209 administrators in France born after 1908 who were available for front-line duty. Thirty-five of these had already been sent out, or were being processed for deployment. Of the remaining men, forty-seven had been born in 1911 or later, which put them in the category that was supposed to be transferred to the front first. The document expressed optimism that even for the more specialised areas of economic management in France, competent administrators might be found among older men, but it insisted that younger administrators could not be deployed elsewhere until such replacements had been found.[83] Soon after, citing the Führer's own wishes, the Oberkommando der Wehrmacht ordered that the military administrative staff in the West be reduced by 25 per cent. All fit soldiers born 1908 or later who had not yet attained the rank of officer were to be deployed to the front.[84]

Although such orders sounded clear and decisive, the unease and foot-dragging that these measures provoked in Paris can be glimpsed in the comments of a female staff member who worked in the economic department of the military administration. In a letter to a friend who had formerly worked in the same office, Eva L. confided that men were being combed out for the front, notably a staff member who "is supposed to disappear from here by the twenty-first of March and is now moving heaven and hell to save his oh-so-precious life! It's a complete shame the way he's trying to duck out. M. [another staff member] is shirking successfully. He's written off sick but no one knows what he's actually lacking."[85] A year later, staff member M. was still working in Paris, listed as temporarily unfit for service, to be deployed after 1 May 1943.[86]

Through the spring and summer, leading administrators in France continued to express their willingness to provide more men for combat duty, but only on condition that they were sent alternate personnel. They

Umfeld der Wehrmacht zwischen 1939 und 1945" in *Die Wehrmacht: Mythos und Realität*, ed. Rolf-Dieter Müller and Hans-Erich Volkmann (München: Oldenbourg Wissenschaftsverlag, 1999); Maubach, *Stellung*.

83 Chef des Verwaltungsstabes, Abt. Z, Tgb. No. 69/42 an OKH, Generalstab des Heeres, Generalquartiermeister Betr. Personelle Verlagerung, 18 FebruaryFebruary 1942 (AN: 40 AJ/455).

84 Kommandostab Abteilung Ia, Aktennote, 24 March 1942 (AN: AJ 40/455).

85 Eva L., 3 March 1942 (BfZ SS). Earlier in the year, staff in Paris had noted that numerous officers and administrators were producing medical documentation to show that they were unfit for the climatic conditions in the East. Militärbefehlshaber in Frankreich Kommandostab Abt. IIa (L) (K) (II) Br. B Nr. 150/42 geh. IIa Betr. Körperliche Eignung für Verwendung im Osten, 21 January.

86 List of military administrators on staff at MBH France, born in 1906 or younger, n.d. [ca. April 1943] (AN: 40 AJ/455).

also worked towards ameliorating the process by which administrators moved into active combat. By September 1942, an arrangement had been made that enabled Wehrmacht administrators to be released to their home districts rather than to the desk staff clearing house at Marburg on the Lahn. This change made it easier for former administrators to receive officer training and be prepared properly for their deployment.[87] The Wehrmacht shifted small numbers of male replacement staff into France, and above all, brought in more women to perform lower-level office jobs. With time, some of these women took on greater responsibilities, combining with existing female staff to become a major component of the military administration in France and other occupied areas.[88]

The need for staff continued to rise despite these efforts, and to at least some extent, reorganisation itself created extra work. A signals lance corporal in Paris, Alfred M., pointed out tha "[r]eforms and organizational restructuring mean that our official duties here are stretching out more and more, which not the least puts more demands on each individual."[89] If anything, the work that needed to be done was growing, rather than shrinking, yet manpower was continually being siphoned off to the front.

Regardless of the pressure it put on remaining soldiers, the attempt to shift men from West to East continued. Hitler's growing anxiety about these issues was signalled by the striking of a special commission led by General Walther von Unruh, which visited France and other occupied areas in spring and summer 1943 as part of efforts to rationalise manpower use. A decorated veteran of World War I and a fervent National Socialist, Unruh had been appointed by Hitler in May 1942 as head of a special unit directly under the authority of Field Marshall Keitel. Since then, he had been responsible for streamlining military staffing in the Eastern occupied territories and reevaluating overall manpower use at

---

[87] MBH Fr. Zentralabteilung [Abt.] Z 219/1 an die Chef des militärverwaltungsbezirks A, B, C, Betr. Militärische Ausbildung und Verwendung der aus der Militärverwaltung für die Truppe Freigegebenen, 5 September 1942 (AN: 40 AJ/455).

[88] Between 28 April and 21 May 1942, some 840 Stabshelferinnen arrived in France. OKH to MBH Fr, "Bildung einer Stabshelferinnenschaft für die Heeresdienststellen in den besetzten Gebieten," 24 March 1942 (AN: 40 AJ/456). Overall numbers of Stabshelferinnen are difficult to estimate. Documents from June 1944 suggest that there were then 192 Stabshelferinnen under the authority of the Militärverwaltung-Zentralabteilung alone. Leitender Intendant beim MBH Frankreich, "Bereitstellung von Arbeitskitteln für Stabshelferinnen, 16 May 1944 (AN: 40 AJ/456). The Wehrmacht used more than 500,000 female auxiliaries overall. Hagemann, "Mobilizing," 1057.

[89] Alfred M., 10 February 1943 (BfZ SS).

home in the Reich.[90] Sardonically referred to as the "faith-healer and hero-grabbing commission" (Gesundbeter und Heldengreifkommission) because they declared ostensibly sick men well and aimed to turn even the meekest souls into front-line soldiers, Unruh's staff sniffed out malingerers, limited redundancies, and identified anyone they thought might make a better contribution to the war effort at the front.[91] As historian Kroener has remarked, the aptly-dubbed Unruh, whose name means "unease," did in fact spread unease whereever he went.[92] At the same time, his overall effectiveness was limited by power-struggles between Keitel, Goebbels, and Himmler, as well as the difficulty of sorting out overstaffed bureaucracies that overlapped deliberately to encourage competition in the context of the Third Reich's well-recognised ideologically-based "administrative Darwinism."[93]

In all, Unruh spent about six weeks in France from mid-June to the end of July 1943, inspecting the occupation apparatus countrywide. Fritz-Dietlof Graf von der Schulenberg, a Reich Ministry of the Interior staff member attached to Unruh's commission, wrote home to his wife soon after arriving in Paris. He complained about the "plethora of very bloated bureaus waging war against one another," and went on to describe, "an army of people who, apparently busy doing things that are crucial to the outcome of the war, are all impossible to do without, and yet live a life that no longer has any connection to this war's severity and also does not meet the measures of honesty and clean living. It's the Augean stables."[94] These comments give some measure of the Herculean task that Unruh's men, arriving from the outside with a mandate to increase efficiency, believed they faced. At the same time, while criticising the atmosphere in France and lending credence to the notion that there was an *Etappengeist* there, these men were, ironically, vulnerable to local temptations themselves. A day or so earlier, Schulenberg had seen sixty-six-year-old Unruh, who liked his wine, "glowing almost purple from the good Burgundy."[95]

---

[90] Kroener, "Heldenklau," 270, 272.

[91] Militärbefehlshaber in Belgien und Nordfrankreich, Gruppe pers., Reinhold an Militärbefehlshaber in Frankreich, Gruppe pers., Gehrhardt, 4 May 1943 (AN: AJ 40/455).

[92] Kroener, "Heldenklau," 271.   [93] Kroener, "Heldenklau," 278.

[94] Schulenberg to his wife, 11 June 1943, cited in Kroener, "Heldenklau," 278. Schulenberg was a member of the group that attempted to assassinate Hitler on 20 July 1944, which suggests that his reaction to the putative Etappengeist in France may have been determined as much by a traditional conservative, outlook than by a National Socialist outlook per se.

[95] Schulenberg to his wife, 10 June 1943, cited in Kroener, "Heldenklau," 281.

In the end, having toured France extensively, Unruh's commission concluded that in fact, the administration there was not as disorganised and inefficient as many imagined. All the talk about an *Etappengeist* aside, Unruh had apparently left the country satisfied that the administration was in good hands, and that notably women were being employed as much as possible in office jobs.[96] Although administrator Medicus reported rather self-servingly that Unruh "had been impressed by the organization of the military administration in France and that there could be no talk of over-staffing, [indeed] rather the contrary was the case,"[97] Unruh's own report was more neutral and called for men up to thirty-seven years of age to continue to be shifted towards combat deployment.[98] Underlining that not everyone agreed with Medicus's rosy view of the situation, just a week later, the army High Command wrote to inform administrators that Hitler had mentioned several times "the danger of becoming too rooted to one's station in the western occupied areas" and the need to keep men in this region "capable of action."[99] The central military personnel bureau had already decided that active-duty officers who had spent more than two years in the West should be switched to other theatres, and now the measure was to be extended to military administrators too. "After all," the document pointed out, "about fifty percent of the administrators in the Western areas have been there two years and more."[100] In a new departure, not only men who had served two years in France, but all administrators over sixty, too old for combat, were supposed to be sent home to either military or civilian roles in the Reich interior, regardless of the length of time they had served as occupiers. This measure too was intended to free up younger men, in this case those working in Germany, for active duty.[101]

Clearly, then, however efficient the administrators in France believed their organisation to be, pressure to reduce staff continued. The new rules about older personnel, which would have targetted experienced men like Medicus, or Kurt Blanke, a key administrator of measures

---

[96] Der Sonderbeauftragte des Führers General der Infanterie von Unruh an den Militärbefehlshaber in Frankreich, 24 July 1943 (AN: 40 AJ/450; AN: 40 AJ/455).

[97] Medicus an OKH Abt. K Verw. staff member Danckwerts, 2 August 1943 (AN: 40 AJ/455).

[98] Many men were already older than this, for as many as 80 per cent of officers in the military administration were over thirty-seven in 1943. Laub, *After the Fall*, 45.

[99] OKH Abt. K Verw. (Verw.) an Militärbefehlshaber in Frankreich, Militärbefehlshaber in Belgien und Nordfrankreich, 31 July 1943 (AN:40 AJ/455).

[100] OKH Abt. K Verw. (Verw.) an Militärbefehlshaber in Frankreich, Militärbefehlshaber in Belgien und Nordfrankreich, 31 July 1943 (AN:40 AJ/455).

[101] The two-year rule also applied to German civilian employees. Lammers to central Reich Ministries, 8 July 1943 (AN: 40 AJ/455).

against French Jews since 1940, underlined the absurdity of the situation.[102] On 24 August, the Paris Command's administrative branch expressed its concern, and soon the head of von Stülpnagel's administrative staff, Elmar Michel, wrote to the central military personnel department to argue that, although active troops might go soft from staying in one place too long, administrators were different, for "as their stay here lengthens, their performance rises."[103] Michel asked that only occasional transfers take place, and his letter included statistics showing that if older men were added to the younger men already switched out, only 11 per cent of the 275 administrators working directly for the Militärbefehlshaber in Paris, and 28 per cent of the 410 working elsewhere in France, notably in the Field Commands, would actually remain.[104] Even the highest military authorities could see that radical transfers like these made little sense, and in October, the policy was put on ice.[105] In Paris, administrators continued to argue that they needed qualified and skilled personnel with local knowledge, and pointed out, yet again, that there was no point in sending experienced men to the front, only to see them assigned to desk work that would have been done by female secretarial staff in the West.[106] Finally, in early January 1944, the two-year rule was also put on hold, underlining that it made little sense to shift experienced and high-ranking officers out of France, regardless of how "soft" they might, from the outside, appear to have become.

Evidently, the Reich was caught in a bind. Losses in the East required frequent injections of men, while staff were also needed to maintain Germany's hold on occupied areas while exploiting their raw materials, food, and labour.[107] The scale of planned personnel transfers and the complexities of administering the process took up so many resources that these measures began to seem utterly counterproductive. In January 1944, increasingly desperate, the central military authorities reversed

---

[102] On Blanke, see Jungius and Seibel, "The Citizen as Perpetrator."

[103] Kommandant von Gross-Paris, Militärverwaltungsstab Abt. person. 545/43 g an MBH Fr. Abt. MVZ, 24 August 1943 (AN: 40 AJ/455); Chef der Militärverwaltung, MBH Fr. an OKW Generalquartiermeister, 4 September 1943 (AN: 40 AJ/455).

[104] Chef der Militärverwaltung, MBH Fr. an OKW Generalquartiermeister, 4 September 1943 (AN: 40 AJ/455).

[105] Zentralabteilung, file note reporting on a telephone call from early October, 19 November 1943 (AN: 40 AJ/455).

[106] Chef der Militärverwaltung, MBH Frankreich an OKH, Generalquartiermeister Betr. Abgabe jüngere Jahrgänge, 18 December 1943 (AN: 40 AJ/455).

[107] Kroener traces the overall evolution of military manpower in this period in Bernhard R. Kroener, "'Menschenbewirtschaftung,' Bevölkerungsverteilung und personelle Rüstung in der zweiten Kriegshälfte (1942–44)" in Organisation und Mobilisierung, 777–1002.

their procedures such that instead of asking departments to make younger, expendable administrators available for front-line service, as of 31 January 1944, they now required key staff who had to stay in occupied and staging areas to be declared essential workers.[108] All this did was create more paperwork, as a whole new set of requests for essential worker status had to be made. Far from an efficient, keenly sharpened war machine, the French experience shows how, by 1944, Hitler's army was burying itself in paper, struggling to respond to mounting problems on all sides.

Within a few months, moreover, circumstances had become so tense in France that it seemed more than ever counter-productive to send occupiers anywhere else.[109] Very soon, of course, France itself became a front-line area, at which point reorganising the military administration seemed futile indeed. Efforts continued, but more as a kind of knee-jerk reaction than because they actually made sense.[110] In a final report in 1945, military administrators claimed that ongoing attempts to shrink their staff in France had merely fostered unease and wasted resources as each section fought to retain its most efficient personnel. The desire to keep men from becoming *westweich* was, they suspected, less the reason for the reductions than behind-the-scenes power plays and the attempts of other Reich instances to perpetuate their own relatively safe positions in the West by weakening the military administration.[111]

Whatever the reality of the situation, there remained a widespread perception that men in France were becoming soft. In January 1944, Hitler sent General Jodl to France to check on matters, and he came back with reports of local staff headquarters furnished with armchairs and carpets that seemed better-suited to princely residences than to battle positions. Hitler had expected nothing less, for the head of Army Group B, Erwin Rommel, had already complained that in Paris more men crossed one's path carrying parcels than carrying guns. Jodl recommended that staff headquarters be moved outdoors, a measure that was actually ordered on 1 March 1944. Conveniently for the officers, there was still often a comfortable chateau nearby.[112]

---

[108] Vermerk über UK-Anträge, n.d. [January 1944] (AN 40 AJ/455).
[109] MVZ PV: 2375, PA 723 an das Oberkommando des Heeres, Generalstab des Heeres, Generalquartiermeister, Betr. Abgabe juengerer Jahrgaenge, 8 May 1944 (AN: 40 AJ/455).
[110] These ongoing efforts are documented in AN: 40 AJ/455.
[111] Militärverwaltung in Frankreich: Abschlussbericht der Verwaltung: Allgemeines und Gruppe "Allgemeine und innere Verwaltung", 25 March 1945, 29 (AN: AJ 40/536).
[112] Jodl's and Rommels comments are cited in Tewes, *Frankreich*, 388.

The contrast between the lifestyle available in France, especially to high-level occupiers, and the dismal realities of the Eastern Front fed the notion that men in the West were living too well. The very real, but often overlooked, mobility of the war contributed to this perception because it made it so easy to make comparisons. As men moved across Europe from West to East and back again, their experiences stayed with them, whether as warm memories to sustain a soldier through a cold winter's night, or as unspoken visions to haunt even the sunniest hours, making war in the West seem like "child's play" by comparison. The differences between East and West affected behavior, too, making it hard for former occupiers to adjust to new contexts, and perhaps also, though this is beyond the scope of this book, influencing the rate with which they took on the brutal attitudes and conduct expected against a new "sub-human" foe in the East. Certainly, when units were transferred back westwards, they experienced a kind of culture shock, which sometimes revealed itself in ugly transfers of violent methods more typical of other war fronts. In the context of harsh fighting and growing losses, any perceived privilege, including the simple fact of being an occupier in the West, caused resentment. The question then became less about whether there really was an *Etappengeist* in France, and more about how the perception that there was such a spirit intensified demands to limit staff and tighten procedures in ways that were counterproductive for the war effort overall.

In the end, two things are clear. The first is that occupiers did enjoy themselves in France, and complaints about good living there, especially compared to the Eastern Front, were based in fact. The second, however, is that concerns about soldiers becoming *westweich* were probably exaggerated. Especially when battle turned against Germany, France became a convenient scapegoat. If occupation leaders were not fully to blame for this, they did bear part of the responsibility, for they had promoted a consumption-, leisure- and, tourism-based model of occupation from the beginning. Even if accusations that there was an *Etappengeist* were overblown, the conflict really did seem far away in France, and the regime had a deep interest in perpetuating this illusion. The trouble was that when the conflict touched again on France directly, some occupiers had difficulty switching gears. As we will see, many continued almost to the end to act in France as if there was not, in fact, a war going on.

7 Twilight of the Gods

"To my mind," wrote German railway administrator Wilhelm Unverzagt after war's end, "the word 'westweich' applied to considerable extent to the way of thinking of a great many German bureaus [in France]." According to Unverzagt:

One felt the attitude of total war very little here. That had nothing whatsoever to do with the fact that a first-rate dinner at the [legendary Paris restaurant] Tour d'Argent was a pleasure ... but one should not have let the *real* job be pushed into the background by these aesthetic things, by Paris, by its unique colours, the width of its streets, the relaxed way that even the simple man carried himself as a matter of course. Many [occupiers] had practically forgotten the war, particularly since they lived better than most people in the Reich."[1]

Unverzagt had been transferred to France in 1944 after twenty months spent in the German-held East. In his writing, he tried to work through what had gone wrong in the West, and he summarised an idea that had become common currency among Germans from about 1943 onwards. Increasingly, people believed that while soldiers on other war fronts fought on grimly and civilians at home bore up bravely under the strains of aerial bombing, troops in the West were enjoying themselves. Rather than making a fair contribution, they had underestimated war's challenges and gone soft. Like the civilians in World War I, whose lack of backbone was blamed for Germany's loss in the "stab in the back" myth, occupiers in the West had become scapegoats. They were fingered as lazy and decadent, hedonists who sought only to maximise their own pleasure as the Reich's enemies tore Germany apart.

Using Unverzagt's comments as a starting point, this chapter addresses three interconnected questions. Focusing on the period from early 1944 through the German retreat from France, it asks first whether, and to what extent, occupiers adjusted their approach to take the new

---

[1] Emphasis in the original. Wilhelm Unverzagt, "Die letzte Wochen in Paris", n.d., 46 (BArch: N 1259/3).

earnestness of the situation into account. Second, although Unverzagt, and others mentioned in Chapter 6, often suggested that occupiers were neglecting their duty, was the notion that there was an *Etappengeist* in France mainly an exaggeration, a myth that may have contained a grain of truth, but primarily served as a convenient story relayed to explain German losses? Finally, if there was an *Etappengeist*, or even the perception of one, what impact did this have on the way soldiers fought the war in France in 1944?

The first part of the answer is that, although the character of the occupation had been changing since 1941, and defence was uppermost in the minds of soldiers by early 1944, there were also symptoms of an *Etappengeist* in France. Worse, top-level occupiers were aware of the problem. They allowed it to persist in part because, as we have seen, activities like shopping, tourism, and photography offered occupiers coping mechanisms, enabled more complete exploitation of French goods, and made the country useful as a staging area for rest, relaxation, and training. Pastimes like shopping and sightseeing continued to the bitter end, subject to new restrictions, but popular nonetheless because they offered respites from combat and from Germany's increasingly discouraging overall situation. These activities also persisted because, having favoured them from the occupation's earliest days, it was difficult for the leadership to change direction. Treating France as a pleasure garden had taken on its own momentum and now, as Rome burned, so to speak, the fiddler who had begun playing four years earlier no longer knew how to put his instrument down.

Quite apart from occupiers' actual behaviour, which the authorities at least tried to control, there was a widespread perception that men in France no longer met the Third Reich's expectations of soldierly bearing and comportment. Chapter 6 has shown how this perception nourished ongoing pressure to reduce the size of the occupation army. Here, we explore how the notion that men in France exhibited an *Etappengeist* may have contributed to radicalising violence among troops transferred into France from other fronts. Bertram Gordon has argued that, among some occupiers, knowledge of France obtained through several years spent living there, and a continuing appreciation for French landscapes, monuments, and a Gallic way of life, may have served as a brake on violence.[2]

---

[2] Gordon suggests that Germans' attraction to France as tourists affected high-level decision-making, for example decisions to offer the French an armistice in 1940, or to spare Paris from total destruction in 1944. He does not examine how the familiarity with France fostered through tourism may have limited occupiers' violence more broadly. Ben H. Shepherd notes that although the Commander-in-Chief in the West, Field Marshal von Rundstedt was ruthless, "some of his subordinates proved more humane," and offers

But was the contrary also true? How did *not* having been an occupier affect soldiers' propensity to violence? And, more to the point, how did battle-hardened incoming soldiers' awareness of the disparities between the harsh realities they had faced and the apparently relaxed good living of long-term occupiers influence new arrivals' approach to warfare in the West?

For exhausted combattants arriving in an apparent "paradise" after devastating battle experiences, the contrast between the horrors of the Eastern Front and the pleasures of life in France seemed shocking. The notion that some occupiers had simply been enjoying themselves was a deep affront. When incoming soldiers who had seen hard fighting became involved in atrocities, they may have partly been demonstrating their inability to adjust to the quite different context of the West, and also taking out their frustration on the French population. Equally, they may have wanted to show themselves and other Germans that, unlike the "soft" occupiers in the West, they knew how a "real" war should be fought.[3] Determined to eradicate the "softness" they believed to be partly responsible for defeats elsewhere, men like SS-Oberscharführer Fritz Swoboda, discussed below, used brutality to demonstrate their own strength and masculinity. The notion that troops in the West had become soft therefore had not only explanatory, but also causal power. It formed part of the background to incoming units' radical violence in the occupation's last weeks.

If we conceive of warfare in France neither as strictly conventional nor as purely ideologically driven, but rather a hybrid that combined conventional and ideological elements to varying degrees depending on time and place, what were the factors that tipped the balance either way? Historian Peter Lieb has shown that the level of ideological indoctrination, as well as soldiers' past war experiences, were important considerations. Ideologically highly-charged SS units and elite formations were responsible for the worst atrocities in France. Alongside these men, soldiers with long experience in anti-partisan warfare, or who had fought in challenging rearguard actions in the Soviet Union, entered France

---

examples. Gordon, "Warfare and Tourism," 628–31, 633; Shepherd, *Hitler's Soldiers*, 586.

[3] Lieb points out that during 1941 in the East, troops in rear areas were often the most brutal, as if they were trying to demonstrate that they too could contribute to the war against communism. Although it played out in the opposite way, with second-line troops that had been stationed in France longer typically less brutal, the dynamic in France was rooted in similar rivalries among units and soldiers over who was "harder" in battle. Lieb, *Konventionneller*, 507.

primed to fight brutally.[4] Beyond the ideology and battle experiences that Lieb examines, occupation experiences, and in some cases the lack thereof, affected soldiers' propensity to extreme violence. This chapter contends not only that long-term occupiers were less likely to commit atrocities, but also that, for those who did not have this experience, disdain for and a kind of visceral envy of long-term occupiers, who were widely assumed to be going soft, spurred on violence. Where Lieb's extremely thorough account examines primarily army and SS Commanders, their combat experiences and ideological indoctrination, the focus here is on lower-level soldiers' and military administrators' occupation experiences and their attitudes towards fellow soldiers. Using a bottom-up approach, this account complements Lieb's analysis by suggesting that alongside the elements he has identified, the notion that there was an *Etappengeist* in the West created pressure for radicalisation.

As the war ended in France, the putative *Etappengeist* became an easy explanation for German failures. Like the "stab-in-the-back" myth, it served to exculpate military leaders by blaming losses on a small number of individuals who had misjudged the earnestness of the hour. Read in this way, France was lost because occupiers had failed to be "real men" in Kurt F.'s words. As Unverzagt had put it, they had neglected to recognise and do their "real job."[5] Rather than admitting that the Reich was increasingly outnumbered and outgunned, it was simpler to blame the situation on decadence and a failure of military manliness.[6] If only, the story ran, civilians and soldiers had worked harder, committed themselves more fully to total war and been willing to exercise greater brutality, they might have been victorious. It was all very well to live like gods in France, but winning the war demanded men.

Germans spent the early part of 1944 both waiting for and dreading the Allied invasion that was to signal the beginning of the end of the war. As tensions rose, however, the occupation continued much as usual. At a meeting in Paris in late January to address troop morale and political "education," military staff discussed a proposal from the city's Commander to end organised sightseeing visits to the capital.[7] Although it might have made sense to suspend these visits, apparently all delegates to the meeting viewed "continuing this opportunity as desirable, both in

---

[4] Lieb, 506–7.
[5] Cited in Chapter 6. F., "Kriegsbriefe," February 19, 1943. Wilhelm Unverzagt, "Die letzte Wochen in Paris", n.d., 46 (BArch: N 1259/3).
[6] Thomas Kühne discusses concepts of military masculinity in *Kameradschaft: Die Soldaten des nationalsozialistischen Krieges und das 20. Jahrhundert*, 140 ff.
[7] See Chapter 6. Transcript of 29 January 1944 meeting of NSFOs, 8 February 1944 (BArch: RH 36/552).

general and in the specific interest of the units arriving from the East."[8] Sightseeing visits offered benefits in terms of rest and relaxation, and the meeting attendees argued that stopping them would disadvantage low-ranking soldiers who, unlike officers, could not afford to make trips to Paris on their own. The fact that these trips persisted exemplifies the often contradictory nature of German occupation policies and practices. On the one hand, leading voices recognised that visits to Paris might seem inappropriate at a time when all resources were supposed to be directed towards the war effort. On the other, officers responsible for welfare and morale argued that, notwithstanding this concern, it was precisely the value of such visits to the war effort that meant they should be maintained.

Even in 1944, soldiers coming to Paris as part of organised tours had trouble understanding that these were not simply free-for-alls. The Militärbefehlshaber issued strict guidelines that insisted on appropriate discipline and demeanour, and warned men to "keep your distance from the French civilian population!" "Going arm-in-arm either actively or passively with women," was forbidden, as was taking French women into German eating or drinking establishments.[9] Since the threat of resisters seemed to be everywhere, soldiers were warned not to go out alone after dark, to keep their gloves on and their weapons loaded.[10]

Men on organised visits to Paris were not the only ones determined to make the most of France while there was still the opportunity. In early spring 1944, in what with hindsight seems a remarkable display of obliviousness, complaints came from Biarritz "that members of the Wehrmacht who want to stay overnight there, or are seeking accommodation for longer periods of time are either finding quarters themselves or else seeking out quarters they lived in before in order to reserve them from the French as summer residences."[11] These individuals clearly assumed that Germany would be able to hold France for another year, and they were planning their summer leave time.

Another sign that some occupiers' approach to France fell short of military expectations is that Spring 1944 saw an increase in the use of the civilian French postal service by soldiers who had been redeployed to another part of the country. Sending private letters by regular mail, rather than the military post, was strictly forbidden because it risked giving away the location of entire units. Worse, "[t]he majority [of these letters] are

---

[8] Transcript of 29 January 1944 meeting of NSFOs, 8 February 1944 (BArch: RH 36/552).
[9] "Merkblatt für den Aufenthalt in Paris", n.d. [ca. March 1944] (BArch: RH 36/42). On relationships with French women, see Chapter 2.
[10] "Merkblatt für den Aufenthalt in Paris", n.d. [ca. March 1944] (BArch: RH 36/42).
[11] OB West Abt. II b No. 583/44 Az. 31 Betr. Besuch der Küstenbäder, 27 March 1944 (BArch: R 70 Fr. 18).

purely love letters," which indicated that transferred soldiers were trying to keep long-distance romances with locals alive.[12] Even at a time that called for heightened vigilance, occupiers continued to think of France as a place for leisure and pleasure, above all.

The Allies landed in Normandy on 6 June 1944.[13] For some men in the fifty-eight divisions of mixed-quality German defenders in France, the invasion marked a release of tension that had been building up for months.[14] "One breathes a sigh of relief that there's now finally shooting here too," wrote signals Captain Richard D. in Bordeaux, "for if all of our work had been in vain, it would have been maddening too."[15] Soldiers closer to the line of fire soon had another view. They began writing home about the vast array of weapons at the Allies' disposal, and observed that the mechanised warfare they faced was more fearsome than Stalingrad. "Beautiful Normandy today is hell for the infantryman, and Stalingrad can't measure up to the materiel-based slaughters taking place here," wrote Lance Corporal Hans S. of the Ninety-First Infantry Division, which faced the American Ninth Infantry Division on the Contentin peninsula.[16] Just as Kurt F. had compared his experiences on the Eastern Front to Verdun, interpreting them as the vindication of his whole generation's bravery, now, men in the West saw Normandy in the context of Stalingrad, perceiving this battle as an opportunity to show that they too could withstand the storm of combat and should be seen as heroes.

Germans all over France felt a change in atmosphere after the Normandy landings. As the Allies moved forwards, occupiers who were accommodated in widely-scattered quarters were regrouped for safety and, by late June, staff in Paris were writing to the army High Command about the "very significant increased demands" that had been placed on the military administration since the beginning of the

---

[12] MBH Fr. Abt. Ic/I, 5 April 1944 (BArch: R 70 Fr. 7).

[13] The following focuses on German attitudes and perceptions rather than on military events. For events, consult notably Antony Beevor, *D-Day: The Battle for Normandy* (New York: Penguin Books, 2010); John Keegan, *Six Armies in Normandy: From D-Day to the Liberation of Paris* (New York: Penguin Books, 1982); Lieb, *Overlord*; Samuel W Mitcham, *Retreat to the Reich: The German Defeat in France, 1944* (Westport, Conn.: Praeger, 2000); Shepherd, *Hitler's Soldiers*.

[14] On the preparedness and overall state of troops in early June, see Shepherd, *Hitler's Soldiers*, 586–7.

[15] Communications captain Richard D., letter, 6 June 1944 (BfZ SS). A similar sentiment was expressed by lance corporal Willi H., letter, 7 June 1944 (BfZ SS).

[16] Hans S., 15 June 1944 (BfZ SS). A similar comparison to Stalingrad was made by an unnamed soldier in Carentan on 17 June 1944 (BfZ SS).

invasion."[17] Finally able to put an end to constant pressure from Berlin to redeploy and reduce especially his administrative personnel, the Militärbefehlshaber declared all administrators across the country to be indispensable (unabkömmlich) in their current positions.[18] A couple of weeks later, Field Commanders were asked to identify the degree of fitness of every single man, even those previously declared not fully fit for combat, an indication that even desk staff might soon be called out to fight.[19] From Bordeaux, signals Captain Richard D. had already written that the Allied capture of the port city of Cherbourg had put his own city on alert, with all men required to return to their quarters by 9 pm. There were daily shooting matches between resisters and French police, and frequent explosions at night. "The peaceful Bordeaux of last year is full of barbed wire and checkpoints," he added, reassuring his Home Front reader that "[w]e are nonetheless in what is for the time being the most peaceful city in France, and if our cables were not being destroyed from time to time by air raids, we would have been finished here long ago."[20]

While war was taking over formerly "peaceful" Bordeaux, Lance Corporal Hans S. reported that "beautiful Normandy" had become "a hell for the infantryman."[21] As they negotiated this "hell," soldiers' interactions with the land and people were often ruthless. Although German actions on the Eastern Front reached a much higher level of overall brutality that mixed war, exploitation and genocide, contemporaries did not necessarily perceive the difference in magnitude. More than ever before, the relative wealth and prosperity of France became a liability. Colonel General Friedrich Dollman's Seventh Army in Normandy, which included mainly poor-quality divisions, recorded 562 cases of theft in the first half of 1944.[22] In the third week of June, Lance Corporal S., whose unit was part of that army, wrote home that "in Russia we lived

---

[17] W. Hoffmann, 25 June 1944 (BfZ SS); Militärverwaltung Zentralabteilung an Oberkommando des Heeres, Generalquartiermeister Betr. Abgabe jüngerer Jahrgänge, 27 June 1944 (AN: 40 AJ/455).
[18] Individuals with an UK-Stellung (Unabkömmlichstellung, or indispensable role) fulfilled essential functions in the economy or administration and could not be sent into combat. Militärverwaltung Zentralabteilung an Oberkommando des Heeres, Generalquartiermeister Betr. Abgabe jüngerer Jahrgänge, 27 June 1944 (AN: 40 AJ/ 455).
[19] Kommandant des Heeresgebietes Südfrankreich, Abt. Verwaltung u. Wirtschaft, Az. Gr. Z Pers. an den MBH Fr. Abt. MVZ Paris, Betr. Tauglichkeitsgrad von MV-Beamten, 16 July 1944 (AN: 40 AJ/455).
[20] Communications captain Richard D., letter, 30 June 1944 (BfZ SS).
[21] Lance corporal Hans S., letter 15 June 1944 (BfZ SS).
[22] Although 40 per cent of Dollmann's troops had combat experience, another 40 per cent did not, and 20 per cent was made up of older men who had been "combed out" of civilian jobs and into the army. Shepherd, *Hitler's Soldiers*, 587.

brutally, but even more so here. The privates [Landser] are really quite shameless."[23] Commenting on the men's tendency to wreck their quarters and steal whatever they could lay their hands on, he noted that he had often passed through abandoned and war-damaged cities, "but I have never yet been able to bring myself to take things that I did not absolutely need, like socks and underwear." Other occupiers did not share his reticence, he added, and "they steal all kinds of things, despite the fact that they have to haul them along with them, [for] the parcel post is going nowhere, and on top of that, the privates have no idea what tomorrow will bring."[24] S., for his part, preferred to skip pillaging, writing that he would be happy if he made it home to his loved ones safe and sound.

Although morale remained solid overall, there is evidence from other parts of France, too, that some units' discipline was failing. In late June, British intelligence officers interviewed a Swiss representative of the Red Cross who had travelled to Marseilles earlier that month. Partly perhaps offering his Allied listeners what they wanted to hear, the representative commented that "German soldiers in Sète and Marseilles looked dirty and in bad condition. Many were to be seen lounging about with open shirt-collars." He concluded that, "[t]hey are undoubtedly soft after two or three years in barracks in Marseilles, and of poor morale."[25] In fact, no soldiers had been in barracks for two or three years in Marseilles, for the city had not been occupied until 12 November 1942. Although notably Dollman's troops in Normandy had second-rate equipment, and some battalions in France had been replaced with Osttruppen (local men from the East who fought for the Germans and whose morale and training were generally weaker), morale as a whole was strong.[26]

Even after the invasion, moreover, life away from the front continued much as usual for many occupiers. Orders from three days after the Allied landing, for example, stated that soldiers and officers in Paris would still be allowed to enter French opera houses, theatres, cabarets and variétés, though only if they carried a pistol, or were accompanied by another German who was armed.[27] Although other less "frivolous" publications were cancelled, the bi-weekly touristic guide to Paris, Der deutsche Wegleiter, continued to appear. As if nothing had changed, the

---

[23] Lance corporal Hans S., letter 21 June 1944 (BfZ SS).
[24] Lance corporal Hans S., letter 21 June 1944 (BfZ SS).
[25] Interview by political intelligence officer Ridley Prentice with M. Gaillet of Red Cross, 30 June 1944 (The National Archives: FO 371/41862).
[26] Ahlrich Meyer, Die Besatzung, 144; Shepherd, Hitler's Soldiers, 586–7.
[27] Kommandant von Gross-Paris, Standortbefehl No. 40/44, 9 June 1944 (BArch: RH 36/42).

final issue in August 1944 included an index of useful addresses for Germans living in Paris, French and German theatre listings, a history of the Paris central market, Les Halles, and a review of an art show at the Salon de l'Orangerie.[28] The *Wegleiter*, like the concerts, tours and other leisure opportunities that continued throughout the occupation, was no doubt partly an attempt to retain a sense of normalcy in the face of growing tensions.[29] But the failure to move more decisively to a war footing had other roots as well. Persistent manifestations of a touristic, relaxed attitude under the direct protection of German leaders suggest that both officers and men found it difficult to change course. Good food and drink, cultural attractions and leisure activities, once enjoyed, were hard to give up. Finally, on 26 July, when Germany's position in France was deeply threatened and assassinations by the resistance had become routine, the Paris Commander informed his men with clear exasperation that, "even if these murders are avenged after the fact in nearly every case, the soldier's blind trust must finally come to an end."[30] It was too late for that, however, and the soldiers themselves were not to blame. Having begun the occupation in a spirit of tourism as much as conquest, then instrumentalised consumption, leisure and pleasure to the regime's own ends, putting occupiers on a war footing now was like trying to reverse a freighter at full steam.

Making this transition was especially complicated because, as we have seen, France had developed into perhaps the most important rest and relaxation area outside the Reich. From 1941 onwards, the exploitation of French territory for regrouping and retraining troops was essential to the pursuit of the war as a whole. A ban on soldiers' sightseeing or limits on French entertainment would have been relatively easy to impose, albeit perhaps difficult to enforce, but the full potential of the "softer" exploitation of France could only be realised if soldiers were allowed to keep enjoying themselves. Occupiers not only profited from leisure opportunities themselves, but also shared their experiences with their families and friends. Beyond direct benefits to the men, their

---

[28] *Der deutsche Wegleiter* No. 103, 12–26 August 1944. See also Gordon, "Warfare and Tourism," 627. On Wegleiter Verlag, publisher of the *Wegleiter*, see Ch. 3 and Geiger, *L'image*, 379–80; Krob, "Paris Through Enemy Eyes: The Wehrmacht in Paris 1940–1944."

[29] Mitchell, *Nazi Paris*, 123. On the importance of "normality" as a force that underpinned popular support for National Socialism, see Andreas Wirsching, "Volksgemeinschaft and the Illusion of 'Normality' from the 1920s to the 1940s" in *Visions of Community in Nazi Germany: Social Engineering and Private Lives*, ed. Martina Steber and Bernhard Gotto (Oxford: Oxford University Press, 2014), 152, 155.

[30] Kommandant von Gross-Paris, Standortbefehl No. 54/44, 26 July 1944 (BArch: RH 36/42).

consumption, tourism, and leisure nourished popular support for Hitler's regime. Viewed from this perspective, allowing an *Etappengeist* to flourish in France was, for a very long time, an acceptable price to pay for significant rewards. Moreover, awareness that high-ranking occupiers were enjoying French pleasures on their own initiative led policy-makers to continue regime-sponsored sightseeing so that all soldiers could benefit from similar opportunities. As noted earlier in the chapter, when the Paris Commander proposed cutting down on group visits to the capital, officers responsible for troop morale and welfare argued that doing so would simply disadvantage ordinary soldiers who, unlike officers, could not pay for such trips from their own pockets. Ground-level occupiers and their needs and desires influenced the occupation to its very end, delaying the shift to a war footing perhaps decisively.

On 9 August 1944, although great swathes of France had already been taken over by the Allies, the soldier named Rudi, who we encountered in Chapter 5 nonchalantly eating grapes and enjoying local swimming, still had time to do some shopping. In a letter to his family, Rudi asked whether the jacket he had posted to his wife fit properly, and noted that he had sent her a pound of cocoa, two bars of soap and a pair of stockings through a friend who was travelling to the German border city of Aix-la-Chapelle (Aachen). He might yet pack up a bottle of cognac, he added, and he hoped to be able to buy more such goods soon. Much depended on whether he stayed in France, for it was likely that his unit would move further to the rear shortly.[31]

A week later, in a less positive mood after falling back to a new position, Rudi told his wife and son that, "[t]he Tommies are now near the town I was in until recently. Nonetheless, we can't hang our heads, although we must reckon with all possibilities. It's war after all, and we are soldiers."[32] Faced with an unfathomable future, at least the evening promised to be jolly, Rudi wrote, because, since the unit would be falling back again, each man had been issued thirty cigarettes, and the cantine was clearing its stocks of wine and spirits. However, this too was a "sign of the times" and the letter ended with the comment that "[e]verything is still so unclear even here in the West. I'm curious to see how this whole thing will pan out."[33] This letter was Rudi's last.[34]

---

[31] Rudi [letters give first name only], letter 9 August 1944 (BfZ: SSch).
[32] Rudi, letter 16 August 1944 (BfZ: SSch).
[33] Rudi, letter 16 August 1944 (BfZ: SSch).
[34] The file contains no further dated correspondence from him, nor any information about Rudi's presumed death (BfZ: SSch).

For many men, like Rudi, the occupation of France ended with death. Indeed, despite fierce efforts to hold France, once Allied forces broke out of the beachhead in Normandy, it did not take long for most of the country to fall. As soon as the High Command had discerned that the main Allied attack was taking place in Normandy, not further to the northeast in the Pas de Calais, it sent experienced troops, many of whom had fought on the Eastern Front, to the battle zone. In fact, with 65 divisions on the ground in later June 1944, versus 165 in the East, German forces were denser in the West compared to the size of the front to be defended. Still, efforts to combat the Allied advance were hampered notably by the enemy's size, material resources, and superiority in the air.[35] In early July, there were 3,800 Allied tanks compared to 1,200–1,300 German ones in Normandy, and by 23 July, 1.5 million Allied soldiers faced just 400,000 German men in the same region.[36] The Allies had ordered extensive air raids to soften up German defences before the invasion, and they continued to use air power to destroy communications networks and impede the arrival of reinforcements. This meant that, especially in Normandy, French civilians were gravely endangered. As many as 19,000 may have been killed by aerial bombing in Normandy alone, and many others were compelled to leave their homes.[37] In October 1944, the French calculated that some 1.2 million bombed-out civilians were still displaced.[38] As civilians fled the battle zone, the Allies had first taken Cherbourg, then Caen, and moved south and east, until free French forces entered Paris on 24 August. Fighting continued in eastern France for another month as Germans frantically packed up equipment, papers and belongings before departure, fought desperately as long as they could, and endured draining marches to the rear. Some men were taken prisoner, while others made it back to Germany, rested, regrouped, and were sent off to other fronts.[39] By mid-September 1944, the occupiers had withdrawn from most of

---

[35] Shepherd, *Hitler's Soldiers*, 608.   [36] Shepherd, *Hitler's Soldiers*, 607.
[37] Shepherd, *Hitler's Soldiers*, 607. In total, Allied bombing in France took some 67,000 lives. Torrie, *For Their Own Good*, 4, and on events in 1944, Ch. 7. See also Claudia Baldoli and Andrew Knapp, *Forgotten Blitzes: France and Italy under Allied Air Attack, 1940–1945* (New York: Continuum, 2012).
[38] Nearly a third of these were from Normandy. Torrie, *For Their Own Good*, 159.
[39] On POWs, see Bob Moore and Barbara Hately-Broad, eds., *Prisoners of War, Prisoners of Peace* (Oxford: Bloomsbury Academic, 2005); Neitzel and Welzer, *Soldaten*; Römer, *Kameraden*. On Germans held in France into the postwar period, see Valentin Schneider, *Un million de prisonniers allemands en France 1944–1948* (Paris: Vendemiaire, 2011); Fabien Théofilakis, *Les prisonniers de guerre allemands: France, 1944–1949, une captivité de guerre en temps de paix* (Paris: Fayard, 2014).

France. They still held a few "fortress" pockets on the Atlantic, but the rest of the country was free.

As Germany lost the territory it had held in the West, the idea that soldiers in France lacked discipline and soldierly bearing, by no means new, gained force. When the Allies moved towards Aix-la-Chapelle, for example, just inside the Reich proper, a National Socialist political officer commented in mid-September that the German population was refusing to evacuate into the Reich interior. He blamed this refusal on the "influence of floods of retreating staff from France [Frankreiche-tappe]."[40] The political officer believed that the insufficient resolve exhibited by retreating staff was giving the local population license to stay put fatalistically, rather than evacuating in order to safeguard resources and regroup for renewed attacks. The officer's use of the pejorative term *Etappe* underlined that he considered not the retreating soldiers themselves, but their putative softness to be the root of the problem.

Contemporaries knew, too, that being accused of "insufficient 'hard-ness,' let alone of 'softness'" was "the greatest reproof that can fall upon one in the Third Reich."[41] Yet the idea that troops in France had gone soft was persistent and widespread. This notion can be found not only in strongly National Socialist sources such as the one just cited, but also in sources whose authors were more distant from the regime. It had been expressed notably by Fritz-Dietlof von der Schulenberg, a nobleman and representative of the Ministry of the Interior who had visited Paris with General Unruh's commission, and was later a member of the 20 July plot against Hitler.[42] Wilhelm Unverzagt, quoted at the beginning of this chapter, was another individual whose overall stance was critical of the regime, if not overtly opposed to it.[43] He had been head of personnel management for the German railway (Reichsbahn) until he lost his position on political grounds in 1938. Yet he too thought that troops in the West were weak. Both von der Schulenberg and Unverzagt were animated not by radical National Socialism, but rather by a traditionally conservative sense of duty and appropriate behaviour. Both were older men who were offended by what they saw as laxity among troops in the rear. That both were also veterans of World War I was no

---

[40] National Socialist leadership officer (NSFO) Flossdorf to Raessler, 15 September 1944 (HstAD: RW 37/21).

[41] The remark comes from the diary of the commanding General in Croatia, Edmund Glaise von Horstenau, cited in Lieb, *Konventionneller*, 509.

[42] On Unruh's commission, see Chapter 6.

[43] Wolfgang Klötzer, Reinhard Frost, and Sabine Hock, "Unverzagt, Wilhelm," *Frankfurter Biographie: personengeschichtliches Lexikon* (Frankfurt am Main: W. Kramer, 1994).

accident – the perception that bloated staging areas had weakened Germany's fighting strength was part of long-standing explanations of why the Reich had lost that conflict as well. Evidently, comments from a variety of sources supported the notion that soldiers in France were going soft. If, for a moment, we take this idea at face value and consider its potential impact on the occupation as a whole, perhaps an approach to France based on "soft" interactions like consumption and leisure actually provided some measure of protection to the French as Germany fought to retain its western prize. In some cases, it appears to have done so. The close relationship that longer-term occupiers had with the land, its monuments, and its people sometimes sheltered these from extreme violence. However, this was not always the case. Moreover, it seems that some occupiers' comfortable, apparently relaxed, interactions with France may have spurred on violence among others. Even as shopping, entertainment, and insouciance continued in some circles, extreme violence and atrocities became the rule in others. The level of violence in the West did not reach that of the Eastern Front, far from it, but there were brutal acts against the Allied forces, as well as reprisals, ostensibly directed at the French resistance, that targeted French civilians directly.

Historian Peter Lieb, who offers the most complete account of anti-partisan activities in France in 1943–4, has linked the greatest atrocities to the SS and to units arriving in the West after hard fighting notably against partisans during the Eastern retreat. Lieb contends that formations that had been in France longer exhibited more restrained behaviour.[44] At the very least it seems that, as Bertram Gordon has argued, knowledge of France and the French reinforced through tourism contributed to limiting violence, rather than inciting it.[45] The fact that, of regular Wehrmacht units, those that had experienced Eastern retreat were most often involved in extreme violence suggests that these men were more frustrated and brutalised than others. Lieb has also pointed to their ideological indoctrination as a radicalising force, but were there other, less tangible factors that led soldiers to move beyond the constraints of conventional warfare?

Answering this question requires differentiating among various groups of soldiers, and in particular between SS and regular units. With rare exceptions, and recognising that regular army troops also committed atrocities, the men of the Waffen-SS were more ideologically-charged and more likely to act brutally. Based on extensive research using covert

---

[44] Lieb, *Konventionneller*, 506 ff. See also discussion in Neitzel and Welzer, *Soldaten*, 379 ff.
[45] Gordon, "Warfare and Tourism," 628 ff., 633.

British and American recordings of conversations among German prisoners of war, Sönke Neitzel and Harald Welzer have, like Lieb, emphasised the "ideological conditioning" of SS units.[46] These men were trained to view the war in extreme terms as a fight to the death between National Socialism and Bolshevism Europe-wide. SS men also had a strong sense of their own superiority that was not shared except by some elite groups in the army, such as paratroopers.[47] They viewed themselves as Hitler's shock troops, and there was a widespread understanding among them that, as one individual in British captivity put it, the SS "should show the Wehrmacht the right example."[48] Although attitudes to violence were not completely uniform, according to Neitzel and Welzer, "there could be no doubt in the SS divisions that one must be 'harder,' and also 'more radical' than the army."[49]

The case of SS-Oberscharführer Fritz Swoboda gives a sense of what this meant in practical terms.[50] Swoboda, who was twenty-two when he arrived in France in 1944, came from the Austrian city of Brünn. He had extensive experience in dealing with resisters, as he had been stationed in Prague in May 1942 when members of the Czech Resistance assassinated the Nazi governor of the area, Reinhard Heydrich. Swoboda was part of a detachment that stormed the resisters' hideout in the St Cyril and Methodius church in Prague using machine guns, tear gas, and even water pumped into the church basement by the fire department in an attempt to capture the men alive. In the end, Swoboda's unit wounded two men before the group took their own lives rather than be captured. Swoboda was decorated for his role in this action, and later mentioned in Allied captivity that to remember it better, he had taken a photograph of the church with bullet holes in it. A few days after the church was

---

[46] Neitzel and Welzer, *Soldaten*, 387. The conversations were recorded for intelligence purposes, principally at the Trent Park and Latimer camps in the UK and at Fort Hunt, VA. These facilities housed, for varying lengths of time, POWs deemed to be of particular interest to the Allies. Some recorded exchanges took place among prisoners, others involved individuals who the POWs believed to be fellow prisoners, but who were in fact spies working with the Allies. The 16,960 British transcripts and 3,298 American files represent a broad cross-section of soldiers, and the fact that they document spontaneous conversations makes them especially valuable sources. Neitzel and Welzer, *Soldaten*, 423–30.

[47] Neitzel and Welzer, *Soldaten*, 387–90.

[48] Special Report Army 649, 16 July 1944, cited in Neitzel and Welzer, *Soldaten*, 387.

[49] Neitzel and Welzer, *Soldaten*, 373, 387. On the SS, see also Jean-Luc Leleu, *La Waffen SS: Soldats politiques en guerre* (Paris: Perrin, 2010); Bernd Wegner, *Hitlers politische Soldaten: Die Waffen-SS 1933–1945. Leitbild, Struktur und Funktion einer nationalsozialistischen Elite* (Paderborn: Schöningh, 2008).

[50] This account follows that of Felix Römer, who has worked with the same source base as Neitzel and Welzer. "Kameraden, Foreword," 405–14.

stormed, Swoboda was put in charge of a firing squad comprised of twelve men assigned to execute some of the hundreds of prisoners the Germans killed in the wake of Heydrich's death.[51] In a further notorious reprisal action, the villages of Lidice and Ležáky were completely razed, their inhabitants killed outright or transfered to concentration camps before being gassed. Swoboda's statements in captivity show that he was fully aware of the extent of the violence, and thought it was completely justified.[52] Swoboda praised Heydrich as someone who "had already achieved a great deal."[53]

Swoboda's killings were not limited to German-controlled Czech areas. Before he was taken prisoner in November 1944, he belonged to the Seventeenth SS-Panzergrenadierdivision "Götz von Berlichingen," which fought on the front-lines in Normandy. Römer recounts that Swoboda "and his men murdered defenceless American prisoners of war there upon at least one occasion."[54] Swoboda saw this as an appropriate reprisal after his superior, a Lieutenant, was killed by Americans alerted to the Germans' presence by two US prisoners who had escaped captivity.

Men like Swoboda exercised violence both against enemy troops, and against resisters in France. Based on his Czech experiences, Swoboda believed that an occupying force must always be "energetic" [energisch], notably against resisters.[55] In a conversation with a cellmate that was recorded at the American military interrogation centre in Fort Hunt, Virginia, Swoboda regretted that the German forces had not employed the same techniques that they had used in the Czech region to eradicate resistance in France.[56] "If we had done that in France too, we would [not] have had the maquis," he claimed, adding that Czech areas "have been quiet since 1943, as far as I know."[57] Swoboda claimed that he himself would stop at nothing to control the territory. "Yes," he insisted, "I've sworn it to myself, and many others have sworn the same thing: if we occupy France again, then every Frenchman up to age sixty who

---

[51] As Römer points out, some of these individuals had done nothing more than speak positively about Heydrich's death. Römer, *Kameraden*, 407. Swoboda's chilling account of the killings, which stretched over "perhaps 14 days" is quoted in Neitzel and Welzer, *Soldaten*, 174–5.

[52] Römer, *Kameraden*, 407. Cf. Neitzel and Welzer, *Soldaten*, 175.

[53] Römer, *Kameraden*, 407. [54] Römer, *Kameraden*, 407–8.

[55] Römer, *Kameraden*, 408.

[56] Swoboda, taped conversation with Konrad, 1 December 1944, quoted in Römer, *Kameraden*, 407.

[57] The Czech resistance never recovered after the "blood baths" of summer 1942, Römer notes. Swoboda, taped conversation with Konrad, 1 December 1944, Römer, *Kameraden*, 407.

crosses my path ... I'll shoot every Frenchman between the ages of fourteen and sixty who crosses my path. I'll do that, and every one of us will do that."[58] Later, in a several-page signed manuscript he prepared at Fort Hunt in December 1944, Swoboda contended that opposition groups in France "had apparently seen it as a weakness" that Germany had not initially made reprisals against "the French national body [Volkskörper] as such."[59] As a result, he believed, resistance had continued to grow and take on more open forms. For this reason, Swoboda contended that "it should not be held against us [Germans]" that the reactions were so brutal.[60] As historian Felix Römer remarks, the tone of this document and the fact that Swoboda signed his own name to it, underline the degree to which he saw his own perspective as justified.[61]

Swoboda represented the stone heart of Hitler's Waffen-SS. He had belonged to the organisation's predecessor, the SS-Verfügungstruppe, since 1939, fought on the Western Front in 1940, later in the Balkans, the Eastern and again the Western Front. By the time he found himself at Fort Hunt, he had been wounded six times and was covered in scars.[62] Young men like him comprised the core of the most notorious units of the Waffen-SS, included the SS-division "Das Reich" that committed the Nazis' most infamous atrocity in France, the murder, on 10 June 1944, of 642 men, women and children, many of whom were locked inside a church that was then set alight at Oradour-sur-Glane.[63] For such men, who had spent most of the past five years moving from engagement to deadly engagement, land to land, village to village, it did not much matter where they were. To them, war was much the same, whether in Prague, on the Eastern Front, or in the West. Military necessity, as they saw it, was paramount, and the kinds of distinctions that longer-term occupiers might make between people they knew and strangers, landscapes and monuments they visited and appreciated, and combat terrain, must have seemed pointless, unmilitary, and downright dangerous. For one such as Swoboda, universal ruthlessness, regardless of circumstances, was the only way to win the war.

Can we generalise from Swoboda's case? To some degree, perhaps, but not completely, or the war in France in 1944 would have been a great deal more bloody and violent than it was. Even in the SS, not everyone

---

[58] Swoboda, taped conversation with Konrad, 29 November 1944, quoted in Römer, *Kameraden*, 408.
[59] Fritz Swoboda, manuscript, 7 December 1944, quoted in Römer, *Kameraden*, 409.
[60] Fritz Swoboda, manuscript, 7 December 1944, quoted in Römer, *Kameraden*, 409.
[61] Römer, *Kameraden*, 409.   [62] Römer, *Kameraden*, 405, 410.
[63] On German atrocities and Oradour, see Chapter 5, Farmer, *Martyred Village*; Ahlrich Meyer, *Die Besatzung*, Ch. 8.

thought and acted as Swoboda did.[64] Moreover, the SS formed only one segment of the German forces, and although SS units were often called upon to take on particularly challenging tasks, they were usually far outnumbered by regular army forces.

How did SS men compare to those of the regular army? Men from other branches of the service recognised that members of the Waffen-SS tended to be particularly harsh, but they were themselves capable of cruelty too. The conversations of Navy private Lehmann, recorded in captivity, illustrate this point well. Lehmann had been stationed on the Normandy coast, and in a discussion about the situation in France, remarked that the French had liked their German occupiers. Relations with local people had been good, he said, until the Waffen-SS had arrived and "made a mess" of everything such that the population was put in a "bad mood."[65] This fit a standard pattern – other Germans often pointed a finger at the SS, arguing that they were responsible for souring relations between the Germans and local people. In the same conversation, however, Lehmann described how his unit had searched the house of an older man near Canisy in Normandy, and, because they had found a covert radio transmitter, put the man "up against a wall"and "shot him down."[66] Even German military law required that a case like this be brought before the courts before the death penalty was carried out.[67] Thus, Lehmann's reference to the SS's well-known brutality was as much an attempt to make himself look better and to shift blame onto others as it was a statement that described varying levels of brutality between a member of the regular forces, who had perhaps spent a longer time in France, and the newly-arrived SS.

Beyond a very human tendency to blame others for their own short-comings, what other attitudes did men of the regular army harbour? We have established that they too tended to believe there was a great deal of laxity, or "softness," in France. While the SS-man Swoboda argued, from the perspective of one used to fighting partisans, that Germans should have undertaken more extensive reprisals after resistance attacks, voices from the regular army focused more on the failings of conventional methods of defence. A pattern of mutual accusation can be traced as well, with lower ranks blaming officers for losses, while officers blamed

---

[64] Neitzel and Welzer, *Soldaten*, 375, 387.
[65] Special Report Navy 3929, 10 July 1944, cited in Neitzel and Welzer, *Soldaten*, 382.
[66] It is unclear when this event took place. Special Report Navy 3929, 10 July 1944, cited in Neitzel and Welzer, *Soldaten*, 382.
[67] Neitzel and Welzer, *Soldaten*, 382.

their men. The reports from captivity examined by Sönke and Neitzel, as well as Römer, illustrate these tendencies.

The Norman city of Cherbourg fell to the Allies in late June 1944. This gave Allied troops access to a deep water port, which was necessary to step up shipments of war materiel. For several months, before Antwerp became available, Cherbourg was the most important port in Europe. German prisoners taken as the city was lost were well aware that their defeat there was a major setback. Over and over again, they insisted that the defeat was not their fault, for it had been utterly impossible to hold the city with such poorly-armed and ill-prepared troops.[68] The leadership was rumoured to have been weak as well, for a lance-corporal complained in July 1944 that, "[t]he officers in Cherbourg were a cowardly lot."[69] One was supposed to have been court-martialed because he wanted to break out and retreat behind German lines, but the trial never began because "the gentlemen officers were in their bunker and didn't dare go out."[70] Another prisoner complained that "[t]he officers had already packed their bags for captivity days ago. If our officers hadn't been so cowardly, Cherbourg would never have fallen as it did."[71] Prisoners of war evidently sought to absolve themselves of responsibility for German losses, and there was an element of fabulation to these accounts as well. Recounted from soldier to soldier, they became convenient explanations for what had taken place that bore little relationship to reality.[72]

This interpretation is confirmed by the fact that officers read the situation the other way around. General Walter Köhn, for instance, claimed that, "when the leader stayed put, and the officer stayed put, the men held. As soon as the [officer] left his position, though [the men gave up]!"[73] In captivity, Köhn spoke to a cellmate about an incident in which a Lieutenant had asked him what to do about a tunnel full of ammunition at Cherbourg. Rather than leave this treasure for the Allies, "[b]low the hole closed. There's nothing for it," Köhn had said. Later, the Lieutenant had called to say that "he had blown the hole closed, but beforehand he had called inside to see if there were any German soldiers

---

[68] Neitzel and Welzer point out that it was typical of soldiers to blame "others" for losses, *Soldaten*, 313.

[69] Special Report Navy 3924, 8 July 1944, cited in Neitzel and Welzer, *Soldaten*, 315.

[70] Special Report Navy 3924, 8 July 1944, cited in Neitzel and Welzer, *Soldaten*, 315.

[71] Special Report Navy 3932, 11 July 1944, cited in Neitzel and Welzer, *Soldaten*, 315.

[72] On the stories soldiers tell about war, see Samuel Hynes, *The Soldiers' Tale: Bearing Witness to a Modern War* (New York: Penguin Books, 1998).

[73] Special Report German Generals 934, 1 July 1944, cited in Neitzel and Welzer, *Soldaten*, 315.

or anything left inside. A hundred and fifty men came out. In the back, huddled in a corner, they'd been lying there for days. A hundred and fifty men!" The men were unarmed, and the General claimed that he had pulled together weapons for them and set them to fighting. Then, "when I had deployed them, I turned around, and they were all gone again."[74]

Lending credence to these reports of cowardice from both officers and men, the Commander of the Port of Cherbourg, Captain Hermann Witt, had radioed to Paris on 27 June 1944 that Generalmajor Sattler in the navy yards had surrendered prematurely with 400 men.[75] A few days later, in captivity, Witt complained about Cherbourg that "it was a complete Jena and Auerstedt" – a reference to Napoleon's rout of Prussian forces in 1806.[76] The troops' morale had collapsed, Witt said, and the soldiers chose to surrender rather than fighting to the death. Indeed, according to a staff lieutenant of the 709th infantry division, the men had come close to mutiny, and "[i]n fact, no soldier was really willing to do anything anymore. I guarantee you that if our bunkers had not been taken, the next day they would have knocked off the officers."[77]

There was, then, some truth to accounts that German forces had not defended Cherbourg as well as they might have, though Lieb points out that the 709th Infantry Division had been obliged to send its best officers to the Eastern Front in 1943–4, and the replacements it received were not nearly as strong. Three German battalions had been replaced with Osttruppen, and before the final battle at Cherbourg, the men had been cut off for several days at the top of the Cotentin peninsula.[78] Allied forces were superior and in contrast to the Eastern Front, where soldiers feared nothing more than becoming Soviet prisoners, Allied captivity seemed relatively attractive. The thought of getting out of war quickly may have have encouraged men to lay down their arms.[79]

Cherbourg fell, but German efforts were more successful in other nearby areas, for example on the Cap de la Hague peninsula, a small, rocky, heavily fortified zone whose access was relatively easy to defend. There, an officer recalled approvingly, soldiers had held on "to the last moment."[80] On the whole, we have noted, German morale in France held up fairly well until August, when discipline in some of the other infantry units began to fail.[81]

---

[74] Special Report Army 622, 6 July 1944, cited in Neitzel and Welzer, *Soldaten*, 314.
[75] The radio transcript is cited in Neitzel and Welzer, 314.
[76] Special Report Navy 3925, 10 July 1944, cited in Neitzel and Welzer, *Soldaten*, 314.
[77] Special Report Navy 616, 1 July 1944, cited in Lieb, *Konventionneller*, 433.
[78] Lieb, *Konventionneller*, 432.   [79] Lieb, *Konventionneller*, 433, 438.
[80] Special Report Army 639, 8 July 1944, cited in Neitzel and Welzer, *Soldaten*, 314.
[81] Lieb, *Konventionneller*, 437; Shepherd, *Hitler's Soldiers*, 625.

This is not the place to explore the strengths and weaknesses of Germany's defence efforts from a tactical or strategic point of view. Clearly, the factors that determined the success or failure of particular engagements, or individual soldiers' actions were complex. But soldiers' attitudes mattered, and it is highly likely, if difficult to prove, that the arrival of new troops, unused to a particular region and to the quieter day-to-day interactions of occupation, increased the likelihood of extreme violence. If extensive acquaintance with France and the relaxed attitudes of longer-term occupiers served as a brake on violence, these same attitudes may also have functioned as a catalyst to violence for incoming men with a bone to pick against putative *Etappenschweine* (rear echelon swine) among their own ranks in France. Such men may have absorbed the arguments Kurt F. echoed about the lazy *Etappe* and wanted to purge the occupation of the "softness" they saw as responsible for the army's losses.

There was a recognisable clash of cultures between combat troops and longer-term occupiers. Active troops harboured significant scorn for military administrators, in particular, and representatives of both the Waffen-SS and the regular army made derogatory comments about the men who struggled to manage administrative tasks and maintain working relationships with the French during the German retreat.[82] The difference in culture was partly due to a generational conflict, for military administrators were typically older than the men in charge of front-line troops, especially tank regiments.[83] It was also closely linked to the widespread attitude that troops in the West were going soft.

In at least one case, negative comments about military administrators stemmed directly from the Commander of a unit that used excessive violence in combat in the same period. In late June 1944, the leader of "Kampfgruppe Wilde" of the Eleventh Panzer Division, Lieutenant Colonel Dr. Traugott Wilde, complained about Generals Sternkopf and Kalkowski, administrators responsible for liaison detachments in Périgueux and Brive respectively.

Their measures are determined by a blind trust that arises from personal relationships. Their measures reveal a weakness that the terrorists [sic] know about. Their influence gets in the way everywhere and is not intended to root out the terrorists, but is based on the point of view that the troops who are deployed here now will one day be pulled out and then the only possible way to live will be to rely on so-called good relationships. Moreover, they establish their

---

[82] Lieb, *Konventionneller*, 383.
[83] Lieb, *Konventionneller*, 384. After 1943, only 20 per cent of the military administrative staff were under thirty-seven years of age. Laub, *After the Fall*, 37.

administrative orders on the basis of measures that might have been right and good for the police president of Potsdam in 1910."[84]

These comments criticising administrators' close connections to local people and outdated attitudes were made on 20 June 1944. Postwar French investigations revealed that between 17 and 21 June, as part of anti-partisan operations in the Dordogne area, the Kampfgruppe Wilde killed 75 partisan prisoners near the village of Mouleydier, which they also burned to the ground, ostensibly because members of the maquis had hidden there.[85]

Wilde's case offers an opportunity to connect atrocities against resisters directly with the attitude that occupiers in the West were weak and enjoying too good a relationship with local people. Interestingly, the Kampfgruppe Wilde's own reports exaggerated the head count of their murderous activities at Mouleydier, claiming that 302 enemies had been killed, and about twice that number wounded. Wilde himself had relatively little combat experience, though he had served as a liaison to the Romanian army and had undertaken several training missions to become a regimental Commander. He was evaluated as an intelligent officer who was sometimes a little erratic and nervous, and made hasty decisions. The men of his unit were a mixed group, some of whom had experience in the East.[86] In May 1944, the behaviour of men of the Eleventh Panzer Division, to which Wilde's men belonged, had given rise to complaints that some soldiers "had not yet accustomed themselves to the orderly situation here [in France]."[87] Apparently, therefore, the Kampfgruppe Wilde combined several of the features that aligned with excessive violence – it had experience in the East, or at least some of its men did, and although it was not itself an elite unit, its parent unit, the Eleventh Panzer Division, was. Perhaps most significantly, its commanding officer, who did not have a great deal of combat experience and tended to make snap decisions, expressed a scornful attitude towards local occupiers.

It is impossible to demonstrate beyond a shadow of a doubt that incoming men were more likely to lash out against the French because they felt that there was an *Etappengeist* in France that had weakened German defensive capacities. However, the final reports of German administrators who had fled France in 1944 offer additional evidence to support this conclusion. Above all, they reinforce the notion that there

[84] Wilde, report, 20 June 1944, cited in Lieb, *Konventioneller*, 383–4. Cf. Shepherd, *Hitler's Soldiers*, 621.

[85] Lieb, *Konventioneller*, 379.   [86] Lieb, *Konventioneller*, 379–80.

[87] Armeeoberkommando 1 patrol duty report for May 1944, 1 June 1944, quoted in Lieb, *Konventioneller*, 377.

was a culture clash between longer-term occupiers and newly-arrived active troops. This clash stemmed partly from the variant tasks and obligations of the two categories of men for, while administrators focused on the day-to-day negotiations and interactions that facilitated exploitation, active troops were oriented towards defence, whatever the cost. The divergence was also due to the way administrators had learned to approach France, as a place with human and material resources to be exploited, certainly, but also as a land to experience as tourists, to enjoy as consumers of goods and leisure opportunities. If this came across to other men as being *westweich*, it was simply the normal way of doing things for many longer-term occupiers.

After they had made their way back to Germany in autumn 1944, military administrators formerly stationed in Paris, and their colleagues in the local field commands, wrote a series of reports that summarised their experiences. Setting their actions in the best possible light, they tried to justify their policies and practices while outlining the difficulties they had faced.[88] Like other contemporary attempts to narrate the war, the reports of the occupation's desktop warriors must be read with caution, for they served to exculpate their authors and they have contributed to long-lasting perceptions of the French occupation as a relatively "harmless" episode in the conflict as a whole.[89] Administrators developed a set of narratives that emphasised their own good intentions, and underlined that cooperation with their counterparts in the French civilian bureaucracy had generally been good. Although Germany had engaged in justified retaliation against resistance activities by a small number of "terrorists" in France, "correct" relations between representatives of both nations had persisted to the very end. Administrators' reports typically concluded with an adventurous story about how they had made their way back to Germany, and an accounting of specific individuals' fates in the turmoil. Where they did mention excessive violence and atrocities, these were minimised and attributed to a small group of men or specific "bad apples." Despite their self-serving quality, read against the grain, the reports offer insights into the occupiers' last days in France. Above all, they give a sense of the challenges administrators thought they faced and of how they sought to narrate their own story.[90]

---

[88] See, e.g. BArch: RW 35/1253, 1278.
[89] Eismann, *Hôtel Majestic*, 27 ff. Cf. Moeller, *War Stories: The Search for a Usable Past in the Federal Republic of Germany*.
[90] Instead of seeking "réalité" in these reports, they can best be read to help understand how occupiers chose to narrate their experiences. Eismann undertakes this in the context

The main overall report on administrative issues addressed notably the question of whether the German staff in France had become overgrown, serving as a soft billet for men trying to avoid front-line service. On the contrary, the report argued, there were rather too few military administrators in France than too many.[91] Ongoing efforts to pare down the military administration had wasted resources and led to infighting as each section strove to retain its most efficient functionaries. Staff members argued that, rather than avoiding softness, the constant pressure to slim down the military administration was mainly the result of other Reich instances' efforts to shore up their own relatively safe positions in the West.[92]

Still, administrators did not deny that there had been symptoms of an *Etappengeist* in France. They insisted that a dispersal of responsibility had hampered efforts to combat this phenomenon, since elements of the occupation apparatus refused to recognise the overriding authority of the Militärbefehlshaber Frankreich. When disciplined, these offices simply appealed to their parent organisations in Berlin to arrange exceptions to the rules.[93]

When they were confronted with extreme violence, in keeping with their relative isolation from such acts thus far, some administrators seemed genuinely shocked. They tried to explain away the violence by couching it in terms of military necessity, and when that excuse no longer aligned with the actual level of brutality, they suggested it was the unfortunate consequence of understandable frustrations. This pattern is evident in the report of a staff member responsible for monitoring the French cloth industry at Epinal. The author devoted several paragraphs of his comments to the actions of a certain Major von Eisenhardt-Rothe.[94] According to the report, Eisenhardt-Rothe had lost his wife in an air raid on Berlin and become radicalised. With nothing left to lose, he

of German security policy; here, the reports are examined for evidence on German attitudes more broadly. Eismann, *Hôtel Majestic*, 41.

[91] The report buttressed this conclusion by citing General Unruh's findings, discussed in Chapter 6. Militärverwaltung in Frankreich, "Abschlussbericht der Verwaltung, Allgemeines und Gruppe 'Allgemeine und innere Verwaltung,'" 25 March 1945, 29 (AN: AJ 40/536).

[92] Militärverwaltung in Frankreich, "Abschlussbericht," 25 March 1945, 29 (AN: AJ 40/536).

[93] Militärverwaltung in Frankreich, "Abschlussbericht," 25 March 1945, 26 (AN: AJ 40/536).

[94] Likely Major Georg von Eisenhart-Rothe, born in Stettin 14 August 1890, killed 28 October 1944 at Saint-Dié, France. His wife, Olga, died in an air-raid on Berlin 23 November 1943. The spelling of Eisenhardt used in the report has been retained. *Genealogisches Handbuch des Adels*, Vol. 41, Adlige Häuser B VIII (Limburg/Lahn: C.A. Starke, 1968): 74.

sought to establish a defensive base in the West and began telling every-one around him that he wanted to fight to the death there. In command of a group of soldiers, Eisenhardt-Rothe had gone after resisters in the Senones valley in the Vosges region of eastern France. When the oper-ation was over, the bodies of the many casualties were only thinly covered with stones, such that Eisenhardt-Rothe said the valley smelled of corpses. Eisenhardt-Rothe then led an expedition against the nearby town of Charmes, where resisters had shot at two German cars. In retaliation, the report detailed how the community was occupied, men and women separated, and men then "transported to Germany to be put to work"[95] Other sources indicate that at least 139 men were taken away – not to become workers in Germany, as the report's benign phrasing implied, but to the prison camp Schirmeck in Alsace, and then on to Dachau.[96] The German administrator's report went on to note that because American flags could be seen flying from some houses in Charmes, these houses had been set on fire, and the fire soon spread through the town, destroying two thirds of it.

In an apparent attempt to justify the reprisal action, the report's author emphasised that resisters had been hiding in the town, something he believed he could confirm because he had found evidence of squatters when he inspected a set of empty workers' homes belonging to a local textile firm. The account singled out Eisenhardt-Rothe as a radicalised individual, who, in mourning for his wife, was ready to do almost anything for revenge. His actions were detailed carefully in the report, yet portrayed in such a way as to appear relatively moderate, even comprehensible. The report's author backed them up with his own eye-witness testimony, and neglected to mention that violent reprisals against civilians were common as the Germans fought to destroy resistance forces and retain control over the Vosges region while American troops moved in.[97]

But why were these events included in the report at all? They could simply have been left out, for they had little to do with the document's ostensible subject, the exploitation of the French cloth industry. Instead,

---

[95] Bericht des Referates gewerbliche Wirtschaft, FK 622 Epinal, illegible signature, n.d. [fall 1944] (BArch: RW 35/1278).
[96] Of individuals sent to Schirmeck at this time, 58 per cent died or went missing. Manuel Maris, "Les départs vers Schirmeck: les arrivées en septembre 1944," Fondation pour la mémoire de la déportation, www.bddm.org/liv/details.php?id=I.287; Dominique Lormier, *La Libération de la France, jour après jour: juin 1944 – mai 1945* (Paris: Le Cherche Midi, 2012), 216–17. Lormier gives the number of deportees as 157, noting that some 300 regular infantry and 600 Waffen-SS were involved in actions at Charmes.
[97] Maris, "Les départs vers Schirmeck: les arrivées en septembre 1944."

the report-writer chose to include Eisenhardt-Rothe's actions, apparently because he had found them shocking, and sought to document them for posterity. A stilted disclaimer headed up the section on the atrocities committed by Eisenhardt-Rothe: "Although the undersigned has no exact knowledge of specific activities among the command staff, a certain line of development can be discerned therein that must not be concealed."[98] Although the atrocities were framed in a way that made them seem understandable given Eisenhardt-Rothe's overwrought condition, the detail with which they were rendered suggested that the events were still fresh in the author's mind, and that he wanted them to be remembered. His inclusion of his own eye-witness testimony indicated that he was trying to rationalise what had happened, aligning reports of the violence with his own personal observations of possible resistance activity. He added to the report the information that the responsible senior officer, Epinal Field Commander General von Krichenbach, had come under strong influence from his chief of staff, Major Herkner, and from Eisenhardt-Rothe himself.[99] Taken as a whole, the report suggests that the administrator sought to bring Eisenhardt-Rothe's activities to the attention of his superiors, for they did not align with the expectations of civility harboured by a long-term occupation administrator. To head off accusations of "softness," he was careful to do this in a way that avoided seeming to condemn the excessive violence of these actions.

The potential for a clash of cultures between longer-standing occupiers and those newly arrived from other battle fronts is further underlined by one final document, this time from early autumn 1944. Bureaucrats forced to flee Nantes, where Field Commander Hotz had been the first high-ranking officer targetted by the resistance, still insisted in their final reports that, "[c]ooperation with the French administrative offices and especially those of the prefect and the mayor was remarkably good despite the overall situation, which was developing to the Reich's disadvantage."[100] When regular forces, unused to this "cooperation," arrived on their way to Normandy, longer-term occupiers recognised a difference in attitudes between them and the new arrivals immediately. As hordes of infantry marauded through, throwing bureaucratic order into

---

[98] Bericht des Referates gewerbliche Wirtschaft, FK 622 Epinal, illegible signature, n.d. [fall 1944] (BArch: RW 35/1278).

[99] General von Krichenbach had died of war wounds in autumn 1944, which perhaps made it easier to suggest he had come under unfortunate influences. Lieb, *Konventionneller*, 520.

[100] FK 518 (Nantes), Verwaltungsgruppenleiter Piatschek "Bericht über die Rückführung der Verwaltungsgruppe der FK 518 in Nantes," 23 September 1944 (BArch: RW 35/1253). Cf. Gildea, *Marianne* Ch. 14.

disarray and destroying the delicate balance of relations between occupiers and occupied population, members of the Nantes military government found themselves defending France as they knew it against these
strangers who did not share their understanding, even affection, for the
place. In the final report he composed once safely in Germany, the head
of the Nantes administrative group, Piatschek, congratulated himself that
his unit had kept incoming soldiers from implementing scorched earth
policies that would have destroyed not only the local power plant, but
also the city's famous *transbordeur*, a suspended aerial platform "bridge"
that ferried cars and trucks across the mouth of the Loire. Although
military necessity mandated the destruction of this crucial piece of infrastructure, Piatschek had worked to save it. It was surely no coincidence
that the *transbordeur* not only served to bridge the river, but was also, as
Piatschek himself noted, a well-known and much photographed tourist
attraction, the key landmark and symbol (Wahrzeichen) of Nantes.[101]

Piatschek's contention that men like him, local German occupiers who
knew the situation on the ground, played a key role in saving symbolic
and essential structures from the depredations of their fellow-Germans,
is challenging to evaluate. On the face of it, it may be true — after all, the
transbordeur survived, and Paris itself, famously, was spared by the
German forces as they retreated.[102] Yet it is also a kind of myth, a story
retailed through final reports like this one, to absolve administrators of
responsibility for the occupation's worst atrocities. Like the administrator at Epinal who offered a whitewashed account of reprisals against
civilians at Charmes, administrators often painted themselves as relatively innocent, by implication blaming the occupation's violence on the
Reich's leaders in Berlin, the active troops in general, and specific radicalised individuals or units in particular.

The idea that administrators were a qualitatively different group of
occupiers from the active troops, especially those who arrived in
1943 and 1944, has had a long life. This notion was taken up in the
postwar period, for instance by a researcher who was anything but a
supporter of the National Socialist regime. Karl Brandt, a former University of Berlin professor of agriculture, had left Germany for the United
States in 1933. In 1945/46, he returned to Germany as the economic
adviser to the Chief of Food and Agriculture of the US Military

---

[101] The transbordeur, opened in 1903, was located in the same place as today's Pont Anne
de Bretagne. It was taken down in 1958.
[102] On tourism and the saving of Paris, see Gordon, "Warfare and Tourism," 628–9.

Government in Germany. As part of his duties, Brandt prepared a report on the management of food and agriculture in German-occupied Europe. The report displayed keen insight into agricultural conditions, insight that Brandt gleaned from the testimony of "eyewitnesses to the agricultural and food administration of the occupied territories willing to co-operate."[103] Reflecting the biases of these individuals, who can only have been former occupiers, Brandt viewed German policies on the ground in France as relatively benign or comprehensible. Following the tendency, at the time, to overlook or downplay Nazi oppression, Brandt made a clear distinction between flexible military administrators and their harsh taskmasters in Berlin, and drew a direct connection in his 1953 report between local administrators' cooperation with the French, and the nascent European Coal and Steel Community. While acknowledging the role of the Cold War in pushing Germany and France together after 1945, Brandt argued that cooperation between the two countries "was made possible by the French experience with German military government – or more precisely, with the persons in the field, their philosophy, and their conduct."[104]

Brandt's suggestion that occupation laid a foundation for European integration has been explored by many others since.[105] It is problematic, of course, because it blanks out the fundamental power imbalance, exploitation and brutality of the occupation. Still, Brandt's comments show the persistence of the idea that local German administrators had a qualitatively different relationship with France than other representatives of the Reich. Brandt saw this positively, but looked at negatively, it was an *Etappengeist*, a softness from being too long in the West that needed to be managed tightly, if not completely rooted out.

---

[103] Karl Brandt, Otto Schiller, and Franz Ahlgrimm, *Management of Agriculture and Food in the German-Occupied and Other Areas of Fortress Europe: A Study in Military Government* (Stanford: Stanford University Press, 1953), xxv.

[104] Brandt, Schiller, and Ahlgrimm, 568.

[105] Ludwig Tewes, for example, speculated about the everyday interactions of the occupation years as a foundation for good Franco-German relations after 1945 and offered several examples of ongoing contact at an individual, and family level between former occupiers and people they had met between 1940 and 1944 in France. Thomas Sandkühler has asked to what extent the history of the Third Reich might be seen as part of the history of European integration, while Mark Mazower offered a summary of National Socialist ideas about Europe. Pamela Swett wondered how German business used lessons learned during the war years to further their advertising goals in formerly occupied areas after 1945. Mazower, *Hitler's Empire*, 556–61; Thomas Sandkühler, "Europa und der Nationalsozialismus: Ideologie, Währungspolitik, Massengewalt," *Europe and National Socialism: Ideology, Monetary Policy, Mass Violence.* 9, no. 3 (October 2012): 428–41; Swett, *Selling under the Swastika*, 229; *Frankreich*, 11, 245, 389, 374.

The notion that soldiers in the West were going soft was remarkably persistent. Having encouraged "softer" interactions with France from the occupation's outset, it was difficult for the authorities to change gears in 1944. Partly a matter simply of organisational momentum, consumption, leisure, and tourism were deliberately allowed to continue because these activities offered respites to soldiers and benefitted morale. Such opportunities were a double-edged sword, however, because they made life as an occupier in France seem enviable, especially compared to fighting on the Eastern Front, and they fed rumours that troops in the West were unfit for battle. The putative "softness" of longer-term occupiers quickly developed into a trope, an easy way to account for German failures, and to blame others for the loss of France.

Nourished by this trope, a clash of cultures developed between longer-term occupiers and incoming combat troops whose role was more narrowly focused on combat and defence. If some occupiers' long acquaintance with the country protected French people and infrastructure like the Nantes *transbordeur* from German violence, on other occasions, the softer approach taken by certain occupiers spurred others to greater brutality. The notion that occupiers in France had misjudged the situation, were too lenient and ill-prepared for battle, contributed to radical violence during the German retreat.

★ ★ ★

Did German soldiers live "like God in France," as they themselves often remarked? Compared to their comrades on the Eastern Front, in many ways they did, though above all this phrase represented the imagined ideal of a good life. From the outset, enjoying France's abundant food, its material goods and pleasures was part and parcel of being an occupier. After a challenging, if brief, period of battle in 1940, soldiers relished the opportunity to spend time in a country that, before the war, had been considered Germany's cultural equal, and a popular destination. Memories of World War I and the pseudo-scholarly discourse of *Westforschung* encouraged them to see their presence in the West as justified. Although it was deeply coloured by exploitation and brutality, the regime went to great lengths to portray theirs as a gentle occupation, and Germans as cultivated, educated occupiers rather than the "barbarians" depicted by outside observers.

Soldiers benefited significantly from their powerful position in France. They ate at fine restaurants, purchased goods and services at advantageous rates, and enjoyed opportunities for entertainment and leisure. Although scholars debate the purely economic value of occupiers' rampant consumption, it is clear that shopping, eating, and the consumption of experiences represented important rewards for soldiers. Shared with families at home through letters and photographs, these opportunities bolstered overall support for Hitler's regime.

Tourism, in particular, offered a way to approach living in a foreign country and smoothed the transition from combatant to occupier. In tour guides and the commemorative publications for soldiers referred to here as "France books," propagandists formulated a narrative of occupiers' presence as benign, and directed soldiers to understand and remember their experiences in ways that aligned with a National Socialist worldview. In a dynamic of mutual appropriation and reappropriation, motifs developed by soldiers appeared in these books, which then went on to influence other soldiers' writing and photographs. Like shopping and the consumption of experiences, tourism was instrumentalised to increase popular consent for Hitler's rule.

Soldiers used snapshots to develop a story of the occupation in which they were welcome visitors, rather than oppressors. Photography was remarkably widespread among soldiers, and this was the first occupation from which such a vast array of amateur snapshots have survived. These photographs highlight a deep disconnection between what soldiers were actually doing – occupying a country militarily – and the ways they depicted their role. Photography served as a tool to distance oneself from reality, to create an imagined world that seemed much closer to peacetime than to war.

After the invasion of the Soviet Union, France was exploited as a crucial staging area whose many resources, including food, consumer goods, and sheer attractiveness as a seemingly "peaceful" sightseeing destination, served the German war effort. The need to maintain relative calm in France was one of the forces that encouraged moderation in German policy, notably towards resisters, at least until 1943–4. The occupation regime continued to facilitate "soft" interactions with the land and its population because they offered rewards to soldiers, helped them to rest and relax, and lubricated consent.

With time, however, critical voices arose. Observers, notably on the Eastern Front, complained that men in the West were not contributing enough to the war effort. As the situation in France became more dangerous due to increased resistance activity, "soft" interactions with the country and its people came to seem a liability. Even as the authorities decried the putative *Etappengeist* in France, they still needed a quiet staging area for rest and relaxation, and continued to sponsor the very activities that made soldiers in the frozen East look enviously westwards. Maintaining the balance between permissiveness and control, allowing, while also closely monitoring, soldiers' pleasures, was a significant challenge.

As part of the larger drive to increase efficiency and channel a maximum of manpower to the war front, experts under General Unruh were sent to comb through the occupation administration and send superfluous staff to the front. These efforts notwithstanding, from the lowest ranks through to the officers, rumours that troops in the West were "soft" persisted. Like the "stab in the back" myth of World War I, the notion that rear area staff were lazy and decadent grew and took on a power of its own. It became a convenient way to explain away one's own failings and the increasingly obvious likelihood of a German defeat.

Although the notion that troops in the West were universally "soft" was a myth, occupiers who had been stationed in France for longer periods of time had different responsibilities and a different approach from those newly-arrived for training or defensive purposes. Administrators remarked upon the contrasts between themselves and incoming troops, complaining that the latter lacked knowledge of local conditions and failed to understand that they could not behave the same way in the West as they had in the East.

Once the Allies began to reconquer France, this difference in culture had a direct impact on the pursuit of war. On the one hand, the daily neutral, if not cordial, interactions that long-term occupiers had with the land and its people helped to protect both from greater violence.[106] On the other hand, the idea that soldiers in the West were going soft may also have contributed to the vindictiveness with which some military units, notably those arriving in France after having fought in bitter rear-guard actions in the East, exacted reprisals from the French population. These units, fresh from deadly engagements of unspeakable brutality, found the situation in France unimaginable. Their willingness to engage in radical violence against civilians can partly be explained by their past war experiences and, especially in the case of the Waffen-SS and other elite units, their ideological conditioning.[107] Part of the explanation surely also lies in precisely what "older" occupiers decried – combat troops' lack of knowledge of prevailing conditions in France, and their tendency to behave as if they were still in the East, where local people were treated much worse than those in the West. New arrivals may also have wanted to demonstrate that, regardless of how occupiers in France had typically behaved, their own way of doing things was different. Other men might have become *westweich* but these men were *osthart*, so to speak, hardened by eastern warfare and willing to do whatever was necessary to eradicate weakness and win the war. Like the soldier Kurt F., who had complained

---

[106] See earlier in the chapter and Gordon, "Warfare and Tourism," 628–9.
[107] Lieb, *Konventionneller*, 506 ff.; Neitzel and Welzer, *Soldaten*, 379 ff.

in 1943 that men in the West had "partly forgotten what this war in the East is really about," these soldiers felt that they had been sacrificed while others were having a good time.[108] In this way, the notion that there was pervasive softness in the West served to spur on violence among soldiers arriving in France from other fronts.

In tracing these developments, this book addresses three levels of questions. First, it looks at soldiers' experiences as occupiers, enriching accounts of the German occupation of France by adding colour and depth to the portrayal of ground-level occupiers. Using sources such as letters, diaries and especially amateur photographs, it focuses on experiences of occupation, rather than more commonly-studied combat experiences. Second, intervening in the intertwined histories of consumption, leisure and tourism, it explores how the occupation authorities instrumentalised activities like shopping and sightseeing to cover up the occupation's exploitative core, to reward soldiers, and to foster popular consent in the Third Reich. Contributing, third, to the history of Nazism and World War II, it explores a discordance between longer-term occupiers' perceived "soft" approach to France and incoming troops' more ruthless attitudes, and argues that this discordance contributed to excessive violence in the occupation's final period.

German interactions with France, and soldiers' perceptions of themselves and their comrades as occupiers and soldiers, were filled with ambiguities. Drawing attention to the "softer" aspects of occupation does not seek to minimise the oppression that French people and other persecuted groups endured under National Socialist rule. Exploring not battle, but occupation, and not combat, but leisure, consumption, and tourism, contributes to understanding wartime more fully. Above all, examining the ways in which leisure and violence interacted reveals more about how the former supported, enabled, and facilitated the latter.

Consumption, leisure, and tourism were integral elements of the German occupation of France. These activities smoothed soldiers' transition from combat to occupation, and the regime instrumentalised them to exploit their potential benefits, notably to morale. With time, however, managing these "softer" elements of occupation proved a challenge that contemporaries felt the authorities only partly mastered. "Softer" interactions offered benefits, but they also needed to be managed tightly, for they threatened to get out of hand. Living like gods in France was acceptable only if soldiers did not forget that they were first and foremost Hitler's men.

---

[108] F., "Kriegsbriefe," February 19, 1943.

Bibliography

PRIMARY SOURCES

ARCHIVES

Akademie der Künste, Kempowski Archiv, Berlin
Kempowski-BIO
40b   Anon. photo album
71/1–2   Rolf S.
196   Alfons B.
217/2   Eckart E.
536   Karl D.
3354   Hermann H.
3885   Herbert K.
6374   Viktor S.
6443/4   Memoir, 290. Infanterie-Division
6471   Werner Rittich

Archives Nationales, Paris
AJ 40   Archives Allemandes 1940–44

Archives Départementales de Paris
1012/57/1   Cabinet du Préfet

Archives Départementales de la Seine-Maritime, Rouen
51 W   Cabinet du Préfet

Bundesarchiv, Berlin-Lichterfelde
NS 5 VI   Deutsche Arbeitsfront, Arbeitswissenschaftliches Institut –
           Zeitungssammlung
NS 6   Partei-Kanzlei der NSDAP
NS 9   NSDAP Auslandsorganization-Landesgruppe Frankreich
NS 18   Reichsministerium für Volksaufklärung und Propaganda,
           Reichspropagandaamt Ausland
NS 22   Reichsorganisationsleiter der NSDAP

NS 30   Einsatzstab Reichsleiter Rosenberg
NS 37   Hauptamt für Volkswohlfahrt
R 55   Reichsministerium für Volksaufklärung und Propaganda
R 58   Reichssicherheitshauptamt
R 70 Fr.   Deutsche Polizeidienststellen in Frankreich

Bundesarchiv, Freiburg (Militärarchiv)
Nachlässe
Msg 1/257   Johannes Gutschmidt
Msg 1/1353–54   Friedrich Kittel
Msg 1/1707   Friedrich Herrlein
Msg 2/15645–56   Paula Stück von Reznicek
N 13/3; 6; 7   Hans Oetting
N 15/13   Erich Scheibel
N 22/5   Fedor von Bock
N 76/1; 6; 8; 24; 28 Helge Arthur Auleb
N 205/5   Edgar Röhricht
N 245/10; 36–38   Leo Freiherr Geyr von Schweppenburg
N 586/3; 8; 9; 11   Friedrich Siebert

Other
RH 19-IV   Heeresgruppe D (from 15 March 1941
            Oberbefehlshaber West)
RH 20–2   Armeeoberkommando 2
RH 20–10   Armeeoberkommando 10
RH 20–14   Armeeoberkommando 14
RH 21–4   Panzerarmee 4
RH 24–6   Generalkommando VI. Armeekorps (Korps Weidling)
RH 24–80   Generalkommando LXXX
RH 24–81   Höheres Kommando z.b.V. XXXII (from 1942, LXXXI
            Armeekorps)
RH 34   Truppenkommandanturen in Frankreich
RH 36   Kommandanturen der Militärverwaltung
RH 45   Einheiten der Propagandatruppe des Heeres
RH 56   Versorgungs- und Verwaltungsdienststellen ausserhalb
            des Feldheeres
RM 45-IV   Marine Dienst- und Kommandostellen mit Regionaler
            und Lokaler Zuständigkeit im Bereich Frankreich
            und Belgien
RW 35   Militärbefehlshaber Frankreich und nachgeordnete
            Dienststellen
RW 36   Militärbefehlshaber in Belgien und Nordfrankreich
RW 41   Territoriale Befehlshaber in der Sowjetunion

RW 49   Abwehrleitstelle Frankreich/Paris
RW 60   Gerichte der Reichswehr und Wehrmacht
RWD 19   Militärbefehlshaber in Frankreich und nachgeordnete
           Dienststellen, Veröffentlichungen

Bundesarchiv, Koblenz
Nachlässe
BSG 4   Walter Bargatzky
N 1023/1   Werner Best
N 1259/3   Wilhelm Unverzagt

Bundesarchiv, Koblenz (Bildarchiv)
Bild 101 l   (selected) Propagandakompanien der Wehrmacht; Heer
             und Luftwaffe; Frankreich

Deutsches Tagebucharchiv, Emmendingen
205/II   Kriegstagebuch der Zweiten Kompanie
             Infanterieregiment 463
270/I   Kurt F.
745/II   Hans-Peter Eckener
812   Hansjörg P.
944/II/1   Siegfried P.
1628   Wilhelm S.
1810   Fritz E.
1818/I   Alfred Haas
1852   Wolfgang E. R. F.
1859   Tagebuch 12. Komp. I.R. 279, 95. I.D.
1862/II   Horst D.
1900   Klaus Peter Suhrkamp
1908   Winfried A.
1942   Hans Klumpp
1960/4–6   Hans W.
1985/1–5   Helmut Justus
2033   Bernhard Schulz
2044   Otto Pscherer
2063   Hugo L.
2105/II   Josef Esser
2108/I   Werner Kogel

Deutsch-Russisches Museum, Karlshorst
Anonymous Photo Albums
    KH 201885
    KH 202763

KH 203442
KH 206542
KH 206543
KH 207591

Historisches Archiv zum Tourismus, Berlin
Tour Guides and Ephemera
F06/02/940/Par
F06/02/941/Esc
F06/00/942/Ogr
*BAE/General-1
*RAS/Frankreich-1
*MEY/Nordfrankreich-4

**Landesarchiv Nordrhein-Westfalen,
Abteilung Rheinland, Düsseldorf**
RW 37/21   Reichsverteidigung, Höherer SS- und Polizeiführer West

Mémorial de Caen, Archives, Caen
Anonymous Photo Albums
   No. 2–7; 9–11; 14

Other
D 10   Documents officiels Wehrmacht, Manche 1943–1944
D 50   Documents privés

Politisches Archiv des Auswärtigen Amtes, Berlin
   Deutsche Botschaft Paris

The National Archives, Kew
FO 371   Foreign Office; Political Departments; General
             Correspondence; Reports from France

**Württembergische Landesbibliothek,
   Bibliothek für Zeitgeschichte, Stuttgart**
   Sammlung Sterz
   Sammlung Schüling

**University of New Brunswick Archives and Special Collections,
Fredericton**
BC MS/186   Wilhelm Stuckart draft plan for Germany/France frontier

Periodicals
   Das Reich
   Der deutsche Wegleiter: Wohin in Paris?
   Der Durchbruch: Soldatenzeitung an der Westfront
   Der Politische Soldat
   So sehen wir Rouen: Soldatenzeitschrift
   Der Urlaubsschein: Unterhaltungsblatt für Westurlauber
   Der Vormarsch
   Pariser Zeitung
   Soldat im Westen

PUBLISHED PRIMARY SOURCES

Alef, Kurt. *Unser Divisionsbereich in der Normandie.* n.p., n.d.

Armee Oberkommando Bordeaux. *Kleiner Wegweiser für die Soldaten der - deutschen Südwestarmee an der Atlantikküste.* Bordeaux: Delmas, 1940.

Baedeker, Karl. *Paris und Umgebung: Chartres, Fontainebleau, Senlis, Reims, Verdun.* 20th ed. Leipzig: Karl Baedeker, 1931.

Banger, Hans. *Paris: Wanderung durch eine Stadt.* Paris:Verlag der Deutschen Arbeitsfront, 1942.

Bernsee, Hans. *Aufgaben der NS-Volkswohlfahrt im Kriege.* Berlin: Zentralverlag der NSDAP, 1941.

Böll, Heinrich. *Briefe aus dem Krieg, 1939–1945.* 2 vols. Cologne: Kiepenheuer & Witsch, 2001.

Brand, Guido K. *Zwischen Domen und Bunkern. Westeindrücke eines OT-Kriegsberichters.* Amsterdam: Volk und Reich Verlag, 1944.

Bruel, André. *Paris und seine Umgebung. Taschenführer Hirvyl.* trans. F. Schenk. Angers: Jacques Petit, 1940.

Droege, Heinrich, ed. *Bretagne: ein Buch für die deutsche Kriegsmarine.* Marine Propaganda Abteilung West, 1941.

Eckener, Hans-Peter and Peter Wolter. *Lieber Vater – mein lieber Per: Briefwechsel mit zu Hause 1940–1944.* Self-published, 1998.

Eich, Hans et al. *Kleines Bilderbuch von Rouen.* n.p., 1940.

Eparvier, Jean. *A Paris sous la botte des Nazis.* Paris: Editions Raymond Schall, 1944.

Göpel, Erhard. *Die Normandie.* Paris: Pariser Zeitung, 1942.

Hardeweg, Bernd. *Im Westen: Aufzeichnungen eines Landsers aus dem Feldzug in Frankreich.* Berlin: Verlag Die Wehrmacht, 1941.

Harren and Hass, *Wacht am Atlantik. Eine Bildfolge von Südwestfrankreich für den deutschen Soldaten.* Bordeaux: Imprimerie Delmas, 1940.

Hitler, Adolf. *Mein Kampf.* 11th ed. Munich: Franz Eher Nachf., 1942.

Hoffmann, Heinrich. *Mit Hitler im Westen.* Munich: Zeitgeschichte Verlag, 1940.

International Military Tribunal Nuremberg. Vol. 28. Nuremberg, 1948.

International Military Tribunal Nuremberg. Vol. 37. Nuremberg, 1949.

Kitzing, Hans Joachim. *Wir liegen in Paris.* Berlin: E.S. Mittler & Sohn, 1941.

Das Schloss in der Normandie. Berlin: E.S. Mittler & Sohn, 1941.

Kernoun, M. *Deutscher Soldaten-Führer durch Paris.* Paris: Imprimerie Sauclières, 1940.

Kleiner Führer durch Paris für deutsche Soldaten: Erinnerung an Paris 1940. Paris: Dompol's Editions, 1940.

Koehler, Walter. *Umkämpfte Küsten. Ein Buch für die Angehörigen der deutschen Kriegsmarine in den besetzten Westgebieten.* Marine Propaganda Abteilung West, 1943.

Kuziela, Zeno, and R. Dyminskyj. *Die Ukraine.* ed. Luftwaffenführungsstab Ic/VIII. Stuttgart: Alemannen-Verlag, n.d.

Lorenz, H. *Frankreich, ein Erlebnis des deutschen Soldaten.* Paris: Odé Verlag, 1942.

Soldaten fotografieren Frankreich, ein Bilderbuch mit Erzählungen. Paris: Wegleiter Verlag, 1943.

Ludendorff, I.G. et al., *Sturmmarsch zur Loire. Ein Infanteriekorps stürmt, siegt und verfolgt*. Berlin: Verlag Die Wehrmacht, 1941.

Medicus, Franz Albrecht, and Hans Hörmann. *Kathedralen in Frankreich unter deutschem Schutz*. Paris: Wegleiter Verlag, 1942.

Schlösser in Frankreich. Paris: Wegleiter Verlag, 1944.

Meier, Rudolf. *Soldatenführer durch Warschau*. ed. Oberfeldkommandantur Warschau. Warsaw: Verlag der deutschen Buchhandlung, 1942.

Meinhold, *Die Normandie*. Befehlshaber Sicherung West, 1940.

Miquel, René, and Roger Schall. *Reflets de France*. Paris: Imprimerie E. Desfossés-Néogravure, 1942.

Moats, Alice-Leone. *No Passport for Paris*. New York: G.P. Putnam's Sons, 1945.

Moes, Eberhard. *Land an der Biskaya. Von der Loire bis zu den Pyrenäen*. Paris: Imprimerie E. Desfossés-Néogravure, 1942.

Ogrizek, Doré, ed. *Pariser Nächte*. Paris: Odé Verlag, 1941.

Ogrizek, Doré, ed. *Paris, Frankreich Nord und West*. Paris: Odé Verlag, 1941.

Paris. Paris: Verlag für Kunstbücher, 1940.

Pehle, Max et al., eds. *Historischer Schul-Atlas*. 54th ed. Leipzig: Velhagen und Klasing, 1937.

Reindl, Andreas. *Die Nieder-Normandie: Führer für deutsche Soldaten*. Caen: Imprimerie centrale de Basse-Normandie, Caron et Cie., 1941.

Schall, Roger. *Reflets de France*. Paris: Editions Raymond Schall, 1950.

Schall, Roger, and Jean Baugé. *Frankreich: ein Bilderbuch*. Paris: Imprimerie E. Desfossés-Néogravure, 1942.

Schemet, Bohdan. *Die Ukraine einst und jetzt: kurzer Überblick der ukrainischen Geschichte*. Berlin: Verlag der Ukrainischen Wirklichkeit, 1941.

Schmidthüs. *Soldatenführer Nîmes und seine Umgebung*. Nîmes: Sadiac, n.d.

Schulz-Wilmersdorf, Paul Arnold. *Paris: deutsch gesehen*. Berlin: Hermann Hillger, 1941 (Reichsamt deutsches Volksbildungswerk der NS-Gemeinsachaft "Kraft durch Freude.")

Sieburg, Friedrich. *Gott in Frankreich: Ein Versuch*. Frankfurt am Main: Societäts-Verlag, 1931.

Standortkommandantur Dijon. *Führer durch Dijon*, Dijon: Imprimerie cooperative ouvrière, n.d.

Wehrt, Rudolf van. *Frankreich auf der Flucht: Ein Erlebnisbericht aus dramatischen Tagen*. Oldenburg: Gerhard Stalling Verlagsbuchhandlung, 1941.

Windfelder, Norbert. *An der Kanalküste: Foto-Erinnerungen*. Paris: Imprimerie E. Desfossés-Néogravure, 1942.

Zeitung der 10. Armee, ed. *Ich weiss Bescheid: kleiner Soldatenführer durch Wilna*. Hamburg: Hanseatische Druck- und Verlags-Anstalt, 1918.

MEMOIRS

Audiat, Pierre. *Paris pendant la guerre*. Paris: Hachette, 1946.

Bargatzky, Walter. *Hotel Majestic: ein Deutscher im besetzten Frankreich*. Freiburg im Breisgau: Herder, 1987.

Buchheim, Lother-Günther. *Mein Paris: eine Stadt vor dreißig Jahren*. Munich: Piper, 1977.

Delmer, Sefton. *Die Deutschen und ich* (Hamburg: Nannen, 1962)
Duméril, Edmond. *Journal d'un honnête homme pendant l'Occupation: juin 1940–août 1944.* ed. Jean Bourgeon. Thonon-les-Bains: Albaron, 1990.
Hartlaub, Felix. *Kriegsaufzeichnungen aus Paris.* Berlin: Suhrkamp, 2011.
Heller, Gerhard. *In einem besetzten Land: NS-Kulturpolitik in Frankreich: Erinnerungen 1940–1944.* Cologne: Kiepenheuer & Witsch, 1982.
Jünger, Ernst. *Strahlungen.* Tübingen: Heliopolis-Verlag, 1949.

OTHER WORKS CONSULTED

Alary, Eric, Bénédicte Vergez-Chaignon, and Gilles Gauvin. *Les Français au quotidien : 1939–1949.* Paris: Perrin, 2009.
Aly, Götz. *Hitler's Beneficiaries: Plunder, Racial War, and the Nazi Welfare State.* trans. Chase Jefferson. New York: Picador, 2008.
Hitlers Volksstaat: Raub, Rassenkrieg und nationaler Sozialismus. Frankfurt am Main: S. Fisher, 2006.
Assmann, Jan. "Communicative and Cultural Memory." In *Cultural Memory Studies: An International and Interdisciplinary Handbook*, eds. Astrid Erll and Ansgar Nünning, 109–18. New York: de Gruyter, 2008.
Baldoli, Claudia, and Andrew Knapp. *Forgotten Blitzes: France and Italy under Allied Air Attack, 1940–1945.* New York: Continuum, 2012.
Baranowski, Shelley. "Family Vacation for Workers: The Strength through Joy Resort at Prora." *German History* 25, No. 4 (2007): 539–59.
Nazi Empire: German Colonialism and Imperialism from Bismarck to Hitler. Cambridge: Cambridge University Press, 2010.
Strength through Joy: Consumerism and Mass Tourism in the Third Reich. Cambridge: Cambridge University Press, 2004.
Bartov, Omer. *Hitler's Army: Soldiers, Nazis, and War in the Third Reich.* Oxford: Oxford University Press, 1992.
The Eastern Front 1941–1945: German Troops and the Barbarisation of Warfare. Basingstoke, Hampshire: Macmillan, 1985.
Beck, Birgit. *Wehrmacht und sexuelle Gewalt: Sexualverbrechen vor deutschen Militärgerichten 1939–1945.* Paderborn: Schöningh, 2004.
Becker, Annette. "From War to War: A Few Myths, 1914–1942." In *France at War in the Twentieth Century: Propaganda, Myth and Metaphor*, eds. Valerie Holman and Debra Kelly, 15–26. New York: Berghahn, 2000.
Beevor, Antony. *D-Day: The Battle for Normandy.* New York: Penguin Books, 2010.
Bergerson, Andrew, and Maria Stehle. "Rudolph Mosaner's 'Wanderjahre': Irony and Impunity in Nazi Europe." In *War, Exile, Justice, and Everyday Life, 1936–1946*, ed. Sandra Ott, 309–34. *Center for Basque Studies Conference Papers Series*; No. 7. Reno: Center for Basque Studies Press, University of Nevada, 2011.
Berggötz, Sven Olaf. "Ernst Jünger und die Geiseln: Die Denkschrift von Ernst Jünger über die Geiselerschießungen in Frankreich 1941/42." *Vierteljahreshefte für Zeitgeschichte* 51, No. 3 (2003): 405–72.

Berghoff, Hartmut. "Enticement and Deprivation: The Regulation of Consumption in Pre-War Nazi Germany." In *The Politics of Consumption: Material Culture and Citizenship in Europe and America*, eds. Martin Daunton and Matthew Hilton, 165–84. Oxford: Berg, 2001.

Berghoff, Hartmut, and Thomas Kühne. *Globalizing Beauty: Consumerism and Body Aesthetics in the Twentieth Century*. New York: Palgrave Macmillan, 2013.

Bödeker, Hans Erich, Arnd Bauernkämper, and Bernhard Struck. "Einleitung: Reisen als kulturelle Praxis." In *Die Welt erfahren: Reisen als kulturelle Begegnung von 1780 bis heute*, eds. Arnd Bauernkämper, Hans E. Bödeker, and Bernhard Struck, 9–30. Frankfurt am Main: Campus Verlag, 2004.

Boll, Bernd. "Das Adlerauge des Soldaten: Zur Fotopraxis deutscher Amateure im Zweiten Weltkrieg." *Fotogeschichte* 22, No. 85/86 (2002): 75–87.

"Vom Album ins Archiv: zur Überlieferung privater Fotografien aus dem Zweiten Weltkrieg." In *Mit der Kamera bewaffnet: Krieg und Fotografie*, ed. Anton Holzer, 167–78. Marburg: Jonas, 2003.

Bopp, Petra. *Fremde im Visier: Fotoalben aus dem zweiten Weltkrieg*. Bielefeld: Kerber, 2009.

"Fremde im Visier: Private Fotografien von Wehrmachtssoldaten." In *Mit der Kamera bewaffnet: Krieg und Fotografie*, ed. Anton Holzer, 97–117. Marburg: Jonas Verlag, 2003.

"'…ich habe ja nun aus Russland genug Bilder': Soldatenalltag im Sucher eines Amateurfotografen im Zweiten Weltkrieg." In *Der engagierte Blick. Fotoamateure und Autorenfotografen dokumentieren den Alltag*, eds. Irene Ziehe and Ulrich Haegele, 73–96. Berlin: LIT Verlag, 2007.

Branche, Raphaëlle, and Fabrice Virgili. *Rape in Wartime*. New York: Palgrave Macmillan, 2012.

Brandt, Karl, Otto Schiller, and Franz Ahlgrimm. *Management of Agriculture and Food in the German-Occupied and Other Areas of Fortress Europe: A Study in Military Government*. Stanford, Calif.: Stanford University Press, 1953.

Brenner, Peter J. "Schwierige Reisen: Wandlungen des Reiseberichts in Deutschland 1918–1945." In *Reisekultur in Deutschland: Von der Weimarer Republik zum "Dritten Reich,"* ed. Peter J. Brenner, 127–77. Tübingen: Max Niemeyer, 1997.

Browning, Christopher R. *Ordinary Men: Reserve Police Battalion 101 and the Final Solution in Poland*. Reprint edn. New York: Harper Perennial, 1998.

Buchheim, Christoph. "Der Mythos vom „Wohlleben." Der Lebensstandard der deutschen Zivilbevölkerung im Zweiten Weltkrieg." *Vierteljahrshefte für Zeitgeschichte* 58, No. 3 (July 2010): 299–328.

Buchheim, Lothar-Günther. *U-Boot-Krieg*. München: Piper, 1976.

Die Festung. Hamburg: Hoffmann und Campe, 1995.

Buisson, Patrick. *1940–1945, années érotiques : Vichy ou les infortunes de la vertu*. Paris: Editions Albin Michel, 2008.

Bunting, Madeline. *The Model Occupation: The Channel Islands Under German Rule, 1940–1945*. London: Pimlico, 2004.

Burke, Peter. *Eyewitnessing: The Uses of Images as Historical Evidence*. Ithaca: Cornell University Press, 2001.

Burleigh, Michael. *Germany Turns Eastwards: A Study of Ostforschung in the Third Reich.* Cambridge: Cambridge University Press, 1988.

Burrin, Philippe. "Writing the History of Military Occupations." In *France at War: Vichy and the Historians,* 77–90. Oxford: Berg, 2000.

Caplan, Jane. *"Jetzt Judenfrei." Writing Tourism in Nazi-Occupied Poland.* London: German Historical Inst., 2013.

Clark, Catherine E. "Capturing the Moment, Picturing History: Photographs of the Liberation of Paris." *The American Historical Review* 121, No. 3 (June 1, 2016): 824–60.

Cobb, Richard. *French and Germans, Germans and French: A Personal Interpretation of France under Two Occupations 1914–1918/1940–1944.* Hanover, NH: University Press of New England, 1983.

Collar, Peter. *The Propaganda War in the Rhineland: Weimar Germany, Race and Occupation after World War I.* London: I.B. Tauris, 2013.

Collingham, E. M. *Curry: A Tale of Cooks and Conquerors.* Oxford: Oxford University Press, 2006.

Collingham, Lizzie. *The Taste of War: World War II and the Battle for Food.* London: Penguin, 2012.

Confino, Alon. "Traveling as a Culture of Remembrance: Traces of National Socialism in West Germany, 1945–1960." *History & Memory* 12, No. 2 (2001): 92–121.

Corni, Gustavo. *Hitler and the Peasants: Agrarian Policy of the Third Reich, 1930–1939.* New York: Berg, 1990.

Corni, Gustavo, and Horst Gies. *Brot, Butter, Kanonen: Die Ernährungswirtschaft in Deutschland unter der Diktatur Hitlers,* 1997.

Crew, David. "What Can We Learn from a Visual Turn? Photography, Nazi Germany and the Holocaust." *H-German Forum: German History after the Visual Turn,* September 18, 2006. http://h-net.msu.edu/cgi-bin/logbrowse.pl?trx.

Crouthamel, Jason. *An Intimate History of the Front: Masculinity, Sexuality, and German Soldiers in the First World War.* New York: Palgrave Macmillan, 2014.

Darnton, Robert. "What Is the History of Books?" *Daedalus* 111, No. 3: 65–83.

De Grazia, Victoria. "Nationalizing Women: The Competition between Fascist and Commercial Cultural Models in Mussolini's Italy." In *The Sex of Things: Gender and Consumption in Historical Perspective,* eds. Ellen Furlough and Victoria De Grazia, 337–58. Berkeley: University of California Press, 1996.

De Grazia, Victoria, and Ellen Furlough. *The Sex of Things: Gender and Consumption in Historical Perspective.* Berkeley: University of California Press, 1996.

Delacor, Regina. "Weltanschauungskrieg im Westen: zur Rolle der Wehrmacht bei Geiselexekutionen im besetzten Frankreich 1941/42." *Militärgeschichtliche Zeitschrift* 62, No. 1 (2003): 71–99.

Attentate und Repressionen: ausgewählte Dokumente zur zyklischen Eskalation des NS-Terrors im besetzten Frankreich 1941/42. Instrumenta 4. Stuttgart: Thorbecke, 2000.

Denoyelle, Françoise. "Walter Dreizner, un amateur sous influence: des télécommunications à la photographie." *Francia* 33, No. 3 (2006): 85–94.

Didczuneit, Veit, Jens Ebert, and Thomas Jander. *Schreiben im Krieg – Schreiben vom Krieg: Feldpost im Zeitalter der Weltkriege.* Essen: Klartext, 2011.

Dietz, Burkhard, Helmut Gabel, and Ulrich Tiedau. *Griff nach dem Westen: Die „Westforschung" der völkisch-nationalen Wissenschaften zum nordwesteuropäischen Raum (1919–1960)*. Waxmann Verlag, 2003.

Dingel, Tina. "Consumption in Nineteenth- and Twentieth-Century Germany: A Historiographical Essay." *Cultural & Social History* 2, No. 2 (May 2005): 247–56.

Drake, David. *Paris at War: 1939–1944*. Epub. Harvard University Press, 2015.

Dücker, Burckhard. "Reisen in die UdSSR 1933–1945." In *Reisekultur in Deutschland: Von der Weimarer Republik zum "Dritten Reich,"* ed. Peter J. Brenner, 253–84. Tübingen: Max Niemeyer, 1997.

Eggers, Christian. "Gurs - und die Anderen: Gedanken zur Erforschung der Französischen Internierungslager 1939–1945." *Francia* 21, No. 3 (September 1994): 171–9.

Eismann, Gaël. *Hôtel Majestic: Ordre et sécurité en France occupée (1940–1944)*. Paris: Tallandier, 2010.

"Représailles et logique idéologico-répressive. Le tournant de l'été 1941 dans la politique répressive du Commandant militaire allemand en France." *Revue historique*, No. 669 (January 2014): 109–41.

Evans, Jennifer, Paul Betts, and Stefan-Ludwig Hoffmann, eds. *The Ethics of Seeing: 20th Century German Documentary Photography Reconsidered*. New York: Berghahn, 2018.

Fahlbusch, Michael, and Ingo Haar, eds. *German Scholars and Ethnic Cleansing 1919–1945*. New York: Berghahn Books, 2005.

Farber, David, and Beth Bailey. "The Fighting Man as Tourist: The Politics of Tourist Culture in Hawaii during World War II." *The Pacific Historical Review* 65, No. 4 (November 1996): 641–60.

Farmer, Sarah. *Martyred Village: Commemorating the 1944 Massacre at Oradour-Sur-Glane*. Berkeley: University of California Press, 1999.

Feigel, Lara. "'The Photograph My Scull Might Take': Bombs, Time and Photography in British and German Second World War Literature." In *Bombing, States and Peoples in Western Europe, 1940–1945*, eds. Claudia Baldoli, Andrew Knapp, and Richard Overy, 121–35. New York, NY: Continuum, 2011.

Fiss, Karen. *Grand Illusion: The Third Reich, the Paris Exposition, and the Cultural Seduction of France*. Chicago: University of Chicago Press, 2010.

Fritzsche, Peter. *A Nation of Fliers: German Aviation and the Popular Imagination*. Cambridge: Harvard University Press, 1992.

An Iron Wind: Europe under Hitler. New York: Basic Books, 2016.

Furlough, Ellen. "Une leçon des choses: Tourism, Empire, and the Nation in Interwar France." *French Historical Studies* 25, No. 3 (Summer 2002): 441–73.

Fussell, Paul. *The Great War and Modern Memory*. Oxford: Oxford University Press, 2013.

Geiger, Wolfgang. *L'image de la France dans l'Allemagne nazie 1933–1945*. Rennes: Presses Universitaires de Rennes, 1999.

George L. Mosse. *Fallen Soldiers: Reshaping the Memory of the World Wars*. Oxford: Oxford University Press, 1990.

Gerhard, Gesine. *Nazi Hunger Politics: A History of Food in the Third Reich*. Lanham: Rowman & Littlefield, 2015.

Gersdorff, Ursula von. *Frauen im Kriegsdienst 1914–1945. Beiträge zur Militär- und Kriegsgeschichte 11*. Stuttgart: Deutsche Verlags-Anstalt, 1969.

Gibson, Craig. *Behind the Front: British Soldiers and French Civilians, 1914–1918*. Cambridge: Cambridge University Press, 2014.

Gildea, Robert. *Marianne in Chains: In Search of the German Occupation 1940–45*. London: MacMillan, 2002.

"Resistance, Reprisals and Community in Occupied France." *Transactions of the Royal Historical Society (Sixth Series)* 13 (December 2003): 163–85.

Gordon, Bertram. "Ist Gott Französisch? Germans, Tourism and Occupied France 1940–1944." *Modern and Contemporary France NS* 4, No. 3 (1996): 287–98.

"Warfare and Tourism: Paris in World War II." *Annals of Tourism Research* 25, No. 3 (1998): 616–38.

Grayzel, Susan R. *Women's Identities at War: Gender, Motherhood and Politics in Britain and France during the First World War*. Chapel Hill, N.C.: University of North Carolina Press, 1999.

Grynberg, Anne. "Les camps du sud de la France: de l'internement à la déportation." *Annales. Histoire, Sciences Sociales* 48, No. 3 (1993): 557–66.

Guerin, Frances. *Through Amateur Eyes: Film and Photography in Nazi Germany*. Minneapolis: University of Minnesota Press, 2011.

Hadwiger, Daniel. "Austausch auf Augenhöhe? Deutsch-französische Begegnungen von Wohlfahrtsorganisationen während der Besatzungszeit in Deutschland und Frankreich (1940–1949)." In *Zum Phänomen des Austauschs in den Geistwissenschaften/Les phénomènes de l'échange dans les sciences humaines*, edited by Silvia Richter and Maude Williams, 110–30. Frankfurt am Main: Peter Lang, 2016.

Hagemann, Karen. "Mobilizing Women for War: The History, Historiography, and Memory of German Women's War Service in the Two World Wars." *Journal of Military History* 75, No. 4 (October 2011): 1055–94.

Harris, Ruth. "The Child of the Barbarian: Rape, Race and Nationalism in France during the First World War." *Past & Present*, No. 141 (November 1993): 170.

Hartmann, Christian. "Massensterben oder Massenvernichtung? Sowjetische Kriegsgefangene im 'Unternehmen Barbarossa.' Aus dem Tagebuch eines deutschen Lagerkommandanten." *Vierteljahreshefte für Zeitgeschichte* 49, No. 1 (2001): 97–158.

Hartmann, Christian, Johannes Hürter, and Ulrike Jureit, eds. *Verbrechen der Wehrmacht: Bilanz einer Debatte*. München: Beck, 2005.

Harvey, Elizabeth. "'Ich war überall': Die NS-Propagandaphotographin Liselotte Purpur." In *Volksgenossinnen: Frauen in der NS-Volksgemeinschaft*, ed. Sybille Steinbacher, 138–53. Göttingen: Wallstein Verlag, 2007.

Harvey Levenstein. *We'll Always Have Paris: American Tourists in France since 1930*. Chicago: University of Chicago Press, 2004.

Heer, Hannes, and Klaus Naumann, eds. *Vernichtungskrieg: Verbrechen der Wehrmacht 1941–1944*. Hamburg: Hamburger Edition, 1995.

Herbert, Ulrich. *Best: Biographische Studien über Radikalismus, Weltanschauung und Vernunft, 1903–1989*. Bonn: J.H.W. Dietz, 1996.

"Die deutsche Militärverwaltung in Paris und die Deportation der französischen Juden." In *Von der Aufgabe der Freiheit: Politische Verantwortung und bürgerliche Gesellschaft im 19. und 20. Jahrhundert*, eds. Christian Jansen, Lutz Niethammer, and Bernd Weisbrod, 427–50. Berlin: Akademie, 1995.

"The German Military Command in Paris and the Deportation of the French Jews." In *National Socialist Extermination Policies: Contemporary German Perspectives and Controversies*, ed. Ulrich Herbert, 128–62. New York: Berghahn Books, 2000.

Hewitson M. "'I Witnesses': Soldiers, Selfhood and Testimony in Modern Wars." *German History* 28, No. 3 (2010): 310–25.

Hoffmann, Stefan-Ludwig. "Gazing at Ruins: German Defeat as Visual Experience." *Journal of Modern History* 9, No. 3 (2011): 328–50.

Holzer, Anton. "Die oben, wir unten: Das Boot, der Krieg, die Fotografie: Der U-Boot-Krieg als deutsche Heldengeschichte?" In *Mit der Kamera bewaffnet: Krieg und Fotografie*, ed. Anton Holzer, 118–45. Marburg: Jonas Verlag, 2003.

Holzer, Anton, eds. *Mit der Kamera bewaffnet: Krieg und Fotografie*. Marburg: Jonas Verlag, 2003.

Horne, John, and Alan Kramer. "German 'Atrocities' and Franco-German Opinion, 1914: The Evidence of German Soldiers' Diaries." *Journal of Modern History* 66, No. March (1994): 1–33.

German Atrocities 1914: A History of Denial. New Haven: Yale University Press, 2001.

Hüppauf, Bernd. "Der entleerte Blick hinter der Kamera." In *Vernichtungskrieg: Verbrechen der Wehrmacht 1941–1944*, eds. Hannes Heer and Klaus Naumann, 504–27. Hamburg: Hamburger Edition, 1995.

"Emptying the Gaze: Framing Violence through the Viewfinder." *New German Critique*, No. 72 (Fall 1997): 3.

"Langemarck, Verdun and the Myth of a New Man in Germany after the First World War." *War & Society* 6, No. 2 (1988): 70–97.

Hürter, Johannes. "Foreword." In *Kameraden: die Wehrmacht von innen*, by Felix Römer, 9–15. München: Piper, 2012.

Hynes, Samuel. *The Soldiers' Tale: Bearing Witness to a Modern War*. New York: Penguin Books, 1998.

Imlay, Talbot. "The German Side of Things: Recent Scholarship on the German Occupation of France." *French Historical Studies* 39, No. 1 (February 2016): 183–215.

Jackson, Julian. *France: The Dark Years, 1940–1944*. Oxford: Oxford University Press, 2001.

Jahn, Peter. "Bilder im Kopf – Bilder auf dem Papier." In *Foto-Feldpost: geknipste Kriegserlebnisse 1939–1945*, eds. Peter Jahn and Ulrike Schmiegelt, 8–12. Berlin: Elephanten Press Verlag, 2000.

"Vorwort." In *Foto-Feldpost: geknipste Kriegserlebnisse 1939–1945*, eds. Peter Jahn and Ulrike Schmiegelt, 7. Berlin: Elephanten Press, 2000.

Jahn, Peter, and Ulrike Schmiegelt, eds. *Foto-Feldpost: geknipste Kriegserlebnisse 1939–1945*. Berlin: Elephanten Press, 2000.

Jungius, Martin, and Wolfgang Seibel. "The Citizen as Perpetrator: Kurt Blanke and Aryanization in France, 1940–1944." *Holocaust & Genocide Studies* 22, No. 3 (Winter 2008): 441–74.

Kedward, H. R. *In Search of the Maquis: Rural Resistance in Southern France 1942–1944*. Clarendon Press, 1993.

Keegan, John. *Six Armies in Normandy: From D-Day to the Liberation of Paris*. New York: Penguin Books, 1982.

Kitchen, James. "'Khaki Crusaders': Crusading Rhetoric and the British Imperial Soldier during the Egypt and Palestine Campaigns, 1916–18." *First World War Studies* 1, No. 2 (2010): 141–60.

Klötzer, Wolfgang, Reinhard Frost, and Sabine Hock. "Unverzagt, Wilhelm." *Frankfurter Biographie: personengeschichtliches Lexikon*. Frankfurt am Main: W. Kramer, 1994.

Koller, Christian. *"Von Wilden aller Rassen niedergemetzelt"*. *Die Diskussion um die Verwendung von Kolonialtruppen in Europa zwischen Rassismus, Kolonial- und Militärpolitik (1914–1930)*. Stuttgart: Franz Steiner, 2001.

Koshar, Rudy. *German Travel Cultures*. Oxford: Berg, 2000.

Köstlin, Konrad. "Erzählen vom Krieg: Krieg als Reise." *BIOS: Zeitschrift für Biographieforschung, Oral History, und Lebensverlaufsanalysen* 2 (1989): 173–82.

Krob, Melanie Gordon. "Paris Through Enemy Eyes: The Wehrmacht in Paris 1940–1944." *Journal of European Studies* 31 (2001): 3–28.

Kroener, Bernhard. "„General Heldenklau:" Die „Unruh-Kommission" im Strudel polykratischer Desorganisation (1942–1944)." In *Politischer Wandel, organisierte Gewalt und nationale Sicherheit*, ed. Ernst Willi Hansen, 269–85. München: R. Oldenbourg, 1995.

"Die personnelle Ressource des Dritten Reiches im Spannungsfeld zwischen Wehrmacht, Bürokratie und Kriegswirtschaft 1939–1942." In *Organisation und Mobilisierung des deutschen Machtbereichs: Kriegsverwaltung, Wirtschaft und personelle Ressourcen 1939 bis 1941*, eds. Bernhard R. Kroener, Rolf-Dieter Müller, and Hans Umbreit, 693–1002. *Das Deutsche Reich und der Zweite Weltkrieg*, 5/1. Stuttgart: Deutsche Verlags-Anstalt, 1988.

"'Menschenbewirtschaftung,' Bevölkerungsverteilung und personelle Rüstung in der zweiten Kriegshälfte (1942–44)." in *Organisation und Mobilisierung des deutschen Machtbereichs: Kriegsverwaltung, Wirtschaft und personelle Ressourcen 1939 bis 1941*, eds. Bernhard R. Kroener, Rolf-Dieter Müller, and Hans Umbreit, 777–1002. *Das Deutsche Reich und der Zweite Weltkrieg*, 5/2. Stuttgart: Deutsche Verlags-Anstalt, 1999.

Kühne, Thomas. *Kameradschaft. Die Soldaten des nationalsozialistischen Krieges und das 20. Jahrhundert*. Göttingen: Vandenhoeck & Ruprecht, 2006.

"Kameradschaft: 'das Beste im Leben des Mannes:' Die deutschen Soldaten des Zweiten Weltkriegs in erfahrungs- und geschlechtergeschichtlicher Perspektive." *Geschichte und Gesellschaft* 22, No. 4 (1996): 504–29.

Kundrus, Birthe. "Colonialism, Imperialism, National Socialism: How Imperial Was the Third Reich?" In *German Colonialism in a Global Age*, eds. Bradley Naranch and Geoff Eley, 330–46. Durham: Duke University Press Books, 2015.

"Greasing the Palm of the Volksgemeinschaft? Consumption under National Socialism." In *Visions of Community in Nazi Germany: Social Engineering and Private Lives*, eds. Martina Steber and Bernhard Gotto, 157–70, 2014.

"Nur die halbe Geschichte: Frauen im Umfeld der Wehrmacht zwischen 1939 und 1945." In *Die Wehrmacht: Mythos und Realität*, eds. Rolf-Dieter Müller and Hans-Erich Volkmann. München: Oldenbourg Wissenschafts-verlag, 1999.

Laharie, Claude. *Le camp de Gurs, 1939–1945 : un aspect méconnu de l'histoire du Béarn*. Paris: J & D Editions, 1993.

Latzel, Klaus. *Deutsche Soldaten – nationalsozialistischer Krieg? Kriegserlebnis – Kriegserfahrung, 1939–1945*. Paderborn: Schöningh, 1998.

"Tourismus und Gewalt: Kriegswahrnehmungen in Feldpostbriefen." In *Vernichtungskrieg: Verbrechen der Wehrmacht 1941–1944*, eds. Hannes Heer and Klaus Naumann, 447–59. Hamburg: Hamburger Edition, 1995.

"Wehrmachtssoldaten zwischen 'Normalität' und NS-Ideologie, oder Was sucht die Forschung in der Feldpost?" eds. Rolf-Dieter Müller and Hans-Erich Volkmann, 573–88. *Die Wehrmacht: Zwischen Mythos und Realität*. Munich: Oldenbourg, 1999.

Laub, Thomas J. *After the Fall: German Policy in Occupied France, 1940–1944*. New York: Oxford University Press, 2010.

Laudan, Rachel. *Cuisine and Empire*. Berkeley: University of California Press, 2013.

Le Crom, Jean-Pierre. *Au secours, Maréchal !: l'instrumentalisation de l'humanitaire, 1940–1944*. Paris: Presses universitaires de France, 2013.

Leleu, Jean-Luc. *La Waffen SS: Soldats politiques en guerre*. Paris: Perrin, 2010.

Leong-Salobir, Cecilia. *Food Culture in Colonial Asia: A Taste of Empire*. Milton Park, Abingdon, Oxon: Routledge, 2011.

Lethen, Helmut. "Der Text der Historiographie und der Wunsch nach einer physikalischen Spur: das Problem der Fotografie in den beiden Wehrmacht-sausstellungen." *Zeitgeschichte* 29, No. 2 (2002): 76–86.

Lewis, Abigail. "Making Propaganda French: The Service Central Photographi-que and the Battle for Photography under Vichy." Unpublished conference paper, Society for French Historical Studies, Washington, DC, 2017.

Lieb, Peter. *Konventioneller Krieg oder NS-Weltanschauungskrieg?: Kriegführung und Partisanenbekämpfung in Frankreich 1943/44*. Munich: R. Oldenbourg, 2007.

"Repercussions of Eastern Front Experiences on Anti-Partisan Warfare in France 1943–1944." *The Journal of Strategic Studies* 31, No. 5 (2008): 797–823.

Unternehmen Overlord: Die Invasion in der Normandie und die Befreiung Westeur-opas. München: C.H.Beck, 2015.

Lieb, Peter, and Robert O. Paxton. "Maintenir l'ordre en France occupée: Combien de divisions?" *Vingtième Siècle*, No. 112 (2011): 115–26.

Loberg, Molly. "The Streetscape of Economic Crisis: Commerce, Politics, and Urban Space in Interwar Berlin." *Journal of Modern History* 85, No. 2 (June 2013): 364–402.

Lormier, Dominique. *La Libération de la France, jour après jour: juin 1944 - mai 1945*. Paris: Le Cherche Midi, 2012.

Luneau, Aurélie, Jeanne Guérout, and Stefan Martens, eds. *Comme un allemand en France: lettres inédites sous l'occupation 1940–1944*. Paris: L'Iconoclaste, 2016.

Lyautey, Margot. "L'Ostland en France pendant la Seconde Guerre Mondiale." M.A. thesis, Ecole des Hautes Etudes en Sciences Sociales, 2017.

MacCannell, Dean. *The Tourist: A New Theory of the Leisure Class.* New York: Shocken Books, 1976.

Mailänder, Elissa. "Making Sense of a Rape Photograph: Sexual Violence as Social Performance on the Eastern Front, 1939–1944." *Journal of the History of Sexuality* 26, No. 3 (September 2017): 489–520.

Maine, Paul. "L'image de Paris et de la France occupée dans les actualités allemandes (Deutsche Wochenschau) de Mai 1940 à Novembre 1942." In *La France et l'Allemagne en Guerre: Septembre 1939 – Novembre 1942*, eds. Claude Carlier and Stefan Martens, 375–410. Paris: Fondation pour les études de Défense nationale; Institut d'histoire des conflits contemporains; Bundesministerium für Forschung und Technologie; Deutsches Historisches Institut Paris, 1990.

Maris, Manuel. "Les départs vers Schirmeck: les arrivées en septembre 1944." *Fondation pour la mémoire de la déportation.* www.bddm.org/liv/details.php?id=I.287

Marrus, Michael R., and Robert O. Paxton. *Vichy France and the Jews.* Stanford: Stanford University Press, 1995.

Maubach, Franka. *Die Stellung halten: Kriegserfahrungen und Lebensgeschichten von Wehrmachthelferinnen.* Göttingen: Vandenhoeck & Ruprecht, 2009.

Mazower, Mark. *Hitler's Empire: How the Nazis Ruled Europe.* New York: Penguin Books, 2009.

Meinen, Insa. *Wehrmacht und Prostitution im besetzten Frankreich.* Bremen: Edition Temmen, 2001.

"Wehrmacht und Prostitution: Zur Reglementierung der Geschichterbeziehungen durch die deutsche Militärverwaltung im besetzten Frankreich 1940–1944." *1999: Zeitschrift für Sozialgeschichte des 20. und 21. Jahrhunderts* 14, No. 2 (1999): 35–55.

Meyer, Ahlrich. *Der Blick des Besatzers: Propagandaphotographie der Wehrmacht aus Marseille, 1942–1944.* Bremen: Edition Temmen, 1999.

Die deutsche Besatzung in Frankreich, 1940–1944: Widerstandsbekämpfung und Judenverfolgung. Darmstadt: Wissenschaftliche Buchgesellschaft, 2000.

"Grossraumpolitik und Kollaboration im Westen: Werner Best, die Zeitschrift 'Reich – Volksordnung – Lebensraum' und die deutsche Militärverwaltung in Frankreich 1940–42." In *Modelle für ein deutsches Europa : Ökonomie und Herrschaft im Grosswirtschaftsraum*, ed. Horst Kahrs et al., 29–76. Beiträge zur nationalsozialistischen Gesundheits- und Sozialpolitik 10. Berlin: Rotbuch, 1992.

"'Kleistische Prosa oder Polizeibericht? Anmerkungen zu Ernst Jünger's Denkschrift zur Geiselfrage." *Vierteljahreshefte für Zeitgeschichte* 52, No. 2 (2004): 281–6.

Middell, Matthias. "Konjunktur der Wissenschaftsgeschichte: Beobachtungen und Problematisierungen anhand neuer Veröffentlichungen zur völkischnationalistischen Historiographie in Deutschland." In *"Westforschung", Eine Diskussion zur völkisch-nationalistischen Historiographie in Deutschland, H-Soz-u-Kult Review Symposium*, eds. Vera Ziegeldorf and Matthias Middell, 3–14.

Veröffentlichungen von Clio-Online, 2003. http://hsozkult.geschichte.hu-berlin.de/rezensionen/type=revsymp&id=320.

Mièvre, Jacques. *L'"Ostland" en France durant la seconde guerre mondiale: une tentative de colonisation agraire allemande en zone interdite.* Nancy: Université de Nancy II, 1973.

Milton, Sybil. "The Camera as Weapon: Documentary Photography and the Holocaust." *Simon Wiesenthal Center Annual* 1 (January 1984): 45–68.

Milward, Alan S. *The New Order and the French Economy.* Oxford: Clarendon, 1970.

Mitcham, Samuel W. *Retreat to the Reich: The German Defeat in France, 1944.* Westport, Conn.: Praeger, 2000.

Mitchell, Allan. *Nazi Paris: The History of an Occupation, 1940–1944.* New York: Berghahn, 2008.

The Devil's Captain: Ernst Jünger in Nazi Paris, 1941–1944. New York: Berghahn Books, 2011.

Moeller, Robert G. *War Stories: The Search for a Usable Past in the Federal Republic of Germany.* Berkeley: University of California Press, 2001.

Moore, Bob, and Barbara Hately-Broad, eds. *Prisoners of War, Prisoners of Peace.* Oxford: Bloomsbury Academic, 2005.

Mouré, Kenneth. "Food Rationing and the Black Market in France (1940–1944)." *French History* 24, No. 2 (June 1, 2010): 262–82.

"La Capitale de La Faim: Black Market Restaurants in Paris, 1940–1944." *French Historical Studies* 38, No. 2 (April 2015): 311–41.

Mouré, Kenneth, and Paula Schwartz. "On vit mal." *Food, Culture & Society* 10, No. 2 (Summer 2007): 261–95.

Mühlhäuser, Regina. *Eroberungen: Sexuelle Gewalttaten und intime Beziehungen deutscher Soldaten in der Sowjetunion 1941–1945.* Hamburg: Hamburger Edition, 2012.

Münch, Matti. *Verdun: Mythos und Alltag einer Schlacht.* Munich: Martin Meidenbauer, 2006.

Neitzel, Sönke, and Harald Welzer. *Soldaten: Protokolle vom Kämpfen, Töten und Sterben.* Frankfurt, M: Fischer Taschenbuch, 2012.

Neumaier, Christopher. "The Escalation of German Reprisal Policy in Occupied France, 1941–42." *Journal of Contemporary History* 41, No. 1 (2006): 113–31.

Nolan, Michael E. *The Inverted Mirror: Mythologizing the Enemy in France and Germany 1898–1914.* New York: Berghahn Books, 2004.

Nora, Pierre. *Les Lieux de mémoire.* 7 vols. Paris: Gallimard, 1984.

Ott, Sandra. *Living with the Enemy: German Occupation, Collaboration and Justice in the Western Pyrenees, 1940–1948.* Cambridge: Cambridge University Press, 2017.

"The Informer, the Lover and the Gift Giver: Female Collaborators in Pau 1940–1946." *French History* 22, No. 1 (March 2008): 94–114.

Paul, Gerhard. *Visual History: ein Studienbuch.* Göttingen: Vandenhoeck & Ruprecht, 2006.

Paxton, Robert O. *Vichy France: Old Guard and New Order, 1940–1944.* New York: Knopf, 1972.

Pedersen, Susan. *The Guardians: The League of Nations and the Crisis of Empire.* Oxford University Press, 2015.

Perrault, Gilles, and Pierre Azema. *Paris under the Occupation.* New York: Vendome Press, 1989.

Peschanski, Denis. *La France des camps: l'internement, 1938–1946.* Gallimard, 2002.

Petersen, Wolfgang. *Das Boot.* Bavaria Film, 1982.

Plassmann, Max. "Wehrmachtbordelle: Anmerkungen zu einem Quellenfund im Universitätsarchiv Düsseldorf." *Militärgeschichtliche Zeitschrift* 62, No. 1 (2003): 157–73.

Radtke-Delacor, Arne. "Die 'gelenkte Wirtschaft' in Frankreich: Versuch einer vergleichenden Untersuchung der technokratischen Strukturen der NS-Besatzungsmacht und des Vichy-Regimes (1940–1944)." *Pariser historische Studien* 72 (2006): 235–54.

"Produire pour le Reich: Les commandes allemandes à l'industrie française (1940–1944)." *Vingtième Siècle,* No. 70 (April 2001): 99–115.

Rebentisch, Dieter. *Führerstaat und Verwaltung im Zweiten Weltkrieg: Verfassungsentwicklung und Verwaltungspolitik 1939–1945.* Frankfurter historische Abhandlungen, Vol. 29. Stuttgart: F. Steiner Verlag Wiesbaden, 1989.

Reemtsma, Jan Philipp, and Ulrike Jureit, eds. *Verbrechen der Wehrmacht: Dimensionen des Vernichtungskrieges 1941–1944: Ausstellungskatalog.* Hamburg: Hamburger Edition, 2002.

Risser, Nicole Dombrowski. *France under Fire: German Invasion, Civilian Flight and Family Survival during World War II.* Cambridge: Cambridge University Press, 2012.

Roberts, Mary Louise. *What Soldiers Do: Sex and the American GI in World War II France.* Chicago: University of Chicago Press, 2013.

Römer, Felix. *Kameraden: Die Wehrmacht von Innen.* München: Piper, 2012.

Roos, Julia. "Racist Hysteria to Pragmatic Rapprochement? The German Debate about Rhenish 'Occupation Children', 1920–30." *Contemporary European History* 22, No. 02 (May 2013): 155–80.

Rosbottom, Ronald C. *When Paris Went Dark: The City of Light under German Occupation, 1940–1944.* New York: Little, Brown and Company, 2014.

Rouquet, François, Fabrice Virgili, and Danièle Voldman. *Sexes, Genre et Guerres.* Payot, 2010.

Sachsse, Rolf. *Die Erziehung zum Wegsehen: Fotografie im NS-Staat.* Dresden: Philo Fine Arts, 2003.

Sanders, Paul. *Histoire du marché noir: 1940–1944.* Paris: Perrin, 2000.

The British Channel Islands under German Occupation 1940–45. St. Helier: Jersey Heritage Trust, 2005.

Sandkühler, Thomas. "Europa und der Nationalsozialismus: Ideologie, Währungspolitik, Massengewalt." *Zeithistorische Forschungen.* 9, No. 3 (October 2012): 428–41.

Scheck, Raffael. *French Colonial Soldiers in German Captivity during World War II.* Cambridge: Cambridge University Press, 2014.

Hitler's African Victims: The German Army Massacres of Black French Soldiers in 1940. Cambridge: Cambridge University Press, 2006.

Schilling, Britta. *Postcolonial Germany: Memories of Empire in a Decolonized Nation.* New York: Oxford University Press, 2014.

Schmiegelt, Ulrike. "'Macht Euch um mich keine Sorgen...'" in *Foto-Feldpost: geknipste Kriegserlebnisse 1939–1945*, eds. Peter Jahn and Ulrike Schmiegelt, 23–31. Berlin: Elephanten Press, 2000.

Schneider, Valentin. *Un million de prisonniers allemands en France 1944–1948.* Paris: Vendemiaire, 2011.

Schöttler, Peter. "Die historische 'Westforschung' zwischen 'Abwehrkampf' und territorialer Offensive." In *Geschichtsschreibung als Legitimationswissenschaft 1918–1945*, ed. Peter Schöttler, 204–61. Frankfurt am Main: Suhrkamp, 1997.

"Eine Art 'Generalplan West': die Stuckart-Denkschrift vom 14 Juni 1940 und die Planungen für eine neue deutsch-französische Grenze im zweiten Weltkrieg." *Sozial.Geschichte* 18, No. 3 (2003): 83–131.

Geschichtsschreibung als Legitimationswissenschaft 1918–1945. Frankfurt am Main: Suhrkamp, 1997.

Semmens, Kristin. *Seeing Hitler's Germany: Tourism in the Third Reich.* New York: Palgrave MacMillan, 2005.

Sharpley, Richard, and Philip R. Stone, eds. *The Darker Side of Travel: The Theory and Practice of Dark Tourism.* Bristol: Channel View Publications, 2009.

Shepherd, Ben H. *Hitler's Soldiers: The German Army in the Third Reich.* New Haven: Yale University Press, 2016.

Shirer, William. *"This Is Berlin": Radio Broadcasts from Nazi Germany, 1938–40.* Woodstock: Overlook Press, 1999.

Sontag, Susan. *On Photography.* New York: Doubleday, 1977.

Regarding the Pain of Others. New York: Picador, 2003.

Spang, Rebecca L. *The Invention of the Restaurant: Paris and Modern Gastronomic Culture.* Cambridge: Harvard University Press, 2001.

Spode, Hasso. "Review of Strength through Joy: Consumerism and Mass Tourism in the Third Reich. By Shelley Baranowski." *Journal of Social History* 41, No. 4 (2008): 1074–6.

Stargardt, Nicholas. *The German War: A Nation under Arms, 1939–45.* London: Bodley Head, 2015.

Starl, Timm. *Knipser: die Bildgeschichte der privaten Fotografie in Deutschland und Österreich von 1880 bis 1980.* München: Koehler & Amelang, 1995.

Stein, Wolfgang Hans. "Archive als Objekt von Kulturimperialismen: Französische Archive in Deutschland – deutsche Archive in Frankreich." In *Archiv und Gedächtnis: Studien zur interkulturellen Überlieferung*, eds. Michael Espagne, Katharina Middell, and Matthias Middell, 89–121. Leipzig: Leipziger Universitätsverlag, 2000.

Swett, Pamela. *Selling under the Swastika: Advertising and Commercial Culture in Nazi Germany.* Stanford: Stanford University Press, 2014.

Tewes, Ludger. *Frankreich in der Besatzungszeit 1940–1943.* Bonn: Bouvier, 1998.

Théofilakis, Fabien. *Les prisonniers de guerre allemands: France, 1944–1949, une captivité de guerre en temps de paix.* Paris: Fayard, 2014.

Todd, Lisa M. *Sexual Treason in Germany during the First World War.* London: Palgrave Macmillan, 2017.

Tooze, J. Adam. "A New Look at Nazi Plunder." *The Telegraph*, August 9, 2007.

The Wages of Destruction: The Making and Breaking of the Nazi Economy. New York: Penguin USA, 2008.

"What Held Nazi Germany Together? The Aly-Tooze Debate Revisited." January 25, 2017. www.adamtooze.com/2017/01/25/what-held-nazi-germany-together-the-aly-tooze-debate-revisited.

Torrie, Julia S. *"For Their Own Good": Civilian Evacuations in Germany and France, 1939–1945.* New York: Berghahn Books, 2010.

"Frozen Food and National Socialist Expansionism." *Global Food History* 2, No. 1 (March 2016): 51–73.

"The Many Aims of Assistance: The Nationalsozialistische Volkswohlfahrt and Aid to French Civilians in 1940." *War & Society* 26, No. 1 (May 2007): 27–38.

"'Our Rear Area Probably Lived Too Well': Tourism and the German Occupation of France, 1940–1944." *Journal of Tourism History* 3, No. 3 (December 2011): 309–30.

"Visible Trophies of War: German Occupiers' Photographic Perceptions of France, 1940–44." In *The Ethics of Seeing: 20th Century German Documentary Photography Reconsidered*, eds. Jennifer Evans, Paul Betts, and Stefan-Ludwig Hoffmann, 108–37. New York: Berghahn, 2018.

Toury, Jacob. "Die Entstehungsgeschichte des Austreibungsbefehls gegen die Juden der Saarpfalz und Badens (22./23. Oktober 1940 – Camp De Gurs)." *Jahrbuch des Instituts für Deutsche Geschichte, Universität Tel-Aviv* 15 (January 1986): 431–64.

Umbach, Maiken. "Selfhood, Place, and Ideology in German Photo Albums, 1933–1945." *Central European History* 48, No. Special Issue 03 (September 2015): 335–65.

Umbreit, Hans. *Der Militärbefehlshaber in Frankreich 1940–1944.* Boppard am Rhein: H. Boldt, 1968.

"Die deutsche Herrschaft in den besetzten Gebieten 1942–1945." In *Organisation und Mobilisierung des deutschen Machtbereichs: Kriegsverwaltung, Wirtschaft und personelle Ressourcen 1939 bis 1941*, eds. Bernhard R. Kroener, Rolf-Dieter Müller, and Hans Umbreit, 4–274. *Das Deutsche Reich und der Zweite Weltkrieg*, 5/2. Stuttgart: Deutsche Verlags-Anstalt, 1988.

Urry, John. *The Tourist Gaze: Leisure and Travel in Contemporary Societies.* London: Sage, 2002.

Veillon, Dominique. *La mode sous l'Occupation: débrouillardise et coquetterie dans la France en guerre, 1939–1945.* Paris: Payot, 1990.

Vivre et survivre en France, 1939–1947. Paris: Payot, 1995.

Verheyde, Philippe. *Les mauvais comptes de Vichy: l'aryanisation des entreprises juives.* Paris: Perrin, 1999.

Virgili, Fabrice. "Enfants de Boches: The War Children of France." In *Children of World War II the Hidden Enemy Legacy*, eds. Kjersti Ericsson and Eva Simonsen, 138–50. Oxford: Berg, 2005.

"Les viols commis par l'armée allemande en France (1940–1944)." *Vingtième Siècle*, No. 130 (April 2016): 103–20.

Naître ennemi : Les enfants de couples franco-allemands nés pendant la Seconde Guerre mondiale. Paris: Payot, 2009.

Shorn Women: Gender and Punishment in Liberation France. trans. John Flower. Oxford: Berg, 2002.

Vorländer, Herwart. *Die NSV: Darstellung und Dokumentation einer nationalsozia-listichen Organisation*. Boppard am Rhein: Harald Boldt, 1988.

Warring, Anette. "Intimate and Sexual Relations." In *Surviving Hitler and Mussolini: Daily Life in Occupied Europe*, eds. Robert Gildea, Olivier Wieviorka, and Anette Warring, 88–128. Oxford: Berg, 2006.

Wegner, Bernd. *Hitlers politische Soldaten: Die Waffen-SS 1933 – 1945. Leitbild, Struktur und Funktion einer nationalsozialistischen Elite*. Paderborn: Schöningh, 2008.

White, Richard. "The Soldier as Tourist: The Australian Experience of the Great War." *War & Society* 5, No. 1 (1987): 63–77.

Wiesen, S. Jonathan. *Creating the Nazi Marketplace: Commerce and Consumption in the Third Reich*. Cambridge: Cambridge University Press, 2010.

Wildt, Michael. *Generation des Unbedingten: das Führungskorps des Reichssicherheitshauptamtes*. Hamburg: Hamburger Edition, 2002.

Winter, Jay. *Remembering War: The Great War between Memory and History in the Twentieth Century*. New Haven: Yale University Press, 2006.

Sites of Memory, Sites of Mourning: The Great War in European Cultural History. Cambridge: Cambridge University Press, 1998.

Wintle, Michael J. *Imagining Europe: Europe and European Civilisation as Seen from Its Margins and by the Rest of the World in the Nineteenth and Twentieth Centuries*. Bern: Peter Lang, 2008.

Wirsching, Andreas. "Volksgemeinschaft and the Illusion of 'Normality' from the 1920s to the 1940s." In *Visions of Community in Nazi Germany: Social Engineering and Private Lives*, eds. Martina Steber and Bernhard Gotto, 149–56. Oxford: Oxford University Press, 2014.

Wölki, Kerstin. "Krieg als Reise: Die Wahrnehmung Frankreichs durch deutsche Soldaten im zweiten Weltkrieg." M.A. Thesis, Albert-Ludwigs-Universität, 2007.

Ziino, Bart. "A Kind of Round Trip: Australian Soldiers and the Tourist Analogy, 1914–1918." *War & Society* 25, No. 2 (2006): 39–52.

Index

Africa books, 22–24, 98, 113–15
African soldiers, French, 17, 27, 49, 129, 146, 169
Aly, Götz, 13, 24, 62–64, 66, 73, 90
Ardennes, 34–36, 40
atrocities, 7–8, 25–26, 129, 168, 183–87, 195, 203–4, 223–24, 233–37, 240–46
    World War I, 23, 41–42, 46, 49–51, 84, 95–96, 148
Aufsichtsverwaltung (oversight), 51, 55–56

Baranowski, Shelley, 14–16, 35, 64
barbarians, idea that occupiers were, 23, 30, 41–42, 46, 49–51, 62, 125, 147–48, 180, 190, 194, 248, See also "correct," idea that occupiers were
Bargatzky, Walter, xi, 184–85
battlefield tourism. See tourism, battlefield
Beauftragten der Sicherheitspolizei und des Sicherheitsdienstes (Representative of the Security Police and Security Service, BdS), 57–58
Best, Werner, 51, 54–58, 94, 103, 108–9
Biarritz, 92, 111, 225
black market, 63, 73, 80–81, See also consumption; plunder
Blanke, Kurt, 217
Böll, Heinrich, xi, 51–52, 54, 111–12, 144
Boot, Das (film). See Buchheim, Lothar-Günther
Bordeaux, 92, 125, 170–71, 175–76, 179, 192, 204, 226–27, See also wine
Brandt, Karl, 246–47
Brest, xii, 92, 107
Brittany, 107, 112, 121–23, See also Brest; Mont Saint-Michel; Saint-Malo
Buchheim, Lothar-Günther, 122–23, 160–63
Burgundy, 36, See also wine
butter, 14, 62, 71, 78, 80, 197

Caen, 121, 231
castles, French, 102, 112, 125–26, 154, See also Versailles
cathedrals, French, 23, 30, 35, 41, 44, 99, 112, 125–26, 154
Charmes, 243–44, 246
Cherbourg, xii, 1, 61, 165, 227, 231, 238–39
children of German-French couples, 86
chocolate, 72–73
civilians
    Belgian, 27, 46–49
    French, 23, 27–29, 40, 46–49, 62, 68, 154–57, 159, 177, 225, 231, 233, See also atrocities; fraternisation; "hostage" crisis; prostitution; rape
    German. See Home Front; morale, German civilian
cognac. See wine
Compiègne, 45, 184
    1940 armistice at, 44, 46, 152
Confino, Alon, 15, 94
consumption, 2–17, 19, 23–24, 27–29, 61–81, 95, 130, 168, 220, 230, 233, 249, 251, See also black market; fraternisation; lingerie; perfume; plunder; prostitution; Soldatenkaufhaus; tourism
    aesthetic, 141, See also tourism; photography
    and gender, 14–15, 65–66, 70–71, 88
    and Home Front, 13–14, 63, See also plunder and Home Front
    and moral norms, 71
    and plunder, 13–14, 24, 62–69
    attempts to manage, 72–74, 76, 88–90, 110, 127, 228–30, See also black market; Soldatenkaufhaus
    entertainment, 82–83
    food, 78–81, See also wine; intoxication
    long-term patterns of, 65–66, 90–91
    of experiences, 77–78

responses
    French, 87–88
    German, 88–90
    "correct," idea that occupiers were, 30, 51,
        87, 190, 242

DAF. *See* Deutsche Arbeitsfront
D-Day. *See* Normandy, Allied landing in
demarcation line, 39, 109 n 63, 169, *See also*
    non-occupied zone
despoilment. *See* plunder
Deutsche Arbeitsfront (German Labour
    Front, DAF), 102–3, 123–24
Dijon, 88, 112, 192
drunkeness. *See* intoxication; wine
Duméril, Edmund, 42–43, 178
Durchbruch, Der, 46 n 72

Eastern Europe, soldiers' attitudes towards,
    97, 114, 118–21, 144, 198–201,
    See also photography
Eastern Front, 192–93, *See also* atrocities;
    Eastern Europe, soldiers' attitudes
    towards; mobility, wartime;
    Stalingrad
    and France as rest and staging area, 5–6,
        8, 11, 25, 59, 167, 180, 192–94,
        201–3, 229–30, 249
    anxiety about transfer to, 196–97, 214
    levels of violence and, 17, 173, 180,
        194–95, 197–98, 203–5, 223–24,
        227–28, 236, 240–46, 248, 250–51
    manpower requirements, 6, 12, 59, 166,
        196, 209–20, 227, 243, 250
Eckener, Hans-Peter, xi, 78, 99–100,
    104–6, 108
economy. *See* consumption; plunder
ego-documents. *See* sources, first-person
Eiffel tower, 44, 104–6, 142–43, 152–53
Eisenhardt-Rothe, [Georg] von, 243–45
Eismann, Gaël, 17, 168, 180
empire. *See also* Holy Roman Empire
    German colonial, 34, *See also* Africa
        books
    National Socialist, 12, 35, 79, 97, 114,
        See also Aufsichtsverwaltung;
        Grossraum; mobility, wartime;
        Stuckart memorandum
    of Charlemagne, 34
Etappengeist. *See* "softness"
exchange rate, 12, 28, 62, 87–88, 138

F., Kurt, xi, 2–3, 6, 79, 88, 192–95, 205,
    224, 226, 240, 250
food. *See* consumption, food

France books, 13, 22–23, 113–27, 150, 249
franc-tireurs, 28
fraternisation, 66, 83, 85–87, 159, 176, 226,
    See also women
French administration, 48, 55–57, 171,
    175, 242
French African soldiers. *See* African
    soldiers, French
French civilians. *See* civilians, French
Front und Heimat, 209

gender. *See* consumption and gender;
    fraternisation; gendered metaphors;
    women
gendered metaphors, 50
generational conflict, 7, 232, 240
German Labour Front. *See* Deutsche
    Arbeitsfront
ghetto. *See also* Jews
    Warsaw, 199–201
Gildea, Robert, 11, 178
Globke, Hans. *See* Stuckart memorandum
Goebbels, Joseph, 100, 179, 207, 209, 216
Gordon, Bertram, 7, 15, 77, 93, 96, 222, 233
Gothic architecture, 23, 30, 35, 41
Großraum (greater space), 55–56
Gutschmidt, Johannes, xi, 43, 79–80,
    92–93, 109–10, 198–201

Haas, Alfred, xi, 198–201
Heller, Gerhard, 94, 109 n 63
Herbert, Ulrich, 18, 56–57, 167, 180, 183
Hitler, Adolf, 46, 58, 106, 207–8, 215, 217,
    219, 232, *See also* "hostage" crisis
    views on France, 31, 33
    visit to France 1940, 44–45, 100, 106,
        152–53
Hoffmann, Heinrich, 44–45, 153
Höherer SS- und Polizeiführer (Superior
    SS and Police Leader), 57–58,
    183–84
Holy Roman Empire, 38
Home Front, German, 71–72, 126, 166,
    207–9, 221, *See also* consumption;
    morale, German civilian; plunder
"hostage" crisis, 25, 167–69, 173–84,
    189–90
Hotz, Karl, 42–43, 177–79, 245

Imlay, Talbot, 85
intoxication, 50, 80, 170, 174, 230

Jews, 25, 97, 118, 120, 123–24, 166–69,
    172–74, 181–84, 199–201, *See also*
    racial ideology; Warsaw

Jodl, Alfred, 38, 219
Jünger, Ernst, xii, 81, 94, 179, 185–86, 190, 197

Keitel, Wilhelm, 6, 177–79, 182, 215
Klumpp, Hans, xii, 27–29, 31, 47, 77–78, 197–98
Knochen, Helmut. *See* Beauftragten der Sicherheitspolizei und des Sicherheitsdienstes
Knoke, Georg Wilhelm, 184
Koshar, Rudy, 15, 94, 97, 121
Kraft durch Freude (Strength through Joy, KdF). *See* Deutsche Arbeitsfront
Kundrus, Birthe, 14, 64–65, 76, 114

Laub, Thomas, 9, 168, 177
Les Invalides. *See* Napoleon
Lieb, Peter, 7, 12, 18, 204, 223–24, 233
lingerie, 14, 24, 73, 88
Locarno, spirit of, 42, 52
Lorenz, Heinz, 116 n 84, 125–26, 128, 152, 155, 158

Madeleine, Eglise de la, 104
maquis. *See* resistance, French
Marseilles, 228
    Vieux Port district, 145–46, 187
Medicus, Franz, 125–26, 210, 217–18
memory
    postcolonial. *See* Africa books
    World War I, 23, 29–32, 34, 41–46, 51–54, 100, 102, 119–20, 206–7, 221, 248, 250, *See also* atrocities, World War I; tourism, battlefield; Verdun; Versailles, Treaty of
Meyer, Ahlrich, 17, 55 n 101, 167
Michel, Elmar, 50, 57, 218
Militärbefehlshaber Frankreich (Military Commander in France, MBH), 9–12, 57–58, 60, 109–10, 210, 218, 225, 227, 243, *See also* Stülpnagel, Carl-Heinrich von; Stülpnagel, Otto von
Mitchell, Allan, 10
Moats, Alice, 90–91
mobility, wartime, 6, 8, 11–12, 25, 59, 194–95, 201, 220
Molyneux (fashion house), 90
Mont Saint-Michel, 92, 107, 206
Montmartre, 77, 101, 104–6, 158–59, 173
morale
    German civilian, 5, 12–14, 73–74, 207–9, 221, *See also* Home Front, German

German military, 5, 12–14, 17, 73–74, 94, 196, 208–9, 224–25, 228, 230, 239, 248, 251, *See also* "softness"

Nachrichtenhelferinnen (communications auxiliaries), 213, *See also* women
Nantes, 43, 177–79, 245–46, 248
    transbordeur, 246, 248
Napoleon, 44, 104, 106, 239
Napoleonic wars, 38, 122, 239
National Socialist People's Welfare Organization. *See* Nationalsozialistische Volkswohlfahrt
Nationalsozialistische Führungsoffiziere (National Socialist Political Leaders, NSFO), 208–9
Nationalsozialistische Volkswohlfahrt (National Socialist People's Welfare Organization, NSV), 43–44, 46–49, 82
Neitzel, Sönke, 18, 21–22, 233–34, 238
nightlife, 118
non-occupied zone, 56, 172, *See also* demarcation line; tourism in France, non-occupied zone
Nordostlinie (Northeastern line), 38–40, 58, *See also* Stuckart memorandum
Normandy, xi, 1–2, 61, 107–8, 112, 121–22, 197, 228, 235, 237, *See also* Caen; Cherbourg; Mont Saint-Michel; Rouen
    Allied landing in, 7, 189, 193, 226–28, 231–32
Northeastern Line. *See* Nordostlinie
NSV. *See* Nationalsozialistische Volkswohlfahrt

Oberg, Karl. *See* Höherer SS- und Polizeiführer
occupation
    conceptions of, 31, 49, 168, 190, 194, *See also* Aufsichtsverwaltung; empire; Großraum; Stuckart memorandum
    continuities with past, 46
    Rhineland, interwar French, 37, 44, 49
    World War I, German, of Belgium and Northern France, 95, *See* atrocities, World War I; barbarians, idea that occupiers were
Opéra Garnier, 104, 153
Oradour-sur-Glane, 204, 236
Ostland company, 40

Osttruppen, 228, 239
oysters, 25, 79

palaces. *See* castles, French
Paris, 4, 14–16, 43–44, 48, 50, 53, 74–78,
    87–88, 90–92, 94, 100–7, 109, 111–
    12, 116–18, 123–24, 142, 151–53,
    156, 158–61, 173–74, 187, 224–25,
    228–31, 246, *See also* consumption;
    Eiffel tower; Montmartre; Napoleon;
    restaurants; Sacré Coeur; tourism
Jewish quarter, 118
nightlife, 83, *See also* Montmartre
perfume, 14, 24, 61–62, 65, 71, 75, 87–88,
    91
Pernod, 80, *See also* intoxication; wine
Pétain, Philippe, 39, 56
photo albums. *See* photography
photographs. *See* photography
photography
    in Eastern Europe, 129, 136, 141–44,
        198, *See also* Eastern Europe,
        soldiers' attitudes towards
    in France, 8, 24–25, 95, 128–64, 222, 249
    and comraderie, 137
    and memory, 130, 137, 147–49, 155
    and plunder, 138–39
    and propaganda, 130, 150–54, 156,
        158–63
    and tourism, 139–41
    and violence, 130–31, 141–46
    everyday quality, 128–29, 131, 138,
        163–64
    exhibition, 125–26, 128, 150–52
    French, 13, 142, 155–57
    photo books, 150–51, 158
    popularity, 133–35
    regulations, 135–36
photographs as sources, 21, 134–35, 137
    n 27, 163–64
pillage. *See* plunder
plunder, 6, 13–15, 24, 27–29, 50, 61, 63,
    65–72, 78–79, 87–91, 131, 183,
    203–4, 227–28, *See also* photography
    in France and plunder, *See also*
    consumption by occupiers
    and cameras, 134
    and Home Front, 71–72, *See also*
    consumption and Home Front
Poland, xii, 31–32, 53, 58, 121, 179, 198,
    See also Eastern Europe, soldiers'
    attitudes towards; Warsaw
prisoners of war
    Allied, 28, 235, *See also* African soldiers,
    French

German, xii, 231
    recorded conversations of, 18–19, 22,
        233–39
    Soviet, 198
prisoners, political. *See* "hostage" crisis
propaganda, 2, 5, 44, 51, 67, 70, 83, 86,
    109, 115, 118, 122–23, 126, 145,
    157, 188, 201, *See also* Goebbels,
    Joseph; France books; morale;
    Nationalsozialistische
    Führungsoffiziere; photography
    in Soviet Union, 136
World War I. *See* barbarians, idea that
    occupiers were; atrocities, World
    War I
Propaganda Companies, 46 n 72, 106,
    122–23, 134, 159, *See also*
    Vennemann, Wolfgang; Buchheim,
    Lothar-Günther
prostitution, 12, 77, 83–84, 173

racial ideology, 10, 18, 35–37, 49, 55, 58,
    82, 85, 107–8, 118–24, 126, 146,
    198–201, *See also* Eastern Europe,
    soldiers' attitudes towards; Jews
rape, 50, 67, 84–85, 169
resistance, French, 7, 25, 170–73, 249,
    See also atrocities; franc-tireurs;
    "hostage" crisis
    German responses, 7, 25–26, 146, 166,
        170–73, 186, 235–38, 240–45
rest and relaxation. *See* Eastern Front, and
    France as rest and staging area
restaurants, 80–81, *See also* consumption,
    food
    Maxim's, 90
    Tour d'Argent, 81, 221
Rhineland occupation. *See* occupation
ROGES. *See* Rohstoff-Handelsgesellschaft
Rohstoff-Handelsgesellschaft (Raw
    Materials Purchasing Agency,
    ROGES), 20
Rohstoff-Handelsgesellschaft (ROGES),
    110–11
Römer, Felix, 18, 235–36, 238
Rouen, 92, 112, 162
Rundstedt, Gerd von, 109 n 2, 222

Sacré Coeur, 105
Saint-Nazaire, 122–23
Schadt, Wilhelm, 188, 205
Schall, Roger, 87–88, 154–57
Schaumburg, Ernst, 124, 151, 173–74
Scheck, Raffael, 17
Schilling, Britta, 22–23, 98, 113, 126

Schöttler, Peter, 38
Schulenberg, Fritz-Dietlof von der, 216,
    232, See also Unruh, Walther von
Schulz, Bernhard, xii, 61–62, 71, 85–87,
    165–66, 170, 186, 196–97
Schutzstaffel (SS), 11, 57–58, 85, 167, 183,
    204, See also Waffen-SS
Security Police and Security Service,
    Representative of. See Beauftragten
    der Sicherheitspolizei und des
    Sicherheitsdienstes
Senones valley, 243–44
shopping. See consumption
Siebert, Friedrich, xii, 43, 140, 146
Sieburg, Friedrich, 32, 51
sightseeing. See tourism
"softness", 6–7, 97, 195, 204–7, 209, 216,
    219–20, 224, 230, 241–43, 247,
    249–51
Soldatenheim, 104–5
Soldatenkaufhaus (soldiers' department
    store), 74–76, 104
sources, first-person, 5, 16, 19–21, 198,
    251, See also photography
Spain, 90, 90 n 75, 92, 109–10
spoliation. See plunder
Stabshelferinnen (administrative
    auxiliaries), 213, See also women
Stalingrad, 201–2, 226
Strength through Joy. See Deutsche
    Arbeitsfront
Stuckart memorandum, 29–30, 33–41, 46,
    See also Westforschung
Stülpnagel, Carl-Heinrich von, 166, 183
Stülpnagel, Otto von, 6–7, 57–58, 166–68,
    173–83, 185–86
Suhrkamp, Klaus Peter, xii, 199
Superior SS and Police Leader. See Höherer
    SS- und Polizeiführer
Swoboda, Fritz, xii, 223, 234–37

Tomb of the Unknown Soldier. See
    Unknown Soldier, Tomb of the
Tooze, Adam, 13–14, 63
tourism
    battlefield, 44–45, 93 n 2, 100, 102
    in Eastern Europe, 199–201, See also
        Eastern Europe, soldiers' attitudes
        towards
    guidebooks, 118–21
    in France, 4–17, 22–26, 44–45, 64,
        76–77, 92–112, 125, 127, 130,
        141–43, 153–54, 168–70, 225,
        248–49, 251, See also Brittany; Paris;
        Mont Saint-Michel; Normandy
    as factor limiting violence, 233, 240,
        242, 246, 248–49

attempts to curtail, 222, 230, See
    "softness"
guidebooks, 127, 154, See also France
    books
non-occupied zone, 110 n 69
Tulle, 204

Unknown Soldier, Tomb of the, 53–54,
    101, 104, 106, 149, 153
Unruh Kommission. See Unruh, Walther
    von
Unruh, Walther von, 196, 215–17, 250,
    See also Eastern Front, manpower
    requirements; Schulenberg, Fritz-
    Dietlof von der
Unverzagt, Wilhelm, xii, 221–22, 224,
    232

Vennemann, Wolfgang, 145
Verdun, 35, 193, 226
Versailles, 32, 45, 102, 105, See also
    Versailles, Treaty of
Versailles, Treaty of, 23, 30, 41, 44–45, 58,
    114, 125, 127, 193, See also World
    War I
veterans, World War I
    French, 30, 42, 52, 178, See also memory,
        World War I
    German, xi, 30, 42–45, 52, 92, 187, 210,
        215, 232, See also World War I
veterans, World War II
    German, 112 n 72, 136
violence, excessive. See atrocities
Vosges region, 34–35, 243–44

W., Hans, xii, 107, 201
Waffen-SS, xii, 7–8, 18–19, 186, 204,
    223–24, 233–37, 240, 250
Warsaw, 53, 106
    ghetto. See ghetto, Warsaw
Welzer, Harald, 18, 21–22, 233–34
Westforschung, 23, 37–38, 248, See also
    Stuckart memorandum
westweich. See "softness"
Windfelder, Norbert, 151
wine, 29, 32, 72, 79–80, 82, 90, 193, 197,
    216, 230, See also intoxication
women, 49, 66, 71, 77, 88, 102, 111, 137,
    158–59, 201, 204, 213–15, 217, 225,
    236, See also fraternisation; gender;
    prostitution; rape
World War I, 4, 96, 119–20, 195, See also
    atrocities, World War I; memory,
    World War I; tourism, battlefield;
    veterans, World War I

Zucca, André, 155 n 69

CPSIA information can be obtained
at www.ICGtesting.com
Printed in the USA
LVHW010106060220
645955LV00012B/147

9 781108 457590